D0077091

MARXISM

NOMOS

XXVI

NOMOS

Lieber-Atherton, Publishers

New York University Press

NOMOS XXVI

Yearbook of the American Society for Political and Legal Philosophy

MARXISM

Edited by

J. Roland Pennock, *Swarthmore College*

and

John W. Chapman, *University of Pittsburgh*

New York and London · New York University Press · 1983

Marxism: Nomos XXVI
edited by J. Roland Pennock and John W. Chapman
Copyright © 1983 by New York University

Library of Congress Cataloging in Publication Data
Main entry under title:

Marxism.
  (Nomos; 26)
  Bibliography: p.
  Includes index.
  1. Marx, Karl, 1818–1883—Congresses. I. Pennock, J. Roland (James Ro-
land), 1906–   . II. Chapman, John William, 1923–   III. Series.
HX39.5.M377 1983   335.4   83-8360
ISBN 0-8147-6586-6

CONTENTS

PART IV: SOME UNRESOLVED ISSUES

CONTRIBUTORS

JOHN W. CHAPMAN
Political Science, University of Pittsburgh
G.A. COHEN
Philosophy, University College London
JON ELSTER
Philosophy and History, University of Oslo
TOM GERETY
Law, University of Pittsburgh
ALAN GILBERT
Political Science, University of Denver
STEPHEN HOLMES
Government, Harvard University
LEON LIPSON
Law, Yale University
RICHARD W. MILLER
Philosophy, Cornell University
PATRICK RILEY
Political Science, University of Wisconsin-Madison
PETER G. STILLMAN
Political Science, Vassar College
MARK TUSHNET
Law, Georgetown University
FREDERICK G. WHELAN
Political Science, University of Pittsburgh
SHELDON S. WOLIN
Politics, Princeton University

PREFACE

The topic of the meetings of the American Society for Political and Legal Philosophy held in New York in September 1981, with the American Political Science Association, was "Marxism Today." Although nine of the twelve chapters in this volume are derived from those meetings (all but those of Cohen, Elster, and Stillman), we title this volume simply *Marxism,* as being more nearly reflective of its contents. Modern developments of Marxist thought are not neglected in these essays, but it would be misleading to suggest that the primary concern of the book is modern Marxism rather than the work of the great man himself.

As anyone who follows the literature of social science and social philosophy knows, the Marx industry has achieved mammoth proportions. No end is in sight and no consensus emerges, as the chapters of this book amply prove. We offer no discussion of the reasons for the explosive output of books and articles on Marx and Marxism, on "critical theory," and so on, but that topic in itself would indeed be an appropriate subject for study and speculation. Two sentences that appear in the ensuing chapters would provide appropriate points of departure for such an enterprise. Tom Gerety remarks that Marx "alternated between heated rhetoric and qualified elaboration." (p. 203) And Peter Stillman, after reminding us of how so much of "Marxist" thought for so long was immobilized in frozen dogma, indicates something of the scope and depth demanded of the modern Marxist, declaring that "Since critique involves not only the bare conclusions but also the process by which they were discovered, the vital strands of Marx's critique today almost always include an emphasis upon and thinking through again Marx's full theory." (P. 271)

The general outline of the volume is apparent from the table of contents. In Part I Richard Miller leads off the discussion of

"Marx and Morality" by contending that Marx is not a moralist, at least in the standard philosophic sense of that term (involving equality, general norms, and universality), but that yet he does give guidance for political choice to a great many people. Marx's philosophy is nonmoral yet "decent." That and other terms relating to personality and character are said to be better explained in causal rather than morally evaluative terms. Patrick Riley takes issue with this method of dealing with character, and argues that if it were true its relativism would undermine Miller's own argument. Riley also maintains that Marx clearly did have a concept of moral *right* even though he did not adhere to a theory of *equality* of rights. Frederick Whelan contends that Miller's tests for a theory of morality (which provide the basis for his conclusion that Marx is not a moralist) are really tests for a theory of justice. Morality includes other elements, such as benevolence and virtue; Marx's larger political theory, Whelan insists, requires a theory of revolutionary virtue. Whelan extends his argument to deal with difficulties encountered by "socialist" states.

Sheldon Wolin, in Part II, asks, how can Marx's method be sound when his predictions have so conspicuously failed? The answer, he holds, appears to be twofold. It is partly that Marx's intentions were not solely scientific: they were both pragmatic and dynamic, intended to produce revolutionary and political action. He never completed the scientific argument in support of his belief that eventually men would overcome the exploitative aspects of the economic system and humanize it; the system was in reality too protean. Moreover, Wolin suggests, only a worldwide revolution could overcome the opposition forces. The second part of Wolin's case, however, is that in the further evolution of Marx's thought forces inherent in the total capitalist system revolutionize it without need for a proletarian revolution. Hence the prediction of revolution appears not as a failed prophecy, but as "solace," a memorial to Marx's early faith in human action. (P. 107)

Both of the commentators on Wolin take sharp issue with his argument, one briefly and one at considerable length. Stephen Holmes finds both Marx and Wolin incurably romantic. In both emotional commitment is at odds with theoretical insight. Alan Gilbert strongly disagrees with Wolin's largely intellectual and technological interpretation of Marx, contending that Marx's own political activity and the revolutionary movements that he in some degree spawned had profound influence on his work. He denies both that Marx came to believe in an all-powerful capitalism and that he became despairing of effective proletarian action against it.

Part III is devoted to Marx and the law. Our leading author in this part, Mark Tushnet, admits to considerable difficulty in specifying a uniquely Marxist theory of law. Neither the subject matter nor the substantive content of a distinctive theory of law emerges. He does believe, however, that the structure of legal categories provides some hills in which the gold of a Marxist theory of law may be found. All else has been destroyed by Legal Realism. Well, perhaps not quite everything else. When searching for the nature of law or the factors influencing its development one should always start with "the relations of production" (without worrying about whether they are "in the last instance" determinative). This is a small piece of turf, but Tushnet advances reasons for holding it sufficient to constitute the basis for a Marxist theory of law.

Tom Gerety embeds his comments on Tushnet in a more far-ranging discussion. Examining the works of Eugene Genovese and E.P. Thompson, he finds that the former illustrates that good Marxist work in legal history is possible, while Thompson shows that such work at its best is only loosely and ambiguously "Marxist." Turning then to Tushnet and to Duncan Kennedy, Gerety finds the Marxist element even harder to detect. Having found these new legal Marxists mildly interesting and at most "suggestive," he goes on to inqure, in a famous phrase, "What is to be done?" No clear answer to this question is vouchsafed, but one thing that does come out of the investigation is that a Marxist lawyer is in a nasty predicament: he cannot fairly represent his clients and at the same time act as a Marxist revolutionary should act. A lawyer who helps his clients in the courtroom risks convincing them that the system works! Thus, in the words of Gerety's title, good lawyers make bad Marxists. The converse, that good Marxists make bad lawyers, he hints may also be true.

Leon Lipson also comments on Tushnet's paper. Noting the difficulty that Tushnet finds in searching for a Marxist theory of law, and having regard both for Tushnet's requirement that such a theory must be *good* theory and for Lipson's own contention that it must look at law from outside of law, Lipson concludes—after a brief examination of Pashukanis's would-be Marxist theory of law—that Tushnet's pursuit faces such obstacles that it must be based on great optimism indeed.

In Part IV, we have lumped together three interesting discussions of various aspects of Marxism that do not relate primarily either to each other or to any one of the first three parts. (Relations do exist, however, and are in some instances adverted to.)

G.A. Cohen, a philosopher, has something to add to his influential book on Marx's economic and technological determinism. While he by no means retracts his earlier argument, he does qualify it. He continues to hold that Marx held this theory, but he is less sure that it is true—less sure, in fact, of how it can be either confirmed or disconfirmed. His rich and complex argument defies summarization. It involves him with Marx's philosophical anthropology, his theory of history, his economics, and his vision of the society of the future, about each of which he has something important to say.

Peter Stillman, in an essay already referred to, analyzes the structure (perhaps "strategy" would be a better word) of Marx's work. It is not the substance of Marx's *corpus*, hardly even his method in the usual sense, that Stillman finds of continuing value. Rather, his focus is on "critique," the word that appears in the title or subtitle of so many of Marx's writings, including even *Capital* itself. This term embraces three steps of analysis, each at both a theoretical and a practical level: first, "immanent criticism," then "critical reconstruction," and finally "critical supersession." After explaining and illustrating Marx's deployment of these levels of criticism, Stillman deals briefly with present-day scholars who, shunning dogmatic Marxism, make use of this approach, the most eminent of whom is Jürgen Habermas.

Finally comes the Norwegian scholar, Jon Elster, who incidentally takes issue with Cohen at one point. His chapter might have been placed in Part I, which deals with "Marx and Morality," for Elster does indeed have much to say about Marx's position on moral issues, arguing for instance that Marx in fact has a theory of justice even though he himself may not have thought so. Nonetheless, to place Elster's essay under this heading would risk distorting the reader's understanding, for its primary purpose is to explicate the meaning in Marx's system of the crucial terms "exploitation," "freedom," and "justice." That Marx's use of these concepts has moral implications is not Elster's chief concern.

With no more by way of introduction we now let the writers speak for themselves. We do thank them for their contributions and for their patient compliance with editorial suggestions, frequently involving the painful process of condensation. We also thank Eleanor Greitzer, assistant to the editors, for so willingly taking the blame for any of our mistakes or oversights that she fails to catch!

J.R.P.
J.W.C.

PART I

MARX AND MORALITY

1

MARX AND MORALITY

RICHARD W. MILLER

In a very broad sense, Marx is a moralist, and sometimes a stern one: he offers a rationale for conduct that sometimes requires self-sacrifice in the interests of others. That the conduct he calls for will sometimes involve "self-sacrificing heroism" is epitomized in his praise of the "heaven storming" men and women who defended the Paris Commune (CWF, p. 568; Kugelman, SC, p. 247).[1] His concern that conduct be reasonable and well-informed is clear when he distinguishes the scientific basis for present-day workers' struggles from the "fantastic," even "reactionary" misconceptions supporting workers' struggles in the past (CM, pp. 359 ff.).

At the same time, Marx often explicitly attacks morality and fundamental moral notions. He accepts the charge that "Communism . . . abolishes . . . all morality, instead of constituting [it] on a new basis" (CM, p. 351). The materialist theory of ideology is supposed to have "shattered the basis of all morality, whether the morality of asceticism or of enjoyment" (GI, p. 115). Talk of "equal right" and "fair distribution" is, he says, "a crime," forcing "on our Party . . . obsolete verbal rubbish . . . ideological nonsense about right and other trash so common among the democrats and French Socialists" (CGP, p. 388).

Evidently, the very broad usage in which Marx might be called a moralist is artificially broad and misleading, in his own view. In the abstract, this is no paradox. Though philosophers commonly ignore it, a vast territory lies between narrow self-inter-

3

est and what would naturally be called morality. For example, Max Weber sometimes asserts his commitment to world power for his nation, a commitment requiring self-sacrifice and supported in part by rational reflection on courses of action and their consequences. He accepts that his nationalism does not give equal weight to the interests of everyone, e.g., to his own, to French nationalists', and to the interests of those Germans who would prefer the situation of "a 'little' people" to that of "a people organized into a Great Power."[2] When he speaks of his nationalist commitment as political, not moral, and capable of overriding moral commitments in his hierarchy of concerns, we understand him, even if we are repelled. Similarly, Nietzsche's outlook is amoral but not at all self-centered, since the elite are committed to the hard-fought defense of their common excellence. In everyday life, loyalty to family or friends that exceeds moral requirements is also located in between self-centeredness and morality.

It is not clear, however, in just what ways Marx's outlook differs from morality. Nor is it clear for just what reasons people are to make his move away from morality. In pursuing these questions, I will try to be fair to the texts. But my main interest is to present plausible arguments for a radical departure from the moral point of view, at least as philosophers have conceived it. When its foundations are brought to light, Marx's rejection of morality as a basis for political action turns out to be complex, well-argued, and humane, though, in an important sense, antihumanitarian. Moreover, it is based on aspects of Marx's social theory that many non-Marxists would accept. Whether or not his views are ultimately valid, they should have a status that they lack at present: a standard alternative that must be addressed in thoughtful discussions of morality.

1. THE DISTINCTNESS OF MORALITY

As a basis for resolving political questions, morality, in the narrower sense, is distinct from self-interest, class interest, national interest, or purely aesthetic concerns. The bases for political decision that we most comfortably classify as moralities tend to display three features:

1) *Equality.* People are to be shown equal concern or respect or afforded equal status. In the manner appropriate to choices of institutions and political strategies, everyone is to be treated as an equal. Of course, there are big disagreements as to what the appropriate form of equality is. But some standard of equality is to be the ultimate basis for resolving conflicts among different people's interests.

2) *General norms.* The right resolution of any major political issue would result from applying valid general norms to the specific facts of the case at hand. These rules are valid in all societies in which there is a point to resolving political disputes by moral appeal; roughly, all societies in which cooperation benefits almost everyone but scarcity is liable to give rise to conflicts (Hume's and Rawls's "circumstances of justice").

3) *Universality.* Anyone who rationally reflects on relevant facts and arguments will accept these rules, if he or she has the normal range of emotions.

In portraying Marx as a critic of the moral point of view in politics, I mean that he argues against all three principles as inappropriate to choosing what basic institutions to pursue. As I have mentioned, there is still a broad sense in which he does describe a moral point of view. He makes arguments for strategies which might require self-sacrifice. Distinctions between decency and indecency, what ought to be done and what ought not, have a role in his outlook. His arguments, primarily directed at choices among political and economic systems, may leave standing most ordinary morality concerning actions towards individuals. But it is also natural to adopt the narrower usage, and to see Marx as advancing a nonmorality. The three principles, after all, capture the important ways in which a basis for choice might be seen as neutral and as displaying a concern for all. The first requires neutrality among different people's interests. The second requires impartial reference to the social circumstances of all historical societies concerned with morality. The third requires arguments that impartially appeal to everyone's rational capacities. It is the neutrality of the moral point of view that we emphasize in distinguishing obviously moral outlooks from obviously nonmoral ones.

Admittedly, some philosophers whom we take to offer a morality reject some of the three principles, at least on a rigid interpretation of them. Aristotle, for example has no ultimate premise of equality (or so I have argued elsewhere.)[3] But when we encounter someone who rejects all three principles (Weber, for example, in his discussions of international relations), most of us naturally take him or her to have departed from the moral point of view.

Despite these considerations, someone might be disinclined to follow Marx in associating the moral point of view as such with commitment to at least some of the three premises. After all, the premises are highly abstract, while "morality" is an everyday term, not a product of philosophical reflection. Beyond a point, the disagreement is purely verbal. What is important is that Marx attacks pervasive philosophical assumptions about morality, that his attack separates him much further from typical moral philosophers than they are separated one from another, and that his consequent outlook on basic social choices is unexpectedly close to outlooks that we would all be inclined to call nonmoral. Granted, the content of this outlook, as I shall interpret it, would lead most people to regard it as decent and humane in its values. In this way, it differs from Nietzsche's or Weber's. That is, in itself, an interesting result. If Marx is right, motivations that initially attract us to the three premises should lead most of us to reject them when we reflect on their consequences for political decision.

2. EQUALITY

Most of the antimoral arguments suggested by Marx's writings attack the first premise, the premise of equality. Before developing them, however, I need to sketch the grains of truth that Marx discerns in the demand for equality. Otherwise, my interpretation will seem perverse.

Marx advocates social arrangements that would, in his view, make people much more equal in power and enjoyment than they are at present. Initially, at least, these arrangements would embody standards that Marx explicitly characterizes as standards of equal right, e.g., "To each according to his or her labor" (CGP, pp. 386–388). Marx's case for these arrangements and standards is that they would enhance people's lives, not that they would conform to some ultimate standard of equality. Yet among the dimensions of life that Marx emphasizes, two are especially connected with equality. Under socialism and communism, most people are less dominated, more in possession of their lives, since they are better able to develop their capacities in light of their own assessments of their needs. Moreover, their interactions will be governed to a greater extent than now by mutual well-wishing and concern. In Marx's view, these goods of freedom and reciprocity are what most people have really desired when they have made equality their battle cry. In sum, an ultimate standard of equality, though a mistake for most people, is a mistake that often leads people in the right direction. It is often a one-sided or confused expression of rational desires really satisfied by communist society (see Engels to Bebel, SC, p. 276; *Anti-Duehring*, p. 118).[4]

Ultimate demands for equality are of four kinds: distributive, requiring that all possess an equal bundle of goods, resources or opportunities; rights-based, requiring conformity to certain rights possessed equally by all; attitudinal, requiring that equal concern or respect be shown to all; and standards of impartiality, requiring that the general welfare be promoted without bias toward the good of some. All of these prove inadequate as ultimate bases for decision, in the face of inescapable conflicts in class-divided societies. From case to case, institutions should treat people equally in certain specific ways, but they should not do so to satisfy a standard of equality. Rather, a good form of equality is a good tool for producing certain effects, assessed without applying such a standard.

3. EQUAL DISTRIBUTION

Distributive ideals are especially important to Marx because of their influence on the workers' movement through proposals of Proudhon's and Bakunin's. He argues that a distributive standard is inappropriate for basic social choices, if it is a general demand for equal goods and powers, while it is utopian, if it takes the form of Proudhon's and Bakunin's more specific criteria of equality.

The general demand that all have an equal bundle of goods,

resources, and opportunities is inappropriate as the main standard for judging social arrangements because people's main concern is with social relations and well-being, not with equal distribution as such. Equality could, in principle, be achieved by dragging everyone down to a common, low level. Marx labels the outlook that would then be satisfied "crude communism." He points out that it would corrupt interactions, because it is motivated by envy. Moreover, it is self-destructive because unconcerned with the growth of people's satisfactions and powers. (See EPM, pp. 152–155; CM, p. 359.)

A parallel argument is suggested by Marx's emphasis on exploitation, as against unequal distribution. Exploitation produces inequalities no greater than those in many nonexploitive situations, such as the inequalities produced by the differing fertility of independent family homesteads. Yet the existence of exploitation provides a much more urgent rationale for change. In sum, the most basic social choices should be guided by mutual concern and respect, the pursuit of material and cultural well-being, and the avoidance of exploitation, not by distributive equality as such.

While these criticisms are relevant to utterly general demands for distributive equality, they may not do justice to the demand for equal distribution that Proudhon and Bakunin had in mind. Equality for them probably meant sufficient equality of resources and opportunities to guarantee full and equal independence for all. This full and equal independence is distinguished both from the economic subordination of those who must work for others in order to live, and the political subordination of those subject to state interference, even if the state is democratically controlled. This ideal of equal independence leads Proudhon and Bakunin to pursue a politically decentralized society of independent producers, sufficiently equal in resources that no one economically dominates others. In Marx's view, this ideal is utopian. Sufficient equality of productive resources is ephemeral, at best, in a modern setting of physically interdependent production. The network of production, if carried out by independent units, must be regulated by market mechanisms. Even if the distribution of productive resources is initially equal, luck, if nothing else, will soon create some inequalities. Market mechanisms will magnify the first inequalities, as the rich get richer through economies of scale, thicker cushions against calamity, greater access to credit, and greater capacity to innovate. The eventual result is financial ruin and dispossession for the many and their subordination to the few who come to control the means of production. "[E]xchange value . . . is in fact the system of equality and freedom, and . . . the disturbances which they encounter in the further development of the system are disturbances inherent in it, are merely the realization of equality and freedom, which prove to be inequality and unfreedom" (G, pp. 248 ff.).

4. EQUAL RIGHTS

These problems with distributive equality make rights-based standards all the more attractive, for a society may respect rights when goods are partitioned in a variety of changing patterns. But rights-based equality encounters its own distinctive problem. There are too many rights. The conflicting interests of different groups set equally basic rights in conflict. These conflicts are properly resolved by treating rights as means for enhancing people's lives, not as ultimate standards.

The first stage of socialism would, for example, fulfill the right of each to an income according to his or her labor. But, just by that token, it violates the communist standard, to each according to his or her needs, since the frail worker with children to bring up gets no more than the strong, childless worker. "This equal right is an unequal right for unequal labor . . . It is, therefore, a right of inequality in its content, like every right" (CGP, p. 387). By comparison with capitalism, too, the first stage of socialism violates rights that should claim the attention of a rights-based moralist. The factories of Horatio Alger types, acquired through hard work and honest bargains, are confiscated, just as robber barons' are. People are kept from investing hard-won resources in private factories and farms. In short, the right to reward in proportion to labor is preserved by violating the right to the results of nonaggressive labor and honest bargains.

One can say that the socialist right is a higher right, the communist standard a right in a very broad sense, which is higher still. But on what scale have these rights been weighed? Not all of the needed weighing can be done on the scale of a further, super-right. Any right is "a right of inequality," conflicting with others in ways that demand resolution (CGP, p. 387). These conflicts are to be resolved by treating rights as means to life enhancement, choosing those which would most enhance well-being if embodied in society at the time in question.

Marx's most detailed discussion of conflicts among rights, in the *Critique of the Gotha Program*, concerns rights to income. But a similar conflict among political rights also emerges from his writings. The equal right of all to be left alone by government and the equal right of all to effective participation in government are independent and important aspects of rights-based political equality. In a class-divided society, they inevitably conflict. Without collective ownership dominated by a workers' state (with the interference that entails), economic power becomes concentrated in the hands of a few, who dominate effective participation in government as a result. Yet the demand for noninterference is not in general misguided or purely ideological. Individuality and independence are real needs. (See CM p. 347.)

As with all the conflicts among rights that Marx describes, analogous conflicts arise for most people who accept interference with laissez-faire capitalism, even if they reject Marx's socialism. The right to participation must be balanced against the right to noninterference. For most of us, attracted both to non-subordination and to noninterference, the only reasonable way to secure both rights is to treat both as instruments, and find institutions and strategies that most enhance people's lives in society as a whole.

Most of these conflicts reflect a more general split among rights-based standards of equality. On the one hand, people have a right to an equal distribution of the benefits, powers, and burdens of the basic social arrangements that dominate their lives and which can only be avoided at great cost, if at all. In economics, this demand for equal terms for cooperation leads to the socialist or the communist standard; in politics, to the demand for equal influence on the political process. On the other hand, people have an independent right peacefully to pursue their interests without interference. This implies a right to invest, retain, and bequeath in the economic realm, and a right to freedom from state interference in politics. In modern systems of interdependent production, these two dimensions of rights inevitably conflict. Yet most of us, so far as we base social choice on rights, regard neither dimension as intrinsically superior. (Marx's arguments are not meant to convince someone who approves of rights to noninterference no matter what the consequences.) The existence of this conflict between noninterference and fair terms for cooperation is the general, though nonconclusive, reason for supposing that rights-based equality generates conflicts that only a nonrights basis for choice can resolve. That the general problem had not been solved, even approximately, despite centuries of trying made it a good bet, by Marx's time, that it was insoluble.

A modern assessment of Marx's attack on morality would have to be anachronistic and consider twentieth-century attempts to solve the general problem. I will just mention one aspect of this further assessment. Rawls's theory of justice is, in part, an effort to reveal the one overriding version of equality appropriate to the choice of basic institutions.[5] But if I have posed the problem about rights correctly, Rawls' theory seems too biased toward one dimension of rights to solve the problem without begging the question. Even if Rawls' hypothetical contract describes fair terms for cooperation, the peacefully self-aggrandizing entrepreneur who has not actually agreed to such a contract can appeal to the consideration that people should be free peacefully to pursue their interests. The original position expresses a very different consideration, the demand that the burdens and benefits of cooperation be fairly distributed. To judge the peaceful self-aggrandizer's appeal from the standpoint of the original position is simply to ignore the independent weight of rights to noninterference.[6]

5. EQUAL CONCERN

It might seem that the failures of distributive and rights-based equality are due to their rigid reliance on abstract rules, rather than concrete emotions. Equality and morality ultimately rest on a humanitarian feeling of equal concern and respect for all.

Marx criticizes this heartfelt equality by opposing it to the attitudes required for effective change in a class-divided society. "[T]rue socialism [i.e., the movement of that name in Germany in the 1840s] concerned no longer with real human beings but with 'Man', has lost all revolutionary enthusiasm and proclaims instead the universal love of mankind" (GI, p. 130). Given Marx's view of social reality, this contrast is psychological common sense. For example, the militant strikes that can improve the status of the working class harm the vital interests of factory owners, and may drive some into bankruptcy. Yet, as Marx often emphasizes, many of these factory owners are personally decent. So are many of the police whom militant strikers must often fight off, sometimes quite violently. And a militant strike is among the mildest of the confrontations that are crucial levers of change for Marx. To give sharp confrontations a crucial role and require that they be based on a feeling of equal concern for all would be either hypocritical or self-defeating. That is so, in any case, unless reference to equal concern is reference to respect for principles of distribution, rights, or impartiality. But then we are back in the troubled realm of rigid and abstract rules of equality.

6. UTILITARIANISM

Everything said so far might, in principle, be said by a utilitarian. In utilitarianism, only one kind of equality is fundamental: the general welfare is to be determined without bias toward some people's well-being. For Marx, this unbiased determination of the general welfare is impossible.

If the general welfare is identified with some homogeneous happiness stuff, valuable in proportion to intensity and extent, we commit "the apparent stupidity of merging all the manifold relationships of people in the one relation of usefulness" (GI, p. 110). A society of frenetically self-aggrandizing shopkeepers, each feeling intense pleasure at routine triumphs in getting the best of others, but not crestfallen by routine defeats, is less desirable, all else being equal, than a society of people who wish each other well and enjoy acting on their mutual concern. Yet in the two societies, people might, in principle, "use" their relations to produce equal amounts of pleasure. Some relations, activities, and experiences are more to be promoted than others whose enjoyment is just as intense and pervasive. By the same token, to adopt the intensity-and-pervasiveness standard is not really to embrace a neutral standard. Only to care about the intensity and pervasiveness of enjoyment is, at best, to adopt a quite definite and idiosyncratic conception of welfare. This conception is rejected by most people (perhaps all) when they refuse to merge all relationship into the one relation of using others for one's pleasure, and rationally reflect on the different relationships that one might enjoy.

A generally acceptable standard must distinguish between different bases for equally intense enjoyment. However, we cannot make the necessary discriminations without social bias. No ranking of all important goods, including, say, leisure as against material income, the enjoyment of competitive striving as against the enjoyment of cooperation, and the chance to occupy the top of hierarchies as against the guarantee of a secure, moderately comfortable life, is faithful to the needs or the reflective desires of all—industrial workers, farmers, investment bankers, housewives, shopkeepers, and professors alike. If we seek a ranking that all would accept if they had relevant data, we are pursuing what does not exist. If we adopt the ranking of those who have actually tasted all kinds of pleasure, we show bias toward the upper strata who are able to practice such connoisseurship. In short, Mill's proposal to weigh different kinds of experience impartially, by relying on the expertise of those who have experienced all the kinds in question, is either biased or ineffective.

These troubling connections between social location and psychological structure are part of the basis for Marx's claim in *The German Ideology:* "The connection of the enjoyment of the individuals at a particular time with the class relations in which they live . . . shattered the basis of all morality, whether the morality of asceticism or of enjoyment" (p. 115). Later on, in *Capital,* the charge that utilitarianism neglects the impact of social processes on basic human wants reemerges in a savage criticism of Bentham, "a genius in the way of bourgeois stupidity" who fails to distinguish what is useful for different epochs and classes and instead "takes the modern shopkeeper, especially the English shopkeeper, as the normal man" (p. 571). Finally, at the end of his life, Marx reaffirms the social relativity of needs in his notes on Adolf Wagner's *Lehrbuch der politischen Oekonomie:* "[If 'Man'] means Man, as a category, he has . . . no . . . needs at all. . . . If it means a man who is already to be found in some form of society . . . one must begin by presenting the particular character of this social man, i.e., the particular character of the community in which he lives."[7]

Again, a development since Marx's time is relevant to the larger argument. Modern economics has produced conceptions of the general welfare that rely on functions ranging over individual preferences. In effect, the summing of experiences in classical utilitarianism is replaced by ideal voting schemes. The economists' utilitarianism seems, however, to be much less appropriate to choices of basic institutions than Bentham's or Mill's. Interpersonal comparisons of intensity play no role. Preference sets are not subject to criticism as making for more or less happiness, even though basic institutions themselves play an important role in determining preferences. Finally, in light of Arrow's famous theorem, preference utilitarianism turns out to lack the virtues of precision and generality that make it attractive in the first place, as against the traditional alternatives.

The conflicting rankings of goods that cannot be reconciled by effective and impartial methods are extremely important in the choice among basic institutions. A socialist state, for example, cannot offer everyone whatever education or occupation he or she wants. Under capitalism, such choices are often constrained by finances or family background. Most people, if they accept Marx's factual claims about capitalist constraints and socialist possibilities, would prefer to work out these problems of choice in a socialist framework. But not every sane person would. Some care too deeply, for their own and for others' sake, that striving for personal betterment, free from direct interference, be allowed, even if lack of resources often makes the prospects dim. Similarly, the institutions of Marx's classless society allow little scope for purely self-interested competition. For some, this activity is an important positive good.

If the different rankings of goods are different enough, there is no possible compromise, since feasible economic systems violate either one conception of the good or the other. Marx addresses himself to the majority's conception, but not out of a complacent belief that the majority must be correct. Socialism and communism are addressed to actual needs. But that those needs are the proper objects of political action, as against their rivals, is not a matter of fact. (As usual, almost all of those who reject Marx's specific social goals will find that their own outlooks are affected by similar conflicts in analogous ways, when they chose between laissez-faire capitalism and somewhat more collective arrangements.)

Marx's theoretical criticism gains in importance when we consider the practical context, the pursuit of means to change society. In his view, the struggles that eventually lead to socialism are often dangerous and uncertain. They sometimes fail, or even make matters worse. To sign on to this movement, one ought rationally to believe that it may make the world a lot better if it succeeds. Thus, even if different conceptions of the good are not different enough to affect a preference for socialism when all facts are known with certainty, they might affect a rational decision to take part in the struggle for socialism, in an uncertain and dangerous world.

7. GENERALITY

The second typical feature of moralities, after the equality they require, is the generality of the norms on which they rely. We can assess any social arrangement by applying to the particular facts at hand norms that are valid whenever moral appeals have a point. Or at any rate, the major questions about stable features of societies can be settled in this way, whatever dilemmas arise in emergencies.

The basic reason Marx denies that general norms rate all societies when applied to relevant facts is that the goods now to be pursued have been in deep and irreconcilable conflict in the past. Marx's paradigm of this conflict is classical Athens. The Greeks, he says, "excused the slavery of one on the ground that it was a means to the full development of another" (C, p. 385). Behind this excuse was a reality. The technological capacities of ancient Greece made cultural development dependent on leisure for some based on enforced drudgery for others. The competing goods, here, are so important and different that there is no basis for determining whether Greek institutions were desirable. Not moral reasoning but the course of history produced a solution to this dilemma, the dependence of the development of human powers on subordination, monotony, and violence. "In proportion as labor develops socially, and becomes thereby a source of wealth and culture, poverty and destitution develop among the workers, and wealth and culture among the non-workers. . . . This is the law of all history hitherto . . . [I]n present capitalist society, conditions have at least been created which enable and compel the workers to lift this social curse" (CGP, p. 384). ("Wealth" here clearly refers to really beneficial resources.) The enhancement of life in society as a whole, governed by Marx's conception of the good, is not meant to be a standard by means of which past societies can be rated. Marx never suggests that there is a fact of the matter as to whether classical Athens was better as a slave society rich in cultural goods than it would have been had it remained a cluster of villages based on subsistence farming. The norms that ought to guide us now and in the future are not suited for judgments of the past. But Marx's nonmorality claims no more than guidance for the present and the future.

8. UNIVERSAL RATIONALITY

The third feature of typical moralities is a kind of epistemological equality. Moral norms are supposed to be accepted by anyone who rationally reflects on appropriate arguments, accepts relevant factual claims, and possesses the normal range of emotions.

I have already mentioned one reason Marx rejects this claim to universality. Different people attach different importance to rival goods as important for themselves and for others, say, competitive striving as against cooperation, or material income as against leisure. Institutions cannot be neutral in all these rivalries. Everyone cannot be brought to agree by rational persuasion.[8]

Beyond this, Marx must have been impressed by facts of historical diversity. In ancient Greece and Rome, he emphasizes, everyone accepted slaves as appropriate to the functioning of a normal household. In medieval Europe, everyone gave customary restrictions and obligations of kinship great moral weight, much more so than in the present day. It simply is not true that all intelligent normal modern people, aware of relevant facts and arguments, accept the earlier rules as morally valid in their respective settings. Nor is it true that ignorance or unreason were the basis for the older views. That Aristotle would have changed his mind about slavery if he had appreciated some fact or argument does not fit what we know about Aristotle and his contemporaries.[9]

9. IDEOLOGY

Marx sometimes summarizes his rejection of morality in the statement that morality, like religion, is ideological (e.g., CM, p. 351; CGP, p. 388). An ideology, for Marx, is a system of beliefs and attitudes that distort reality and that result from social forces, characteristic of class societies, that have no tendency to bring ideas in line with reality.

Though it is clear that Marx analyzes the origins of moral ideas in this way, it is not clear what, if anything, the analysis adds to his criticism of morality. For one thing, the label of "ideology" presupposes the arguments already investigated, in which morality is criticized as intellectually defective. Ideology is *false* consciousness. In Marx's meta-ethics, just as much as in his economics, the case that a system of ideas is ideological must include arguments that it is invalid. So far, those arguments have been independent of historical examinations of social origins.

In addition, Marx's actual historical discussions of the social origins of moral ideas are fragmentary. The scattered remarks are intriguing. In his view, the modern ideas about equality, freedom, justice, and the general welfare that he criticizes are in part a cultural inheritance from the bourgeoisie's triumph over feudal restrictions (GI p. 84; G, p. 245). In part, they are the result of a kind of wishful thinking to which a middle-class background gives rise, a false hope that domination by entrenched elites can be overcome within a system of individual

competition (CM, pp. 354 ff.; G, pp. 248 ff.). In part, they result from the tendency of bourgeois media to limit and stultify
discontent, say, by presenting fair treatment by employers as
the only proper goal of workers' activism or by limiting the
proper role of government to the satisfaction of people's equal
rights. Consider, for example, traditional conservative efforts
to limit social demands by confining them to the fulfillment of
rights, as in David Stockman's recent remark, "What people
don't realize is that there are plenty of things they want that they
don't have a right to." For Marx, such a comment simply reveals that rights are less important than many suppose. For a
rights-based liberal or socialist, Stockman's remark imposes a
real burden of argument.[10] These speculations about social
origins are as convincing as any current hypothesis about the
origins of modern moral ideas. But they are fragmentary speculations, nonetheless.

With its limited role and speculative status, does the distinctive, causal aspect of Marx's thesis that morality is ideology make
any contribution to his case against morality? I think it does.
By offering an alternative interpretation of our feelings of attraction toward the moral point of view in politics, the thesis of
ideology undermines the use of those feelings as evidence.

Many people who are intellectually attracted to the antimoral
arguments previously sketched still feel reluctant to embrace
the conclusions. I feel this way myself. Such feelings are not
irrelevant to the decision whether to accept Marx's antimoral-
ism. One might, after all, find it so obvious that social choices
should be made on the basis of equal concern for all that Marx's
arguments merely convince one that a sufficiently abstract and
flexible basis for equal concern has not yet been described.
Nonetheless, one may feel, some such standard must exist.
However, feelings of obviousness and implausibility, attraction
and repulsion need to be interpreted before they can be given
evidential weight, and interpretation, here, includes causal explanation. Suppose that crucial feelings that the interests of all
must be treated equally are due to a cultural background ultimately shaped by bourgeois needs to tame discontent, and to a
lack of personal exposure to hard social realities. Interpreted
in this way, they should not lead one to resist the force of Marx's
case against morality. And the Marxist explanation is at least as

well-grounded as any claim that these feelings are based on an accurate moral sense. By analyzing their origins, Marx makes appeals to moral feelings less compelling, in much the same way as Freud undermined reliance on religious feelings by offering an alternative interpretation of their origins in terms of the dependency and fears of childhood and the unity of self and world felt in early infancy.

The argument from origins to the assessment of validity is supposed to be a fallacy, so monstrous that it has a name, "the genetic fallacy." What would be fallacious is the assumption that ideas are debunked simply by retracing their origins to social interests. This assumption is especially implausible for moral ideas. For example, a strong duty to be hospitable to strangers is accepted by traditional Eskimos because of a common interest in such hospitality in a seminomadic society where any family may be struck down in the constant battle with Nature. This explanation does not debunk. If anything, it justifies. Still, some causes are so inappropriate to some beliefs that the belief should be abandoned if we find it, in the final analysis, to be due to such a cause. Historical bourgeois interests in domination, together with a protected middle-class upbringing, are not appropriate as ultimate causal bases for a belief that all should be treated equally. Similar arguments about inappropriate causes are, after all, a normal aspect of scientific criticism. If contamination from the lab technician's hands caused the streptococcus colony in the Petri dish, and the consequent belief that the patient had strep throat, that is a ground for withdrawing the belief. Perhaps the patient does have a strep throat. Still it is no fallacy to deny that we are in a position to make this claim, since the causes of our belief would be inappropriate.

10. THE STRUCTURE OF A NONMORALITY

If Marx did not believe that there were norms that dictated the right political choices for every historical situation, he certainly wanted political choices in his time to be guided by large-scale and long-term norms, not by caprice or short-term interests. "The Communists fight for the attainment of the immediate aims . . . of the working class; but in the movement of the present they also represent and take care of the future of that movement" (CM, p. 361). If he does not address his arguments for guiding principles to the needs and the basic desires of all, he is certainly concerned to address those arguments to the working class as a whole, along with as many as share in the interests of the working class, on account of social situation or personal commitment. It is important to Marx that this intended audience is enormous. In a number of writings he takes it to be an attraction of communism that it reduces the barriers to irrational social choice by appealing to interests that most really share, and by constructing a society in which basic choices will eventually be guided by the interests of all, as outlooks become increasingly harmonious (e.g., GI, pp. 55 ff., 66; CM, pp. 344, 353). In short, with respect to a very large audience, Marx advocates principles that are supposed to guide present-day social and political choice in the same way as a political morality.

In broadest outline, Marx's nonmorality has the following shape. His arguments for certain social arrangements are partly based on an appeal to a diverse assortment of goods: freedom, reciprocity, self-expression, the avoidance of pain and premature death, and other relatively familiar goods that are obviously a part of Marx's case for socialism. However, the catalogue of general goods does not entirely determine that socialism be chosen, when combined with the social facts as Marx sees them. The more specific goods determining the choice of socialism can only be defined or chosen in response to reflection on the actual consequences of specific, feasible social alternatives. Marx addresses himself to the enormous audience of those who do respond with such a choice. But other responses would not be irrational or unfair.

The adoption of socialist goals does not complete Marx's premises for social choice. His outlook is more articulated than that. His political strategy for achieving socialism, while partly recommended as a means, is independently supported by its own value, assessed through similarly complex connections with general human goods. Finally, the basic question of whether and how to participate in the movement is determined by a further, partly independent standard, a conception of which character traits are to be admired and cultivated. I will fill in this outline of a highly articulated outlook through a series of contrasts with simpler bases of choice that are often ascribed to Marx.

The foundations for the choice of social arrangements in Marx are usually assumed to resemble utilitarianism in form, if not in content. Social arrangements are to be judged by their capacity to maximize along some favored dimension or dimensions. On some accounts, this dimension is material productivity. The best social arrangement is the one that contributes the most to the development of material productive powers, either in the circumstances in question or in the long run. Alternatively, the standard of choice is supposed to be the capacity to maximize certain aspects of human experience: pleasure or happiness, if Marx is taken to be a utilitarian, or a plurality of independent goods, including reciprocity, self-expression, and freedom.

In fact, basic societal choices in Marx are not determined by any logically prior maximizing standard. Consider, first, the productivity standard. As a description of a relation between successively evolving social forms, this standard is faithful to Marx's general statements about historical change. But as a standard of evaluation, it conflicts with several aspects of his writings. For one thing, if he had a productivity standard, his response to the violence, pain, and drudgery imposed by past social arrangements would be to excuse them, as necessary to the heightening of productivity. The proper outcome would be a justification of Athenian slavery, rather than Marx's actual nonjudgment. In the second place, Marx, both early and late, attacks the one-sidedness and monotony of work characteristic of industrial capitalism, while acknowledging the contribution of industrial capitalism to the growth of productive powers (EPM, p. 124; C, pp. 340 ff., 604; CGP, p. 388). Moreover, he portrays it as an advantage of socialism that people will be able to choose leisure over material production, when this suits their preference (C, III, p. 820). It would be arbitrary for someone who acknowledges the importance of goods conflicting with material production to rate material productivity the sole measure of a social system's worth. Finally, the one-sidedness of a productivity standard does not even have the advantage of rendering people's political choices more determinate. Those who resist processes of productive change, for example, English workers opposed to the regimentation of industrial work, certain early utopian socialists, and Sepoy mutineers, make a positive contribution to history as Marx sees it, at least as much as those who develop the productive forces. Through resistance to productive change, workers may acquire the knowledge and the unity to make successful revolutions and to control a postrevolutionary society. Working-class unity is a result of processes increasing productivity. But it is based, in part, on resistance to the necessary costs of such progress (see CM, pp. 342 ff.; C, ch. 15, sec. 5). Thus, a productivity standard would not tell most people what they ought to do in basic political choices.

I have already discussed certain distinctive problems of portraying Marx as a utilitarian. But Marx might still be taken to seek the maximization of each of a plurality of independent goods. This pluralist maximizing standard may not be effective for all societies, or justifiable to everyone. However, apart from this relativism, Marx's outlook would be an example of "ideal utilitarianism," like G.E. Moore's in *Principia Ethica.*

The problem with this interpretation is that it gives a commitment to general goals, not specified in terms of institutional arrangements, an absolute priority which it does not receive in Marx's writings. Certainly, Marx never presents his arguments in this ideal utilitarian style. More important, a criticism of this attempt to keep ultimate general goals separate and all-determining is implicit in Marx's actual arguments: stated in general terms, the goals are too vague fully to determine basic social choices; there is no way to make them appropriately determinate, except by redefining them in terms of social choices that are partially independent of the general goals.

Consider, for example, the goal of freedom. A concern for freedom is certainly one of the reasons why people should take seriously Marx's descriptions of how capitalism works, and his comparisons with socialist possibilities. A concern for freedom gives that sociology a bearing on choice. But someone might accept those social descriptions and reject socialism if he or she put enough weight on noninterference as an aspect of freedom, as against the possession of resources that make desires effective.

There is no reasonable way of specifying the emphasis on

resource freedom that a choice of socialism requires, without defining it as "sufficient emphasis to support the choice of socialism, given Marx's view of the facts." It will not do to say, in the abstract, that Marx's standard of choice rates resource freedom more highly than noninterference freedom. In some imaginable situations the interference required to maintain resource freedom for most people is so pervasive and repellent to so many that Marx himself and his intended audience would opt for noninterference. Imagine that most workers were so deeply committed to capitalist success that a socialist state must constantly intervene to prevent them from trying to set up independent factories and farms. Even in the real world as Marx sees it, the case for socialism does not depend on a rigid, lexical priority for resource freedom. To some people, it is a crucial aspect of the case for socialism that capitalism is apt to generate the direct and brutal forms of repression that Marx labelled "Caesarism" and "imperialism," and later Marxists "fascism." They are deeply concerned with noninterference and need a specific empirical argument as a basis for the decision that capitalism does not have overriding advantages on this dimension. People for whom choice would be indeterminate apart from this factor surely are not excluded from Marx's intended audience.

An absolute priority among aspects of freedom would be too rigid. But there seems to be no other, more flexible rating that is general, that determines basic social choices in the present day, and that accurately expresses standards that people bring to those choices. In particular, quantitative ratings that are specific enough to render choice determinate are overspecific to the point of absurdity. Is resource freedom supposed to trade for noninterference at a rate of six to one at the margin?

Marx's social choices are supposed to be justified among those concerned with freedom, reciprocity, the avoidance of suffering, and other goods, *if* the emphases they place on different aspects of these goods are sufficient to support the choice of socialism. This circularity is not to be removed by a more careful definition of the required emphases. It corresponds to the logic of justification, here. People concerned in general with freedom, reciprocity, the avoidance of suffering, and other familiar goals are presented with an empirical argument about the inevitable consequences of capitalism and the possibilities for change under socialism. If they accept those arguments, and respond with a basic social choice, it is usually a choice of socialism. That choice further defines their underlying goals. In an epistemological turn characteristic of both Marx and Hegel, rational people move from the general (the abstract goals) to the particular (the grasp of actual social consequences) and back to a revision of the general (the further specification of goals). Similarly, the determination of goals by choices in Marx corresponds to the account of moral insight in Hegel's *Philosophy of Right* (see especially the Introduction): the will transforms itself and renders itself determinate by reflective choice among increasingly concrete alternatives.

To a significant extent, the goods that socialism uniquely promotes must be specified and chosen as part of the choice of socialism itself. Thus, it was potentially misleading of me to say that Marx recommends social arrangements according to their tendency to enhance people's lives. There are diverse standards of enhancement, leading to different choices of social arrangements, possessed by actual rational people. None is uniquely reasonable, just as none is uniquely fair.

There are similar indeterminacies in other general goals besides freedom; reciprocity, for example. In many countries that are not technologically advanced, socialism would almost certainly require some official discrimination in favor of working-class families and against formerly bourgeois families in the provision of higher education. It would be hypocritical, here, to claim that the child of a formerly wealthy family is being treated on a basis of reciprocity. Also, the desire of the formerly wealthy for expensive goods will not be given any special weight, even if it is so urgent and entrenched as to constitute a real need and even if special needs are elsewhere accorded special treatment. Most people, if they accept Marxist accounts of the disruptions, social divisions, and restrictions of life under capitalism, would accept that the socialist alternative is preferable as a means of increasing reciprocity in society as a whole. But surely there is no calculus of reciprocity, based on a prior general standard, that justifies this choice.

This movement from the general to the specific and back to the revision of the general is not familiar in political philosophy and economics. It is utterly foreign to the academic theory of choice and decision. But it is ubiquitous in real-life choices. Consider the banal example of a multidimensional choice, along dimensions with no natural numerical measure: the choice of a car. Handling, acceleration, fuel economy, looks, and comfort are all relevant. Given his or her expectations as to what alternatives will be encountered, a prospective buyer can often sketch in a rough way his or her priorities among these dimensions. But an unexpected car may be encountered which handles so well, let us say, that it is worth the loss in fuel economy, even though that had seemed more important. It is bad psychology to claim that in every such case the prospective buyer has shifted from one set of goals to another. Rather, they have become clarified in light of the facts. It is mythmaking, rather than science, to suppose that the clarified goals can always be expressed without reference to particular car models. Given the complexities of the choice, such a standard would have to take the form, "At this level of handling, a loss of a unit of handling will begin to be acceptable if the following gains are made along other dimensions: three units of comfort. . . ." But any number assigned to the degree of fulfillment of a dimension of choice here is arbitrary, a numerical mask over the real facts of preferences among *particular* models. In effect, the neoclassical economist's paradigm of preferences among different baskets of commodities, each kind available in certain numbers of identical units, is being pressed into service where it does not belong.

If my reconstruction of Marx's logic is valid, commitment to a catalogue of general goods, together with acceptance of his empirical arguments, would not make one answer to the question, "What social arrangements are best at present?" rationally compelling for all. In this way, a commitment to socialism is part of the foundations of Marx's outlook. Once this basic societal goal is chosen, are the other basic political choices rationally determined? In particular, is the effective achievement of socialism now the only, or at least the overriding, consideration in the choice of strategies and actions? If so, Marx is, once again, fairly close to utilitarianism in the form of his basic standard. The ultimate standard is the efficiency with which a good is pursued, in this case, the speed with which socialism is reached.

Marx never explicitly answers these questions, but the purely instrumentalist standard is implausible, given extremely common attitudes which Marx can be assumed to share. It is unnecessary, given Marx's beliefs about the means to socialism. In the best reconstruction of his arguments, Marx is recommending his conception of the workers' movement both as something that effectively creates socialism, and as something with positive value in the context of capitalism. Both features play an important, independent role.

On the purely instrumental standard, where only the goal is important, the secure establishment of socialism is to be pursued if it requires, say, five generations of enormous avoidable suffering, with widespread intentional brutality and self-brutalization. The losses in the intermediate future are outweighed by the long-term gains. Few people are willing to accept such an extreme instrumentalism. In his writings, including his private correspondence, Marx, though he sometimes justifies workers' violence that the press condemns, never appeals to the consideration that everything is excused if it contributes to socialism. He seems to have shared in the general rejection of extreme instrumentalism.

More important, Marx's nonutilitarian framework provides no motivation for this instrumentalism. Utilitarians can base their instrumentalism on an argument about rational choice: people's experiences are all that a rational person cares about, in the final analysis; so the rational choice of an alternative solely depends on how it affects experiences; thus, a means is no more or less desirable than the experiential results of adopting it. This argument may be wrong, but it is worth taking seriously. It extrapolates from a plausible model for rational, self-interested choice. A theory that makes self-interested rationality continuous with socially responsible rationality is certainly attractive, especially in light of the distinctive problems of rights-based morality. However, an instrumentalism basing everything on the promotion of a specific social arrangement has no such appeal. It is not at all plausible that the institutional end results of political processes are all that a rational person cares about. No doubt, effects on long-term outcomes are important constraints on choices of courses of action. But reflection on feasible means of reaching a social goal might lead to a new choice of social goals. No argument from a model for self-interested choice makes such reflections look unreasonable. Indeed, at analogous levels of specificity, self-interested choosers often revise their goals after reflection on feasible means.

Admittedly, on a pessimistic assessment Marx might have adopted an extreme instrumentalism as his way out of a dilemma: the concerns that attract us to socialism make any feasible means of attaining this goal repellent. This is not Marx's view, however. Communists, he emphasizes, lead important fights for reforms, even while they connect them with long-term goals (CM, p. 361). Were it not for these reform struggles, the economic pressures of capitalism, even apart from its pressures toward war, would cause most people "to be degraded to one level mass of broken wretches past salvation" (WPP, p. 75). Moreover, aside from reforms that are won, the workers' movement that Marx supports is said to be a humanizing movement, on account of the cooperation, internationalism, rationality, and initiative which it prompts. "The working class . . . know that in order to work out their own emancipation . . . they will have to pass through long struggles, through a series of historical processes, transforming circumstances and men" (CWF, p. 558). Similarly, socialist "revolution is necessary . . . not only because the ruling class cannot be transformed in any other way, but also because the class overthrowing it can only in a revolution succeed in ridding itself of all the muck of the ages and becoming fitted to found society anew" (GI, p. 57). In sum, the workers' movement is not just a means to socialism, but a process of independent value.

Despite the independent status of the workers' movement, the repertoire of standards for choice is still incomplete, for the question of whether to take part in the movement, in ways that are required for its success, is not yet settled.

Suppose that socialism would improve the life of every worker. Still, it is true of every worker that socialism might triumph, to his or her benefit, even if he or she does not take an active part in the struggle. If the risks of participation were not severe, one might regard the free rider as not really accepting the standards previously introduced, the desirability of socialism and of the workers' movement that Marx describes. But the achievement of socialism requires substantial risks on the part of many people. So people can say without hypocrisy, "I think that the goal and movement are for the best, but I will stand aside." For example, in his writings on the Commune, Marx presents "the heroic self-sacrifice" (CWF, p. 568) of the Communards as a necessary episode in the struggle for socialism, scolding his friend Kugelmann for philistine neglect of this aspect of the struggle (SC, p. 247; see also CWF, pp. 569, 574). Immediate self-interest and approval of the workers' movement are too narrow a motivation for its success. Admittedly, if it were true that workers have nothing to lose but their chains, no special outlook would be needed to justify the risky choices, given the alleged advantages of socialism. But, as Marx must have known when he wrote the *Manifesto,* workers who revolt can lose their jobs, their lives, or be imprisoned, not to mention the torture of revolutionaries and their families, which was much rarer in Marx's gentler era. Perhaps, when he wrote the line about having nothing to lose, Marx was influenced by the theory of wages he held at the time, according to which actual wages were bound to decline to the level of bare physical survival, often dropping below it (see CM, p. 345). In that case, a new standard of motivation is at least required by the later Marx, since he had rejected this "iron law of wages" by 1865 at the latest (see WPP, pp. 71 ff., 75; C, p. 168; CGP, pp. 391 ff.).

Marx's general program cannot succeed unless many people accept risks that are not adequately motivated by a sincere desire that his goals and strategy be fulfilled. His politics require that people's actions be guided by a certain type of character, something in addition to preference for the other general standards. This is the character that Marx associated with the hero Prometheus, and saw embodied in generations of class-conscious workers, including Chartists, the participants in the Silesian weavers' uprising, the workers of Paris, Berlin, and Vienna in 1848–49, and the men and women of the Paris Commune. The development of this character is central to the capsule history of the modern working class in the *Manifesto* (pp. 340–345). As portrayed there, and in Marx's historical vignettes, it unites hatred of oppressors with concern for the oppressed, truculence when interests are basically opposed with a positive desire to cooperate when possible, discipline with creativity and tolerance for risks. There is no question that Marx admired this combination of traits and sought to encourage it. The logic of Marx's argument gives this admiration and encouragement an independent role in his outlook.

Some of the most important questions about Marx's replacement for morality concern this model of character. For one thing, how can he expect and recommend widespread subordination of immediate self-interest, while criticizing the philanthropic outlook of the "True Socialists?" Marx's answer is implicit in his interpretations of a variety of empirical data, derived, in part, from popular movements in the French Revolution, the Chartist struggle for the ten-hour day, uprisings of Silesian weavers and Moselle peasants, and Marx's own experiences as a leader of workers and poor peasants in 1848–49. As a basis for self-sacrifice, morality is less effective than concern for a group with whom one shares common enemies and with whom one frequently cooperates on the basis of real and growing reciprocity.

As capitalism develops, it eventually creates and strengthens such solidarity among more and more workers and lower-middle-class people. Within the working class, capitalism breaks down barriers of locale and status, unites people in farflung interdependent production which encourages interdependent resistance, and concentrates and coordinates the capitalist power that workers resist. In this way, "[t]he advance of industry, whose involuntary promoter is the bourgeoisie, replaces the isolation of the laborers, due to competition, by their revolutionary combination, due to association" (CM, p. 345). The special power of commitments based on such association is crucial for changing society, because the necessary steps involve risky and violent actions, requiring boldness and initiative from many people acting at the same time against a better-armed, well-coordinated enemy. Equal sympathy for everyone does not supply a strong enough motive, and, indeed, may undermine necessary actions. Thus, communism, as against movements based on moral appeals, is not "an ideal to which reality will have to adjust itself," but "the real movement which abolishes the present state of things" (GI, p. 57).

This response to the first question makes another especially urgent. Do Marx's model revolutionaries have respect and consideration for strangers who are not allied with the proletariat? In practice, Marx does show such concern, for example, in his condemnations of British brutality toward people in India who are not yet relevant to important class struggles. But it is not clear how he could develop his model of character so as to describe an outlook of broad but not equal and universal concern. Certainly, general, precise but nonegalitarian rules, "100 units of concern for proletarians, 60 for small farmers, five for nonvicious capitalists," seem both callous and silly.

Probably the balance of humanitarianism and narrowness is best understood in terms of a model of character formation. The character that Marx recommends is the product of certain experiences and interactions: love and reciprocity sufficient to create a willingness to make sacrifices for others, even outside of one's personal acquaintance, the hatred of oppression and angry contempt for oppressors, and, finally, the mutual wellwishing that arises from cooperation against oppression. The attitudes to which such a personal history give rise, when informed by awareness of relevant facts, determine the levels of concern of which Marx approves. As in ideal observer theories of morality, the right decision, here, is the one that would be made by fully informed people with an appropriate cognitive and emotional makeup. However, the choice of qualifications is not justifiable to all or justifiable from unbiased perspectives.

Of course, this model is a speculation, an attempt to describe one basis for Marx's various specific statements of approval and disapproval. What is important is that Marx does not have to abandon his ideal of the proletarian revolutionary when he shows concern for those who make no contribution to proletarian struggles.

My description of Marx's positive outlook is now complete. It comprises a series of fundamental commitments that all rational, fully informed people would not share, commitments that do not give equal weight to everyone's interests. At the same time, a catalogue of goods that are the object of humane concern for everyone is relevant, though not determinant, for each commitment.

11. CONCLUSION

How far does one have to go with Marx before one is compelled to accept his criticisms of morality? There are, I think, four basic propositions from which the rejection of morality would follow:

1. Various needs of the vast majority are in such conflict with those of minorities that an ultimate standard of equality would have intolerable costs.

2. Strategies for effective change require obstruction and sometimes violence, which are incompatible with concrete sentiments of equal concern for all involved.

3. In the course of history, normal people have had deep moral differences that were not due to unreason or ignorance. Similarly, in the present day, there are conflicting conceptions of the good that cannot be resolved through rational persuasion.

4. The conflicts between the long-run and the short-run, culture and minimal well-being for all, and productivity and leisure have sometimes been so acute that no set of basic institutions was the best. Only historical change has removed this incoherence.

Many non-Marxists would accept, on reflection, that these premises are probably valid. They should, then, conclude that morality is not an appropriate basis for political action and social choice. That is part of the fascination of the antimoral arguments implicit in Marx's writings. For all the radical sound of the antimoral conclusion, it is based on some of the less controversial Marxist claims about society. Of course, decent people do not abandon morality if they believe that the alternative is narrow self-interest, caprice, or bloodthirsty realpolitik. Here, too, Marx has a special philosophical contribution. More than other writers, he describes an outlook for politics that is decent without being moral.[11]

NOTES

1. In referring to Marx's writings, I will use the following abbreviations: CM for *Communist Manifesto*, CGP for *Critique of the Gotha Program*, CWF for *The Civil War in France*, all with page references to Robert C. Tucker, ed., *The Marx-Engels Reader* (New York, 1972); SC, preceded by the name of the correspondent, for Marx and Engels, *Selected Correspondence* (Moscow, n.d.); GI for *The German Ideology*, C.J. Arthur, ed. (New York, 1980); G for *Grundrisse*, M.

Nicolaus, trans. (New York, 1973); C for *Capital*, vol. I (Moscow, n.d.); EPM for *Economic and Philosophical Manuscripts*, in Bottomore, ed., *Early Writings* (New York, 1964); WPP for *Wages, Price and Profit* in Marx and Engels, *Selected Works in Three Volumes*, II (Moscow, n.d.). The edition of Engels' *Anti-Duehring* to which I refer is Dutt, ed. (New York, 1966).

2. Max Weber, "Zwischen Zwei Gesetze" in *Politische Schriften*, J. Winckelmann, ed. (Tübingen, 1971), p. 143.

3. Richard W. Miller, "Marx and Aristotle: A Kind of Consequentialism," in K. Nielsen, ed., *Marx and Morality, Canadian Journal of Philosophy*, Supplementary Volume VIII (1981).

4. I give a more detailed account of the role of equality and fairness as means that often produce important goods for Marx in ibid. and in "Rights or Consequences," *Social and Political Philosophy, Midwest Studies in Philosophy* VII (1982).

5. See John Rawls, *A Theory of Justice* (Cambridge, Mass., 1971), sections 3, 13 and 40 and John Rawls, "The Basic Structure As Subject," *American Philosophical Quarterly*, 14 (1977), pp. 159–166.

6. Of course, an effective criticism of Rawls' theory must be much more detailed. I develop this sketch further in "Rights or Consequences," op. cit., and present further criticisms in "Rights and Reality," *Philosophical Review* 90 (1981), pp. 383–407, a study of the main present-day attempts to resolve conflicts of interest on the basis of respect for rights.

7. See Marx and Engels, *Werke* (Berlin, 1958), 19, p. 362. On the same theme, see also EPM, pp. 161 ff.; WLC, p. 180; G, p. 92.

8. Compare Rawls's estimate of the power of persuasion to settle such differences in "Fairness to Goodness," *Philosophical Review* 84 (1975).

9. See M.I. Finley, "Was Greek Civilization Based on Slave Labor?" in M.I. Finley, ed., *Slavery in Classical Antiquity* (New York 1960); originally in *Historia*, 8 (1959).

10. Marx also notes that demands for fairness tend to presuppose basic social relations, while calling for their readjustment: "Instead of the *conservative* motto, 'A fair day's wage for a fair day's work, they [i.e., the working class] ought to inscribe on their banner the *revolutionary* watchword, 'Abolition of the wages system' " (WPP, p. 75; Marx's emphasis).

11. Some of the work leading to this paper was done during a sabbatical year partly supported by a Rockefeller Foundation Humanities Fellowship.

2

MARX AND MORALITY: A REPLY TO RICHARD MILLER

PATRICK RILEY

PREFATORY NOTE

Out of a wholly laudable wish to make his presentation as concise as possible, Richard Miller excised several pages of his text; but in the meantime the present commentary had been written, based on the uncut *Urtext*. In order to make the commentary comprehensible, and (still more) in order to restore to public view one of Miller's most striking claims, the following passage—which came near the end of Miller's paper in New York—ought to be re-instated:

Suppose that our tendency to conform to moral principles, in deeds and emotions, has the same origins as other character traits, grumpiness, say, or a cheerful disposition, fearfulness, diffidence, or extraversion. Then the actual power of morality to constrain revenge and vicious envy [during a revolution] need not be greater than the mixture of love and hate, cooperation and conflict that goes into making of Marx's revolutionaries. Indeed, it is surprising, on reflection, that people have believed that moral constraints have irreplaceable powers. Certain deep aversions concerning defecation or eating, together with non-moral ties between parents and children are, after all, among the most deeply inhibiting constraints, even though they do not depend on moral conscientiousness, and may have little to do with rules.

It is the central sentence—"it is surprising, on reflection, that people have believed that moral constraints have irreplaceable powers"—which is most important, and which will be treated at several points in the following commentary.

I

Richard Miller begins "Marx and Morality" with a striking paradox: Marx is, "in a very broad sense," a "moralist"—sometimes, indeed, "a stern one;" but Marx is also an antimoralist who "attacks morality and fundamental moral notions," even complaining of "ideological nonsense about right."[1] So at first sight it looks as if one has to worry about a Marx who vacillates incoherently between antithetical extremes. On "reflection," however (for Professor Miller), this turns out to be a false worry, and that for two main reasons. First, despite some appearances to the contrary, Marx is neither a moralist nor (usually) an antimoralist, but simply a nonmoralist who successfully occupies the "vast" and mainly neglected terrain existing *between* "narrow self-interest and what would naturally be called morality." (This same "territory" was also occupied, in Miller's view, but in a less attractive way, by Nietzsche's "elitism" and Weber's "nationalism.")[2] On Miller's reading, Marx "replaces" morality with a (politically more "effective") "concern for a group with whom one shares common enemies and with whom one frequently cooperates on the basis of real and growing reciprocity." Second, in any case, arguments directed against Marx *from* the "moral point of view"—Kant's respect for persons as "ends in themselves," Hume's "sympathy"—are misguided (as Marx himself saw), because they assume the radical distinctiveness of moral judgment as something "different in kind from the history of love and hatred, cooperation and conflict that otherwise produces our adult character."[3] Those who believe in a "moral psychology" based on "a special inborn sense of motivations, such as respect for moral law in Kant" or sympathy in Hume are insisting on a view "that Marx attacks and that few accept today." For social virtues are "best understood in a causal way, in terms of a model of character formation;" the "character which Marx recommends" for "model revolutionaries" is "the product of childhood experiences of love and reciprocity sufficient to create a willingness to make sacrifices for others."[4]

This "causal" understanding of character as a "product" is the only really radical argument in Miller's paper, since his reading of the details of Marx's "nonmoral" social theory is helpful but (with one large exception) not terribly controversial. (Indeed, the most arresting sentence in Miller's paper has nothing—necessarily—to do with Marx: "It is surprising, on reflection, that people have believed that moral constraints have irreplaceabie powers.")[5] And the "causal" understanding of character has, for Miller, two great advantages: (1) it makes Marx immune to Kantian or Humean criticisms, since those criticisms are grounded in a "moral psychology" long since rendered "implausible" by "the psychology and anthropology of morals" (which has revealed not a kingdom of ends but "social and historical diversity"); and (2) if "causality" is not antithetical to morality (as Kant wrongly imagined in opposing "nature" and "freedom"),[6] but instead the illuminator of morality viewed as a "product," then there might be good reason to think that another celebrated "antithesis"—that between *thought* and causality—is false as well. And that would mean that the concept of "ideology" is no longer problematical or ruinous for philosophy, as even Sartre thought despite semi-Marxian sympathies ("a doctrine that destroys thought"), but is rather the illuminator of philosophy.[7] Both morality and thought are then connected by being "effects." And this would support Miller's central claim that "the causal explanation of moral ideas *as* ideologies also makes its contribution to Marx's case against morality."[8]

To be sure, a "Kantian humanitarian"—Kant himself, or even Eduard Bernstein[9]—might think that a notion such as "ought" cannot (in principle) be accounted for in terms of "causality" or "ideology," that (in Kant's words) "ought has a kind of necessity . . . which is found nowhere in the whole of nature" and its realm *of* causality.[10] But "the causal explanation of moral ideas *as* ideologies" could account for such Kantian feelings, just as it might account for Miller's own (stated) reluctance to "embrace" Marxian conclusions that are "intellectually attractive." On the "supposition" that Miller shrinks from embracing Marx because of "a cultural background ultimately shaped by bourgeois needs to tame discontent, and to a lack of personal exposure to hard social realities," a "causal explanation" of his "feelings" is perfectly possible. Of course it is difficult to be sure how far Miller is accepting a false consciousness explanation of his own reluctance to "embrace" Marx, since he cautiously says, "*suppose* that crucial feelings" of reluctance are due to bourgeois causes.[11] But, were he to strike this mere "supposing," and argue plainly for false consciousness, then it would seem that reluctance to embrace Marx stems from causes, not reasons; criticism would be an epiphenomenon of bad socialization.

The trouble with this sort of "supposing" that reasons reflect causes is that it can, fatally easily, be given a turn that Miller would deplore: a Nietzschean turn, say. On the "supposition" that Miller's not-too-reluctant desire to embrace Marx is a reaction against bourgeois culture, then love of Marxism might be caused by the rationalized plebian *ressentiment* that Nietzsche professes to find equally in Christianity and in socialism: "The 'last judgment' is the sweet comfort of revenge—the revolution, which the socialist worker also awaits, but conceived as a little farther off."[12] Once one starts supposing that one's reasons for political or moral judgment and action are traceable to causes—mainly socio-economic causes, as in Marx, or mainly psychological causes, as in Nietzsche (and Freud)[13]—there are plenty of *raisons que la raison ne connait point.*[14]

If one suspects that his own (and others') reasons are rationalizations or ideologies, that "reluctance" has its causes, then one will come all the more readily to the truly drastic conclusion that Miller states near the end of his paper: "In the course of history, normal people have had deep moral differences that were not due to unreason or ignorance. Similarly, in the present day, there are conflicting conceptions of the good that cannot be resolved through rational persuasion."[15] This is drastic even (or rather especially) from Miller's perspective, since the impotence of "rational persuasion" in praxis, in suggesting what is to be done, seems to leave only two possibilities: a permanent equilibrium *between* "conflicting conceptions of the good," so that no single conception routs the others (the Machiavellian solution);[16] or the triumph of that conception of the good that is quantitatively heavier (more widely desired) than, if not qualitatively superior to, competing conceptions (the Benthamite solution).[17] Neither a "permanent equilibrium" nor the "triumph of the most-desired" does much (necessarily) for Marxism: on the contrary, the first generates pluralism *faute de mieux,* and the second glorifies whatever is actually desired. But desire, in its turn, can be eliminated as a mere strand of false consciousness whose causes are uncoverable ("suppose . . ."); that leaves the field to the permanent equilibrium whose whole point is the absence of any victor, whether of left, right, or center.

In short: Miller's insistence that "there are conflicting conceptions of the good which cannot be resolved through rational persuasion" deals a devastating blow to his own project of offering "plausible arguments for a radical departure from the moral point of view." For "plausible arguments" are, or aim to be, a kind of "rational persuasion." There surely must be a *sufficient reason* to give up conventional morality, as Miller himself concedes: "Decent people do not abandon morality if they believe that the alternative is narrow self-interest, caprice, or bloodthirsty *Realpolitik."*[18] Miller plainly thinks that there is sufficient reason (tinged with a little reluctance) for most people to embrace Marx,[19] but whether his "causal" understanding of "character formation," coupled with his radical doubts about the efficacy of reason, permits reason(s) to serve as (real) motives is doubtful.

In a recent article called "Rights and Reality," Miller insists that "a rational person should be able to give reasons supporting his or her choice of societal goal and social movement,"[20] but whether those "reasons" have independent value and serve as causes (by becoming motives), or merely *reflect* causes, is not clear. (It is unclear mainly because the notion of "supporting" choices with reasons is so equivocal: "support" is something usually supplied ex post facto, like a flying buttress shoring up a crumbling wall.) If reasons lack an autonomous efficacy, then Marxism will have to be generated by causes, not by reasons: by Miller's "character formation" viewed as "the product of childhood experiences." That means that Marxism must be—

appropriately enough—*produced*, not just argued for; one must overcome a bourgeoisie-produced reluctance to embrace Marx by causing a new kind of character. But then one might as well stop talking about "reasons," if by reasons one means independently valuable grounds of action that a rational being can *take* as a motive.[21]

How, for that matter, can "plausible arguments" for embracing Marxian nonmoral "decency" be *efficacious*—bring people to change the world, not just to interpret it differently[22]—if even an Aristotle (to use Miller's own example) would not have "changed his mind about slavery if he had appreciated some fact or argument?"[23] Evidently "plausible arguments" for anything beyond the Athenian ethos would have had no weight with him; how then will those arguments bear on the conduct of those without Aristotle's moral seriousness and understanding? If plausible arguments for decency would not have swayed Aristotle, how can they sway soi-disant Kantians in the grip of a false consciousness that generates antisocialist "reluctance?" One almost suspects Miller of wanting it both ways: of wanting "plausible arguments" for Marx to be truly efficacious, truly motive-providing, while wanting "reluctance" to embrace Marx to be *caused* by bourgeois culture, not *suggested* by Kantian reasons. But ideology, as someone once observed, is not a cab that one can stop at will: Miller would have to acknowledge that it is simply too convenient to say that reasons for embracing Marx are good, while reasons for reluctance to embrace him are mere ideologies that have unsavory causes. That, unreasonably, makes some reasons unreasonable.[24] (In any case it remains surprising that a philosopher should be so comfortable with the notion of ideology, given Marx's insistence in *The German Ideology* that "when reality is depicted, philosophy as an independent branch of activity loses its medium of existence . . . morality, religion, metaphysics, all the rest of ideology and their corresponding forms of consciousness, thus no longer retain the semblance of independence.")[25]

Miller's stress on "the causal explanation of moral ideas" may even be the reason for (cause of?) his virtual exclusion of the notion of "moral necessity" or "ought" from his itemization of the "features" of morality. Moralities, he urges, typically involve "equal concern or respect" for people, "applying valid general norms," and universal acceptance of "relevant facts and arguments." But "ought" is not on the list: in Miller's account of the "moral point of view," people *"are to be* shown equal concern;" anyone who "rationally reflects . . . *will* accept these rules. . . ."[26] The locutions "are to be" and "will" take the place of "ought." Is this because "ought" is impossible to fit into "the causal explanation of moral ideas"—as Kant thought?

If—to draw these preliminary observations together—Marx is neither a "moralist" nor an "antimoralist," but a "nonmoralist" who rejects "morality as a basis for political action" (while offering a social theory which is nonetheless "complex, well-argued and humane"); and if "moral" objections to Marxism are traceable to a "moral psychology" which is false because it attempts to lift reasons out of the causal realm, then Miller is wholly right. (The mere *possibility* of his being right makes his paper an extremely interesting one, for he would have succeeded in establishing Marxism as a "standard alternative" to the "moral point of view.") But if the paradox with which he begins cannot be resolved and Marx really does vacillate between morality and antimorality; or if there might be a reason for failing to embrace Marx which is something more than an "ideology," then Miller is less than wholly right. The obvious course, then, is to inspect the claims that (1) Marx is a nonmoralist and (2) moral ideas have "causal" explanations.

II

Miller's view that Marx is a nonmoralist rests largely on the claim that Marx had radical doubts about the three main "features" of the "moral point of view:" equality, generality, and universality; his account of these doubts is skillful and (mainly) persuasive. Moreover, Miller is right in asserting that "most of the antimoral arguments suggested by Marx's writings attack . . . the premise of equality,"[27] touching more lightly on generality and universality. But one can still question, first, whether Marx's doubts about "equal right," especially in the *Critique of the Gotha Program,* are as devastating to "right" as they are to "equality;" and second, whether Marx' other social concerns—involving, in Miller's own words, "love," "reciprocity," "concern," "humaneness"[28]—do not amount to a morality, even if not a morality defined (exclusively) *by* equality, generality, and universality. The second question is the more important, since it asks what *counts* as morality, and whether Miller has not constructed a "nonmoral" test that Marx can and must pass. But the first question relates back to Miller's opening concern that Marx might vacillate between morality and antimorality: despite a strong attack on equality and an insistence on "ideological nonsense about right," it is certainly arguable that the *Gotha Program* describes and defends a nonideological true right that finally arrives at the end of social time. What is clear is that Miller does not consider the crucial paragraphs of the *Gotha Program* that *might* bear this reading.

Miller does a fine job with those passages in Part I that reveal the defects in theories of "equal right." In the "first phase of communist society," Marx argues, the individual producer receives back from society . . . exactly what he gives to it. . . . The same amount of labor which he has given to society in one form he receives back in another." But this "equal right" is still, in Marx' view, "stigmatized by a bourgeois limitation."

> The right of the producers is *proportional* to the labor they supply; the equality consists in the fact that measurement is made with an *equal standard,* labor. But one man is superior to another physically or mentally, and so supplies more labor in the same time, or can labor for a longer time; and labor, to serve as a measure, must be defined by its duration or its intensity, otherwise it ceases to be a standard of measurement. This *equal* right is an unequal right for unequal labor. It recognizes no class differences because everyone is only a worker like everyone else, but it tacitly recognizes unequal individual endowment and thus productive capacity as natural privileges. *It is, therefore, a right of inequality, in its content, like every right.*

Hence, Marx goes on, with an "equal performance of labor" and an "equal share in the social consumption fund," one worker will "receive more than another." And to avoid "all these defects, right instead of being equal would have to be unequal."[29]

All of these passages—which build on the Aristotelian notion that one-sided theories of justice rest on one-sided ideas of "equality"[30]—Miller reads faithfully. But he says next to nothing about the two celebrated paragraphs that follow in the *Gotha Program:* paragraphs that argue for a "right" that is neither "equal" *nor* "ideological nonsense." First, of course, one should recall Marx' actual words:

> But these defects [of "equal right"] are inevitable in the first phase of communist society as it is when it has just emerged after prolonged birth pangs from capitalist society. Right can never be higher than the economic structure of society and the cultural development conditioned by it.
>
> In a higher phase of communist society, after the enslaving subordination of the individual to the division of labor, and therewith also the antithesis between mental and physical labor, has vanished; after labor has become not only a means of life but life's first need [*das erste Lebensbedürfnis*]; after the productive forces have also increased with the all-round development of the individual, and all the springs of cooperative wealth flow more abundantly—only then can the narrow horizon of bourgeois right be crossed in its entirety and society inscribe on its banners: "From each according to his ability, to each according to his needs!"[31]

That Marx, in speaking of the "higher phase," is also thinking of a "higher right"—one no longer *shaped* by equality—is plain from the claim that "right can never be higher than the economic structure of society," for in that "higher phase" the springs of cooperative wealth "flow more abundantly," which makes it possible to transcend equal right and to meet needs. Thus, for Marx, an old Humean problem is solved by abundance: "increase," Hume had said, "to a sufficient degree the benevolence of men, or the bounty of nature, and you render justice useless;" all one need do is to alter either nature, or human nature.[32] Hume, to be sure, doubted that *either* "nature" could be overcome;[33] Marxian right (in a "higher phase") rests on the possibility of what Hume had thought impossible.

But how does Miller read the later paragraphs from the *Gotha*

Program—the ones dealing with nonequal right in a "higher phase?" Only in this quite limited way: "One can say that the socialist right is a higher right, the communist standard a right in a very broad sense, which is higher still. But on what scale have these rights been weighed? Not all of the needed weighing can be done on the scale of a further, super-right."[34] What Miller (rather disparagingly) calls "super-right"—"true right" would be better—is precisely *present* in Marx's insistence on transcending the worst features of the division of labor, overcoming the antithesis between mental and physical work, providing for needs once the springs of cooperative wealth flow more abundantly. Then would be *realized* the right or rightful society described by Marx in the incomparable Book III, Chapter 48 of *Capital:* the "Trinity Formula" chapter.

> Just as the savage must wrestle with Nature to satisfy his wants, to maintain and reproduce life, so must civilized man, and he must do so in all social formations and under all possible modes of production. With his development this realm of physical necessity expands as a result of his wants; but, at the same time, the forces of production which satisfy these wants also increase. Freedom in this field can only consist in socialized man, the associated producers, rationally regulating their interchange with Nature, bringing it under their common control, instead of being ruled by it as by the blind forces of Nature; and achieving this with the least expenditure of energy and under conditions most favorable to, and worthy of, their human nature. But it nonetheless still remains a realm of necessity. Beyond it begins that development of human energy which is an end in itself, the true realm of freedom, which, however, can blossom forth only with this realm of necessity as its basis. The shortening of the working day is its basic prerequisite.[35]

One sees, though, why Miller declines to cite or discuss either the two paragraphs from the *Gotha Program,* or the passage from *Capital* III, 48: both passages certainly seem to describe societies that are "right" or just or "worthy of human nature" (though not indeed "equally" right). If the choice is that of making Marx a "nonmoralist" (with *no* theory of "right") in order to preserve the full force of his phrase "ideological nonsense about right," or making him embrace true right (at the end of time) even at the *cost* of "ideology," surely the second choice is preferable. For if Marx's "higher phase of communist society" is not *right*, why struggle to attain it? Why strive to overcome alienation, the extraction of surplus value, and the dangers of a reserve pool of labor, if those things are not *wrong*? To be sure, one could say with Miller: because a proletarian has formed relations of "solidarity" and "concern" with a group "with whom one shares common enemies, and with whom one frequently cooperates on the basis of real and growing reciprocity."[36] But that is not enough, given the *abstractness* of "solidarity," "concern," "cooperation," and "reciprocity:" all of those virtues can be, and are, practiced by pirates ("honor among thieves").[37] (*"Droit naturel,"* Diderot says, is to be found even *"dans les conventions tacites des ennemis du genre humain entre eux."*)[38] In any case Miller tacitly recognizes the importance of "right" in an important and fine distinction that he draws: as he himself says, people who are oppressed will "hate" oppression and feel "angry contempt" for oppressors;[39] but that careful distinction between "hatred" and "contempt" surely is grounded in the moral notion that while *acts* may be hated, *actors* ought not to be.

It seems, then, that in stressing (perfectly accurately) Marx's reservations about "equal right," Miller has made "right" as untenable as "equality." But all "right" in Marx is not attached to equality: if it were, one could not finally redefine right in terms of needs, which are necessarily unequal (simply because individuals are unequal), as Marx himself insists.[40]

The minimizing of any "right" not attached to equality leads to the second aspect of Miller's view of the "features" of morality: if right need not be connected to equality, then there is one "feature" of morality (right itself) that needs to be (as it were) "added" to equality, generality, and universality. But if there is one, there may be others; one may well wonder whether Marx doesn't have a "morality," not just in the shape of "right at the end of time" but also in the form of the "love" and "decency" (together with rejection of war, colonialism and racism) that Miller himself insists on as aspects of Marxian "social theory." (All of these aspects arrive at the end of Miller's paper, when he is explaining why Marx' nonmorality should not be *alarming,* why Marx "describes an outlook for politics that is decent without being moral.")[41] Had not morality been defined *through* equality, generality, and universality, to the exclusion of "ought," "right," and "decency," one would not draw a line between "morality" and "decency": nor would one stress "love" as important (above all in "character formation") but as "nonmoral." Miller's ruling out of love as a moral motive is, ironically enough, a Kantian prejudice.[42] Love is the core of morality in St. Paul ("though I speak with the tongues of men and angels, and have not charity, I am become as sounding brass or a tinkling cymbal"),[43] or in Erasmus, or in Pascal,[44] or in Leibniz's claim that "charity must prevail over every other consideration in the world,"[45] or in Shelley's insistence that "the great secret of morals is love . . . a going out of our nature, and an identification of ourselves with the beautiful which exists in thought, action, or person, not our own."[46] Perhaps, then, it is the narrowness of Miller's account of the "moral point of view" that permits (or forces) him to view Marx as a nonmoralist: had "right" been treated as an autonomous "feature" of morality, not as something riveted to equality, the *Gotha Program* could have received a better reading; what counts as "moral" could have been viewed more generously.

III

The only remaining question is whether Miller is right in saying, in the original version of his paper, that Kantians and Humeans who worry that Marxism might countenance "excesses of revenge and envy"[47] during a revolutionary upheaval are worrying quite groundlessly—probably because they believe in a "moral psychology" that is "implausible." If, as Miller thinks, it is "surprising" that people should think "that moral constraints have irreplaceable powers," then they should probably abandon the moral ideas—such as "the injunction to treat everyone as an end, not a means"—in virtue of which they worry about imagined Marxian excesses. And they should, doubtless, *substitute* a "causal understanding of moral ideas as ideologies."

(Or at least they should do so in politics, where "morality is not an appropriate basis for political action and social choice.")[48]

Obviously one cannot adequately treat here the question or questions: "What is morality? And is it distinctive and irreplaceable?" Merely trying to treat this is sure to plunge us into what Miller correctly calls "conflicting conceptions of the good"—even if one declines to add, with him, that these conflicting conceptions "cannot be resolved through rational persuasion." For present purposes it will have to be enough to point out that when Miller registers his "surprise" that "people have believed that moral constraints have irreplaceable powers," and goes on to say that at least equally formidable constraining powers are to be found in certain social taboos which "may have little to do with rules"[49]—perhaps he is thinking of Freud's remark in *Totem and Taboo* about "the dark origins of our categorical imperative"[50]—he is precisely *making* morality "replaceable" by casting it in the language of "power" and "constraint." As he himself shows, substitute nonmoral "constraints"—quite effective ones—are both conceivable and actual.

There is, of course, another conceivable notion of morality, based less on "constraint" and "power" than on respect for persons as ends in themselves, as members of a "kingdom of ends" who ought never to be treated as mere means to "relative" or arbitrary ends.[51] This morality is meant by its author to shape rightful politics into "republicanism" and "eternal peace," since "true politics cannot take a single step without first paying homage to morals."[52] (Presumably, morality conceived in Kant's way *is* "irreplaceable," since one cannot substitute nonmoral "constraints" and still treat persons as ends in themselves.)[53] To be sure, one could only be persuaded by this view of an "irreplaceable" morality (with its associated politics) by believing in a certain kind of moral psychology—the very one that Miller finds "implausible" and that he thinks was "unacceptable" to Marx. In place of a struggle between titans, which there is no room to stage here—and Marx and Kant were surely that—it will have to be enough to suggest that if morality has more to do with respect than with constraint, then it is not obvious that morality is "replaceable," even by a "social theory" that is "decent" and "humane." Or perhaps a social theory built on hu-

maneness and decency *is* a morality. Or perhaps the kingdom
of ends is fully "realized" (à la Lucien Goldmann) only in social
democracy: that is one way, and not a bad one, of understanding what Marx means in *Capital* III, 48, when he speaks of a
"realm of freedom" for men that is an "end in itself," that is
"favorable to, and worthy of, their human nature." [54] That passage from *Capital,* after all, is a late and cautious reformulation
of Marx's early and uncautious insistence (in "Toward a Critique of Hegel's *Philosophy of Right*") that Marxian criticism "ends
with the doctrine that man is the highest being for man, that
is, with the categorical imperative to overthrow all circumstances in which man is humiliated, enslaved, abandoned, and
despised, circumstances best described by the exclamation of a
Frenchman on hearing of an intended tax on dogs: " 'Poor dogs!
They want to treat you like men.' " [55] If this is Marx's view early
and late, then the distance from Highgate to Königsberg, while
considerable, may not be quite as great as is sometimes imagined.

NOTES

1. Richard W. Miller, "Marx and Morality," in this volume. Cited
   hereafter as Miller.
2. Ibid., p. 4.
3. Miller, original version (as read at the meetings of the American
   Society for Political and Social Philosophy), pp. 42, 47.
4. Ibid., p. 46.
5. Ibid., p. 48.
6. Kant, *Critique of Judgment,* J.C. Meredith, trans. (Oxford, 1952), p.
   14: "Between the realm of the natural concept, as the sensible,
   and the realm of the concept of freedom, as the supersensible,
   there is a great gulf fixed." To be sure, Kant thought that *telos*
   might "bridge" that "gulf;" but that cannot be gone into here. For
   a full treatment of Kant's teleology as it bears on his moral, political, and legal thought, see the author's *Kant's Political Philosophy*
   (Totowa, N.J., 1983), Chapter 4.
7. Jean-Paul Sartre, "Materialism and Revolution," in *Philosophy in the
   20th Century,* W. Barrett and H.D. Aiken, eds. (New York, 1962),
   Vol. 3, pp. 387 ff., particularly pp. 390 ff.: "The leading materialist magazine calmly calls itself '*Thought* (*La Pensée*), the organ of
   modern rationalism' . . . [but] how could a captive reason, gov-

erned from without and manoeuvered by a series of blind causes, still be reason? . . . The materialism they want me to choose, a monster, an elusive Proteus . . . is a doctrine that destroys thought." To be sure, Sartre is careful to add that he is not arguing against Marx himself, but "against the Marxist scholasticism of 1949." Then he adds, more candidly: "or, if you prefer, against Marx *through* neo-Stalinist Marxism" (p. 387). This is more candid because the Stalin pamphlet that is Sartre's direct object of attack in a close paraphrase of *The German Ideology*, part I.

8. Miller, op. cit., p. 14. In his revisions for the present volume, Miller slightly weakened his original text by converting it into a rhetorical question: "Does the distinctive, causal aspect of Marx's thesis that morality is ideology make any contribution to his case against morality? I think it does." But the original and the revised passages, in effect, make the same point.

9. Whether Miller is right in counting Bernstein as a "Kantian humanitarian" is debatable: after all, in the cryptic and elusive final pages of *Evolutionary Socialism* Bernstein says that "social democracy" requires "a Kant"—as distinguished from *the* Kant—"a Kant who should judge the received opinion and examine it critically with deep acuteness," in order to show that its "apparent materialism" is the "highest" and "most easily misleading ideology." To call materialism *itself* the "highest" ideology is a strong and ironic blow, but it is of course Bernstein's conviction that a Kant should "expose" the "magnifying of material factors" as a "self-deception." But Bernstein is careful to add that he is not advocating "going back to the letter of what the Königsberg philosopher wrote," but only back to "the fundamental principles of his criticism." At the same time, to be sure, Bernstein characterizes revolution and proletarian dictatorship as regressive and "atavistic;" that *might* be thought a "Kantian humanitarian" criticism. Cf. Eduard Bernstein, *Evolutionary Socialism,* E.C. Harvey, trans. (New York, 1961), pp. 222 ff.

10. Kant, *Critique of Pure Reason,* N. Kemp Smith, trans. (London 1929), pp. 472–473 (A 547/B 575).

11. Miller, this volume, pp. 24–25.

12. Nietzsche, *The Twilight of the Idols,* in *The Portable Nietzsche,* W. Kaufmann, trans. (New York, 1954), p. 535.

13. Freud, *Civilization and its Discontents,* in *Civilisation, War and Death,* J. Rickman, ed. (London, 1953), p. 80: "The judgments of value made by mankind . . . are attempts to prop up their illusions with arguments."

14. Pascal, *Pensées,* in *Oeuvres de Blaise Pascal,* Léon Brunschvicg, ed. (Paris 1904), Vol. XIII (*Pensées* II), p. 201. But cf. *Pensée,* No. 253,

ibid., p. 186: "Deux excès: exclure la raison, n'admettre que la raison."

15. Miller, §12, #3.

16. Machiavelli, *The Discourses,* in *The Prince and Discourses,* M. Lerner, ed. (New York, 1950), Book I, Chapter 4, p. 119: "Laws that are favorable to liberty result from the opposition of . . . parties to each other."

17. Bentham, *The Principles of Morals and Legislation,* Introduction by L. Lafleur (New York, 1948), Chapter 4, p. 29: "Pleasures then, and the avoidance of pains, are the *ends* which the legislator has in view." Strictly speaking, of course, it is J.S. Mill, more than Bentham, who stresses *desire* and *desirability* as the foundations of ethics.

18. Miller, §12, #4.

19. Ibid., p. 19: "Most people, if they accept Marx's factual claims about capitalist constraints and socialist possibilities, would prefer to work out these problems of choice [between social goods] in a socialist framework. But not every sane person would." Despite his stress on "most people," however, Miller does not view Marxism as mere left-leaning majoritarianism.

20. Richard W. Miller, "Rights and Reality," in *The Philosophical Review,* XC, no. 3, July 1981, p. 403.

21. Cf. Martin Heidegger, *The Essence of Reasons,* Terrence Malik, trans. (Evanston, Ill., 1969), p. 127: "Freedom is the reason for reasons."

22. Marx, "Theses on Feuerbach," No. XI, in *Marx and Engels: Basic Writings on Politics and Philosophy,* L. Feuer, ed. (Garden City, N.Y., 1959), p. 245.

23. Miller, §8, third par.

24. Leo Strauss, *Natural Right and History* (Chicago, 1953), pp. 9–34.

25. Marx and Engels, *The German Ideology* (London, 1965), p. 38. To be sure, this is Marx's most extreme utterance in this vein, and needs to be balanced by the third "Thesis on Feuerbach:" "The materialist doctrine that men are the products of circumstances . . . forgets that it is men that change circumstances" (Feuer ed. p. 244). For a fine commentary on the "Theses" that gives primary weight to the third, see Lucien Goldmann, "L'Idéologie Allemande et les 'Thèses sur Feuerbach,' " in *Marxisme et Sciences Humaines* (Paris, 1970), pp. 170–196. Goldmann offers a persuasive critique of Louis Althusser's overstressing of the deterministic eleventh "Thesis."

26. Miller, pp. 3–4.

27. Ibid., §2.

28. Ibid., original version, p. 28.

29. Marx, *Critique of the Gotha Program*, in *Marx and Engels: Basic Writings*, op. cit., p. 118.

30. Aristotle, *Politics*, 1280a ff.

31. Marx, *Gotha Program*, op. cit., p. 119. Translation slightly altered, since the Feuer edition renders "das erste Lebensbedürfnis" as "life's primary want." That is not satisfactory, given the importance of distinguishing between "want" and "need:" it is the second term that Marx uses. See Marx, *Kritik des Gothaer Programs*, in *Karl Marx–Friedrich Engels: Werke* (Berlin, 1962), vol. 19, p. 21.

32. Hume, *A Treatise of Human Nature*, Book III, in *Theory of Politics*, F. Watkins, ed. (Edinburgh, 1951), pp. 44–45.

33. Hume, "Idea of a Perfect Commonwealth," in *Theory of Politics*, op. cit., p. 229: "All plans of government which suppose great reformation in the manners of mankind are plainly imaginary."

34. Miller, §4, second par.

35. Marx, *Capital*, S. Moore and E. Aveling, trans. (New York, 1967), vol. 3, p. 820.

36. Miller, original version, p. 42.

37. Indeed one can be a pirate *and* a "slave of duty:" cf. Gilbert and Sullivan, *The Pirates of Penzance*.

38. Diderot, "Droit Naturel," in *Rousseau: Political Writings*, C.E. Vaughan, ed. (Oxford, 1962), vol. I, p. 432. Much of the so-called *Geneva MS* or *Première Version* of Rousseau's *Du Contrat Social* is a refutation of Diderot's essay.

39. Miller, ibid., p. 46.

40. Marx, *Gotha Program*, in *Marx and Engels: Basic Writings*, op. cit., p. 119. For a strong and striking defense of the thesis that Marx has no theory of right—certainly no ideology-free notion of right arriving at the end of social time—see Allen W. Wood, "The Marxian Critique of Justice," in *Marx, Justice and History*, M. Cohen, T. Nagel, and T. Scanlon, eds. (Princeton, 1980), pp. 28–29: "If revolutionary institutions mean new laws, new standards of juridical regulation, new forms of property and distribution, this is not a sign that 'justice' is at last being done where it was not done before; it is instead a sign that a new mode of production, with its own characteristic juridical forms, has been born from the old one . . . If the new [stage] is higher, freer, more human than the old, it would be for Marx both entirely inaccurate and woefully inadequate to reduce its superiority to juridical terms and to commend it as 'more just.' " This is effective, and has the merit of preserving "ideology" in a strict form, but it forgets that Marx calls the "higher stage" of (attained) socialism a condition of "higher right"—which must mean that, for Marx, there is (finally) a kind of right that is

not merely "juridical." Wood's interpretation seems to open a *gulf* between "higher, freer, more human" institutions and "justice"— as if a just order could be disconnected from freedom and humanity. (This is surprising, coming from a distinguished Kant scholar.)

For a more persuasive reading of Marx, see Philip Pettit, *Judging Justice* (London, 1980), p. 181: "If the demands of justice are not something that we can sensibly think of construing in an objective [non-ideological] manner, then what is it that vindicates the Marxist critique of capitalist society? It will not do for the Marxist to invoke the march of history, for the fact that present structures are doomed, if indeed they are so, does nothing to show that their demise should be applauded or hastened." That is trenchant, if a little unsympathetic.

41. Miller, §12, #4.
42. Cf. Kant, *Fundamental Principles of the Metaphysic of Morals*, T.K. Abbott, trans. (Indianapolis, 1949), p. 59: "Those who cannot *think* believe that *feeling* will help them out." In the very late *Tugendlehre*, however, Kant tries to draw the categorical imperative and Christian *caritas* closer together: "The duty to love one's neighbor can also be expressed as the duty to make the ends of others (as long as they are not immoral) my own." Kant then, characteristically, resolves love into *respect* for persons as "objective ends:" "The duty to respect one's neighbor is contained in the maxim, degrade no other man merely as a means to personal ends. . . ." Both passages from the *Tugendlehre* are to be found in James Ellington's translation, under the title *Metaphysical Principles of Virtue* (Indianapolis, 1964), p. 114. Like *Religion within the Limits of Reason Alone*, the *Tugendlehre* transforms Christianity into Kantianism.
43. St. Paul, I *Corinthians* xiii.
44. Pascal, *Pensées*, T.S. Eliot, ed. (New York, 1958), No. 792 (Brunschvicg numbering), p. 235: "All bodies together, and all minds together, and all their products, are not equal to the least feeling of charity. This is of an order infinitely more exalted."
45. Leibniz, letter to Mme. de Brinon, in *The Political Writings of Leibniz*, P. Riley, trans. and ed. (Cambridge, 1972), p. 4.
46. Shelley, "A Defence of Poetry," cited in Judith Shklar, *After Utopia* (Princeton, 1957), pp. 44–45.
47. Miller, original version, p. 47.
48. Ibid., p. 50.
49. Ibid.
50. Freud, *Totem and Taboo*, in *Basic Writings of Sigmund Freud*, A. Brill, trans. (New York, 1938), p. 824. Freud adds that the taboo of

"savages is after all not so remote from us as we were at first inclined to believe."

51. Kant, *Fundamental Principles*, op. cit., pp. 45 ff.

52. Kant, *Eternal Peace*, in *Kant's Political Writings*, H. Reiss, ed. (Cambridge, 1970), p. 125. For an interpretation of Kant's politics built around this sentence, see the author's *Kant's Political Philosophy*, op. cit.

53. Ibid., p. 117: "If, of course, there is neither freedom nor any moral law based on freedom, but only a state in which everything that happens or can happen simply obeys the mechanical workings of nature, politics would mean the art of utilizing nature for the government of men."

54. Marx, *Capital*, Moore and Aveling, trans., Vol. 3, p. 820. See also Lucien Goldmann, *Immanuel Kant*, R. Black, trans. (London, 1971). If a Kant-Marx *rapprochement* is possible, Goldmann is surely right to look for it by linking Kant's injunction to "always treat humanity . . . never simply as a means, but always at the same time as an end" with Marx's notion of a "realm of freedom" that is an "end in itself" and "worthy of human nature." (Cf. Goldmann's pp. 174–177.) If there can be left-Hegelianism there surely can be left-Kantianism; Goldmann has found a *Grundlegung* for it. But for Goldmann's view that some interpreters—notably Vorländer—have overassimilated Kant and Marx to each other, see his "Propos Dialectiques," in *Les Temps Modernes*, J.-P. Sartre, ed., No. 140 (Paris, 1957), pp. 732–735.

Of course a Goldmannesque *rapprochement* between Kant's realm of ends and Marx's realm of freedom is possible only if Goldmann himself is right when he maintains that the third "Thesis on Feuerbach," in "opposing" dialectical materialism to eighteenth-century *matérialisme mécaniste,* leaves some autonomous value to thought (even pre-Marxian thought) as something more than merely "epiphenomenal," as something that can turn back on, understand, and transform "substructures." That is why Goldmann quotes and requotes Marx's insistence that "the materialist doctrine that men are products of circumstances . . . forgets that it is men that change circumstances," and tries to minimize the deterministic *German Ideology* and its notion that "when [productive] reality is depicted, philosophy as an independent branch of activity loses its medium of existence" (Goldmann, *Marxisme*, op. cit., pp. 175 ff.). On Goldmann's view the third "Thesis," in "passing from mechanistic materialism to the dialectical position," supposes "the abandoning of a rigorous determination of human psychology by circumstances" and the (proper) recognition that "circumstances are themselves the product of mind [*psychisme*] and of previous human conduct" (ibid., p. 179).

It is this granting of limited breathing-space to philosophy that enables Goldmann to take Kant's ethics seriously (while nonetheless tilting them toward Marx): "Once we realize that this formula [of treating persons as ends] condemns any society based on production for the market, in which other men are treated as means with a view to creating profits, we see . . . [that for Kant] the totality would be the realization of a 'kingdom of ends;' that is to say, the very reverse of present-day society where, with the exception of a few rare and partial communities, man is never more than a means" (Goldmann, *Immanuel Kant,* op. cit., pp. 176–177). This reading, which respects Kant while inclining him leftward, would not be possible at all (as Goldmann stresses) on an Althusserian view: one that insists on a *coupure épistemologique* between Marx and *all* of his predecessors (including Hegel), one that insists that even *within* Marx himself there is a *coupure,* a "passage from petit-bourgeois humanist political and philosophical positions" in the early 1840s to "communist-materialist positions" by the time of *The German Ideology* (Louis Althusser, "Sur la Dialectique de l'évolution intellectuelle du Jeune Marx," in *Hegel-Jahrbuch 1974,* W.R. Beyer, ed. [Köln, 1975], p. 133). That supposed passage, that alleged "severing" within Marx himself, however, is made less persuasive when one sees that *Capital* III, 48 clearly echoes the Kantian phraseology of "Towards a Critique of Hegel's *Philosophy of Right.*" It is true, of course, that *The German Ideology* speaks disparagingly of Kant's "good will:" "Kant was satisfied with 'good will' alone, even if it remained entirely without result . . . he made the materially motivated determinations of the will of the French bourgeois into *pure* self-determinations of the will . . . into purely ideological conceptual determinations and moral postulates" (*The German Ideology,* op. cit., pp. 210–212). But even Hegel had complained that "the laurels of mere willing are dry leaves that never were green," that Kantian good will is "formal" and never accomplishes anything. Both Hegel and Marx are arguably wrong: Kant's good will is supposed to respect persons *as* ends, to strive to realize the kingdom *of* ends (as Goldmann at least sees): that teleological side of Kant, stressing respect for persons as the "final ends of creation," is the side that Marx reflects and respects.

55. Marx, "Towards a Critique of Hegel's *Philosophy of Right,"* in *Karl Marx: Early Writings,* T.B. Bottomore, trans. and ed. (New York, 1964), p. 52 (translation slightly altered). Cf. Maximilien Rubel, *Rubel on Karl Marx,* J. O'Malley, trans. (Cambridge 1981), p. 112: "This ethic [of "Towards a Critique"] underlies all social criticism

that Marx will undertake in his political and literary tasks." This seems to be true at least of *Capital* III, 48; less persuasive, however, is Rubel's insistence that Marx finally "abandoned philosophical speculation in favor of an ethical credo." The notion that ethics involves more belief than thought is peculiar; it is a little reminiscent of what Georg Lukács says about Kant in *History and Class Consciousness* (R. Livingstone, trans. [Cambridge, Mass., 1968], p. 123): "Kant had attempted . . . to show that the barriers that could not be overcome by theory (contemplation) were amenable to practical solutions." This makes Kant a fideist, as Rubel makes Marx a fideist; what it forgets is that in *Critique of Judgment* Kant tried to "bridge" theory and practice by saying that finite intelligences must *necessarily* interpret nature teleologically and that persons must *necessarily* view themselves as the "final end" of a teleologically subordinated creation (in which there is no knowable being "beyond" man).

3

MARX AND REVOLUTIONARY VIRTUE

FREDERICK G. WHELAN

There is no disputing that Marx was a moral philosopher in the sense of advancing a theory concerning the nature and sources of morality, or moralities; the more controversial questions are whether Marx offers a normative moral theory of his own, and, if so, what moral judgments and values he defends. It may be granted that Marx's writings lack any well-developed theory in the latter sense. Marx may, moreover, have deliberately refrained from attempting to formulate an ethical doctrine (or, perhaps, a certain sort of ethical doctrine)—because he thought that such an enterprise was either philosophically misguided, or tactically and rhetorically erroneous from the point of view of the practical needs of the workers' movement, or both. The absence of a moral theory, finally, has appeared to some interpreters to be consistent with (or even necessitated by) Marx's theory about morality. If Marx held that all moral beliefs and practices are thoroughly determined by historically evolving systems of production, or that all moral concepts are ideological—that is, partisan ideas masquerading as distinterested truths—then (it may be argued) there would have been no point in his trying to provide justifications for whatever moral opinions or feelings he may have had.

One cannot, however, infer that Marx had no moral theory from the view that having one would be inconsistent with certain other of his doctrines. Moreover, the nonmoral interpretation of Marx is at variance with the strong impression that

Marx's readers receive from the moral sentiments, including attitudes of advocacy and indignation, that are frequently expressed in his writings. The claim of scientific objectivity, which was held to secure Marx's intellectual stature by his followers of two or three generations ago, now appears to some to conceal the "real" Marx: "It is no secret that for all his pretense at being a scientist, Marx was fundamentally a moralist. . . ."[1] Recent scholarship in this area has looked at Marx's texts mainly with an eye to discovering his views on justice, and it has tended to reaffirm the older, nonmoral interpretation. Even if we accept the predominant (but not unanimous) finding that Marx has no theory of justice, however, we may not infer from this that he lacks any ethical doctrine, although commentators tend to do this.[2] Justice is the moral concept that may seem to be most salient for a social theorist or political philosopher, but it is not the only moral concept to which we ought to attend; nor is a theory of justice the only possible sort of moral theory. It may be that Marx has a different kind of moral theory, or at least intimations of one.

Among the more promising themes in Richard Miller's paper are his brief comments on Marx's views regarding the special virtue of proletarian revolutionaries, or the ideal type of character that Marx suggests should be admired and cultivated, and which he implies will characterize socialist citizens. These are themes that one can find in Marx's own writings, and they have also been prominent in certain currents of the subsequent Marxist tradition. Miller notes that Marx admires a certain kind of character and praises the heroism of workers in their struggles, and he says that it is this, in part, that makes Marx's theory *seem* moralistic. Miller, however, is unwilling to consider these judgments as comprising a moral theory, regarding them, rather, as falling in an intermediate area between morality and self-interest. He takes this position, however, only because he arbitrarily stipulates overly stringent criteria that a doctrine must meet in order to count as a *moral* theory. Virtue, however, is a moral concept, and a doctrine that delineates traits or qualities that should be construed as excellences of character, or grounds for admiration and praise of an individual's character (and the actions that flow from it), is a kind of moral theory. Suggestions, at least, of some such theory run through much socialist

(including Marxist and Soviet) literature, and there are indica-
tions of it in Marx himself as well.

Miller lays down three criteria for what he would regard as
a genuine moral theory, or for "morality," or the "moral point
of view;" these are equality, generality of norms, and universality (or universal rationality). Equality seems to be the principal standard—equal treatment of all persons, or (attitudinally)
equal concern and respect for everyone. Miller's main reason
for regarding Marx's practical doctrine as something other than
moral is that its undisputed reference to class interest as a legitimate basis for political action is at variance with what Miller
takes to be the moral requirement of equal concern for everyone. In general, for Miller a moral theory must consist of a
body of rules or principles that apply to all people indiffer-
ently, and prescribe equal treatment for all, and that are justifiable by reasons that any rational and impartial person could
accept (barring disagreements with respect to relevant facts).
This account of *morality,* it seems to me, is plausible as a characterization of a theory of *justice,* which is one type of moral
theory, or which may comprise part of a comprehensive moral
theory, but which is surely not equivalent to the whole of morality. It is justice, among moral concepts, that has commonly
been held to be logically connected with the concept of equality
(taken in some sense), or to prescribe some version of equal
treatment. A theory of justice typically contains general norms
of the sort that can guide the design of large-scale social institutions (but which, because of their generality, are often inapplicable for resolving personal dilemmas of moral choice).
Norms of justice, finally, are typically expressed in a formal
fashion (to each his due, equality of rights, the difference principle, etc.), so that they can plausibly be presented as universal
or rational principles.

Now Marx probably does not have a theory (either explicit
or implicit) that meets these criteria—in which case we may
conclude that he does not have a theory of justice. This thesis
has been forcefully argued with reference to Marx's texts; it can
also be buttressed by other distinctive arguments often attributed to Marx—the views that (given Marx's sociology) no
moral point of view not bound up with a particular mode of
production and a particular class interest is possible; that it is

pointless to criticize capitalism in terms of the moral concepts (such as justice) available in the capitalist era, since these (like those of previous eras) have a conservative bias, and are functional in sustaining the status quo; that the putative standards of socialist justice are as yet too faint to provide the basis for an effective critique of contemporary institutions; and that moralizing in any case simply encourages the illusion that moral convictions and changes in moral convictions can effect material historical change, an illusion that leads to misguided strategies for promoting change. Arguments such as these are suggested in Miller's paper, but for the most part his approach is more formal; he concludes that Marx is not a moralist principally because his theory fails to conform to the stipulated general standards. Even the more common grounds for concluding that Marx rejected appeals to morality, however, seem to apply to theories of justice more than to other moral concepts. Marx usually thought of justice as a juridical rather than a moral concept—as positive legal justice, in effect—concerning which it is far more plausible than in the case of purely moral concepts to suppose that it is tied to particular social orders and modes of production.[3] We cannot conclude, however, that since Marx lacks or repudiates any theory of justice he therefore is not a moral thinker in other significant senses of the word.

VIRTUE IN MORAL THEORY

Moral theories are sometimes classified as (1) theories of the good, which consider the elements of happiness or other things deemed worthy of pursuit by human beings; (2) theories of the right (or deontic theories, including theories of justice), which consider moral obligations and prohibitions, and which typically issue in general rules of conduct, or general principles governing social practices and institutions; and (3) theories of virtue (or aretaic theories), which set forth an ideal character or delineate personal qualities deemed valuable and worthy of admiration and cultivation.[4] While there are no doubt numerous interrelations among these categories, let us consider two ideas that might figure in a theory of virtue, but that could not easily be accommodated within a theory of the right.

1. Benevolence, or what Hume calls limited benevolence (or "confined generosity") rather than the systematically (and thus artificially) universalized benevolence called for in utilitarianism, is a virtuous quality of character by which a person performs, or is regularly disposed to perform, beneficent acts. One of the interesting features of Hume's ethics is the contrast he draws between benevolence and justice as opposite types of virtue. Justice (in keeping with Miller's criteria for morality) consists of general rules that apply equally and impersonally to all cases that arise under them; as a personal quality justice is the disposition to observe the rules, which must be established as a social practice before it is possible—or at least before it makes any sense—for an individual to be just. Hume calls benevolence, in contrast, a natural virtue because it is a more spontaneous quality of character, not depending upon a social scheme or upon reflection on the social utility of general rules. Since benevolence arises from feelings (both natural and habitual), it quite naturally and appropriately varies with the strength and objects of these feelings. Benevolence therefore in contrast to justice usually involves special consideration for those who are close to us, such as family members, friends, and comrades, or for people in particularly difficult circumstances, especially when they are sufficiently close enough to us for their plight to engage our sympathy. This feature of benevolence is quite consistent with our approbation of it as a genuine virtue. In fact, for a naturalist like Hume (for whom morality is an expression of human nature) it would be odd and indeed *morally* (as well as psychologically) questionable for a person *not* to have special feelings for, and to be inclined to give preferential treatment to, *his own*. Hume goes on to argue that the rules of justice (in their proper sphere) must be inflexible—"either by spite or favour"—and so that benevolent impulses (like hostile ones) must yield to justice in cases of conflict.[5] In many instances, however, benevolence may properly be manifested in practice, and its status as a virtue (like the feelings that underlie it) persists even when its tendencies must be suppressed.

Benevolence, therefore, unlike justice, need not be expressed according to a rule of equal treatment, or according to any general norms. This is partly (as Hume indicates) because true benevolence is supposed to be a matter of genuine inner feeling, of the sort that (when habitual) comprises a trait of character, and our feelings simply do not observe general rules with the regularity that is properly expected of justice. And it is partly because beneficence, unlike justice, is (in J.S. Mill's terms) a duty of imperfect obligation: its recipients have no correlative right to it, and thus its manifestations are to an extent discretionary, and may appropriately reflect the inclinations and special commitments of the benevolent person.

Benevolence—and other, similarly natural qualities—is a moral virtue, or a morally admirable quality of character, notwithstanding its variability or irregularity. As a virtue it may perfectly well figure in a moral theory—a theory of virtue rather than a theory of the right. Aristotle's *Ethics* contains a well-developed moral theory built around the delineation of an ideal character; some of the virtues comprising such a character, moreover, depend on uncommon, and in some cases innate, capacities, and thus the actions that flow from them could not reasonably be regarded as generally obligatory. This would apparently not meet Miller's criteria for a moral theory, although surely it would be perverse to deny it that title. Miller acknowledges that Marx admires a certain exemplary kind of character, and he even compares Marx's ideal in this respect to Aristotle's ideal of the "great-hearted man;" yet Miller declines to regard the presentation of this ideal as a moral theory, or as a component of a moral theory.[6]

While we have recently been encouraged to think of justice as the primary virtue of social institutions, and therefore as the main ethical concern of political theories, it is worth noting that theories of virtue have often figured centrally in political thinking. The type of character held up for admiration may in important respects be conceived politically; it might, for example, involve being a citizen, among other things, as in the case of Greek ethics. Or a certain kind of political regime or society may be approved and advocated primarily because of its tendency to encourage the development of a certain type of character, as for example in Mill's defense of liberalism. Analogous lines of argument may be present in Marx, forming links between his moral and his political theories.

It is not, of course, that Marx espouses the virtue of benevolence as such—certainly not in such quaint terminology. However, the class solidarity that is undoubtedly a concern of Marx's, and which is much emphasized by Miller, can be construed as a case of what Hume means by "limited benevolence"—that is, a special concern and inclination to work for the welfare of one's own group, for the members of which one has developed special feelings and loyalties through proximity, sympathy, and shared experiences, over and above what could be expected as the result of shared interests (taking interest in a fairly narrow, economic sense).[7] Such solidarity (as with Hume's benevolence) may on occasion be at odds with the demands of justice, or of "equal concern," in which case we have a conflict between two moral principles. In such cases Hume says that justice (with its rigid and general rules) must prevail; perhaps it is a distinctive mark of Marx's theory that class solidarity is ranked higher— or would be so ranked, had Marx developed his theory more systematically. Hume is thinking of the requirements of a stable social order; Marx is thinking mainly of the dynamic process of change from one social order to another, or of conditions within an unstable order. In any case, I do not see any reason to follow Miller and deny that a determination to act on the basis of class solidarity (or of other kinds of group solidarity) cannot be a moral motive simply because it reflects a particular interest, and offends against norms of equality and generality. It is not justice, to be sure, but it might still be an expression of moral virtue, or an admirable trait of people's character in some situations.[8]

2. There is secondly the issue of supererogatory acts, and the praise and admiration we often accord to individuals who go beyond the requirements of moral duty (that is, who do more than is prescribed by general norms that apply equally to all), and especially to those individuals whose developed characters exhibit an habitual readiness to do more than is required. Supererogatory virtue exists in different degrees. A person who simply adheres to a generally obligatory moral principle, such as promoting the general welfare, when he has no assurance that others will do likewise—and who thereby risks being taken advantage of—may according to some theories (such as Hobbes's) be doing more than can be required of him. People whose morally praiseworthy actions entail even greater and more tangible personal costs, or risks, even to the point where

we may speak of self-sacrifice and moral heroism, display a stronger form of supererogatory virtue.

Supererogation is notoriously a subject that does not fit well in modern ethical theories (such as the Kantian or the utilitarian), precisely because these theories, in line with Miller's criteria, try in effect to assimilate morality to law, or to present morality as a set of general principles or generally obligatory rules, treating virtue (when they treat it at all) as derivative from right. A theoretical enterprise of this sort seems to leave no room for spontaneity or for extraordinary individual endeavors within the sphere of morality; this seems contrary to our common language and intuitions, which do accord moral admiration to such efforts, and to the common outlook that sees as morally admirable those qualities of character that exceed what can be prescribed as general norms. Theories of the right also make no place for praise (which is surely part of our moral vocabulary) since, while we blame someone for violating obligatory rules (such as rules of justice), we do not praise him for observing them. Aristotelian ethics and other moral theories that are primarily theories of virtue, of course, have no difficulty in dealing with outstanding qualities. They typically recognize different types and degrees of virtue, and provide for the allocation of praise accordingly; they do not make virtue simply a matter of performing right actions, which are demanded equally of all. Praise is often important for psychological reasons within such theories, furthermore, since it is generally recognized that virtues must be cultivated, and that this process is furthered by social practices such as praising as well as by more formal educative and political influences.

One might be tempted to regard an emphasis on exceptional virtue as a characteristic theme of aristocratic rather than democratic systems of ethics, the latter insisting on "leveling" morality by reducing it to a set of general rules that can be equally required of everyone, and denying that special abilities should be regarded as virtues, especially if they are in any degree due to differential innate capacities or natural talents. Nevertheless, the theme of moral heroism and the heroic virtue of committed revolutionaries is certainly present in some of Marx's writings, as Miller notes, reflecting perhaps Marx's appreciation of the necessity of such qualities for the making of revolution, with all

its attendent risks. Marx presumably does not espouse an aristocratic system (although talk of elites and vanguards—that is,
those who excel in revolutionary virtue—is not absent from the
Marxist tradition). Similar themes may perhaps in Marx's case
be attributed to the romantic sources of his thought—to the
"Promethean" urge to transform the world (and thus also mankind), for example, that has been discerned behind Marx's ethical views.[9] This theme of heroism, together with the related
theme of class solidarity, suggests that there is a distinctive
Marxian theory of virtue—whether one calls it proletarian, revolutionary, or socialist virtue—even if it is the case that Marx
lacks a theory of justice.

VIRTUE, REVOLUTION, AND SOCIALISM

If Marx indeed offers us a theory of revolutionary virtue, it
may be in part because his larger political theory requires one—
a possibility to which I now turn. Of course, we may not infer
that Marx actually held certain views simply because his other
doctrines demand them, and I shall return below to evidence
of these themes in Marx's texts. However, it is a legitimate exercise to work out the implications and requirements of an author's theory even if he does not fully do so himself, and the
recognition that a particular position is required by his other
doctrines entitles us to ascribe special significance to whatever
he does say regarding the former.

Whatever else he may have been, Marx was undoubtedly a
revolutionary theorist, predicting and advocating the overthrow of capitalism in circumstances and by methods entailing
dangers and difficulties for the protagonists, and a proponent
of a future socialist (or communist) form of social and economic organization. Thus it is to the revolutionary process itself, and to the future order of socialism, that a Marxian theory
of virtue is likely to have particular reference. With respect to
revolution the relevant analysis has been carried out by Buchanan (following Olson), in an article to which Miller alludes
in connection with Marx's comments on the revolutionary character;[10] this connection needs to be pursued further. The revolution, most simply, presents a collective action problem. The

benefits it will bring (if successful) are collective or indivisible goods with respect to the working class, each member of which will enjoy them whether or not, and regardless of the degree to which, he made any contribution toward or incurred any of the costs (especially personal danger) involved in producing the general benefits. This state of affairs poses a classic "free rider" problem, insofar as the workers are conceived as rational egoists, concerned to further their personal interests. More interestingly, Buchanan argues that even workers who were rationally determined to advance their *common* class interest ("maximize overall utility for the group") would likewise fail to achieve the coordinated action necessary to effect the revolution.[11]

How then can the proletarian revolution be imagined to come about? The (unsuccessful) analysis based on interest, rationally pursued, seems to be indicated by the many passages ("The proletarians have nothing to lose but their chains. They have a world to gain.") in which Marx himself portrays the revolution as being in the interest of the workers and as destined to come about on this basis. This is a theme that Buchanan links to the common interpretation of Marx as eschewing appeals to moral principles, and which some would adduce as further evidence that Marx has no moral theory at all. If we leave aside moral considerations, there appear to be two, perhaps complementary, ways within the collective action model by which revolutionary action (successful or not) could be explained. One explanation, which Buchanan acknowledges, contains the seeds of a theory of revolutionary terrorism: apathetic, timid, or simply rational workers are coerced by their leaders, by means of threats that outweigh the risks of participating, into joining the movement; these threats simultaneously ensure that all or most workers will join in and share the risks, thus making it possible for all to achieve what is in their common interest. A second explanation corresponds, perhaps, to the Leninist alternative within Marxism: in addition to collective goods for the entire working class, the revolution also offers the prospect of certain particular goods—especially power: high positions in the party and in the post-revolutionary state—that will attract ambitious individuals to come forward and assume the special risks and hardships of serving as leaders, organizing the revolution, and carrying the rest along (possibly using methods suggested in the first explanation).

Both of these explanations solve the problem as posed in this formal manner, and both shed some light on how historical revolutionary movements actually work; neither, however, can find much support in Marx's own writings. We come, then, to a third solution, one that makes reference to moral motivation, and which may have the best claim to reflect Marx's own view of the revolution. Buchanan points out that the collective action problem could be solved if the workers acted on moral principle rather than on the basis of interest—if, for example, they acted on an internalized moral imperative to advance the (or their) common good, or to create humane institutions, whatever the personal risks. Buchanan, however, accepting the argument that Marx lacks a theory of justice, concludes that Marx rejected *any* appeal to moral principles, and that therefore a moral solution was not available to him (although he notes that socialists have in practice not entirely given up what Marx once called "obsolete verbal rubbish" about justice and right).

This conclusion, however, which resembles other scholars' inferences from the absence of any affirmation of moral rules to the absence of any moral dimension in Marx's theory, is too hasty. It is evident that the collective action problem of the revolution could be overcome if a large proportion of workers possessed—and in the critical junctures were motivated by—the virtue of solidarity with their fellow workers, acting to promote the common interest out of loyalty to their comrades, and scarcely even reflecting that their own interest is subsumed in the common. The chances of revolutionary success, moreover, would be enhanced if only a few of the workers displayed supererogatory proletarian virtue in the strong sense—that is, if they were prepared to incur exceptionally high risks or engage in the self-sacrificing heroism that could catalyze the entire movement or effect a decisive victory. (As suggested above, the willingness to incur *any* risks in a common cause, without guarantees of reciprocity or success—that is, the most basic kind of behavior needed to break a collective action impasse—may be thought of as supererogatory in a weaker sense.) Workers who exhibit class solidarity in the revolution might be acting on principle; to interpret their conduct as the product of a distinctive kind of virtue, however, is to emphasize that certain psychological elements, such as feelings of group loyalty and habits of collective action, rather than moral reasoning, are responsible for it. If revolutionary success is thought to depend on such virtue, furthermore, it is important that proponents of revolution seek to instill and cultivate it; this may be why Marx, though averse to moralizing in terms of abstract principle, was quick and generous in his praise of the kind of character and heroism that could bring success (eventually) to the revolutionary cause. Such virtue, of course, tends to eliminate not only egoistic motives, but even the very calculating rationality that creates the collective action and free rider problems.[12]

While the virtue of dedicated revolutionaries plays this instrumental role in a full account of the Marxian revolution, it also may have moral value (for Marx) apart from its beneficial social consequences (the establishment of socialism); thus it remains virtuous and admirable even when it is manifested in unsuccessful actions. Revolutionary activity is valuable as an occasion for revolutionary virtue, just as charitable practices in Christian thought are seen as valuable as a vehicle by which individuals may exercise the virtue of charity in addition to being a means for the alleviation of misery (and even if they are not the most efficient means to this end). Marx's praise of workers' heroism in failed causes such as the Paris Commune may follow in this way from his judgment of its intrinsic value as well as from his view of the need to cultivate habits of virtue for eventual instrumental purposes.

The collective action problem, and the need for virtue, would appear not to end for Marxists with the revolution, but may continue indefinitely in the socialist era beyond. Socialist production will require diligent efforts in collectivized enterprises without the incentive of private profit; at some stage, when distribution is according to need, the goods produced will be in effect collective goods, since all citizens will have a claim to enjoy them, relative to their needs, without regard to their personal contribution. In this situation the opportunities for free riding will be very numerous, and particularly so to the extent that the coercive state (which could threaten shirkers with punishment) withers away—something that on some accounts is supposed to happen around the time that the fully developed socialist system begins to flourish. This visionary future would clearly be threatened by the persistence of any trace of the rational self-interest that is prevalent in the capitalist era, and which creates collective goods problems; socialism therefore will depend on a general and spontaneous willingness of individuals to act according to socialist principles, internalized as virtue that will presumably be inculcated in socialist citizens on a regular basis through education.[13] It is thus not surprising that the culture of actual socialist societies frequently contains a strong emphasis on such values as camaraderie and dedication to the common good, and that, especially in the period of the "building of communism," intensified efforts are undertaken in the field of moral education.[14]

A distinction perhaps ought to be drawn between what may be called the *socialist* virtue of the post-revolutionary society and the *revolutionary* virtue that is displayed in the revolution itself (as well as in earlier, abortive rebellions), despite the formal similarities that are brought out in the collective goods analysis. Although both types of virtue consist fundamentally in an habitual willingness to promote the common (class) good without the incentive of special private rewards for so doing, it would appear that revolutionary virtue (with which Marx himself was mainly concerned) contains a larger element of heroism than would be necessary in a functioning socialist system. Revolutionary action usually involves risks of personal danger, in view of its violence and uncertainty of success, and some, at least, must be prepared to expose themselves to very great risks without having any expectation of corresponding rewards. Of the two kinds of virtue discussed above, some degree of supererogatory or extraordinary virtue thus must complement the more extensive virtue of class solidarity during the extraordinary period of the revolution; while by its nature the former cannot be prescribed as a general moral principle, its cultivation can be encouraged through praise for its exemplars. Revolutionary virtue, furthermore, must (according to Marx) appear among the members of a working class that lives under the thrall of the prevailing bourgeois ideology (which encourages egoism and free riding) and that is otherwise degraded by the conditions of its existence; its cultivation, therefore, may be a project of great difficulty for the workers' movement, and, in view of the obstacles, its attainment in any degree may be regarded as a heroic achievement.[15]

In a functioning socialist society, by contrast—or at least in one that is lenient with "parasites"—the only cost of backsliding is a reduction in total productivity, a cost that is largely externalized from the point of view of any individual; nor are any risks involved in performing one's proper tasks. Thus no supererogatory effort is required; it is only necessary that each person do his fair share, out of a continuing spirit of solidarity. Moreover, while the temptations to petty forms of free riding may be more frequent than previously, the whole educational and cultural apparatus of the society will support the development of socialist virtue, perhaps without competition from corrupting influences, and thus the internalization of the requisite values should be smooth and regular. Hence to the extent that actual socialist societies continue to portray and reward virtue as heroic—that is, extraordinary—this must be taken as a sign of a failure of Marx's (and Marxists') hopes for a moral transformation of people in the wake of the revolution, and of actual moral instability in the society. Moral heroism may be necessary to bring socialist institutions into existence, but a "hero of socialist labor" would appear to be a contradictory concept.

The proletarian virtue that Marx admires resembles, and may be a derivative of, the civic virtue that was a distinctive component of earlier republican traditions in political thought. Republican theory frequently shared with liberalism a substantially individualistic psychology and ethos, and the regime it envisaged and advocated likewise made a place for the competitive pursuit of personal interests. Republicanism diverged from liberalism, however, in recognizing both the necessity and the positive value of a sizable public sphere complementing the private, and, accordingly, in the importance it attached to the participation of public-spirited citizens in the public sphere. While the classical liberals tended to assume that the coordination of private actions could be achieved—to the advantage of all—through the market's invisible hand, republicans saw that the maintenance of a legal regime, under whose auspices private transactions could be undertaken on a regular basis, requires a broad, public-spirited commitment to the regime and to certain public values themselves—or, in our terms, that the public or-

der that forms a necessary background for successful individualism is a collective good that would be unattainable if egoistic
rationality were not restrained and complemented by civic virtue. The virtue of republican citizens is manifested especially
in three ways: in legislation, where (as Rousseau most notably
argued) citizens are called upon deliberately to subordinate
considerations of private to public interest; in a general spirit
of law-abidingness, effective even when violations could yield
private gains at negligible risk, which renders unnecessary a
potentially oppressive system of coercive sanctions; and in a
readiness to defend the regime, when necessary, against external threats, even to the point of self-sacrifice. Civic virtue may
realistically be hoped for, according to republican psychology,
because the loyalties, attachments, opportunities for self-
expression, and other concomitants of civic activity are a source
of intrinsic satisfaction for many people. It is nevertheless
properly called a *virtue,* a morally admirable (and, if exceeding
the average level, praiseworthy) quality of character whose cultivation, in the face of potentially corrupting influences, is a
matter of concern.

It is possible that Marx's political thought was marked from
the beginning by an affinity to this republican tradition, as
transmitted (in a distinctive form) by Hegel; the notion of a
genuine community of citizens may have been his original and,
implicitly, persisting political ideal.[16] In his mature writings,
however, in which Marx is concerned primarily with the revolutionary changes necessary to bring about the social and economic conditions for such a community, the theme of political
virtue is retained in the special form with which we are concerned here. The civic virtue of republican theory is supposed
to characterize all citizens, being grounded in a kind of civic (or
patriotic) solidarity of the citizen body, which comprises all—or
all the politically active—members of the society.[17] That such
civic unity is possible and desirable in a class-divided society is
of course in Marx's view an illusion perpetrated by Hegel and
by other ideologists of the bourgeois state; in Marx's theory,
therefore, proletarian *class* solidarity and corresponding proletarian virtue, manifested in collective struggle against the bourgeoisie, appears as psychologically and morally analogous to the
civic qualities sketched (in idealistic fashion) by republicans, and

they have a similar importance in the political doctrine. As I have noted, the virtue that Marx suggests is displayed by workers prior to and during the revolution has, in many of its exemplars, heroic dimensions that earlier republican writers looked for mainly in time of war—which, like the Marxian revolution, requires exceptional initiatives, sacrifices, and leadership.[18] The socialist virtue that will succeed this revolutionary virtue will be less heroic, and more routine, but similar in its foundation in the solidarity of workers and in their commitment to socialist ideals. Since the post-revolutionary society will be comprised of a single class (or be classless in the historical sense of classes), however, this socialist virtue will extend to, or be expected of, all citizens, and thus can correctly be regarded as a genuine *civic* virtue rather than as a distinctively class-based or partisan virtue. It will be, in the view of Marxists, the first truly civic virtue, inasmuch as this will be the first society to extend genuine citizenship to all of its members.[19]

It should be added that theories of virtue typically pertain to small groups or societies. Aristotle's theory, for example, appears to be designed especially for members of the aristocratic strata in the Greek cities of his time, and even theories of civic virtue, while they endorse qualities that are expected of all citizens, usually assume either that the citizen body is a relatively small and compact section of the total population, or that civic virtue is a distinctive feature of small republics (in contrast to large monarchies or empires). Such assumptions regarding context are linked to the moral psychology of virtue, which is generally held to depend not (or not exclusively) on rational acquiescence in general principles but rather on certain feelings for other people that arise spontaneously (when they are natural feelings) or can be developed (when they are habitual) only in comparatively small and intimate settings—either natural groups like the family or tight-knit groups of like-minded people sharing common traditions and experiences. Virtue (especially civic virtue), moreover, must be cultivated, a process that is facilitated by a shared moral outlook and system of education that are more likely to exist, or may more readily be established, in a small community. In contrast, a morality of general rules (rules of justice, rights, legality) suits a large society, where relations among fellow citizens are frequently (and inescapably) impersonal, and where we accordingly acknowledge a moral as well as a legal requirement of impartiality, as Hume most notably emphasized. It would appear that the workers' movement within capitalist society, as envisaged by Marxists, might have the relevant attributes of a small and solidary community within which an ethos of virtue could be cultivated and thrive. It remains more questionable whether a large society (such as a post-revolutionary socialist society in a large country) could be based on virtue; this might be possible only if some of the features that appear more naturally in a small community—such as homogeneity of culture and moral outlook—were to be artifically (and repressively) imposed upon it.

Marx himself tells us very little about the organization of the future society or the moral qualities of its members, confining his attention for the most part to the tensions in capitalist society and the development of the workers' movement there. Marx's treatment of the theme of virtue, therefore, addresses the revolutionary virtue and heroism manifested by those who are destined to overthrow capitalism and by their predecessors in the proletarian revolts of Marx's own time. While Marx may have believed (as some of his followers have certainly believed) that a suitably informed observer could predict the revolution, or state the objective conditions in which it would occur, he nevertheless understood the revolution—and especially its political dimension: the seizure of state power by the proletariat—as *action,* involving the concerted and deliberate efforts of large numbers of adequately motivated individuals. The revolution, that is, though the result of "laws . . . working with iron necessity," would nevertheless have to be *made,* by the political will and on the basis of the intellectual and moral as well as the material resources of the working class. Hence the cultivation and development of this will and these resources constituted a proximate objective for Marx himself as they would for anyone who advocated the revolutionary transformation of society. References to virtue in Marx's writings must be seen in this light: while they may contain materials for a theory of virtue, they are not themselves offered in a theoretical but in a practical spirit—as expressions of praise and encouragement, the intention of which is to further the development within the proletariat of the qualities held up for admiration, since these are among the prerequisites of revolution.

The most important Marxian text in this respect, as Miller suggests, is *The Civil War in France*. This work is ostensibly an account of the Paris Commune of 1871, one of several unsuccessful workers' risings that Marx witnessed and regarded as episodes in the inexorable prehistory of the coming revolution. We are presented in Marx's text, however, with a moral drama of which the rhetorical and practical (rather than sociological or analytical) intent is sufficiently apparent on the surface, and which is even more clear in light of Marx's real opinions concerning the misguided tactics and imperfectly proletarian composition of the communards.[20]

The Commune was important to Marx partly because of some faint intimations of the socialist future (especially in its ambition to overcome the distinction between state and society), but mainly because of the inspiring example it offered of the heroic (though doomed) virtue of workers—or at any rate of right-minded radicals who could be enshrined as moral models for future recruits to the workers' movement. "Paris all truth, Versailles all lie," Marx proclaims; the "heroic resolve" of the revolutionaries "to work out their own emancipation" is contrasted with the "prostitute realities" of the capitalist society that flourished under the Empire and is personified in the personally corrupt Thiers, head of the provisional government that was quick to betray its own vaunted patriotism by seeking Prussian help in suppressing the revolt. The "self-sacrificing champions of a new and better society" oppose the decadent and hypocritical bourgeoisie as characters in a simple but forceful moral fable, the futility of the event effaced by the nobility of the cause and of the efforts expended in it. "Working men's Paris, with its Commune, will be for ever celebrated as the glorious harbinger of a new society. Its martyrs are enshrined in the great heart of the working class."[21] Although the genuine proletarian revolution of the future will require more favorable circumstances, a more fully developed movement, and a better calculation of means, it will not be able to do without the personal qualities displayed by the people whose deeds Marx seeks to preserve in this pamphlet. Virtue, as Marx senses, thrives in a tradition embracing myths and memories as well as habits and institutions, and it is clearly to the development of such a tradition that Marx contributes (and probably intended to contribute) here.

NOTES

1. Paul E. Sigmund, *Natural Law in Political Thought* (Cambridge, Mass.: Winthrop, 1971), p. 166. See also Svetozar Stojanović, "Marx's Theory of Ethics," in Nicholas Lobkowicz, ed., *Marx and the Western World* (Notre Dame: University of Notre Dame Press, 1967).

2. Robert C. Tucker, "Marx and Distributive Justice," in Carl J. Friedrich and John W. Chapman, eds., *Justice: Nomos VI* (New York: Atherton, 1963); and Allen W. Wood, "The Marxian Critique of Justice," in Marshall Cohen, Thomas Nagel, and Thomas Scanlon, eds., *Marx, Justice, and History, A Philosophy and Public Affairs Reader* (Princeton: Princeton University Press, 1980).

3. This is especially argued by Wood, "The Marxian Critique," pp. 13–16. See also Steven Lukes, "Marxism, Morality and Justice," in G.H.R. Parkinson, ed., *Marx and Marxisms* (Cambridge: Cambridge University Press, 1982), pp. 196–202.

4. Cf. William K. Frankena, *Ethics,* 2nd edition (Englewood Cliffs: Prentice-Hall, 1973), pp. 9, 61 ff. See also his "Prichard and the Ethics of Virtue," *Monist* 54 (1970), pp. 1–17. On the moral worth of heroic acts, see J.O. Urmson, "Saints and Heroes," in Joel Feinberg, ed., *Moral Concepts* (Oxford: Oxford University Press, 1969).

5. David Hume, *A Treatise of Human Nature,* L.A. Selby-Bigge, ed., 2nd edition, revised by P.H. Nidditch (Oxford: Clarendon, 1978), p. 502.

6. Marx's description in his early writings of the well-rounded personality and fully developed potentialities of the person who is not alienated and warped by the division of labor resembles in some respects the Aristotelian ideal. These passages may thus contain elements of a full Marxian theory of virtue. Cf. Alan Gilbert, "Historical Theory and the Structure of Moral Argument in Marx," *Political Theory* 9 (1981), p. 178.

7. Hume himself relates benevolence, or natural feelings of "social sympathy" to which benevolence is connected, to political partisanship. *An Inquiry Concerning the Principles of Morals,* Charles W. Hendel, ed. (New York: Liberal Arts Press, 1957), p. 51.

8. Miller's approach to morality is Kantian, which explains why he regards Marx as only ambiguously a moralist. Marx's attacks on "morality" and moralizing, however, were probably directed mainly against Kant and German Kantians, for whom morality was a matter of abstract duty divorced from passion, interest, and concrete circumstance. Marx (like many other theorists of virtue) is best

regarded as an ethical naturalist, for whom moral values are closely related to human (or workers') interests and to action in historical contexts. See H.B. Acton, *The Illusion of the Epoch* (Boston: Beacon Press, 1957), pp. 220–223; and Sidney Hook, *From Hegel to Marx* (Ann Arbor: University of Michigan Press, 1962), pp. 51–53.

9. Eugene Kamenka, *The Ethical Foundations of Marxism* (New York: Praeger, 1962). If the transformation of man (or of human nature) by man's own creative labors is indeed Marx's most basic point, then presumably no Marxian moral theory (including a theory of virtue) could be both general and detailed.

10. Allen Buchanan, "Revolutionary Motivation and Rationality," in Cohen, Nagel, and Scanlon, eds., *Marx, Justice, and History*, pp. 264–287.

11. Ibid., p. 268. Miller appears to miss this point.

12. There is of course the danger here that revolutionary action may become irrational—as perhaps in the Paris Commune, where revolutionary élan failed to compensate for the lack of correct calculations regarding tactics. Some may suggest that a new type of "socialist rationality" will appear within the socialist movement, but no coherent account of this has yet been given, according to Buchanan.

13. A collective action theorist such as Olson would see this as a "moral incentive" to contribute to the production of a collective good. If "moral" is contrasted with "self-interested," however, and if self-interested motivation is eliminated altogether in socialist society, the public-spirited activity in question would not appear "moral" in any distinctive sense. Mancur Olson, Jr., *The Logic of Collective Action* (New York: Schocken Books, 1968), p. 61n.

14. Richard T. DeGeorge, *Soviet Ethics and Morality* (Ann Arbor: University of Michigan Press, 1969). The period of the "building of communism" in the USSR was announced in the 1961 Soviet Communist Party Program, which also included a "moral code" and called for the active promulgation of the new socialist morality. This novel development apparently reflected a general, uneasy sense that the expected "new Soviet man" was not emerging automatically with the changed social conditions; it rested theoretically on Stalin's doctrine of the relative independence of certain parts of the superstructure. Lenin himself, apart from his constant emphasis on the need for discipline and self-discipline among the workers (which could be construed as a contribution to the Marxian theory of virtue), affirms the "Nechaevan" or Plekhanovist doctrine that whatever advances the revolutionary cause is moral, and vice versa. See V.I. Lenin, "The Tasks of the Youth

Leagues," in *Selected Works* (New York: International Publishers, 1971), p. 613. A work that reflects the pervasive tone of moral exhortation in recent Soviet culture is Georgi Smirnov, *Soviet Man* (Moscow: Progress Publishers, 1973).

15. Cf. Lenin's view of the "heroism" displayed in the workers' "victory over our own conservatism, indiscipline, petty-bourgeois egoism, a victory over the habits left as a heritage to the worker and peasant by accursed capitalism." "A Great Beginning," *Selected Works*, p. 478.

16. For Hegel, individuals are citizens of the state, and thus participants in its universality, as well as members of particularistic civil society; or they would be if the state conformed to the idea of a true state, embodying freedom. Marx denied that any state could mediate or resolve the conflicts endemic to civil society in such a way as to realize freedom; human emancipation would require overcoming the dualism between the private and the public spheres, and thus the abolition of both the state (as a distinct entity) and civil society (based on private property). Marx referred to his ideal community sometimes as "democracy" (in his 1843 writings) and sometimes as *Gemeinwesen;* see Robert C. Tucker, *The Marxian Revolutionary Idea* (New York: Norton, 1969), p. 87. While Marx takes individual self-fulfillment to be a fundamental value of this community, he at the same time appears to want to deny that there will be individual *interests* that could be opposed to or even distinguishable from common interests; see Kamenka, *Ethical Foundations*, p. 44.

17. Republicanism could take an aristocratic form, as for example in Montesquieu, or even in Rousseau's *Considerations on the Government of Poland;* the tendency of modern republicanism, however, is democratic (in keeping with the implications of the *Social Contract*).

18. And, perhaps, special honors for leaders (even "dictators"), that seem anomalous in view of the egalitarian values of both republicanism and socialism. Gilbert, "Historical Theory," p. 184, compares revolutionary and civic virtue: Marx's description of the Paris Commune is said to recall the ancient polis.

19. "In these conditions [in socialist, e.g., Soviet society] concern for the public good becomes the most personal concern of all members of society. Personal needs and interests become organically linked in people's consciousness with the interests of society, with ideological and political interests." Smirnov, *Soviet Man*, p. 175.

20. Shlomo Avineri, *The Social and Political Thought of Karl Marx* (Cambridge: University Press, 1971), pp. 239–249.

21. Karl Marx, *The Civil War in France,* in Karl Marx and Frederick Engels, *Selected Works* (London: Lawrence and Wishart, 1968), pp. 300, 294–295, 306, 311. Heroism and virtue are not present in the bourgeois world, which is one reason why the proletariat may be expected eventually to win, even though the capitalists can use the state to solve their own collective action problems.

PART II

THE POLITICAL
DIMENSIONS
OF MARXISM

4

ON READING MARX
POLITICALLY

SHELDON S. WOLIN

Instead of collapsing as Marx predicted that it would, capitalism has emerged stronger than ever.

In advanced capitalist societies, the material condition of the working class has improved rather than worsened.

Working-class movements have become less rather than more revolutionary.

For the better part of a century, critics of Karl Marx have pointed to unfulfilled predictions of the sort represented above as evidence of the falsity of Marx's theory. Typically, their criticism rests on a view that a theory which claims to be scientific is seriously defective if its predictions fail to materialize. The main point of much of this criticism is not the predictions themselves as the discredit that their failure casts upon Marx's analysis of capitalism. If the predictions can be shown to be false, the analysis becomes suspect; if Marx's self-proclaimed science fails as prediction, how can it succeed as scientific analysis?

1. MARX'S INTENTIONS

When Marx is judged by scientific standards, whatever the standards may be and whatever conception of science they may reflect, a certain intention is attributed to him. Marx, we would want to say, aimed to produce a theory that would qualify as scientific. To support this view of his intentions we could point to statements by him such as: "Every opinion based on scientific criticism I welcome."[1] If Marx were judged to have conscientiously pursued his aim, the resulting theory could be said to be shaped by a scientific purpose. The theory's structure of statements—its descriptions, explanations, analyses, and predictions—would expectably be governed by the intention to be scientific, however successful it should turn out to be. For our purposes it is not crucial that we identify precisely Marx's conception of science, but rather that we treat "science" as a metaphor indicative of a commitment to the search for truth. When Marx declared that his theoretical conclusions were "the outcome of conscientious research carried on over many years,"[2] the statement can be read as an intention to be a truth-teller.

While the ideal of science was undeniably important in shaping Marx's theoretical intentions, there were other and conflicting determinants as well. One was a highly developed notion of theoretical *activity* or, more precisely, of theorizing as action. Its basis was laid before Marx became immersed in the study of economics. His intensive research into ancient philosophy while preparing his doctoral dissertation and his close association with the Young Hegelians helped to produce a pronouncedly "political" view of theoretical activity. There were, he believed, distinct philosophical epochs in the history of philosophy that represented the founding of a dominant "total system" by a "master," "a philosophical giant." These periods were frequently followed by times of "gigantic discord" that Marx likened to the wars of the Titans in Greek mythology, where the sons of Uranus depose the father as king of the gods, install Kronos, and then war against Zeus after he successfully challenges Kronos. For would-be philosophers, born as it were in the shadow of a Plato, an Aristotle, or a Hegel, the choice is either to live an Alexandrian existence and be content to refine the all-encompassing system of the master; or to challenge it and to seek its overthrow.[3] Then theory abandons the contemplative mode and becomes action rather than activity. Marx described it as "critical" and "destructive," but its intentions are plainly revolutionary and political: theory aims at overthrowing a philosophical "order" and reconstituting it.[4]

2. THOUGHT AND ACTION

The third element in the structure of Marx's intentions is action itself. Marx's earliest thoughts on that subject were not primarily concerned with the proletariat but with the theorist-as-actor. Throughout most of his life Marx was a passionate political actor: the test of that passion was not so much his involvements in the revolutionary events of 1848, when his theoretical vision was primarily political rather than economic— the *18th Brumaire* (1852) rather than the *Contribution to the Critique of Political Economy* (1859)—as his continued action after many failures and setbacks for the proletarian cause, as though individual commitments still mattered. What made the test so demanding was that Marx did not think of action as merely "doing." Beginning with some of his earliest notations on the nature of theory and action, Marx envisioned action as an extension of thought and theory as a political mode of activity. "It is a psychological law," Marx noted while preparing his doctoral dissertation, "that the theoretical mind, having become free in itself, turns into practical energy . . . The practice (*praxis*) of philosophy, however, is itself *theoretical*. It is *criticism* which measures individual existence against essences, particular actuality against the Idea."[5]

If these early formulations found Marx straining to convert theory into action, to *act*ualize thought, they also suggest that he was seeking to impregnate action with thought, with theory. This latter impulse was expressed in the phrase " 'revolutionary,' 'practical-critical' activity" ('*praktisch-kritischen' Tätigkeit*) and in his criticism of Feuerbach for having exalted theory while denigrating practice as mere "appearance."[6] Action would no longer be confined to the pragmatic and to the fluctuating realm of appearance and opinion: it would become "revolutionary," action that would self-consciously transform a whole society, realizing in fact what the theoretical mind could envision only as idea.

Thus Marx's theoretical intentions were not purely theoretical. Their most extreme formulation was in the second of his theses on Feuerbach. There Marx inverted the Aristotelian principle of the superiority of theoretical contemplation over political action by switching predicates so that theory would be judged by its power, action by its truth: "The question whether human thinking can arrive at objective truth—is not a question of theory but a *practical* question. In practice man must prove the truth, that is, actuality and power, this-sidedness of his thinking."[7]

Aristotle had formulated his conception of *theoria* as a contrast between two lives which ought not to be combined, the political life and the theoretical life.[8] In rejecting that formulation, Marx seems closer to Plato's ideal of the philosopher who alternates between contemplation and action. But while Plato had been concerned to render the two lives compatible while preserving the superiority of the *bios theoretikos*, Marx wanted to make them complementary modes of activity. This aim was evident in his early critiques of Hegel and Feuerbach. In his famous preface to the *Philosophy of Right* Hegel had argued a version of Aristotle's separation of the two modes of activity. Theory "comes on the scene too late" to be of any practical importance because theoretical truth about the world is only possible when the world's actuality is "cut and dried after its process of formation has been completed."[9]

While theory's vision for Hegel was necessarily interpretative and retrospective, a lineal descendant of an ancient tradition of the theorist-as-spectator,[10] for Marx it was to be constitutive and prospective, inspired not by the image of a divine unmoved Mover, but by "the same spirit that constructs railways with the hands of workers . . ."[11] and so drawn toward the dynamics of life-in-becoming rather than its cut-and-dried maturity. As he stated, ". . . the time must come when philosophy not only internally by its content but also externally through its form, comes into contact and interaction with the real world of its day."[12]

3. PREDICTION AND TRUTH

In these early writings Marx's notion of theoretical activity was radically different from Plato's archetype of the *demiurgos* who "took over all that is visible . . . and brought it from disorder into order. . . ."[13] Marx was both the antidemiurgos, committed to disordering the world—"Worlds I would destroy forever/Since I can create no world"—and the Young Hegelian philosopher whose thought has been nuanced by the "interventionist" Aristotle of the *Politics* rather than the comtemplator of the *Ethics* and so is sustained by the belief that not only is "philosophy becoming worldly" but "the world is becoming philosophical."[14] Marx's intention of making philosophy political while making action philosophical presupposed that the quest for truth would remain the decisive mark of philosophy. Philosophy, he insisted, "asks what is true" and makes no compromises with opinion, or with political or parochial loyalties.[15] Commitment to truth was not a mere rhetorical flourish for Marx. Few theorists in the entire history of political theory have been so steadfast in their devotion to the theoretical calling, have made so many personal sacrifices and taken so many risks on its behalf, or have dared to rethink basic presuppositions and begin anew when evidence or argument had cast doubts on years of their previous work.

The commitment to truth, to action, to the symbiosis of theory and action made for a highly complex structure of intentions with numerous possibilities for inner tensions and contrary tugs. The major condition for preserving the structure and preventing its disintegration was that theoretical inquiry would not turn up results that would undermine the aims or project of action. A commitment to truth always carried that possibility and with it the possibility that theory and action might be compelled along divergent paths.

That possibility will be explored in this paper. The form that it took for Marx was theoretic failure. The meaning of theoretic failure was not in Marx's unfulfilled predictions but in the complex fact that faces every interpreter of Marx, that Marx failed to complete his theory. This fact, I shall suggest, is the expression of a conflict that develops between Marx's theoretical findings and his political commitments.

I shall approach this conflict by posing a question that is prompted by the common criticism which attempts to discredit Marx's theory by claiming that history has failed to confirm Marx's prediction about the demise of capitalism. Could Marx's theory be "true" in an important sense despite the patent falsity of the prediction? Conceding for the moment that it might be both possible and illuminating to isolate a theory from its predictions, we would want to know what the remaining theory was a theory of. Would we find an implicit, incompletely articulated theory that was inconsistent with the prediction that capitalism was doomed? Would we have the outlines of a social system with the potentiality to survive periodic crises? If such a system can be detected, then the theory describes a successful rather than a doomed system, a *perpetuum mobile,* as Marx called it, that could endlessly reproduce new conditions for its own perpetuation.

Clearly, if it can be shown that Marx developed a theory that furnished strong grounds for the perpetuation rather than the revolutionary overthrow of capitalism, the implications would be severe. It would cast into doubt the central role assigned the proletariat. It would alter the tenor of the theory, from hopeful to problematic. In addition, it would present Marx's theoretical activity in a different light, having to take account of the possibility that as his inquiries into capitalism were extended, they turned up increasing evidence of the system's unrivalled capability for adaptation and innovation. Thus a conflict internal to the theory was generated, between the results of inquiry and the political intentions of the inquirer. One consequence of the conflict would be registered in the predictions attached to the theory. They would serve as the medium by which Marx would strive to reinstate the political intentions that he had invested in the revolutionary role of the proletariat. Prediction would be the· means of recovering what analysis had rendered problematic, of averting rather than confirming the analysis. It was a way of theory being false to itself in order to be true to action.

One further preliminary. I depart from the conventional assumption that what Marx was intent upon describing as "capital" was an historically specific economic formation. Rather, the view I take is that the great economic writings of Marx's later years—*Grundrisse, Capital,* and *Theories of Surplus Value*—represent a continuation of the project that had preoccupied him from the beginning of his theoretical career, to find the right way of describing a system of power. He would discover that the system could not be adequately comprehended by relying exclusively upon categories drawn from either philosophy, political theory, or economics, although each was essential to identifying different dimensions of power.

4. THEORETICAL INCOMPLETENESS

I turn first to the matter of theoretical incompleteness. As is well known, the bulk of Marx's writings is mostly unfinished. Much of it has become available only within the last half-century, and then only after heavy editing.[16] The writings that are most discussed today were unknown to his contemporaries, while the work that was most widely read in his day, *The Manifesto of the Communist Party*, is frequently downgraded by today's commentators. Marx is the only major writer in the history of theory whose reputation rests substantially on what he chose not to publish.

No theorist of comparable stature has left so many loose ends, so many unfinished themes. It is not merely that the writings are unfinished; the theory is incomplete. Yet no thinker was ever more conscious that the purpose of theory was to pull together "the whole thing in its totality."[17]

"There is no royal road to science," he remarked toward the end, "and only those who do not dread the fatiguing climb of its steep paths have a chance of gaining its luminous summits." Yet unlike others who had struggled to the heights, Marx claimed no full vision of the city below, only a "method of analysis . . . which had not previously been applied to economic subjects."[18] At one time he was persuaded that the completion of the theory was close at hand, that "the system of bourgeois economy" was now within his grasp. "The entire material lies before me in the form of monographs, which were written not for publication but for self-clarification at widely separated periods; their remolding into an integrated whole . . . will depend upon circumstances."[19] Circumstances decreed instead that Marx would leave a vision scattered among numerous "critiques"—no rounded and complete view of the whole, no *Republic*, or *Discorsi*, or *Leviathan*. Even if Marx had succeeded in "remolding" his material, the "system of bourgeois economy" would not have fulfilled the promise of what Engels had called "the famous Positive, what you 'really' want . . ."[20] There was only the unredeemed promise "to present the interconnected whole, to show the relationship between the parts. . . ."[21] When Kautsky once asked the elderly Marx if the time had not come to publish his complete works, Marx replied, "They would first have to be completed."

In accounting for the incompleteness of Marx's theory our task is not to expose theoretical shortcomings, but to interpret the meaning of theoretical defeat. It means asking, what is the contribution failure makes to a great theory? Another and closely related question, or problem, needs some elaboration at this point, because it haunts the whole of Marx's mature vision. Stated simply, there was something troubling about the world and the special way in which Marx perceived it that caused the theory to falter, and hence to be incomplete. One is unprepared for this in a theory whose vision was magnificent in its sweep, sure in its grasp of concreteness, remarkable for its penetration of complex interrelationships, and memorable for its language. Although Marx is typically described as dogmatic, optimistic, and apocalyptic, his later thought sounded an uneasy note as he mused on the "insanity" that "determines the economic and practical life of nations."[22] It was most evident in the pessimism that tinged certain expressions; they are familiar to any reader of Marx, but their enigmatic quality is usually overlooked. The two expressions are "the forces of production" and "the order of things." Marx perceived the world in a special way, as an enormous structure of cumulating power generated by the "process" of production. These processes, ever changing, ever more efficient and voluminous, were genuine "forces." They appeared benign because of their evident capability of satisfying man's most expansive material dreams. But if their potential was benign, their power was staggering and could only be described in hyperbole: "The bourgeoisie, during its rule of scarce one hundred years, has created more massive and more colossal productive forces than have all preceding generations together."[23] As Marx was perhaps the first to show, the development of these forces had exacted a price, appallingly in the case of the workers whose humanity was threatened with extinction, more subtly among those responsible for tending and perfecting a system founded on innovation, and more ominously in the case of the world in which, as Marx was among the first to recognize, the modern economy had fulfilled the Baconian dream of dominating nature and was now bent on consuming her. The highest price of all, and the source of Marx's deepest disquiet, was that this magnificent apparatus of power, constructed by man's labor and ingenuity and requiring centuries of painful evolution, had become an uncontrollable order of things, increasingly less needful of its human operatives and more contemptuous in its treatment of them. At the center of the palace of production reigned a kind of Miltonic chaos:

> . . . the commercial crises by their periodic return put on trial, each time more threateningly, the existence of the entire bourgeois society. . . . A great part not only of the existing products but also of the previously created productive forces are periodically destroyed . . . [in] the epidemic of overproduction . . . and why? Because there is too much civilization, too much means of subsistence, too much industry, too much commerce.[24]

5. DISCORDANT THEMES AND DISQUIET

The disturbing paradox of the system was that it was manmade, yet mysterious; it operated by rational methods, yet it issued in irrational, unpredictable results; it had been contrived for the most prosaic purposes of producing goods, services, and livelihoods, and yet, suddenly, it would veer out of control or break down altogether. Although Marx prophesied that eventually men would master the forces of production and humanize the order of things, he never completed the argument to support it. The system was too protean to remain caught for long. As he wrote to Lassalle:

The job is making very slow progress because things which
one has for many years made the chief object of one's investigations constantly exhibit new aspects and call forth
new doubts whenever they are to be put in final shape.[25]

The last three decades of Marx's life were spent not in pre-
scribing solutions or itemizing the future of man, but spinning
out in tireless detail the inner complexities of the greatest productive system in history. He left behind three massive volumes
which we know as *Capital,* three more collected under the title
Theories of Surplus Values, and a bulging manuscript later des-
ignated as the *Grundrisse.*[26] Scattered throughout all of these
works were substantial clues about the shape of the future, but
these have mostly to be ferreted out from beneath the mass of
detail relating to the mechanisms of capitalism.

What is troublesome about these unconsolidated heaps is the
latent discord among some of the major themes. In the *Grundrisse* and in *Capital* he was concerned to show that the growing
use of technology had already produced a state of affairs in
which workers were increasingly superfluous and human labor,
in its modern form, was becoming anachronistic. Some revision
seemed called for, because Marx's ideas on revolution had been
formulated in a period when he had conceived of the identity
of the worker and the formative experience of work in significantly different terms. The worker who dominates Marx's writing before 1850 is a pretechnological figure; the system of capital that dominates Marx's writings during the 1850s and beyond
is in the throes of technological change. In the pages of the
Grundrisse Marx affords a glimpse of a new kind of worker, one
that might be called the versatile technician, but the discussion
sheds no light on the question of whether the new worker will
exhibit a new form of revolutionary consciousness, or whether
he can be expected to act in a revolutionary manner at all. One
feels cheated by the silence of a theorist who, more than any
modern, had done so much to revive the ancient word *praxis*
and to bind it to theory.

What was the source of Marx's disquietude, the obstacle to
completing his theory? The explanation falls into two parts. The
first has to do with the peculiarities of Marx's thought processes
and the way in which they developed; the second with a crucial

disproportion that began to emerge between his theory of society and his theory of revolution, between the power of the system and the power to be mobilized against it.

6. A GENERAL THEORY OF SOCIETY AND POWER

Beginning in 1843 with his critique of Hegel's *Philosophy of Right*, Marx set out on a search for a general theory of society. The two most striking aspects of a search that was to occupy him for the rest of his life were, first, the astonishing number and variety of philosophical and political theories that he consumed in the process, and, second, the persistence with which he judged each theory according to the standard of power, that is, whether the theory in question had an adequate grasp of the real powers in the world and whether the possession of it significantly empowered the theorist in his efforts to change the world. The search, then, was not for an intellectually satisfying theory but for a power-laden theory.

Marx's quest took him from one theoretical position to another. At the outset, he understood theory to be philosophy, and philosophy to be the system of Hegel. Once within the Hegelian system, which he never wholly escaped, he gravitated toward the "critical" philosophy of the Hegelian Left. Upon discovering Feuerbach, he turned against his former position, and before long, against Feuerbach as well. For each renunciation he gave the same explanation: the theory had failed to grasp the nature of power in the world and, as a consequence, it left the theorist impotent. In the end Marx renounced philosophy itself, and in savage terms: "Philosophy and the study of the actual world have the same relation to one another as onanism and sexual love."[27]

From philosophy Marx turned to the study of economics and theories of communism and socialism. After mastering most of the extant literature of political economy, he pronounced it "shit," saying that no progress had been made in the subject since Smith and Ricardo.[28] He had only a slightly higher opinion of the communist and socialist writings of his time. Increasingly, each of these bodies of thought served Marx as symptoms rather than as theoretical aids. Political economy revealed

the assumptions upon which capitalism operated and the delu-
sions that prevented the economist from perceiving the problematic status of bourgeois society as an historical entity. Socialist and communist theories, on the other hand, showed what it
meant for thought to be immature. These theories suffered
either from an excessive reliance upon moral criticism to the
detriment of any serious analysis of the structure and processes
of capitalism, or, when serious analysis was attempted, it was
conducted with little understanding of the rigorous requirements of truly scientific work. For his own part, Marx's eventual understanding of capitalism as a massive structure of power,
"stupendous" in size and global in scope,[29] while it owed something to all of these other theories, was the product of his own
unique conception of what had to be known in order to understand the theory and practice of capitalism. The question of the
origins and genesis of this "world-historical power" sent Marx
rummaging into the remote past,[30] reading not only history but
anthropology in the hope of discovering how, from the simple
need to sustain existence, men had produced a system of
matchless promise and actual destitution. Then to unlock its
inner secret, he drove himself to examine the actual conditions
of life that, historically, capitalism had created in the cities and
rural areas, as well as in the domains of politics, culture, and
ideas. Finally, there was an imperative need to master the new
science of economics, for capitalist society was unique in having
produced a body of theory concurrent with producing an economic revolution.[31] Never before had an undertaking of this
magnitude been attempted by any theorist, but then, no theorist had ever confronted the massive powers Marx found ranged
against humanity.

7. CAPITALIST CIVILIZATION

Marx's genius was to expose the contemporary structure of
capitalism in all of its historicity. The crucial significance of this
achievement was not the trite discovery that capitalism had a
history but that it constituted a civilization.[32] The structure of
capitalist civilization comprised what is ordinarily distinguished
as society, politics, the economy, and culture. This totality be-

came the focus of Marx's theory. Although he did not complete the theory, the reason had as much to do with his mode of vision as with the scope of the undertaking. That mode of vision is familiarly described as dialectical and misleadingly analyzed as Marx's "method." In truth, the dialectic served Marx not only as a method of inquiry but also as a way of seeing the world. His vision of capitalism bears this out. In laying bare its structure, he draws attention to more than the processes and relations of production and exchange. He analyzes techniques, instruments, and knowledge, as well as the forms of behavior and values enforced by the system. In each of these elements, whether techniques, relations, or behavior, Marx saw a "congealment" of the whole history of capitalism, as well as traces of previous modes of production. In the accumulation of capital he saw the accumulation of history.[33] The rhythm of accumulation was dialectical: capitalism had evolved through various stages in which new developments superseded existing forms and relations without totally annihilating them. Elements of the old were caught up in the new and perpetuated. The weight of things that capitalism carried forward included not only its own history, but the historical deposits of the systems preceding it.

8. TRADITION

The massive proportions of the capitalist system had a telling influence both upon Marx's theory and his estimate of revolutionary prospects. "The tradition of all dead generations," Marx once wrote,

> weighs like a nightmare on the brain of the living. And just when they seem engaged in revolutionizing themselves and things, in creating something entirely new, precisely in such epochs of revolutionary crisis they anxiously conjure up the spirits of the past to their service and borrow from them names, battle slogans and costumes in order to present the new scene of world history in this time-honored disguise and this borrowed language.[34]

In the undertones of this passage one can detect something of Marx's despair at the cumulated massiveness of the modern world, which disposes men to cling to the past even while they are engaged in changing the present. But the passage also suggests something more autobiographical, a hint of a common malady afflicting the theorist as well as the world.

The malady is tradition. Earlier we had pointed out that Marx looked upon capitalism as a system that combined innovation along with perpetuation of elements of the past. Capitalism would eventually topple, according to Marx, because it could no longer support the weight of its accumulated contradictions. Yet the collapse of capitalism would not signify the beginning of an absolutely fresh state of affairs. Just as the capitalist revolution had brought forward the past, so would the post-capitalist era.[35]

9. REVOLUTION AND CONTINUITY

Marx's conception of social change reveals him to be a revolutionary with an acute awareness of continuity. It is as though he combined Burke's sensitivity to tradition with Saint-Simon's insight into the destructive dynamics of technological change. The combination produces an almost painful sense of the overwhelming odds against anyone bent on "creating something entirely new." It is reflected in the way that Marx's practice of theory strikingly reproduces the processes at work in hisotry. Theorizing becomes a mimetic rendering in thought of the ultimate powers whose rhythms dictate the course and contours of the world; a symbolic reenactment of the processes of history: "All that exists . . . exists and lives only by some kind of movement. . . . There is a continual movement, of growth in productive forces, of destruction in social relations, of formation in ideas; the only immutable thing is the abstraction of movement—*mors immortalis.*"[36]

Like the world, Marx's theory took shape as movement, growth, destruction, and perpetuation. Like the world, it was an unfinished process; in this sense Marx never "produced" a completed theory, only a series of approximations, each more inclusive than the last. The way in which Marx practiced theory insured that his theory could never be located in space, as, for example, Hobbes's *Leviathan* could in England's Interregnum, but only observed over time. He used the methods of "critical" theory to force "contradictions" between what he had affirmed and what he was coming to believe; his theory progressed by a dialectical rhythm of discovery and reintegration of the new and the old; and, in imitation of the history of social formations, the theory grew bulkier as it added new concepts, insights, and empirical illustrations to its expanding structure—and more desperate. Its crisis, too, was a crisis of overproduction as it struggled to assimilate into its scheme of interconnections the profuse and intricate relations that its own insights had uncovered. The incompleteness should be read as theoretic failure occasioned by the defeat of heroic intentions. *Mors immortalis.*

Although Marx's revolutionary temper and his passion for theoretic supremacy goaded him into practicing theory as a form of combat, a way of destroying rivals and enemies, his practice was equally distinguished by its remarkable concern for existing intellectual traditions, and for treating truly great theorists with utmost seriousness. He always felt under an obligation to take careful account both of the reigning ideas and their antecedents. Because Marx's search for a theory took him into areas of thought that had long been well-cultivated, the search resembled a succession of forced entries into occupied domains.[37] Typically, it took the form of a critique, either of some writer, such as Feuerbach or Ricardo, or of some problem, such as the nature of revolution. Marx's first move would be to locate the writer or problem in the appropirate tradition. Thus, behind Ricardo stood James Mill, the Physiocrats, and Adam Smith; before Ricardo's concept of value could be understood critically, it was necessary to examine all of the strands of economic thinking that had led to it.[38] Or, to take another example, before Marx would commit himself to "materialism," he first had to compose its history so as to locate Feuerbach's version, which had helped to stimulate his own interest in the doctrine; only then was Marx prepared to describe his own position.[39] Similarly, he hesitated to declare himself a communist until he had thoroughly digested the history of its ideas and of related theories.[40]

In Marx's practice it was as though no theory, concept, or problem could be understood apart from its location in a well-defined and cumulative tradition, and as though Marx's own achievement depended upon its being correctly situated in relation to previous achievements. At the same time, this practice proved to be a formidable obstacle to the completion of his own theory. In addition to the labor of mastering large and complex bodies of theory, there was the task of selecting relevant notions from the various theories, and of integrating them into one's own theory or of relating the appropriate parts of one's own theory to previous writings. "As long as there is an unread book which you think important," Engels complained, "you do not get down to writing."[41] In a sense, however, Marx was always engaged in writing his theory. The world's difficulty was his: of carrying forward more than he destroyed.

10. THE TRANSFORMATION OF CAPITALISM

In Marx's introduction to his *Contribution to the Critique of Political Economy* (1859), he recounted how the 1848 revolutions had interrupted his "economic studies" and that when he was able to resume them in London in 1850, the "enormous amount of material relating to the history of political economy assembled in the British Museum," the advantages that London afforded "for the observation of bourgeois society," and "the new stage of development which the society seemed to have entered with the discovery of gold in California and Australia" caused him "to start again from the very beginning" of his theoretical labors.[42] These remarks underscore once more that Marx was intent upon portraying a system that was constantly undergoing significant change. The changes have a triple character: they are harbingers of the social formation that is to succeed capitalism; they are also changes within capitalism, transformations of it; and they are the source of opposing tendencies that "are so many mines to explode" the capitalist system and "can never be abolished through quiet metamorphosis." He wrote ". . . if we did not find concealed in society *as it is* the material conditions of production and the corresponding relations of exchange prerequisite for a classless society, then all attempts to explode it would be quixotic."[43]

The phrase "as it is" points to the fact that capitalism has been undergoing modifications that eliminated some of its earlier features, transforming it into a formation that is somewhere between classical capitalism and early communism. The status of the worker changes dramatically under the impact of technological innovations; the capitalist as bold entrepreneur and tireless innovator will have been replaced by functionaries; and the pervasively social character of production and increasing "material dependence" of all members of society will have all helped to diminish some of the hierarchical features of society and to replace them by more universalistic relations appropriate to a "system of general social interchange."[44] In its latest phase the system can be described in terms that dwell lingeringly upon the enormous power compacted into the structures of production and into the tremendous "velocity" generated by exchange relations, but the description makes virtually no reference at all to the actors caught up in the system of power. Capital is represented as the "endless and limitless drive to go beyond its existing barrier," "the infinite urge to wealth [that] strives consistently towards infinite increase of the productive forces of labor. . . ."[45] Even wealth itself is treated less as a symbol of avarice and exploitation than as the summary expression of the power already in evidence under capitalism:

> . . . when the limited bourgeois form is stripped away, what is wealth other than the universality of individual needs, capacities, pleasures, productive forces, etc., created through universal exchange? The full development of human mastery over the forces of nature, those of so-called nature as well as of humanity's own nature? The absolute working-out of his creative potentialities . . . i.e. the development of all human powers as such the end in itself, not as measured on a *pre-determined* yardstick?[46]

11. REVOLUTION, PROLETARIAT, AND POWER

It was only after 1850 that Marx came to appreciate fully the system of power that capitalism had amassed and that he was able to work out the complex and tortuous relations and transactions that composed it. That achievement clearly represented a considerable redirection of Marx's political impulses and their absorption into the "politics" being played out in a domain seemingly (if only temporarily) beyond human control and the common understanding. Before 1850, roughly speaking, Marx's political impulses had been fixed upon the two concepts of "revolution" and "proletariat." These concepts were formulated in his preindustrial and preeconomics period and they served as the main vehicles by which traditional political concerns were being carried forward by Marx. That they were formulated before Marx's thinking was profoundly shaped by economics enables one to see how they perpetuated certain traditional themes of political theory.

Revolution and proletariat embody the constitutive or founding element, the beginning of a new order, that classical and early modern political theory had associated with the art of the legislator and especially with a legislator who would be guided by the counsels of those who had acquired political knowledge. They also express a notion of action that is preliberal as well as preindustrial: action of heroic proportions, waged against powerful adversaries, and undertaken to save humanity ("the total redemption of humanity").[47] Not surprisingly, in these early discussions of the working class and revolutionary action Marx introduced traditional themes regarding the importance of political education and political virtue: "What we say to the workers is: 'You will have 15, 20, 50 years of civil war and national struggle and this not merely to bring about a change in society but also to change yourselves and prepare yourselves for the exercise of political power.' "[48]

The crucial political importance of the concepts of revolution and proletariat is that they formed the core of Marx's conception of power. He embraced and developed them before he had begun his intensive studies of the literature of political economy in 1844 and hence before he had incorporated the language of economics into his theoretical outlook. When Marx wrote that "Germany . . . can only make a revolution which upsets the whole order of things" and that the proletariat is the appointed instrument for "the emancipation of man,"[49] his concepts of revolution, proletariat, and power correspond to what Hobsbawm and others have dubbed "precapitalist formations." They were formulated before he had grasped the nature of capitalism as a system of power. His conception of a revolutionary movement, for example, was primarily inspired by reading about the French Revolution of 1789 and composed of images of an aroused mass, goaded into fury by privation, moving against a visible enemy that flaunted its status from atop the social and political pyramid. The most vivid expression of this understanding of revolution was the essay of 1844, *A Contribution to the Critique of Hegel's "Philosophy of Right" Introduction*. There he invests the German workers with a revolutionary potential that will produce a general European contagion, even though, as he specifically noted, Germany's political and economic development lagged behind that of France and Britain.[50]

When Marx (in collaboration with Engels) came to write *The German Ideology* (1845–46), he had begun to acquire a firmer grasp of economics, not least because of his association with Engels, and with it the first appreciation of the power embodied in the system whose overthrow he was advocating. Capitalism, he realized, was a worldwide phenomenon that demanded a revolutionary response commensurate with this new scale. This realization produced the beginning of a crisis in Marx's thinking, for he now saw the futility of investing revolutionary hopes in a precapitalist society such as Germany. A revolution in Germany would necessarily be a revolution against feudalism, a repeat of 1789; but everywhere, including Germany, industrialism was rapidly eradicating the vestiges of feudalism and hence revolution had to be reconsidered.

"The organisation of revolutionary elements as a class supposes the existence of all the productive forces which could be engendered in the bosom of the old society."[51] This formulation crucially determines the nature of revolution. Given the extraordinary magnitude of power consolidated in the modern world, only a massive power can overcome it, a violent "driving force," a "total revolution."[52] The revolution must be worldwide in scope if it is to be commensurate with the universal power of capitalism, "the act of the dominant peoples 'all at once' and simultaneously."[53] Similarly, if the revolutionary force is to succeed it must be the expression of the most modern and hence most powerful phase of productive forces. Revolution under backward conditions merely generalizes a condition of want "and with destitution the struggle for necessities and all the old filthy business would necessarily be reproduced."[54]

The nature of the force that alone can overthrow the monolith of capitalism is summarized in the word "movement," to denote that it, too, is a power equally rooted in the nature of *things* and not in the realm of wishes. "Communism is for us not a *state of affairs* to be established, an *ideal* to which reality [will] have to adjust itself. We call communism the *real* movement that abolishes the present state of things. The conditions of this movement result from the premises now in existence."[55] The power of the "movement" must then be commensurate with those dynamic laws of motion that governed the development of historical forces.[56] Only movement could overcome movement.

It is significant that in the *Communist Manifesto,* where some effort is made to depict the developing crisis of capitalism and to indicate its signs, there is also a different emphasis on revolution. The *Manifesto,* in general, meets the question of how the revolutionary dynamic is generated by borrowing one of Hegel's famous metaphors, *die List der Vernunft.* In place of the cunning of reason, Marx introduces the cunning of necessity. The bourgeoisie, he declared, are *compelled* to create the agents of their own destruction. By exposing the proletariat to the advanced culture of industrial society, the "political and general education" of the bourgeoisie is unintentionally transmitted to the workers; by inveigling the proletariat to help in the bourgeois struggle against remnants of the old regime, the workers are "dragged into the political arena," rendered more politically conscious; and by associating workers in the social activity of production, their sense of common association is stimulated. Thus the bourgeoisie "is compelled to set the proletariat in motion."[57] This view in the *Manifesto* represented a highly subtle shift of emphasis, an accenting of one of the two sides of the "antimony" that Marx had first elaborated in *The Holy Family.* In that earlier work he had described them as the antinomies of "proletariat and wealth"—the latter usage being a significant sign that Marx had not as yet enlarged the notion of wealth or, as he also called it, private property, into a concept of a dynamic system of productive forces. To the extent that the antinomy of wealth, or the later notion of the bourgeois economy, is emphasized, the task of the proletariat is greatly aided by the impersonal forces of history.

12. THE PROBLEM OF ORGANIZATION

The result of this emphasis is not, as critics have often claimed, to advise the proletariat that they need only passively await their triumph, but rather something more subtle: it is to shift attention from the personal or moral characteristics of the proleteriat to the problem of their organization. It is, in other words, to seek ways of generating an impersonal unity of forces to overcome the totality of forces represented by the bourgeois organization of productive forces. On the other hand, if, without ignoring the great power of "wealth," emphasis is placed on the effects of alienation upon the consciousness of the proletariat, then the natural human reaction to oppression and suffering comes to the fore and the qualities of the oppressed become the key consideration. To put it boldly, the question then is what the workers can make of themselves and of their cruel experiences, rather than the wounds that the system inflicts upon itself. It is the difference between emphasizing the self-destruction of the system and emphasizing the self-creation of the proletariat.

This difference, it must be reiterated, was not an absolute contrast in Marx's mind, but a shifting emphasis on elements that "form a whole" and are dialectically related.[58] Thus in *The Holy Family* the emphasis falls on the reactions of the proletariat to their condition and their growing awareness of their plight, which makes revolution appear a *human* necessity. Thus the proletariat "feels annihilated . . . sees its own powerlessness." When inevitably private property advances "towards its own dissolution" this occurs solely because "it produces the proletariat *as* proletariat, poverty which is conscious of its spiritual and physical poverty, dehumanization which is conscious of its dehumanization, and for this reason trying to abolish its dehumanized self."[59] It is "absolutely imperative need," "the practical expression of necessity" that causes the proletariat "to revolt against this inhumanity." It "can and must emancipate itself."[60]

But this theme that the proletariat is driven to revolt in protest against their inhuman lot ends on an equivocal note. In *The Holy Family* Marx feels compelled to deny that he is elevating the proletariat to the status of "gods" and he ends in a kind of uneasy ambivalence that combines the experience of the proletariat and its suggestion of strengthened character with an ordained historical destiny:

> Not in vain does [the proletariat] go through the stern but steeling school of *labor*. It is not a question of what this or that proletarian, or even the whole proletariat, at the moment *regards* as its aim. It is a question of *what the proletariat is,* and what, in accordance with this being, it will historically be compelled to do. Its aim and historical action is visibly and irrevocably foreshadowed in its own life situation as well as in the whole organization of bourgeois society today.[61]

13. THE REVOLUTIONARY TASK

In *The German Ideology* the emphasis on the qualities of the proletariat was heightened as a result of Marx's growing appreciation of the enormous power of the opposing system. The expression of this concern takes the form of conceiving revolution as more than a matter of political overthrow: it becomes the basic medium of political education that will enable the proletariat to rid itself of its brutalized past and prepare for the unprecedented task of controlling aggregates of power such as no ruling class has ever had to contend with. The proletariat will now be measured by the difference between what it has been and what it must become. Here again Marx began from the system's effects on the proletariat: the "contradictions" between the productive system and its relations produces unprecedented "antagonisms" that are humanly registered:[62] they are "unbearable."[63] At one level the struggle is not merely to wrest control over forces which deny men the freedom of "self-activity" but to defend life itself, "to safeguard [men's] very existence."[64] In this account revolution resembles a raw Hobbesian response to the threat of extinction. But this threat is experienced by human beings whose condition, in a sense, has become not only inhuman but dangerously so. Never before has mankind faced such an enormous power that rules in systematic disregard of the ruled. Accordingly human subjects are reduced to an unprecedented condition, "robbed of all life-content," "abstract individuals," "stunted," denied all "self-activity." [65]

The magnitude of the revolutionary task is extraordinary because of the yawning gap between the universal significance of the productive forces potentially available to man and the shriveled stature of the vast majority of individuals. To hand over the former to the latter would be a disaster, for the economy is not a mechanical device, so simplified that the unskilled working man can take it over. The forces to be appropriated "have been developed to a totality." They are universal in scope. Hence they lay a demand on the proletariat of measuring up to their inheritance: men to match the machines.

> This appropriation [by the proletariat] must have a universal character corresponding to the productive forces and the intercourse. The appropriation of these forces is itself nothing more than the development of the individual capacities corresponding to the material instruments of production. The appropriation is, for this very reason, the development of a totality of capacities in the individuals themselves.[66]

How, then, are the proletarians to prepare themselves for this staggering task? How is the mass of mankind, wholly without experience in controlling power, to be made competent to do what no class has ever done and has never been called upon to do?[67] How to develop "the universal character and energy of the proletariat, without which the revolution cannot be accomplished; and in which, further, the proletariat rids itself of everything that still clings to it from its previous position in society?"[68]

Marx's answer was that revolution itself could produce the necessary transformation in men:

> Both for the production on a mass scale of this communist consciousness, and for the success of the cause itself, the

alteration of men on mass scale is necessary, an alteration which can only take place in a practical movement, a *revolution;* this revolution is necessary, therefore, not only because the *ruling* class cannot be overthrown in any other way, but also because the class *overthrowing* it can only in a revolution succeed in ridding itself of all the muck of ages and become fitted to found society anew.[69]

14. METAPOLITICS OF AN INDUSTRIAL COSMOGONY

Thus in *The German Ideology* revolutionary struggle appears as the political means of preparing the workers for accession to power. Indeed, the political element assumes a particular importance at this stage of Marx's thinking because, as yet, he has not developed a clear notion of a "crisis" within capitalism, a condition in which the system begins to founder because of the consequences of its own "logic." As we shall see, the idea of crisis will imply the presence of a second layer of politics over and beyond (although related to) the politics of class confrontation. It will involve the collision of impersonal forces generated by the laws of capitalist production and exchange, and often occurring unperceived by the human actors ("behind their backs," in a favorite phrase of Marx's). This metapolitics would eventually become a dominant theme in Marx's theory.

The shift of significant politics to the level of metapolitics was not the result of the reification of economic processes but was rather the culmination of a line of thought in Marx that had begun as early as the *1844 Manuscripts* to locate politics in economic relations. "Wages," he wrote, "are determined by the bitter struggle between capitalist and worker. . . ." "Capital," he declared, "is the *power of command* over labor and its products."[70] These notions were given a sharper focus when Marx identified the crucial element in the power of capitalists, the ability to buy labor. It is "merely the appearance," Marx wrote in *Wage, Labor and Capital,* that capitalists are buying "labor with money" or that laborers are selling their labor. "In reality what they sell to the capitalist for money is their labor *power.*"[71] The power the laborer sells becomes the source of his servitude—"he belongs not to this or that capitalist but to the capitalist class"[72]—and of the enormous productive power of the system. "Capital is concentrated social force."[73]

As Marx's understanding of the power of capitalism was deepened by his intensive reading in economic theory and history, his undisguised fascination for, even admiration of, the achievement of the system grew. Nonetheless, he remained steadfast in his belief that the workers could gain power. "To conquer political power has become the great duty of the working classes," he declared in his inaugural address to the first International. But at the same time he was clear that only an international movement, characterized by "numbers," "combination," and "led by knowledge," could prevail against the power of capital.[74] It becomes all the more revealing of the growing disproportion in power between "the concentrated social force" of capitalism, "entirely beyond the control of the actors,"[75] and the revolutionary organization of labor that Marx himself should have participated in, some would say encouraged, the liquidation of the first International at the Hague conference of 1872. For in his major theoretical undertakings of the 1850s and 1860s, *Grundrisse* and *Capital*, it is the metapolitical plane that preoccupies him, evoking an imagery of power drawn in almost equal parts from industry and classical mythology:

A system of machinery . . . constitutes in itself a huge automaton, whenever it is driven by a self-actuating prime mover. We have in place of the isolated machine a mechanical monster whose body fills whole factories, and whose demon power, at first veiled under the slow and measured motions of his giant limbs, at length breaks out into the fast and furious whirl of his countless working organs.[76]

Elsewhere he describes "Modern Industry" as chafing under the "unbearable trammels" of existing means of communication and transportation and releasing its frustrations by "its feverish haste of production, its enormous extent, its constant flinging of capital and labor from one sphere of production into another, and its newly created connections with the markets of the whole world." Modern Industry constructs machinery "on a cyclopean scale," including machines for the production of other machines that embody the secret of "a prime mover capable of exerting any amount of force, and yet under perfect control."[77]

15. CRISES AND IMPERSONAL FORCES

It is in this context of the metapolitics of an industrial cosmogony that the idea of "crisis" acquires significations that differ from its usual associations with impending collapse. Crisis is not necessarily a fatal condition, but rather an ordeal in which the subject reemerges, its powers strengthened but infected with new susceptibilities, "contradictions which are constantly overcome but just as constantly posited." In other words, crisis may imply repeated transformations rather than final catastrophe. As Marx phrased it in *Grundrisse,* crises are "the general intimation which points beyond" the present state of a social formation and they are "the urge which drives towards the adoption of a new historic form."[78] They emerge in the natural course of capitalism's "constant revolution," which dwarfs the existential politics of ordinary beings as it "tears down all the barriers which hem in the development of the forces of production, the expansion of needs, the all-sided development of production, and the exploitation and exchange of natural and mental forces."[79] These barriers, Marx insisted, will never really be overcome, but far from signifying the readmission of human politics, they merely reenforce the self-absorbed character of the metapolitics of the system: "The universality towards which it irresistibly strives encounters barriers in its own nature, which will, at a certain stage of its development, allow it to be recognized as being itself the greatest barrier to this tendency, and hence will drive towards its own suspension."[80]

The transfer of politics to the plane of impersonal forces signified that Marx's theoretical inquiries into capitalism were making it increasingly difficult for him to locate the revolutionary force that would overthrow the system other than in "the immanent laws of capitalistic production itself,"[81] laws that work "with iron necessity towards inevitable results."[82] To be sure, Marx preserves an element of revolutionary efficacy as when he describes the Last Days of capitalism: there "grows the mass of misery, oppression, slavery, degradation, exploitation; but with this too grows the revolt of the working class, a class always increasing in numbers, and disciplined, united, organized by the very mechanism of the process of capitalist production itself."[83]

16. DISAPPEARANCE OF THE PROLETARIAT

Yet the curious quality of the last encounter between proletariat and capitalist is that the protagonists are both, in an historical sense, vestigial. The capitalist class has not only been decimated by the cannibalism of the law of monopolistic concentration, but it has also all but disappeared as a human category. "The capitalist is merely capital personified and functions in the process of production solely as the agent of capital. . . ."[84] The disappearance of the capitalist, *while capitalism is still operative,* appears as an instance of a more general systematization of economic relations. "Characters who appear on the economic stage," Marx notes, "are but the personifications of the economic relations that exist between them."[85] The laborer, too, is an impersonation, in his case of "labor-power."[86] But, equally important, the protagonists have each been steadily displaced by technology, so that both in numbers and in contribution the proletariat will have surrendered much of the symbolism that Marx had used to interpret capitalism. As large industry advances, Marx wrote in *Grundrisse,* the creation of real wealth depends less and less upon the laborer's production than upon "the power of those agencies" whose significance "is itself out of all proportion to the direct labor time spent on their production but depends rather on the general state of science and the progress of technology. . . ." The laborer ceases to be "chief actor" and so he "steps to the side."[87]

It is not unimportant to note in this connection that while the lengthy analysis in *Capital*—and the same holds of *Grundrisse*—shows in detail the etiology of the crisis of capitalism, it does not demonstrate or describe the course of proletarian rebellion. No such work can be found among Marx's writings from the period after the *18th Brumaire* (1852) until *The Civil War in France* (1871), occasioned by the Paris Commune. The proletariat thus is left in a curious position: Marx's economic researches have produced results that steadily relieve the proletariat of a revolutionary burden that it lacks the power to carry, yet its name is invoked ("dictatorship of the proletariat") to summarize a course of development that led to its extinction—which is to say that the theory has overcome its original intention.

The fate of the proletariat was sealed when Marx insisted in *The German Ideology* that the proletariat, like Odysseus, must never look backward out of nostalgia for a simpler economy. It must accept the foundations laid by "Big Industry" as the equivalent of the new *logos,* the ultimate reality that dictates the disappearance rather than the triumph of the proletariat. What is being legitimated in its name is a unique system of power that had, prior to the revolution, rendered exploiter and exploited alike superfluous: "This organic system itself, as a totality, has its presuppositions, and its development to its totality consists precisely in subordinating all elements of society to itself, or in creating out of it the organs which it still lacks."[88]

17. SCIENCE AND TECHNOLOGY

The proletariat has to be abolished because it is unlike any victorious group imagined by previous political theorists: it lacks the *virtù* to constitute the new society. The future belongs to the practitioners of science and the technological innovators, because the future takes off from the point attained by the "stupendous productivity" of capitalism: ". . . there is a limit, not inherent to production generally, but to production founded on capitalism." Capitalism is not "the absolute form for the development of the forces of production. . . ."[89]

Thus in the end Marx had found the truly revolutionary force, the permanent revolution in the powers that capitalism had organized into what appeared to be an autonomous system. "Modern Industry has a productive organism that is purely objective. . . ."[90] The contributions of science and technology have worked to establish a system that seems close to being separable from the fate of capitalism, reducing the latter to an incident in the evolution of power:

Modern Industry rent the veil that concealed from men their own social process of production. . . . The principle which it pursued, of resolving each process into its constituent movements . . . by the hand of man, created by the new modern science of technology. . . . Technology also discovered the few main fundamental forms of motion which, despite the diversity of instruments used, are necessarily taken by every productive action of the human body. . . .[91]

By their ability to develop byproducts and to discover unsuspected uses of existing materials, science and technology have opened the prospect of a system that renews itself:

Like the increased exploitation of natural wealth by the mere increase in the tension of labor-power, science and technology give capital a power of expansion independent of the given magnitude of the capital actually functioning. They react at the same time on that part of the original capital which has entered upon its stage of renewal. This, in passing into its new shape, incorporates gratis the social advance made while its old shape was being used up.[92]

18. REVOLUTION AS SOLACE

Thus the revolution has been institutionalized before the proletarian revolution has taken place. The prediction of revolution appears not as a failed prophecy, but as solace, a memorial to an older faith in the power of human action. In this, as in practically everything he wrote, Marx was his own best analyst. In 1867, half in irony, he prepared some guidelines that would serve as a model for future reviews of *Capital*. His work, he suggested, embodied two lines of thought. One was the treatment of economic relations; it represented a "fundamental enrichment of science" comparable to Darwin's achievement. The other was "the tendentious conclusions" of the author, which "imagines or presents the end result of the present movement" of history when it has no demonstrated connection "with his [theoretical] development of the economic relations proper." As one of Marx's most sympathetic interpreters concludes, "If one were to take the trouble, one could perhaps show that his 'objective' analysis refutes his own 'subjective' fantasies."[93]

NOTES

1. *Capital: A Critique of Political Economy*, F. Engels, ed., S. Moore and E. Aveling, trans., 3 vols. (New York: International Publishers, 1967), Vol. I, p. 11.

2. *A Contribution to the Critique of Political Economy*, M. Dobb, ed., S.W. Rayzanskaya, trans. (New York: International Publishers, 1970), p. 23. Hereafter this will be cited as *CCPE*.

3. Karl Marx and Frederick Engels, *Collected Works* (New York: International Publishers, 1975–), Vol. I, pp. 84–86, 492.

4. Note the analogy Marx drew with Themistocles, who urged the Athenians to abandon their city and "found a new Athens at sea, in another element." Ibid., p. 492.

5. Marx-Engels, *Collected Works*, Vol. I, p. 85.

6. *First Thesis on Feuerbach.*

7. *Second Thesis on Feuerbach.*

8. *Nicomachean Ethics*, Bk. X, chs. 7–9. For a close discussion see B. Eriksen, *Bios Theoretikos* (Oslo: Oxford University Press, 1976); W.F.R. Hardie, *Aristotle's Ethical Theory*, 2nd ed. (Oxford: Oxford University Press, 1980), pp. 345 ff.

9. *Hegel's Philosophy of Right*, T.M. Knox, trans. (Oxford: Oxford University Press, 1942), pp. 12–13.

10. See, among countless early examples, the Pythagorean fragment in G.S. Kirk and J.E. Raven, ed., *The Presocratic Philosophers* (Cambridge, Cambridge University Press, 1957), p. 228 (fr. 278).

11. "The Leading Article in No. 179 of the *Kölnische Zeitung*," Marx and Engels, *Collected Works*, Vol. I, p. 195.

12. Ibid.

13. Marx, "Feelings," *Collected Works*, Vol. I, p. 526 (from a poem of 1836).

14. Ibid., p. 195.

15. Ibid., pp. 191–192.

16. For various views on the importance of these works see the following: Louis Althusser, *For Marx*, Ben Brewster, trans. (London: Allen Lane, 1969), Chs. 2, 5, 7; B. Ollman, *Alienation* (Cambridge: Cambridge University Press, 1971), pp. x ff.; Istvan Meszaros,

Marx's Theory of Alienation (London: Merlin Press, 1970), especially Pt. III; Erich Fromm, *Marx's Concept of Man* (New York: McGraw Hill, 1961), pp. v ff.; David McLellan, *Marx's "Grundrisse"* (New York: Harper, 1971), pp. 12–15.

17. *The German Ideology*, S. Rayzanskaya, trans. (Moscow: International Publishers, 1964), p. 50. Hereafter cited as G.I. The concept of the "whole" in Marx has been suggestively developed by George Lukacs, *History and Class Consciousness*, Rodney Livingstone, trans. (London: Merlin Press, 1971) in the essay, "Reification and the Consciousness of the Proletariat."

18. *Capital*, Vol. I, p. 21. The citation is from Marx's Preface to the French edition of *Capital*.

19. *CCPE*, p. 19.

20. Cited in McLellan, *Grundrisse*, p. 6.

21. *Karl Marx, Early Writings*, T.B. Bottomore, ed. (New York: McGraw Hill, 1964), p. 63. Hereafter this will be cited as *Early Writings*.

22. Cited in Franz Mehring, *Karl Marx: The Story of His Life*, E. Fitzgerald, trans. (University of Michigan Press: Ann Arbor, 1962), p. 341.

23. "Manifesto of the Communist Party," *Marx and Engels: Basic writings on Politics and Philosophy*, Lewis Feuer, ed. (Garden City, N.Y.: Doubleday, 1959), p. 12.

24. Ibid., p. 13

25. Letter of Feb. 22, 1858, Karl Marx and Frederick Engels, *Selected Correspondence* (Moscow: International Publishers, n.d.), p. 124. Hereafter this will be cited as *Sel. Corr.*

26. As is well known, only the publication of the first volume of *Capital* was supervised by Marx; the other two volumes were edited by Engels. *Theories of Surplus Value* is considered to be "the first and only draft of the fourth, concluding volume of 'Capital.' " See the edition translated by Emile Burns and edited by S. Ryazanskaya (London: International Publishers, 1963), Vol. I, p. 14.

27. *GI*, p. 255.

28. Karl Marx and Friedrich Engels, *Werke*, 39 vols. (Berlin, 1956), Vol. 27, p. 228. Hereafter this will be cited as *MEW*.

29. *Capital*, Vol. III, p. 266.

30. *Early Writings*, p. 151.

31. ". . . political economy . . . can be considered as both a product of the real *dynamism* and *development* of private property, a product of modern *industry*, and a force which has accelerated and extolled the dynamism and development of industry and has made it a power in the domain of *consciousness* . . . it is always empirical businessmen we refer to when we speak of economists, who are

their *scientific* self-revelation and existence. . . ." *Early Writings*, pp. 147, 170.

32. The concept of the "civilization" of capitalism appeared most prominently in Marx's *Grundrisse*. See *Grundrisse der Kritik der Politischen Ökonomie* (Berlin: Deitz, 1953, and Europäische Verlagsanstalt Frankfurt), pp. 312 ff.

33. "Bourgeois society is the most advanced and complex historical organization of production. The categories which express its relations, and an understanding of its structure, therefore, provide an insight into the structure and the relations of production of all formerly existing social formations, the ruins and component elements of which were used in the creation of bourgeois society. Some of these unassimilated remains are still carried on within bourgeois society, others, however, which previously existed only in rudimentary form, have been further developed and have attained their full significance, etc." *CCPE*, pp. 210–211.

34. *The Eighteenth Brumaire of Louis Bonaparte* in *Karl Marx: Selected Works*, V. Adoratsky, ed., 2 vols. (Moscow: International Publishers, n.d.), Vol. II, p. 315. Hereafter these volumes will be cited as *SW*.

35. "Critique of the Gotha Program," *SW*, Vol. II, p. 563.

36. *The Poverty of Philosophy*, C.P. Dutt and V. Chattopadhyaya, eds. (New York: International Publishers, n.d.), pp. 90, 93.

37. These characteristics were exhibited very early. See his protests against the Hegelian Left for its superficial use of socialist and communist ideas in Lloyd P. Easton and Kurt H. Goddat, *Writings of the Young Marx on Philosophy and Society* (Doubleday: Garden City, N.Y., 1967), pp. 134–35; David McLellan, *Karl Marx: His Life and Thought* (London and Basingstoke: Macmillan, 1973), p. 58.

38. The most awesome example of this is Marx's *Theories of Surplus Value*. It should also be noted that at one time Marx contemplated writing a history of economic theories.

39. See *The Holy Family* (Moscow: International Publishers, 1956), pp. 168–205.

40. See Marx's "Communism and the Augsburg *Allgemeine Zeitung*," *Collected Works*, Vol. I, pp. 220–221.

41. *MEW*, Vol. 27, pp. 233 ff.

42. *CCPE*, pp. 22, 23.

43. *Grundrisse: Foundations of the Critique of Political Economy* (*Rough Draft*), Martin Nicolaus, trans. (London: Allen Lane, 1973), p. 159. Emphasis added.

44. *Grundrisse*, David McLellan, trans., p. 67. The Nicolaus translation (p. 162) is nearly unintelligible.

45. Ibid., pp. 334, 341 (Nicolaus trans.).

46. Ibid., p. 488 (Nicolaus trans.). Emphasis in original.
47. *Critique of Hegel's 'Philosophy of Right'*, Joseph O'Malley, ed. (Cambridge: Cambridge University Press, 1970), Introduction, pp. 140–142. Hereafter cited as *CHPR*.
48. *The Cologne Communist Trial*, Rodney Livingston, trans. (New York: International Publishers, 1971), p. 62. This is part of some remarks made by Marx before the London central committee of the German Communist society in 1850.
49. *Early Writings*, p. 59.
50. *CHPR*. Introduction, pp. 132, 135, 139, 142.
51. *Pov. of Phil.*, p. 146.
52. *GI*, pp. 46, 50; *Birth of the Communist Manifesto*, Dirk J. Struik, ed. (New York, 1971), p. 19 (hereafter cited as *Man.*). *Pov. of Phil.*, p. 147.
53. *GI*, pp. 46–47.
54. Ibid., p. 46.
55. Ibid., p. 47; *Man.*, pp. 12–13; *Pov. of Phil.*, pp. 146–147.
56. *Pov. of Phil.*, p. 93.
57. *Man.*, pp. 15, 17, 19.
58. *The Holy Family*, in Karl Marx and Frederick Engels, *Collected Works*, Vol. 4, p. 35.
59. My translation. The Moscow translation renders "darum sich selbst aufhebende Entmenschung" as "therefore self-abolishing" and thus creates a gratuitous determinism.
60. *Holy Family*, p. 37.
61. Ibid. Emphasis in the original.
62. *GI*, pp. 43, 45, 81, 91; *Theses on Feuerbach*, IV.
63. *GI*, p. 76.
64. Ibid., p. 83.
65. Ibid., pp. 82–83.
66. Ibid., p. 83.
67. Ibid., pp. 83–84
68. Ibid., p. 84.
69. Ibid., p. 86
70. *Selected Writings*, pp. 69, 85.
71. *SW*, Vol. I, p. 254.
72. Ibid., p. 257.
73. "Instructions for Delegates to the Geneva Conference," *The First International and After*, David Fernbach, ed. (New York: Vintage, 1974), p. 91.
74. Ibid., p. 81.
75. *Capital*, Vol. I, p. 228.
76. Ibid., pp. 416–417.
77. Ibid., pp. 419, 420, 421.

78. *Grundrisse,* pp. 410, 228.
79. Ibid., p. 410.
80. Ibid.
81. *Capital,* Vol. I, p. 763.
82. Ibid., p. 8 (preface to first German edition).
83. Ibid., p. 763.
84. Ibid., Vol. III, p. 819.
85. Ibid., Vol. I, p. 85.
86. Ibid., pp. 189–190, 232–233.
87. *Grundrisse,* pp. 704, 705.
88. Ibid., p. 278.
89. Ibid., p. 415.
90. *Capital,* Vol. I, p. 421.
91. Ibid., p. 486.
92. Ibid., p. 605.
93. Maximilien Rubel, *Karl Marx: Essai de biographie intellectuelle* (Paris: Marcel Rivière, 1957), p. 435.

5

ON READING MARX
APOLITICALLY

STEPHEN HOLMES

On Sheldon Wolin's account, the early Marx was motivated by a desire to remake society as a whole as well as to redeem humanity. Later, when he saw that his wild ambitions were unrealistic, he sank back into a thinly veiled despair. These two poses are closely related. They coalesce into an image of Marx as an utterly *apolitical* theorist, as a thinker childishly incapable of enduring the disappointment of his most absurd yearnings.

I shall not ask if this is an accurate portrait of Marx. What I wish to examine is why Wolin finds the apolitical Marx he portrays so attractive and why he misleadingly titles his analysis "reading Marx politically." I shall begin by recapitulating the basic thesis of the paper as I understand it and by dissecting the assumptions that underlie it. Implicit in my summary will be a criticism of Wolin's views. One of the charming things about this paper, of course, is the way it teaches us that we may be critical without being unfriendly. If you show that someone is wrong, you have also shown that he is right. If he is wrong he is right. If he is dead, he is immortal.

I have chosen to summarize the paper as follows. It is jerry-built mythology, but it has its point: *Prometheus swallowed Prometheus and gave birth to heroic failure.* Let me explain. Prometheus, that is to say, the industrial revolution, preempted and supplanted an earlier political revolution or revolutionary tradition that had nurtured heroic, Promethean ambitions (the redemption of man). This sublimation of personal action by impersonal movement is a pattern that can be found *both* in nineteenth-century European societies as they developed *and* in Marx's theory as it developed. Marx's theory was a symbolic reenactment of the process of history: Marx too had a preindustrial phase. The earlier Marx's emphasis on human action (or "the political") was embodied in his two concepts of "revolution" and "the proletariat," which are paradoxically described by Professor Wolin as *traditional* residues in Marx's thought, because they echo the ideas of a mythic legislator founding a new order and, more banally, of purposive political action. Gradually, as Marx pondered the massive, impersonal forces of nineteenth-century capitalism, he abandoned his earlier hope that political action might give birth to a new order and embraced, or seemed to embrace, the theory that capitalism's own internal logic would lead to its collapse and to the creation of a classless society. Politics of the barricade was replaced by "the metapolitics of industrial cosmogony." Wolin has coined such an ugly phrase in order to drive home the point that Delacroix could never have painted a picture of such an impersonal revolution.

So far, we have Prometheus swallowing Prometheus. But what about the birth of heroic failure? Even though he is crucially concerned with "Marx's despair" (§7), Wolin wants to avoid labeling Marx a simple failure. Marx's defeat was complex and pregnant with meaning.

Marx's prognosis that capitalism would eventually collapse because of its own internal development, Wolin argues, must not be understood as a scientific prediction. Instead, it should be interpreted psychologically as Marx's last-ditch protest against his discovery of capitalism's uncanny ability to survive. The pessimism of Marx's analysis might be said to belie the optimism of his predictions. But Wolin prefers the opposite formulation: the optimism of Marx's predictions are a cry of impotent rage against the scientific and technological innovations that have rendered capitalism indestructible.

Wolin focuses on two anomalies of Marx's work: that he could never complete anything he started, and that he persisted absurdly in labeling the mechanical collapse of capitalism with the misleading name of a "proletarian revolution." This was a fraudulent personification of an utterly impersonal process. Wolin interprets both the incompleteness and the misnomer as implicit *confessions* on Marx's part that the game was up, that there was no chance for heaven on earth and that capitalism was immortal. The system would lurch from crisis to crisis, but it would never die. Marx's theoretical discoveries forced this bitter conclusion on him, even though it clashed radically with his optimistic political intentions. Thus Wolin inverts the Marxist tag that without theory will be no revolution, and tells us that *with* theory there will be no revolution. Marx could not publicly admit his disappointing discovery (nor privately to himself), but he could not fully suppress it either. He was too honest for this. It came out in the fragmentary state of his work, and in his continuing to brandish the passé language of political action to depict the collapse of capitalism under the weight of its own contradictions. System dysfunction could never *be* action. By *calling* it action, however, Marx admitted both that action was his dream and that the breakdown of capitalism was nothing but a dream. Likewise all those false predictions simultaneously *concealed* the bitter truth, and *revealed* Marx's juvenile longings.

For the sake of argument, let us assume that Wolin is right and that Marx's thought is characterized by utopian yearnings, querulous despair and self-delusion. Why would this lead Wolin to admire Marx? And in what sense does it embody a *political* interpretation of Marx's works?

It is best to read Wolin in the same way he reads Marx. His stance is complex because it too registers a conflict between emotional commitment and theoretical insight. Wolin admires Marx as a great protestor, "the antidemiurgos, committed to disordering the world." (§3) Yet his admiration is soured by a recognition that Marx was enthusiastic about the technological revolution. Marx enjoyed those huge machines clanking in their industrial infernos. Worst of all, he thought that socialism would *outproduce* capitalism. To celebrate socialism was to celebrate the ethos of productivity.

Wolin belongs to a Rousseauist, romantic tradition that identifies virtue with poverty. Marx adhered to an altogether different tradition that coupled virtue with wealth and economic growth. Thus, Wolin is repelled by Marx's "undisguised admiration" for the achievements of science and technology.[1] He is bothered that Marx's theory was built in the same spirit that constructed railroads. (§2) At one point, he even suggests that Marx betrayed the proletariat by refusing to adopt a nostalgic, neo-Luddite stance of the Wolinite kind: "The fate of the proletariat was sealed when Marx insisted in the *German Ideology* that the proletariat, like Odysseus, must never look backward out of nostalgia for a simpler economy. They must accept the foundations laid by Big Industry as the equivalent of the new *logos*, the ultimate reality that dictates the disappearance rather than the triumph of the proletariat." (§16, third par.) By speaking the impersonal language of modern economics, it seems, Marx squeezed heroic political actors off the historical stage. Wolin romantically believes that technology and humanity are irreconcilable forces. Yet his clear suggestion that Marx the machine-lover was a traitor to mankind appears only fleetingly in the text. It is quickly repressed because it conflicts with Wolin's affection for Marx as a cantankerous protestor. But it does not vanish. It is sublimated into Wolin's bizarre claim that Marx was a success because he was a failure. The falsity of Marx's predictions is what makes them true. This is such an odd suggestion that it requires some interpretation. I read Wolin's celebration of Marx's "theoretical defeat" (86) as follows: just because it is a failure as science, Marx's theory is a success, a human and moral success, and an expression of his tragic despair. Marx's thought represents the heroism of failure. To succeed as science in an age when science exhibits so many hideous, indeed demonic characteristics (for instance, the mad rush to "consume" nature) is to fail humanly. To fail scientifically in the technological-scientific-managerial age is to succeed humanly, at least in the sense of expressing an ultimate unwillingness to compromise with the odiousness of the technological age. Failure is success. Wolin praises Marx because, faced with modernity, his "theory grew . . . more desperate." (§9) This is an extremely ironic claim, since Marx always poured contempt on fellow theorists for their impotence. Wolin's paradox is that Marx's strength *was* his impotence. Predictive power, whatever else it is, is a form of power. The economic entrepreneurs of early capitalism were ruthlessly eliminated by technical prog-

ress. The new power elite consists of "the practitioners of science and the technological innovators." (§17) In this context,
defeat is victory. To botch your predictions is to refuse to play
the power game. Marx did just this. The defeat of his heroic
intentions was itself a refined form of heroism, not just because
Marx's intentions were lofty, but because his refusal to go along
was a sign of genuine saintliness. His "politics" was embodied
in his despair. Marx's Owl of Minerva fluttered pathetically at
dusk. That is what Wolin admires.

I would like to conclude by making some ancillary comments
on Wolin's point of view.

Sometimes Wolin seems to advance two contradictory criticisms of Marx: that his theory is false, that the modern world
does not exclude the possibility of heroic action or "the political" as thoroughly as Marx says; and that Marx's theory is absolutely true, but that the politics-excluding, action-suppressing
society he accurately describes is a noxious place to live, *and*
that Marx has somehow betrayed us by depicting it truthfully.
I suspect that this is not really a contradiction, and that Wolin
could dispel my doubts by saying something about the way
"theory" is a form of political action, an integral part of the
social world it pretends to describe from the outside and so
forth. In any case, without such an argument his case is incomplete.

My second criticism has to do with the nature of the "politics"
that, according to Wolin, is supplanted by the metapolitics of
industrial cosmogony. Sometimes Wolin speaks of the "existential politics of ordinary beings" (§15), which sounds very egalitarian and democratic. At other times, however, he rhapsodizes
about "action of heroic proportions, waged against powerful
adversaries," (96) which sounds Nietzschean, and neither very
egalitarian nor very democratic. When writing in this mode,
Wolin seems to discern the true crime of advanced capitalism
in its ability to turn us all into functionaries. (§10). There are
no Homeric heroes left, neither rampart-mounting revolutionaries nor tradition-bursting entreprenuers. But what is the relation between heroic politics (with mythic legislators founding
new orders) and politics in the everyday sense? And which one
did Marx sublimate?

My final criticism is this. Wolin has advanced an extremely

romantic view of science, technology, and bureaucracy. If you want to know what bureaucracy is, read Kafka.[2] If you want to understand science and technology, visit a nineteenth-century assembly line. What most of us view as signs of progress are really massive forces ranged *against* humanity. The worker is unable to act because he has become a versatile technician, (106) as if poorer instruments would make workers more human or more active in the heroic-revolutionary sense. Against this romantic view it seems more reasonable to say that science, technology, and bureaucracy are simultaneously ambivalent in their human effects. They can destroy possibilities, but they can open up new possibilities as well. That seems to me to be Marx's position, or perhaps it is slightly richer and more subtle than Marx's position, since he sometimes seems to sequentialize the ambiguous consequences of science and technology, making their *bad* effects appear under capitalism and their *good* effects appear under communism, while (in fact) *both* appear simultaneously under any sort of regime. Or at least that might be one plausible interpretation and criticism of Marx's view.

NOTES

1. Sheldon Wolin, *Politics and Vision*, Boston: Little, Brown, 1960, p. 379: "Although *Das Kapital* contained a biting indictment of capitalism for its dehumanization of the worker, it also expressed unabashed admiration for the new leviathan of productive power created by capitalists."
2. *Politics and Vision*, p. 354.

6

THE STORMING OF HEAVEN: POLITICS AND MARX'S *CAPITAL*

ALAN GILBERT

1. ECONOMIC DETERMINISM AND MARX'S LATER THEORY

Sheldon Wolin's "On Reading Marx Politically" severs Marx's theory from Marx's own political activity and that of later Marxian revolutionary movements, and suggests, largely by omission, that such movements have never significantly threatened the power of capitalism. Wolin shares this important assumption with "modernization" arguments in contemporary social science and most economic determinist scholarship on Marxism (an economic determinist interpretation of Marx's theory holds roughly that the level of development of productive forces in any country uniformly determines political possibilities). Contrary to these views, however, one might stress the persistence and worldwide political impact of Marx's theory.

Thus, since *The Communist Manifesto* of 1848, three international Marxian movements have challenged capitalism. These organizations, the International Workingmen's Association (hereafter IWA) and the Second and Third Internationals, involved millions of workers, peasants, and intellectuals. At least in their more radical phases, they defended the view that workers of all nationalities have a common interest. In Marx's time, English workers supported the cause of abolitionism in the U.S.

Civil War and blocked English entry on the side of the slave-holders. The IWA engaged in widespread international strike support, and the ruling classes persecuted its membership for its vehement defense of the Paris Commune. In 1890, the Second International inaugurated the worldwide celebration of May Day to advance the struggle for an eight-hour day and a more cooperative society. That International also conducted a campaign against nationalism, the war preparations of the European bourgeoisies, and some features of colonialism. Though it could not prevent the collision of great powers in World War I, this movement offered a significant alternative to it. Even the German party held antiwar demonstrations before its leaders capitulated; the Bolsheviks, the Italian socialist party and the U.S. IWW persisted in opposition to the war.

Workers in many countries expressed solidarity with the October Revolution; most notably, the German workers' republican revolution of 1919 destroyed the expansionist treaty of Brest-Litovsk.[1] The Third International linked socialism and anticolonialism; it inspired antiracist movements in the advanced capitalist countries (for instance the U.S. Communist Party's campaigns united black and white workers, especially in the South),[2] organized international brigades to side with the Spanish republic, and eventually played a decisive role in the resistance to fascism in Russia, China, and across Europe.

Yet the political leaders of these movements sometimes hesitated to fight for internationalist or revolutionary politics, or rejected such aims altogether. Thus, the political history of these internationals, as revolutionary forces in a hostile and repressive environment, is complex. Despite such setbacks, the successive, renewed development of these cooperative and internationalist alternatives to capitalism demonstrates the cogency and moral force of Marx's political strategies. Further, one might suggest that subsequent movements improved in important ways on the understanding or practice of their predecessors. For example, the Second International emphasized the actual formation of working-class parties and grasped the dangers of world war more strongly than the IWA; the Third saw the need to fight against chauvinism toward colonized peoples and women, to underline the systemic nature of imperialism, to strengthen peasant radicalism, and to advocate revolutionary politics in the union movement more clearly than the Second. One might also point to aspects of decline—thus, the IWA stressed international strike support while the later Internationals did not. Any contemporary radical evaluation of Marx needs to specify the ways in which the original theory and later innovations provided at least a partially adequate social and moral interpretation of capitalism, and explain the successes and persistence, not just the failures and decadence, of these Internationals. Similarly, reasonable non-Marxian historical theories would have to recognize and explain the development of powerful movements for socialism against great odds.

Yet these internationals failed to transform the U.S. and Western Europe (except for the Third International's role in stopping fascism), and the Soviet and Chinese Communist parties have renounced their former radicalism. As a result, many of today's interpretations of Marx ignore the political implications of Marx's theory, the significance of Marx's own political activity, the complex relationships between Marx and later Marxian movements, and the possibility that such movements might have succeeded. An economic determinist view of Marx's theory fuels such a misinterpretation. Marx, in this image, provided at most a theory of economic "powers" that would ultimately drive workers to revolt; his political activity and that of later revolutionary movements, such theorists infer, *must* have been insignificant.

Economic determinist analyses sometimes attempt to refute Marx by noting that, in Europe and the U.S., average real incomes have increased over the long run. They then offer a simple, a priori translation of economic advance into a putative procapitalist working-class consciousness. Such arguments not only abstract from the continued oppressiveness of capitalist working conditions and the militant movements necessary to win or maintain these gains, but neglect the wider political and social consequences of capitalism, which have frequently instigated radicalism. On a Marxian view, the clash of capitalist powers has imposed the enormous costs of two world wars. Given the threat of radical working-class movements, a number of European ruling classes resorted to fascism. In the U.S., racism has persisted, despite challenges from below, and even in recent times, the U.S. government has intervened in different ways to sustain grisly regimes from South Vietnam to Salvador to South Africa.[3] Liberals and Marxians could agree on the moral character of these phenomena, though they would differ about explanations. But the reader need only recognize that sophisticated Marxian theories might be important or plausible contenders for truth about these phenomena to understand the impact of the U.S. communist movement in the industrial unionism of the 1930s or the emergence of French and Italian Communism as mass parties in the resistance to fascism.[4] Modern European and U.S. history materially and morally undermines a determinist picture of uniform capitalist progress, and a putatively necessary conservative adaptation of working-class consciousness. Workers and many others in these societies might have had a more complex, diverse response to this experience—one more open, actually and potentially, to radicalism—than any economic determinist argument can allow.

Though Wolin has criticized some negative features of advanced capitalism in other contexts, his discussion of Marx omits the wider social, political, and moral consequences that a Marxian would emphasize.[5] Instead, Wolin refurbishes one common line of economic determinist analysis with a shift in evaluation. In *Marxism: An Historical and Critical Study*, George Lichtheim maintained that Marx in 1848, bewitched by the imagery of the French Revolution, strove to lead a comparable German uprising; by the 1860s, however, Marx had adopted a sober economic determinist picture of the gradual triumph of democratic socialism. Yet Lichtheim recognizes that Marx never actually held the latter view: "The Marx of 1864 was the theorist of a *labor* movement and *therefore* committed to democratic socialism, however much this circumstance was clouded in his own mind by the continuing struggle to overthrow the old regime." Lichtheim interprets Marx's vigorous revolutionary response to the Paris Commune as being "clouded in his own mind"—a nice example of a scholar inflicting his own economic determinist views on Marx.[6] Wolin accepts Lichtheim's dichotomization of an "archaic," precapitalist Marx, a proponent of "heroic" political action, revolution, and the proletariat, and a later economic determinist Marx, a theorist of the "metapolitics of an industrial cosmogony," fascinated and horrified by the omnipotence of capitalism and the impotence of working class radicalism (Wolin refers to the "shrivelled stature of the vast majority of individuals" §§15, 13).[7] In so far as Marx remained true to his new theory of automation rather than his "archaic" political intentions, Wolin insists, he (ought to have) despaired. More critical of "industrial society" than Lichtheim, Wolin transvalues the older interpretation and foresees not the happy end of democratic socialism, but the deepening gloom of uncontrolled technological domination. Contrary to Marx's own intentions, Wolin reinterprets Marx's theory as a lament: "The analysis relieves the proletariat of a revolutionary burden that it lacks the power to carry; yet its name is invoked ("dictatorship of the proletariat") to summarize a course of development that led to its extinction."

In important essays on the nature and history of political theory, Wolin, adapting Kuhn, has stressed the importance of paradigms, and properly emphasized the role of decadence and severe political conflict in stirring the concern for the common good that characterizes great ("epic") political theorists, including Marx.[8] But Wolin's interpretation of Marx does not pursue his own insights. He misses Marx's view that the workers are a subversive, not just a suffering (let alone shrivelled) class, and ignores Marx's political activity and the impact of later Marxian movements. In Kuhn's terms, however, these facts are striking anomalies for Wolin's interpretation of Marx as the seer of resilient industrial domination. Properly understood, they justify an opposed interpretation of the political and moral significance of Marx's theory. As I have argued in *Marx's Politics: Communists and Citizens,* Marx's insistence on the role of theory in advancing revolutionary movements (the "point" of theory is "to change the world," as the eleventh thesis on Feuerbach puts it) and the need to refine the theory based on fresh political experience, is dramatically contextual. Wolin, however, isolates Marx's theory from immediate political and theoretical debates; his interpretation is anticontextual.[9] Given Wolin's concern for *res publicae* in political theory, one might have expected him to challenge an economic determinist view of Marx's politics. Unfortunately, like many other scholars, he has adopted an old, misguided paradigm.

Wolin's interpretation of Marx makes eleven major claims. A number of these claims (1–4,11, as I summarize them below)

are primarily negative; his thesis requires their defense, although he argues for them only briefly. The alternate viewpoint of this paper will highlight their importance.

First, Wolin contends that, despite Marx's theoretical "passion" and commitment to individual action, he engaged in no
significant political activity. Thus, the revolution of 1848 merely
"interrupted" his theoretical studies (§10); Marx appears in the
IWA *only* to participate in dissolving it (§14, second par.). Second, Marx did not forge specific strategies from his study of
actual radical movements. Though Wolin mentions the French
Revolution, he misses its impact on Marx's strategy for proletarian revolution in 1848; he mistakenly suggests that Marx
urged only a democratic revolution against feudalism, based on
an economic determinist analysis of German political possibilities (§11, third and fourth pars.). Wolin also leaves out Engels's
and Marx's study of the first English working-class movement,
Chartism, or the role of Marx's (and contemporary radical) political experience. Third, Wolin maintains that Marx saw the
working-class movement as a spontaneous outburst, spurred by
capitalist contradictions; for Wolin, communists bring no specific political conception of "the future" of the movement to
struggles in "the present."[10] Fourth, Marx did not influence
significant radical movements. Fifth, more positively as noted
above, Marx's revolutionary intentions stemmed from a "precapitalist" or archaic view of the proletariat; his later theory
imagined "versatile technicians" as sorcerer's apprentices, caught
up in the quasi-mythic domination of capitalist productive powers (§§5,11). Thus, Wolin contends that Marx's theory became
even less political or practice-oriented over time rather than, as
this paper will claim, *more political.*

Sixth, on Wolin's view Marx's theory was primarily concerned with power; he dismissed other theories as "impotent,"
hoped idly for a "powerful" theory to incite proletarian revolt,
and contrary to his intentions, identified the surpassing power
of capitalism (§6). For Wolin, Marx's economic theory increasingly contradicted radical predictions of political action. Sev-
enth, Marx, above all, aimed for a true theory of capitalism
(§1). This thesis conflicts in two ways with Wolin's contention
that Marx sought a mainly "powerful" theory.

Since both six and seven are claims about Marx's purposes

and integrity as a theorist, these internal inconsistencies deserve careful examination. First, Wolin fails to investigate whether the "power" of a theory is linked to its truth—both the theory's capacity to explain historical events and its moral truth (what it tells us about real human capacities for cooperation, freedom, and individuality). Though Wolin's Marx acknowledges some evils of capitalism, Marx appears to hold only an ethical reductionist conception of power, one that erases the moral differences between capitalist "power" and proletarian "power."[11] But the moral deficiencies of capitalism and the attractiveness of a more cooperative alternative might have motivated participants in mass radical movements; Marxian explanations may link (moral) goodness and rationality.[12] Ignoring such movements, Wolin also underestimates the justifiable sources of the theory's political power; he leaves his two notions of what is primary in Marx's theorizing—truth and power—at odds. Second, Wolin asserts that Marx's mature theory grasped the omnipotence of capitalism; yet he insists that Marx stuck to his inadequate predictions of revolution despite his new theoretical insights, and hence, could not face the truth. Wolin saves the putative accuracy of Marx's theory only at Marx's expense, and contradicts his claim about Marx's overriding aim to be a "truth-teller" (§1, first par.). Further, though on Wolin's view, truth and power are each central to Marx's enterprise, the theory loses on both counts. The theory grasps only the power of the impersonal enemies of humanity, but is, in its own right, neither true nor powerful.

Eighth, Wolin attributes the lack of impact of Marx's revolutionary intentions to "the shrivelled stature" of workers. Ninth, Wolin notes that Marx carefully studied the great philosophers and economists (§9, third par.). Wolin sees Marx's *main contribution,* beyond that of other theorists, as the recognition of capitalist civilization as an historical rather than a natural or eternal phenomenon (§7). Tenth, Marx's theory of capitalism focused solely on the "haunting" concept of productive forces; their development would drive history beyond capitalism or (for Wolin) their ostensible resilience would paralyze radical politics. Thus, Wolin omits Marx's discovery of surplus value, the complexity of Marx's economic theory, and Marx's claims about exploitative relations of production.[13] Wolin adopts Marx's rejection of the moralism of other radicals, and discounts Marx's moral judgments, including his indictment of capitalist production relations, as lacking power. Curiously, Wolin's division of Marx into "precapitalist" and "capitalist" phases lapses into a strictly productive forces determinist or historicist Marxism (§ 11).[14] Eleventh, Marx's analysis has little relevance to opponents of social inequalities, war, and other forms of oppression in advanced capitalist society.

This paper will reject Wolin's claims except his contention that Marx aimed to forge a true theory of capitalism, and will offer a contrasting interpretation of Marx's later activity and theory. Wolin's central thesis maintains that the major shift in Marx's views arose simply from a recognition of certain very general economic features of capitalism. In fact, the actual bearing of later theory changes in Marx can only be understood in a more specific context of theoretical and political debates and political experience; some brief background in Marx's activity and his economic and historical theory of the 1840s is necessary.[15]

Just as Hegel had studied Smith and Ricardo and seen the dangerous tendency of modern capitalism to create a spiritually deadening division of labor, extend social inequality, and undermine the universality of law and government, so Marx appraised the conclusions of classical political economy even more critically.[16] While Marx recognized capitalism's productive achievements, he emphasized its human costs to the producers. The classical economists had already stressed a pessimistic prospect for capitalism. For instance, Ricardo had foreseen a shift from industrial profits to increased rents that would ultimately stultify capitalist growth. As he had emphasized, adapting Malthus, a high market wage would lead to an expansion in population which would drive wages down to bare physical subsistence (Ricardo's "natural wage"). Lassalle would later call this view an "iron law of wages." Thus, Ricardo provided the most sophisticated theoretical underpinning for a widespread radical conviction.

The arguments of classical political economy, including the iron law of wages, cohered with the overall materialist hypotheses of *The German Ideology* (1845), *The Poverty of Philosophy* (1847) and *The Communist Manifesto* (1848). Examined critically for their social, political, and moral implications, these economic arguments showed how capitalism could push workers, artisans, and peasants to rebel. Thus, even before 1848, in Marx's supposedly "archaic" period, he had already arrived at the main features of the economic theory that Wolin stresses.[17] Marx's sophisticated theory of the 1860s represents a dramatic shift away from the economics that Wolin identifies as his later view.

Following Aristotle and Hegel, Marx studied completed and emerging forms of political life and the human potentials they revealed. Marx's own theory and strategy emphasized the dynamics of actual radical movements, particularly the French Revolution and Chartism, and the role of communist politics. As early as 1843, Marx recognized in the outcry of Moselle winegrowers that the formally universal laws of modern society coexisted with severe economic oppression. Contrary to economic determinism, Marx's radicalism began from a study of the peasantry. The Silesian weavers' revolt strengthened this view, and pointed to the possibilities for a worker-peasant alliance. Marx's changing analysis of the revolutionary potential of the peasants in 1848 and afterwards may serve as an important example of the *increasingly political character of Marx's theory.*

In 1843, Marx foresaw the political timidity of the German bourgeoisie, paralyzed by fear of the French Revolution's explosive radicalism. That class would ally with absolutism. Between 1843 and 1845, based on French and German experience, Marx contended that Germany would undergo a direct proletarian revolution, fusing artisan, working-class, and peasant anger, to create a communist society (in interpreting *The German Ideology*—Wolin §11, middle—Wolin ignored Marx's claim that English competition, dispossessing the Silesian weavers and others, had already brought capitalist contradictions to a head).[18] After 1845, however, Marx reevaluated the French Revolution. As Babeuf and others had gained communist insights through participation in the French Revolution, so overturning the monarchy and winning the suffrage would highlight, for German workers and peasants, the continuing corruption of formal political equality by capitalist inequality. Taking part in democratic revolution would drive most republicans to the left, and Marx now advocated it. Contrary to Wolin (claim 2), however, the *Manifesto* envisioned the democratic revolution as but the "prelude to an immediately following proletarian" one. Throughout 1848, Marx strove to forge a worker-peasant alliance for democracy and communism in the Rhineland. He also acted on the distinctive features of communist politics outlined in the *Manifesto:* internationalism, as embodied in Marx's defense of the Paris June insurrection and Polish democracy, and exposure of capitalist exploitation.

Though absolutism defeated the revolution of 1848, Marx emphasized a need for even more persistent organized communist activity within the real movement. In studying new French experience, Marx saw that the dynamic of republicanism could lead, depending on political organizing, to a peasant explosion to the left or to the right. His 1850 *Class Struggles in France* traced the emergence of widespread French peasant democratic-socialist secret societies as a response to capitalist usury and mortgages, and to socialist activity. He contended that smallholding peasants, exploited by the bourgeoisie, had become like workers ("their exploitation differs only in form") and stressed the possibilities of a worker-peasant alliance. In 1851, as Marx's radical analysis had suggested, the greatest rural insurrection of nineteenth-century France opposed Napoleon's coup. Yet as Marx also recognized, a strong countercurrent among peasants equipped Napoleon with his mass political support. These conservative peasants, he argued, blamed their increased oppression on the "republic of the rich;" they hoped that a revivified Napoleon would restore their economic independence. Reactionary ideas—"Napoleonic hallucinations" as Marx called them—led to Napoleon's victory. Thus, Marx's nuanced economic and political analysis identified the manifold capitalist victimization of peasants and the dramatic role of political ideas in determining the character of their revolt. This analysis, despite temporary defeat, reinforced Marx's emphasis on the need for a revolutionary party. Energetic activity to secure internationalism, abolish private property, and forge a worker-peasant alliance, could lead, as he wrote to Engels in 1856, to a German proletarian revolution backed by a "second edition of the peasant war. Then the affair will be splendid."[19] The economic argument, sketched above, reinforced this strategy and a second one, based on Chartism and described below in section 2.

During the political respite of the 1850s, Marx also developed his economic theory in a new, sophisticated, and more political direction. Influenced by the classical iron law of wages, other radical theorists contended that workers could gain nothing from strikes. Marx sought to provide a theory of capitalist trends that would explain and justify working-class economic and political action, and yet underline the need for revolution. His new theory of surplus value and the general law of capitalist accumulation, as we shall see, accomplished both these aims. This theory demonstrated greater resilience in capitalism than classical political economy had suggested. But although a contextual understanding of Marx's later economic theory reveals a grain of truth in Wolin's account, it points in the opposite political direction. This theory sustains Marx's view that capitalism will also undercut limited working-class gains, instigate revolt, and permit Marx's revolutionary strategies to take effect. Furthermore, in the context of the IWA, Marx's published theory, especially the first volume of *Capital,* was as section 3 will show, politically charged. Section 4 will illustrate how Marx's new historical and strategic analyses of the impact of colonialism in Ireland on divisions among English workers and the novel political structure of the Paris Commune accentuated the need for clear political understanding and a revolutionary party. His later economic theory paralleled and reinforced these striking political explanations. Yet Marx's occasional depictions of his theoretical project as an interpretation of "the development of the economic formation of society as a natural-historical process" (*die Entwicklung der ökonomischen Gesellschaftsformation als ein naturgeschichtlische Prozess*) conflicted with these political and theoretical conclusions.[20] In his 1859 *Preface,* Marx had contended that economic trends, operating behind the backs of the producers, had reigned in past history (human "prehistory"); the proletarian movement and revolutionary politics would, however, dominate the future communist "history."[21] This paper will suggest a need to mark this political and moral contrast even more strikingly in Marxian theory than Marx did.

The fifth section of the paper will examine the major political impact of twentieth-century eugenics and racism in the light of Marx's theory. Subsequent experience would also justify a more central political emphasis in the theory. This section takes up the issue of whether Marxian theory remains consistent and plausibly scientific across major changes.

2. CHARTISM AND MARX'S NEW THEORY IN *CAPITAL*

Wolin contrasts the "preindustrial" workers of an early "political" period of Marx's activity (1843–1850) with the isolated fully "capitalist" technicians of the *Grundrisse*. He never clarifies whether these "precapitalist" proletarians are declining artisans, who still own their means of production, or industrial workers who have only their labor power to sell. Except for a passing remark, Wolin omits Marx's study of the distinctive productive process of capitalism, which forces large numbers of workers to associate in modern factories (the "Grossindustrie" of *Capital*); he also overlooks Marx's strategy based on the first working class movement stemming from capitalist oppression, Chartism. Marx's 1852 letter to Weydemeyer emphasized that many theorists had recognized class struggle in past societies; as the *Manifesto* suggested, "the history of all hitherto existing societies (except original communism) is the history of class struggles." On Marx's view, earlier modes of production had divided and isolated the oppressed classes, and obstructed movements for a nonexploitative society. In contrast, capitalism concentrated large numbers of workers in factories; the expansion of communications also facilitated general, effective class war from below. Ironically, Wolin's economic determinist interpretation misses Marx's analysis of the specific work situation, *characteristic of modern capitalism,* and substitutes Marx's unpublished glimpse of the very long-run automation of labor or *"suspension of the mode of production"* (a dialectical "suspension" probably impossible, as Marx's phrase suggests, under capitalism).[22] It is thus no surprise that Wolin loses the *political quality* of Marx's theory of capitalist productive powers as instigators of working class revolt.

Engels's 1845 *Condition of the Working Class in England* outlined the main phases of Chartist radicalism on which Marx would base his second revolutionary strategy. The original and "least successful" stage of worker hostility to exploitation—theft—left the individual workers at the mercy of the government. The second, Luddite machine-smashing, the "first organized resistance of the workers," occurred in mutually isolated localities and industries, and resulted in severe punishment. The third—unionism—organized workers countrywide against the capitalists, at least in a given trade. Although "the history of trade unionism is the story of many defeats and of only a few isolated victories," Engels saw unions as a standing protest against the pressures of capitalism:

> The incredible frequency of strikes affords the best proof of the extent to which the social war now rages in England. Not a week passes . . . without a strike occurring somewhere; . . . these strikes are often nothing but skirmishes in a social war . . . a training ground for the industrial proletariat and a preparation for the great campaign which draws inevitably nearer. Strikes are the manifestos by which particular groups of trade unionists pledge their adherence to the cause of the working class.[23]

This revolutionary interpretation of unionism distinguished Marx and Engels both from the utopians and from most union leaders. In an 1875 letter to Bebel, Engels pointed out that all French socialists in the 1840's opposed "combinations" (unions) and strikes, adding "with the exception of us two, who were unknown in France." As the *Manifesto* argued socialist "sects" abstained from or opposed this movement and even English union leaders with whom Marx cooperated in the IWA rejected strikes and class war.[24] Engels's view of strikes as "skirmishes in a social war" laid the foundation for the distinctive Marxian concept of unionism.

The weakness of unionism, however, led to a fourth stage: a "purely political movement," such as Chartism, which could unite the workers in general as a party against their oppressors. This party's aims would include legislation for universal suffrage and shorter hours. Engels also foresaw a fifth stage, in which socialism—then a middle-class movement in England—would fuse with Chartism.[25]

In *Poverty of Philosophy* and the *Manifesto,* Marx elaborated a strategy for a working-class movement that combined the last three stages of Engels's account. Marx argued that workers formed unions as part of a "veritable civil war." To achieve their goals, unionized workers would have to engage in "political struggle" like the Chartists. Marx stressed the need to study this "real movement" of the working class, comparable to the "much researched" development of the bourgeoisie as a class: "But when it is a question of making a precise study of strikes, combinations and other forms in which the proletarians carry out before our eyes their organization as a class, some are seized with real fear and others display a transcendental disdain."[26]

While Engels's *Condition,* still influenced by "true socialism," foresaw the role of communists as pacifying the workers, Marx viewed class struggle as the violent "shock of body against body." Only proletarian revolution could lead to fundamental social transformation: the abolition of classes.

In the *Manifesto,* Marx added that communists had a twofold political role within this working-class movement. In the "movement of the present" (the union struggle), communists, the "most advanced and resolute" group among the workers, should "push forward all the others." Left at this, however, communists would become reformers. Marx argued that communists must also link the current struggle and the "future" of the movement by defending internationalism—"the common interests of the entire proletariat independently of all nationality"—and urging the abolition of bourgeois property in the means of production.[27] Advocacy of the future of the movement—abolition of classes—partly grew out of the movement of the present as a mass struggle against the capitalists for better working conditions, and yet partly conflicted with its goal of a "better" rate of exploitation from the workers' point of view. Contrary to economic determinism, later Russian "economism," and Wolin's claim 3, Marx dialectically stressed revolutionary political activity within the current union struggle.

In Germany in 1848, the union movement had barely begun. In Cologne, Marx could not initiate unionism and simultaneously lead the left wing of the democratic revolution in a worker-peasant alliance; he chose the latter. Nonetheless his followers won leadership in the large (7,000 member) Cologne Worker-

Society and influenced it to play a role in the democratic revolution. After 1864, however, Marx implemented his strategy of radical unionism in the IWA. In becoming its main leader, Marx stressed international strike support, the fight for the shorter work week and support for the antislavery cause in the U.S. Civil War. He sought a broad internationalist framework encompassing union issues that would galvanize the most workers into participation. In the wave of European strikes between 1864 and 1868, the IWA vigorously supported the Leipzig compositors' strike, the English tailors' strikes of 1866 and 1867, the Paris bronze workers' strike, and others.[28] As the IWA gained widespread influence among workers, some radical sects, like the Lassalleans, reversed their position and defended unionism.

Despite the IWA's organizational dissolution in 1872, this Marxian strategy contributed to the eight hours movement in the United States in the 1880s and the formation of a new socialist international (1889) closely linked to the union movement. Yet Marx's revolutionary conception of unions distinguished him from other radical unionists. The IWA's internationalist strategy or the Bolsheviks' revolutionary activity in the unions differed markedly from the U.S. Communist party's militancy—without advocating socialism—in leading the sitdown strikes of the 1930s, or the pre-1914 German Social Democrats' submission to conservative union leaders. Such political differences, in Marx's view, would not arise from "inevitable" and spontaneous adjustments to circumstances. Rather, they represented political choices that could decisively affect the outcome of these movements.

While Marx and Engels advocated a strategy based on unionism in the 1840s, they held a general theory that wages must fall to a "bare existence" or a "wage minimum." But as Weston and others later argued, if unions and strikes could not gain permanent increases in real wages, why have them? Let us examine this contradiction more closely. In *Condition,* Engels questioned the effectiveness of unionism: "All these efforts on the part of trade unionists cannot change the economic law by which wages are fixed according to supply and demand in the labor market. Consequently, trade unions are helpless in the face of the major factors influencing the economy."[29]

Engels stated that depressions (a major factor) forced unions to accept a reduction in wages, while in prosperity unions could drive wages higher. From these true points, however, Engels concluded that unions "are not in a position to secure for their members higher wages than those which they would in any case obtain as a result of free competition between capitalists for skilled men." Again, one might ask, why have them?

But Engels then contradicted himself: "If the manufacturers did not have to face mass organized opposition from the workers, they would always increase their own profits by continually reducing wages." In other words, unions could significantly alter the level of wages. Engels also recognized that employers often used the argument that unions made no difference to undermine unionism while the workers themselves consistently adopted strikes and unions as a method of fighting.[30] But, until Marx formulated his new theory in the later 1850s, they didn't resolve this confusion in their argument.

To grasp the many-faceted impact of Marx's theory, a contextualist must examine it not only in relation to Marx's political activity and conflicts with other radicals, but also in the setting of previous theoretical political economy. As I have noted, Ricardo's contrast between the "natural price" of labor, subsistence, and its variable "market price," determined by supply and demand, provided the most sophisticated theoretical argument for the "iron law of wages" and opposition to unionism. Ricardo's theory took over Malthus's principle of population as a decisive causal mechanism. Temporary market improvements above subsistence would induce workers to have more children, increase supply, and over time, drive wages down to or even below subsistence. Based on Ricardo's view of wages, radicals had envisioned the self-emancipation of the workers through class conflict (Marx) or the forging of cooperatives as an alternative to class struggle (Lassalle, Proudhon). Ricardo, on the contrary, had called for capitalist eugenic regulation of workers through abolition of the English Poor Laws:

> It is a truth which admits not a doubt that the comforts and well-being of the poor cannot be permanently secured without some well-being on the part of the legislature, to regulate the increase of their numbers, and to render less

frequent among them early and improvident marriages.
. . . [But the poor laws] have rendered restraint superfluous and have invited improvidence by offering it a portion
of the wages of prudence and industry.[31]

In a striking causal and moral contrast, Marx's new theory of
wages and population in *Capital* would fix the blame for unemployment and division among workers on the capitalist system rather than on the victims of oppression.

The clash between Marx's earlier theory, drawn from classical political economy, and Marx's strategy of radical unionism
was quite fundamental. In applying his general historical theory to formulate strategies or explain specific events, Marx often
used auxiliary statements, derived from an analysis of the contemporary international situation, particular historical circumstances within a country, or new political movements.[32] No auxiliary statement, however, could extricate Marx from this
difficulty. Which would Marx give up, the higher-level economic principle of the iron law of wages or his analysis of the
real movement? An economic determinist, having grasped the
"basic" tendencies of capitalism, might argue that unionism
should go. Marx, however, could resist neither the evidence of
workers constantly striving to form unions, nor of the victory
represented by the Ten Hours Bill in England. He abandoned
the inadequate principle.

Addressing the General Council of the IWA in *Wages, Price
and Profit* (1865), Marx defended a radical conception of unionism against the Chartist, Weston. He argued that the worker
got paid not for the "labor" of classical political economy, but
for labor power. Its value hovered around subsistence, which
Marx redefined to include both a physical and a very elastic
"historical" or "social" element. Hence, economic and political
organization could affect wages: "The fixation of its [the rate
of surplus value's] actual degree is only settled by the continuous struggle between capitalists and laborers." Contrary to economic determinism, the value of labor power did not simply
reflect an objective law "independent of man's will" but depended on political organization and varied with the tides of
class struggle.[33] Unlike the Ricardian and Lassallean demo-
graphic theory of wages, resting on physical features of the av-

erage worker, Marx provided an original, distinctively historical, class conflict theory of the determination of wages.

Though Wolin fails to notice this basic change, Marx's mature economic theory allows real wages to rise under capitalism,
especially during periods of rapid capital accumulation and intense class struggle, and therefore disqualifies the erroneous
prediction Wolin stresses at the outset of his article. Contrary
to Wolin (claims 6, 10), Marx's theory in *Capital* requires no
arcane reinterpretation, a counterposing of a vision of omnipotent productive powers against revolutionary intentions, to
counter the iron law of wages (though this theory might vindicate Wolin's thesis 7 on Marx's concern to offer a true analysis
of capitalism).

Yet, one might ask, by this change in his theory, hadn't Marx
just undercut his basic argument and justified gradualism? As
a related philosophy of science question, a critic might add:
isn't this change so fundamental that it alters the whole direction of the Marxian theory (or research program as Lakatos
calls it)? Why should we call the new theory a Marxian one at
all?

In response to the first question, Marx regarded reforms under capitalism as limited, and saw substantial, protracted wage
increases as exceptional. In discussing the general law of capitalist accumulation, Marx contended: "A rise in the price of
labor as a consequence of accumulation of capital, only means,
in fact, that the length and weight of the golden chain the wage
worker has already forged for himself allow of a relaxation of
the tension of it."[34] Over the long run, if unions drove up wages,
capitalists would introduce machinery and lay off workers. As
this tendency became sufficiently pronounced it would "pro-
gressively turn . . . the scale in favor of the capitalists against
the working man." Furthermore, as Marx emphasized throughout *Capital*, the power of associated labor or human cooperation, invigorated by scientific achievement, appears in *alien form*
("the golden chain") as the power of capital itself; one way of
reading Wolin's argument is that for Marx—peculiarly—the alienation of capitalist accumulation becomes unchallengeable,
alien domination omnipotent. Thus, the intensity of capitalist
production would physically exhaust, where it did not injure,
the workers; as we shall see, the general law of capitalist accu-

mulation identified a variety of other social, political, and moral consequences. To defeat the ruling classes, Marx contended in *Wages, Price and Profit,* workers must inscribe on their banner not the conservative slogan of "a fair day's pay for a fair day's work!" but the "revolutionary watchword," "abolition of the wages system!"[35] The political argument of this address would dovetail with the general law of capitalist accumulation.

In answer to the second objection, as I argued in *Marx's Politics,* a new scientific theory emerges to challenge one or at most a few leading opponents; it retains its coherence across significant changes if it maintains its major differences with the leading alternate point(s) of view, and provides better explanations and, depending on the branch of science, predictions than before. Thus, when early twentieth-century biologists adopted Mendelian genetics and rejected Darwin's conceptions of some role for genetic blending and inheritance of acquired characteristics, they still considered their theory of evolution Darwinian. The strengthened theory retained Darwin's explanation, against creationism, of the existence of design in nature without a designer.[36] Similarly, in *Capital,* Marx's theory of surplus value and the general law of capitalist accumulation reinforced his earlier conception of capitalism as a conflict-ridden system that victimizes workers, instigates justified rebellion, and requires revolutionary political activity in its transformation. Marx made no fundamental concession to liberal theorists of capitalism's "harmoniousness" or to those who thought of the parasite state of modern Europe (the vast structure of officials and military officers separated from society) as standing above class struggle or as a potential instrument for the reform of capitalism into a more cooperative society. The theory in *Capital* is thus a more sophisticated version of Marxism.

For Marx, the practical anomaly between unionism and the iron law of wages focused attention on the contradiction within classical political economy between its definition of socially necessary labor time as the measure of value and the value of "labor" as subsistence. It therefore contributed to what many have regarded as Marx's fundamental theoretical revolution in *Capital:* his conception of surplus value.[37]

The effect of the union movement and radical strategy on Marx's theory of surplus value provides a valuable illustration of the process by which Marx refined or, in this case, revolutionized his theory: a movement from an older, somewhat contradictory theory (wages will decline to bare subsistence and unionism) through practice (continued development of unions and strikes) to Marx's new theory in *Capital*. This process grew dialectically out of the one we traced earlier: practice (Chartism) to theory (the *Manifesto's* strategy for communist activity) to practice (International Workingmen's Association). This example reveals a very general pattern of theory change in Marx—developing arguments from revolutionary experience and applying them, evaluating the new experience and further elaborating the theory—which Wolin's economic determinist interpretation overlooks (claims 5, 10, 1–3).

Marx moved from a sophisticated economic and political strategy in the late 1840s, though it contained an important contradiction, to a far more complex and even less economic determinist theory in the 1860s. Where the *Manifesto* had compared the capitalist cash nexus to "sentimental" feudal relations and suggested that the former would force men and woman "to face with [their] sober senses [their] real relations with [their] kind," *Capital* provided a novel analysis of commodity fetishism which made even the wage exchange *appear* fair (as an equal exchange of wages for labor instead of labor power). Marx had not abandoned his early idea of alienation. Since labor in production creates surplus value, Marx's new theory makes the *alienation* of capitalism (the belief in the productive powers or *fetishism* of capital, the nature of the "golden chain") fully comprehensible. That capitalism requires associated labor and that the productive process incorporates scientific knowledge enhance the likelihood of this (alienated) misinterpretation, but the theory of surplus value offers the fundamental explanation: "As in religion, man is governed by the products of his own brain, so in capitalist production, he is governed by the products of his own hand."[38] Where the *Manifesto* had foreseen a descent of workers' incomes to bare subsistence, *Capital* now permitted substantial increases in wages. Where Ricardo had envisioned a decline in the rate of industrial profit to the benefit of landlords, Marx's analysis of the tendency of the rate of profit to fall, checked by important countertendencies, made total collapse (as opposed to a cyclical development, still harmful to workers) less likely.[39] Calling for diminished reliance on economic trends to foster "spontaneous" revolution, Marx's new economic and political theory in *Capital* accentuated the need for sustained communist activity in the midst of class conflict.

3. THE POLITICAL IMPACT OF *CAPITAL*

Many scholars, including Wolin, see *Capital* as one of Marx's most determinist, apolitical works, an analysis of "objective economic forces" that will automatically give rise to socialism or, in Wolin's case, to endless capitalist domination. This notion, based on an overemphasis on Marx's phrase about a "natural-historical" succession of modes of production, misses the political force of Marx's argument. In fact, Marx's 1864 "Inaugural Address of the IWA" and his 1865 address, *Wages, Price and Profit,* provided a medium through which the theory of the general law of capitalist accumulation, machinery and modern industry, and the length of the working day entered the international working-class movement. These documents and the resolutions Marx drafted for IWA congresses reveal the theory's striking political implications.

For example, the debate in the General Council, which drove Marx to write *Wages, Price and Profit,* preceded a similar argument with the Proudhonists at the 1866 Geneva Congress. Marx's resolution on "the trade unions: their past, present and future" envisioned their historic role:

> Unconsciously to themselves, the Trades' Unions were forming centers of organization of the working class, as the medieval muncipalities and communes did for the middle class. If the Trades' Unions are required for the guerilla fights between capital and labor, they are still more important as organized agencies for superseding the very system of wages labor and capital rule.

This resolution flowed not just from Marx's argument on subsistence in *Capital,* but also from Marx's theory of the general law of capitalist accumulation. (This law contends that "the greater the social wealth, the functioning capital, the extent and energy of its growth, and therefore, also the absolute mass of the proletariat and the productiveness of its labor, the greater is the industrial reserve army." Marx notes that this tendency, "like all other laws . . . is modified in its working by many circumstances").[40] Through the introduction of machinery, Marx argued, capitalism created a reserve army of the unemployed. For Marx, the destiny of employed (speed-up and injury) and unemployed—"the condemnation of one part of the working class to enforced idleness by the overwork of the other part, and the converse"—were indivisibly linked. To combat this tendency Marx sought to unite the organized workers and the unorganized, particularly agricultural workers, as well as the unemployed.

> Apart from their original purpose, they [the unions] must now learn to act deliberately as organizing centers of the working class in the broad interest of its complete emancipation; . . . they cannot fail to enlist the non-society men into their ranks. They must look carefully after the interests of the worst paid trades, such as the agricultural laborers, rendered powerless by exceptional circumstances. They must convince the world at large that their efforts, far from being narrow and selfish, aim at the emancipation of the downtrodden millions.

Marx also argued in *Capital* that wherever the unions "try to organize a regular cooperation between employed and unemployed, capital and its sycophant, Political Economy, cry out at the infringement of the 'eternal' and so to say 'sacred' law of supply and demand."[41]

The argument in *Capital* reinforced Marx's fight for other causes in the IWA. In the "Inaugural Address" and in a resolution to the Geneva Congress, Marx stressed the limitation of the working day to eight hours as a "preliminary condition, without which all further attempts at improvement and emancipation must prove abortive." Such legislation, he argued, would maintain the health of the workers and secure time for intellectual development, social intercourse, and political action. *Capital* traced in detail the history of the struggle over the length of the working day. It stressed the Chartist movement for the Ten Hours Bill and even used a dialogue between a worker and a capitalist modified from a leaflet that London builders had issued during their strike for a nine-hour day in 1860.

> Suddenly the voice of the laborer, which had been stifled in the storm and stress of the process of production rises. "By an unlimited extension of the work day, you may in one day use up a quantity of labor-power greater than I can restore in three. What you gain in labor I lose in substance. I demand therefore a working day of normal length, and I demand it without any appeal to your heart for in money matters sentiment is out of place. You may be a model citizen, perhaps a member of the Society for the Prevention of Cruelty to Animals, and in the Odour of Sanctity to boot [Sir M. Peto, one of the construction owners, belonged to the Odour of Sanctity], but the thing that you represent face to face with me has no heart in its breast. I demand the normal working-day because I, like every other seller, demand the value of my commodity."[42]

The shorter-hours movement among English workers and the reports of the factory inspectors strongly influenced the writing of *Capital; Capital,* in turn, sought to spur on the movement.

In *Capital,* Marx showed how capitalism, when not restrained by the power of the workers, displayed a "werewolf hunger for surplus labor" and prematurely wasted the workers' lives.

> It steals the time required for the consumption of fresh air and sunlight. It higgles over a meal-time, incorporating it where possible with the process of production itself, so that food is given to the laborer as a mere means of production as coal is supplied to the boiler, grease and oil to the machinery. . . . It extends the laborer's time of production during a given period by shortening his actual life-time.

Workers could stop this "vampire" quality of capitalism only by force: "Between equal rights force decides." Marx argued that "the creation of a normal working day is . . . the product of a protracted civil war, more or less dissembled, between the capitalist class and the working class." As the struggle for shorter hours "takes place in the area of modern industry, it first breaks out in the home of that industry—England." These English workers championed the cause of workers under capitalism everywhere.[43]

In *Capital,* Marx linked one of the most acute international issues of the 1860s, the fight for the abolition of slavery, to the struggle for shorter hours. The death of slavery in 1865, he maintained, had dialectically given rise to new life, the unified movement for the eight-hour day, initiated by the 1866 Baltimore Congress of Labor. In this context, *Capital* advocated an internationalist defense of the most oppressed workers as a fundamental component of the movement for shorter hours: "Labor cannot emancipate itself in the white skin where in the black it is branded." Marx's 1864 "Inaugural Address" had hailed English workers, whose "heroic resistance" had checked the "criminal" attempts of the English ruling class to support the South in the U.S. Civil War. Stemming from before the French Revolution, a political campaign against slavery had aroused English workers to fight for abolitionism. Despite the blockade of cotton and widespread unemployment, English workers opposed the perpetuation of human misery; they also recognized the danger to themselves of the victory of a slave-holding republic in North America and the consequent reshaping of international politics in a reactionary direction. At mass meetings in London, Birmingham and Sheffield, they supported abolitionism. Thus, when a conservative union leader, Roebuck, called for a pro-slaveholder English intervention, the Sheffield workers responded: "Never! We should have a civil war in England first!"[44] In its campaign for the eight-hour day, the IWA emphasized the solidarity of the English and American workers, white and former slave. Nowhere more forcefully than in the chapter on the working day did the arguments of *Capital* flow from the political struggle of the international working class and return to it.

In response to working-class protest, the British Parliament's Children's Employment Commission had begun to restrict the use of child labor in metal and "home work" (putting out) manufacturing. Marx's "Inaugural Address" had awakened the IWA to renewed efforts to suppress the manufacturers' penchant to exploit children. In a satiric moral image worthy of Jonathan Swift, Marx compared the systematically barbaric practices of English capitalists unfavorably with those of perverse Moloch worshippers: "In ancient times, child murder was a mysterious rite of the religion of Moloch, but it was practiced on very solemn occasions only, once a year perhaps, and then Moloch had no exclusive bias for the children of the poor."

In 1867, the manufacturers called for a new parliamentary investigation of factory conditions and an interim postponement of restrictions, allowing, as Marx put it, a fresh "five years' term of exploitation" of children. Some of *Capital's* fiercest pages depicted this exploitation in pottery, matchmaking, and the lace trade. Marx cited the report of a Nottingham magistrate: "Children of nine or ten are dragged from their squalid beds at two, three or four o'clock in the morning and compelled to work for a bare subsistence until ten, eleven or twelve at night, their limbs wasting away, their frames dwindling, their faces whitening and their humanity absolutely sinking into a stone-like torpor." Marx also instigated action by the union leaders in the General Council to oppose any relaxing of the already weak child labor laws. In June, he wrote to Engels, "Fortunately my position in the International enables me to upset the tricky calculations of these curs [the manufacturers]. The thing is of the utmost importance. It is a question of *abolishing the torture* of one and a half million human beings." On August 15, Parliament limited the working day for women and children under 18 to ten and a half hours, not only in large factories but in small enterprises and domestic industry.[45]

The section on machinery and modern industry in *Capital* also served as the theoretical basis for a General Council resolution to the 1868 Brussels Congress. Marx noted that capitalists used machinery as a weapon directed against striking workers: "Machinery not only acts as the competitor who gets the better of the workman, and is constantly on the point of making him superfluous. It is also a power inimical to him and as such capital proclaims it from the roof tops. . . . It is the most powerful weapon for repressing strikes, those periodical revolts of the working class against the autocracy of capital." Whenever workers gained shorter hours, capitalists would introduce machines to intensify their labor and spur productivity. Therefore, Marx suggested, so long as capital "convert[s] every improvement in machinery into a more perfect means of exhausting the workman," workers would renew their effort to reduce the hours of labor.[46]

Furthermore, *Capital*'s analysis of the general trends in capitalism strengthened the new socialist movement gradually developing within the IWA. The 1868 Brussels Congress hailed the publication of *Capital* directly. The arguments in *Capital* gave deeper force to IWA resolutions on the need for a working-class party to conquer political power. These arguments also laid the groundwork for the IWA's international support of the Commune as the "political form at last discovered in which to work out the economic emancipation of labor."[47]

Thus, Marx's arguments on the struggle over the length of the working day, the role of machinery, and the general law of capitalist accumulation forged a strong theoretical underpinning for vigorous internationalist efforts to remedy what Marx's *Rules of the International Workingmen's Association* identified as "the want of solidarity between the *manifold divisions of labor in each country* and [overcome] the absence of a fraternal bond of union between the working classes of different countries."[48] These arguments also underlined the need for revolutionary parties. In *Capital*, Marx emphasized six further broad social, political and moral consequences of capitalist accumulation, ones that go beyond the production process itself and justify revolution. The chapter on the "General Law" includes the first five; the sixth is a general theme of *Capital* and the *Grundrisse*.

First, Marx stressed the use of the reserve army of the unemployed as soldiers in preparations for war; as Mandeville had put it, "a multitude of laborious poor are . . . the never-failing nursery of fleets and armies." Even if such workers were to adopt the capitalists' nationalist justifications for war, they would still be forced to pay with their lives, liberty, and taxes. Capitalist wars fundamentally damage the interests of most workers; they frequently—with exceptions like the Northern side in the U.S. Civil War—spur on and justify internationalist opposition movements[49] (as a related point, the ruling class uses the military internally to menace or suppress working-class revolt).

Second, given the international impact of expanding capitalism, Marx emphasized the increasingly direct linkage and contact of workers of different nationalities. In a precursor to today's analyses of dependency, Marx traced the devastation and depopulation of mid-nineteenth century Ireland that accompanied English industrialization: "Ireland is at present only an agricultural district of England marked off by a wide channel from the country to which it yields corn, wool, cattle and industrial and military recruits."[50] The capitalist revolution in Irish agriculture, propelled by English landlords, had dispossessed subsistence farmers in grain and substituted livestock production on large estates. Combined with the potato famine, this revolution had fueled massive emigration to the U.S. and England and the development of multinational working classes. Furthermore, between 1850 and 1870, Irish population had decreased absolutely. Marx satirically identified Ireland as a kind of inverted Malthusian paradise. Far from improving conditions for the remaining workers and peasants, scarcity of labor coexisted with continuing abject misery. Contrary to Malthus and Ricardo, this outcome illustrated capitalism's specific law of relative surplus population.

Third, on Marx's view, the general law required an ideological component. In the early nineteenth century, the sympathy of English Chartists for Jacobinism in the French Revolution had threatened the English capitalists; they responded with fierce repression and the propagation of Malthus's early eugenics:

> The French Revolution had found passionate defenders in the United Kingdom; the "principle of population" slowly worked out in the eighteenth century, and then, in the midst of a great social crisis, proclaimed with drums and trumpets as the infallible antidote to the teachings of Condorcet, etc. was greeted as the destroyer of all hankerings after human development.[51]

The English ruling class needed to legitimize unemployment, stigmatize immigrants, and blunt class struggle; it had to justify the miserable condition of colonized peoples. Matthew's eugenics (and later versions) conformed to these needs; this argument illustrates the role of functional explanation, stressed by G.A. Cohen, in Marx's theory of capitalism. Further, Marx explained the strong class pressures that sustained this false view. The theory emphasized an important sociological reason for the adoption of Malthus's argument as background or collateral information even in Ricardo's sophisticated political economy.

Fourth, following Mandeville, Marx identified dialectical effects of capitalist inequalities in undercutting, not just expanding public education: "To make the society [which consists of non-workers] happy, [Mandeville argued] . . . it is requisite that great numbers of them should be ignorant as well as poor; knowledge both enlarges and multiplies our desires."[52]

Fifth, Marx traced the impact of such inequalities on working-class housing, nourishment, and medical care. Commenting on parliamentary investigations, Marx's "Inaugural Address" queried: "What did the doctor discover? That the silk weavers, the needle women, the kid glovers, the stocking weavers, and so forth, received on an average not even the distress pittance of the cotton operatives, not even the amount of carbon and nitrogen 'just sufficient to avert starvation diseases.'" *Capital* extended this analysis.[53]

Sixth, capitalism greatly increases potentials for leisure and the emergence of social individuality; yet it simultaneously suppresses these potentials. Wolin emphasizes only one aspect of this conception. For him, Marx glimpsed in the *Grundrisse* an all-powerful automated capitalism in which the industrial working class has disappeared and the remaining technicians have "stepped to the side."[54] But Wolin's interpretation misses both the general context and the specific political upshot of this argument.

In general, Marx argued, capitalist application of science has advanced human productive powers ("knowledge objectified"). Despite the alien domination of capital, this system dialectically magnifies and diversifies the potentials of human beings as producers. As the hours of necessary labor diminish, the disposable time for individuals to secure education and achieve their own aims expands; this "time for the full development of the individual . . . in turn reacts back upon the productive power of labor as itself the greatest productive power."[55] On Marx's account, workers have won limited leisure mainly through class conflict to shorten the working day. But capitalist productivity promises a greater leisure that capitalists fight relentlessly to forestall. With ups and downs, capitalist accumulation works a constant sea change, eroding and transfiguring the justifications for exploitation and its consequences (without revolution, however, such changes can also, except under special circumstances, lead to more ferocious forms of capitalist domination).[56]

In *Capital,* Marx contrasted Aristotle's eudaemonist conception of leisure as a prerequisite for the realization of human potentials with narrow capitalist subordination to the needs of profit-making:

> "If," dreamed Aristotle, the greatest thinker of antiquity, "if every tool, when summoned or even of its own accord, could do the work that befits it, just as the creations of Daedalus moved of themselves . . . then there would be no need . . . of slaves for the lords." Oh! those heathens! . . . They did not comprehend that machinery is the surest means of lengthening the working day. They perhaps excused the slavery of one on the ground that it was a means to the full development of another. But to preach slavery of the masses in order that a few crude and half-educated parvenus might become "eminent spinners," "extensive sausage-makers," and "influential shoe-black dealers," to do this, they lacked the bump of Christianity.[57]

As opposed to Wolin's "versatile technicians," restricted to the sphere of remnant necessary labor, Marx entertained a broad moral conception of the "rich" flourishing of individuality in communism.

For Marx, irreconcilable conflicts of human goods had marked exploitative societies, for instance, the achievement of ancient political community at the expense of slavery, or the capitalist war between mechanization and equality. Such fundamental conflicts may have been (in any case, were in practice) unavoidable in human "prehistory." But on Marx's view, the cooperative productivity, unleashed by capitalism, steadily erodes the necessity of a division between mental and manual work.[58] Thus, the revolutionary movement for a new society can fuse intrinsic goods (solidarity, political community) and instrumental ones (the steps needed to secure communism); it represents a new type of historical and moral advance.

Wolin also overlooks the specific political upshot of even a minimal version of Marx's eudaemonist argument. As G.A. Cohen has emphasized, the contrast between potential leisure and pointless subjection to capitalist imperatives would drive workers to repeated struggles for shorter hours; it would make many consider revolution.[59] Marx's 1868 leaflet for the IWA on "The Belgian Massacres" of iron workers striking for shorter hours arrestingly employed such criteria; the Belgian capitalist "shudders at the very idea that a common working man should be wicked enough to *claim any higher destiny than that of enriching his master* and natural superior."[60]

Or consider a semipermanently unemployed teenager, black, Asian or white, in Great Britain today. In the starkest cases of oppression, racist or antiworking-class ideology (Eysenck, Burt) has stigmatized these teenagers;[61] educational tracking and unemployment have prevented them from acquiring or using available skills, or forced them into the army. This system offers a mean choice of lives to such young people: military recruitment; drugs and crime; persistent victimization by racist, overtly fascist gangs (thus, in summer 1981, "skinhead" attacks in Southall and the firebombing murder of a Pakistani family in Liverpool triggered multiracial rebellions in 30 cities).[62] Liberals can contend that a wider range of individual alternatives and mitigating policies is possible (alternative government programs could expand employment and education, or soldiering in potential just wars could be a rewarding occupation). Nonetheless, the actual treatment of these individuals, despite the vast productivity and ostensibly democratic education of advanced capitalism, remains a serious charge against it. Marx's theory, however, not only explains the need for unemployment, educational inequality, antiworking-class ideology and recruitment for (unjustified) wars, but also sketches a picture of why such a teenager's choice of a good life, in an Aristotelian sense, could involve participation in multiracial rebellions or revolutionary politics. Contrary to Wolin (claim 11), Marx's conception of social individuality has a sustained radical cutting edge. The same paragraph that envisions the worker "stepping to the side" identifies this process as "a material condition to blow this [miserable] foundation [of capitalism] sky-high (*um sie in die Luft zu sprengen*)."[63]

4. NEW POLITICAL EXPLANATIONS IN THE IWA AND MARX'S THEORY

In the 1840s, Marx and Engels recognized the role of Irish radicals in English Chartism. Despite his marked emphasis on the need for revolutionary politics, including internationalism, in that movement, however, Marx expected economic and political forces within England to produce a proletarian revolution that would, in turn, liberate the colonies. In this respect, Marx's 1840s analysis of class conflict had some (distant) affinity with an economic determinist stress on the level of productive forces *within a country*. Assessing the decline of Chartism after 1848, however, Marx offered a new international perspective; he insisted that chauvinist attitudes, rooted in the preservation of colonial rule in Ireland, divided English and Irish workers and crippled socialist organizing in England. To galvanize a revolutionary movement, Marx argued, the IWA had to make anticolonialism and opposition to racism toward the Irish ("religious, social and national prejudices") central features of its program.[64] Thus, Marx's IWA analysis drew far more drastic political conclusions from the connected oppression of English and Irish workers than Marx spelled out in *Capital*.

Marx won the IWA to act on this strategy. In 1867, Manchester courts sentenced five Fenians to death; demonstrations and petitions for amnesty swept Ireland. Based on Marx's conception of the crucial role of colonialism, the General Council condemned Gladstone's conduct toward Ireland as "the genuine offspring of that 'policy of conquest' by the fiery denunciation of which [he] ousted his Tory rivals from office"; it endorsed "the spirited and high-souled manner in which the Irish people carry on their amnesty movement." English, German, Swiss, and Belgian radical papers circulated this resolution, as did the IWA's union branches in England. In 1869, Marx combatted the chauvinism of Mottershead, an English representative to the General Council, and the IWA helped to organize a demonstration of 100,000 in Hyde Park to defend amnesty. (According to Jenny Marx, the demonstrators so jammed the park that some had to perch in the "highest treetops;" Marx reported enthusiastically to Engels that the demonstration *"war famos."*) In 1872, Irish and English workers staged a similar "giant" Hyde Park rally. Thus, the IWA helped to launch a movement to break down these divisions; that movement revealed the potential for Anglo-Irish working-class unity. It declined, along with the IWA, only in the fierce repression throughout Europe that followed the suppression of the Paris Commune. Nonetheless, Marx's new internationalist explanation of the weakness of English socialism and heightened emphasis on multinational unity and anticolonialism underlined the increasingly political character of Marxian theory.[65]

Similarly, in response to the Paris Commune, Marx drew striking political conclusions about socialism. The dictatorship of the proletariat for Marx could not mean simply state ownership of the means of production. Instead, advancing on his 1851 analysis of the parasite state, he contended that workers must "destroy" the old standing army and bureaucratic apparatus; they would replace it with a new political form that would involve a citizen army, officials paid a wage no higher than that of a skilled worker, and recall (in 1872, Marx and Engels made this point their sole amendment to the *Communist Manifesto*). Drawing on an Aristotelian conception of political participation as an intrinsic good, Marx recognized that the Commune's worker-officials carried out their political activity for its own sake, not for money.[66] In addition, where *Capital* had envisioned a short transition to full communism (compared to the lengthy transition to bourgeois domination), the experience of the Commune pointed to a more protracted, violent political conflict.[67]

Thus, the succession of communism out of capitalism could not occur as a "natural-historical" process in the important sense that mere legal measures ostensibly corresponding to new economic structures (such as state ownership of the means of production) would not serve to guarantee it. To emancipate themselves, the workers and their allies had to organize a political party with a precise conception of the nature and political weapons of their enemies, and of the political institutions and internal conflicts of the future regime. Unlike alien prehistory, that movement would have to dominate (communist) human history. Given this new experience, the distinction between history and exploitative prehistory deserves a stronger moral and political emphasis than Marx gave to it in his 1859 *Preface.*

Contrary to Wolin's claim that Marx articulated no political conception of working-class revolution during this period, Marx's writings on the policies of the IWA, on the Commune, and on German and French socialism delineate a clear revolutionary and postrevolutionary strategy.[68] Taken outside this context, *Capital* is an incomplete and, in important ways, misleading presentation of Marx's argument, for Marx's new discoveries highlighted the role of politics in his general theory; in fact, they even suggest a need to recast it. The conceptions of internationalism, the character of socialism, and the need for a revolutionary party, reinforced by *Capital*'s analysis but not spelled out there, are the core of the theory.

5. MARX'S THEORY AND MODERN RACISM

Wolin could grant some of these points, and still deny Marx's theory contemporary relevance (claim 11). For instance, he could suggest that nefarious as capitalism's treatment of working-class teenagers turns out to be, these teenagers form only a limited part of the population. Following an argument of Lakatos, one could give such an objection a strong philosophy of science formulation.

Lakatos defended sophisticated methodological falsificationism as opposed to a naive falsificationism (including Popper's argument about the role of basic statements). Lakatos conceded many points to Kuhn and contemporary realism. He recognized that scientists explore the leading contending theories or research programs at a given time, that a particular theory will not be rejected in the absence of an alternative, and that given the role of auxiliary statements, refutation of theories by crucial experiments is strongly underdetermined by evidence. He suggested, however, that a broad research program is progressing when it has more empirical content than a competing one, and some of that "excess content" is found to be true. Lakatos argued that Marxian theory has become degenerate: "What novel fact has Marxism predicted since, say, 1917?"[69]

This falsificationist argument could acknowledge that Marx's refined views on the peasants, his new theory in *Capital*, and even the more political emphasis proposed in the last section would have strengthened the theory against its liberal competitors. That refined theory could have been a more plausible version of Marxism, just as Darwin's theory combined with Mendel's was more strongly Darwinian; yet capitalist progress and socialist decadence could have falsified its research program.

In this section, I want to show that Lakatos's objection is mistaken, and that the debate in historical and social theory between Marxian and various liberal research programs continues. I have explored the relevance of Marx's theoretical and moral arguments on the conflicts in socialism, based on the Commune, to understanding contemporary communist decadence in Russia, China and elsewhere.[70] This paper will focus on the unexpected light that Marx's general theory in *Capital* casts on two major twentieth-century political and social phenomena: eugenics and Nazi genocide, and the persistence of racism in the United States. Using falsificationist criteria, Popper takes the putative elimination of racism in the U.S. and England as a strong disproof of Marxian theory, and along with the abolition of slavery, as a telling example of moral progress.[71] Since Marxians agree with his point about slavery, the persistence of racism in these societies provides a good test of the comparative explanatory and moral plausibility of Marxian and liberal theories. The following sketch is controversial: my aim is only to show, based on some leading differences between Marxian and liberal theories, that Marxian arguments have strong claims as at least a good first approximation to the truth.

Where liberal theorists often accept the group distinctions postulated by racism just as they appear and think that racism harms only its explicit victims, Marxian theory examines racism's impact on the supposed oppressor group and arrives at the surprising conclusion that racism harms, for instance, English or white American workers along with its obvious targets. Unlike liberals, Marxians view racism *functionally* as a divide-and-rule tactic, whatever the complex methods of its dissemination. Where liberal theories see racism as stemming from the attitudes of most people of the predominant nationality, or as Weber stresses, from the declassé members of the dominant status group, Marxians look to the ruling class (capitalists, government, the "respectable" media, and prestigious intellectuals) to propagate these ideas.[72] For liberals, racism emerges from below; for Marxians, from above. As a third leading difference, Marxians argue that the state, under capitalism, tolerates or often encourages extralegal racist violence, for example, that of the Ku Klux Klan in the U.S., the Black Hundreds in tsarist Russia, and the Nazis in Weimar Germany. Marx suggested this distinctive point about reactionary social movements in the *Eighteenth Brumaire;* given the centrality of racism in such movements, later Marxian analysis goes further in this regard. Liberal theorists, in contrast, disconnect the state and reactionary mass movements, and view the political and judicial structure as neutral or above class struggle.[73]

In the first case, an explanation of early twentieth-century Social Darwinist eugenics can easily parallel Marx's analysis of class conflict and Malthusian eugenics. Throughout Europe and the U.S., unions, socialist, and, later, communist parties made the misery of the working class, understood as its *exploitation* by the capitalists, a political issue. As recent arguments by Chorover, Kamin, and Allen have shown, Social Darwinism, eugenics, and especially the IQ testing movement provided a firm procapitalist response.[74] According to eugenicists, capitalists did not benefit from a system that preyed upon workers. Instead, these naturally gifted individuals achieved their rewards through merit, and proletarians, especially minority workers and immigrants, spawned by inferior stock, could only make the best of their sad biological lot.

As Marxians might suppose, leading capitalists, the government, and professors at prestigious universities encouraged these views. In the United States, the Carnegies, Harrimans, Kelloggs, Rockefellers, and many others funded eugenics research; in Germany in 1900, Krupp sponsored a prize essay contest on the question, "What can we learn from the principles of Darwinism for application to inner political development and the laws of the state?" and financed the publication of ten influential volumes that foreshadowed Nazi population policies. Through IQ testing of immigrants and soldiers, the U.S. government fostered these virulent racist views. Professors like McDougall and Castle of Harvard, Thorndike of Columbia, Terman of Stanford, and Brigham of Princeton (first head of the Educational Testing Service) called for immigration restriction and the squelching of "dysgenic" population trends.[75] Federal and state governments passed racist immigration, miscegenation, and sterilization laws. The impact of the Russian Revolution and widespread strikes led to racist hysteria toward "inferior" East European and Jewish radicals, the Palmer raids, and the massive deportations of 1919. Attacking gentlemen socialists in a lecture at Princeton in that year, Henry Goddard, who administered IQ tests at Ellis Island, illustrated the usefulness of eugenics, "the new science of mental levels", as an ideology of the status quo:

> These men in their ultra altruistic and humane attitude, their desire to be fair to the workman, maintain that the great inequalities in social life are wrong and unjust. For example here is a man who says "I am wearing $12.00 shoes, there is a laborer who is wearing $3.00 shoes; why should I spend $12.00 while he can only afford $3.00? I live in a home that is artistically decorated . . . there is a laborer that lives in a hovel with no carpets, no pictures and the coarsest kind of furniture. It is not right, it is unjust. . . ."

> Now the fact is, that workman may have a ten year intelligence while you have a twenty. To demand for him such a home as you enjoy is as absurd as it would be to insist that every laborer should receive a graduate fellowship. How can there be such a thing as social equality with this wide range of mental capacity?[76]

During its 1920s rebirth as a mass organization in the Southern and Central U.S., the Ku Klux Klan used such ideas, generated from above, as its intellectual staple. The role of capitalists and the government in fostering eugenic racism and bending recent "scientific" advances such as IQ testing to respond to class struggle strongly conflicts with the expectations of liberal theories.

In post-World War I Germany, massive working-class uprisings, spurred by the example of the Russian Revolution, overturned the monarchy, and communist movements threatened the capitalist republic. During this period, the government and judiciary tolerated right-wing movements (Weimar recruited the proto-fascist Freikorps to suppress proletarian revolt); leading officers could participate in the Munich (Ludendorff) or Kapp putsch with impunity; the *prosecutor* at Hitler's Munich trial praised his "virtues" as a relentless fighter against "international Marxism and Jewry."[77] Eugenic proposals were also widely disseminated. Physicians, psychiatrists, and lawyers campaigned to dispense with lives "devoid of value" (*wertlos*), especially those of mental patients, and influenced the Weimar government. In 1923, the chief government physician for Zwickau, who favored sterilization laws, wrote to the Minister of the Interior: "What we racial hygienists promote is not all new or unheard of. In a cultured nation of the first order, in the United States of America, that which we strive toward was introduced and tested long ago. It is all so clear and simple." The German foreign office and the embassy in Washington investigated American eugenic practices. Nazi psychologists and anthropologists subsequently praised U.S. eugenics legislation as the most advanced in the world. Eugenics gave a pseudoscientific stamp to an older Aryan mythology, and facilitated the emergence of Nazi racism as a mass ideology.[78]

In a specific configuration of historical circumstances, including defeat in World War I, republican revolution, the prominence and failure of mass left-wing parties, inflation, and depression, the Nazis came to power. Unlike other European capitalist regimes, they successfully mobilized a substantial part of the population for war. But the *general* European and American ideological trend, eugenics, provided "master race" ideas to march by for the Nazis' nearly successful campaign to conquer Europe.

An emphasis on eugenics as a ruling class response to class struggle from below casts important light on the distinctive moral features of Nazism. As Chorover shows, psychiatrists and physicians in leading German medical and academic institutions implemented broad Nazi guidelines. They murdered thousands of German mental patients and "defective Aryan" children as a forerunner to Nazi genocide against Jews and

Slavs. Contrary to the expectations of an ethical relativist interpretation, these doctors did not start from a bizarre or "incommensurable" moral premise; they adhered to the simple moral standard that children are to be preserved. Based on the findings of the international eugenics movement, however, they adopted a false theoretical notion of what a "healthy" child is, and gave a monstrous turn to the ordinary idea that *healthy* children are to be preserved. As Putnam's recent example of the "super Benthamites," suggests, eugenic theory gave rise to a different *description* of the facts about health and lack of health. These doctors' inability "to get the way the human world is right [was] a direct result of their sick conception of human flourishing."[79] But the decisive element in the conception of the human world that made these doctors (Nazis and others) moral *monsters* was the eugenic premise about health. This pseudo-scientific premise led to a further conception that the preservation of "unfit" children threatened "healthy" ones, and hence, that the "unhealthy" were more like animals (stray dogs to be taken to the pound and put to sleep) than humans.

Liberals theorists often view Nazism as a phenomenon of backwardness, autocracy, and Junker domination under extreme historical circumstances; they separate it sharply from the politics of liberal democratic capitalism and view it as an atavism in the course of modernization.[80] But the important facts I have outlined about the eugenics movement and Nazism conform at least roughly to a Marxian theory of class conflict, which explains the central role of racism and racist ideology, the interconnection of the American and European eugenics movements, the distinctive features of Nazism as opposed to other forms of fascism, and even the specific social and moral causes of Nazism's monstrousness.

This sketch highlights some features of Marx's account of capitalist accumulation and his analysis of divisions of English and Irish workers; yet many previous Marxian analyses of Nazism, even those like Neumann's which emphasize racist ideology, miss these decisive points. Furthermore, the German Social Democrats and Communists neither combatted racist ideology in the universities, media, and hospitals, nor strove to crush the emerging Nazi movement. As a party of government, the SPD often tolerated extralegal Nazi violence; the German communists responded to the Nazis only when attacked.[81] Neither grasped the special ideological and political dangers of a Nazi mass movement. The foregoing account suggests that later Marxian movements and scholars neglected those features of Marx's economic and political theory that would have enabled them to understand and check Nazism before its rise to power.

To some extent, the pseudoscientific features of the eugenics movement crystallized after Marx and Engels had died. Thus, despite the anti-Semitic current in German racism, Marx did not see this distinctive ideological outlook as something important to oppose in *Critique of the Gotha Program* (though his emphasis on internationalism and the need for multiracial unity implies such criticism). In his later years, Engels saw anti-Semitism as a medieval atavism rather than as a component in a wider modern racism; in *Anti-Dühring* (1978), he commented

That same philosopher of reality [Dühring] who has a sovereign contempt for all prejudices and superstitions is himself so deeply imbued with personal crotchets that he calls the popular prejudice against the Jews, inherited from the bigotry of the Middle Ages, a "natural judgment" based on "natural grounds," and he rises to the pyramidal heights of the assertion that "socialism is the only power which can oppose population conditions with a strong Jewish admixture."[82]

In this passage, Engels's conception of anti-Semitism was consistent with a liberal theory, not a Marxian one. Yet the propagation of Malthus's population theory had already revealed the importance of a pseudoscientific answer to demands for social and political equality. The political impact of Marxian internationalism enhanced that capitalist need. Further, Marx had stressed the social forces sustaining the Malthusian answer. Thus, one might have expected, with increased class struggle, that new pseudoscientific versions of racism, like so many heads of a hydra, would spring up.[83] In retrospect, if this sketch of a Marxian analysis of Nazism (which coheres nicely with Marx's theory) has merit, it suggests even more strongly the inadequate political emphasis in *Capital*.

In the second case, liberal and Marxian views also clash over whether white American workers (regardless of racist attitudes) benefit from racism. Recent empirical evidence, Michael Reich's sophisticated statistical study of the impact of racism on income distribution and social welfare, strikingly illustrates a Marxian view.

Reich's study shows that in every standard metropolitan statistical area in the U.S., wherever racism, measured by the ratio of black incomes to white, is at its greatest, incomes for white workers are relatively the lowest, and the income differential between most whites and the top one percent of white families is at its greatest. He also shows that where racism is less potent, AFDC (Aid to Families with Dependent Children) to white families has been greater and the rate of profit lower.[84] These results hold up through multiple regression analysis and strongly suggest that racism, due to its negative impact on the multiracial unity of workers (and others), is decisive in explaining variations in inequalities among whites.

Following a Marxian paradigm, Reich also emphasizes the historical importance of multiracial movements among American workers and farmers against the odds (the Southern farmers' alliance and the early Populists, the multiracial movements of Alabama miners and New Orleans workers, the IWW-led Southern lumber workers' strike, the CIO and so forth). Class unity arguments have had a major impact in such mass movements. As Tom Watson argued during the rise of Populism:

> Now the People's Party says to these two men [black and white] "You are kept apart that you may be separately fleeced of your earnings. You are made to hate each other because upon that hatred is rested the keystone of the arch of financial despotism which enslaves you both. You are deceived and blinded that you may not see how this race antagonism perpetuates a monetary system which beggars both."[85]

Fierce repression and the intensified dissemination of racism were needed to crush such movements.

Reflecting the general weaknesses on ideology in Marxian accounts, Reich denies any systemic connection between ruling-class interests and the propagation of racist ideologies. Despite

the suggestiveness of this argument, he does not see the renewal of such ideologies as characteristic of capitalism. But in
addition to the early twentieth-century eugenics movement, the
civil-rights movement and riots (in Marxian terms, rebellions)
in American cities in the 1960s led to a new wave of well-pub-
licized theories of biological inferiority, for instance the eugenic
views of Jensen and Shockley.[86] Thus, contrary to Wolin (claim
11) and Lakatos, if these arguments (or similar ones) are right,
Marxian theory leads to surprising conclusions vis-à-vis competing liberal research programs, and unearths important evidence to support its claims; it identifies common interests among
workers in opposing the increasingly blatant inequalities of advanced capitalism.

The foregoing examples suggest that Marxian theory might
be progressive even by Lakatos's standards. But a Popperian
could offer two further objections: (a) individual Marxian theorists may contribute to our understanding of capitalism (or
socialism) but socialist and communist movements have generally obstructed Marxian theoretical achievement; (b) Marxian
arguments seem to be at least as much explanatory as predictive. But genuine scientific theories must be predictive and hence
(ultimately) falsifiable; otherwise their use of auxiliary statements is ad hoc in an unjustified sense.[87]

To the first objection, however, one might respond that radical movements based on Marxian ideas—the IWW organizing
of Southern lumber workers, communist-led unemployment
councils, union organizing and campaigns like the one about
Angelo Herndon—forged substantial multiracial unity despite
ruling-class resistance. They kept alive or reinforced the idea
that workers of different nationalities have common interests,
and provided explicit arguments for and examples of such interests. If these movements failed to interpret the role of eugenic ideology as Marx had, they nonetheless contributed to
the political atmosphere in which strong civil-rights movements
could unfold and in which social scientists like Reich could attempt to test (at the time) counterintuitive proposals such as the
contention that racism hurts most whites.[88] Far from hindering
the advance of Marxian theory or good social science, such
movements undercut standard racist stereotypes in academia
and identified an alternative, approximately true "research

program." Further, a Marxian would contend, social prejudices (against the producing classes, foreigners, minorities, women), which serve systemic, ruling-class interests, will receive persistent reinforcement. Given the widely recognized dependence of science and social science on background or auxiliary statements, social scientists will take up such stereotypes as collateral information in the absence of a strong competing theory (Kuhn, Lakatos, and realists all emphasize this general point about competing paradigms).[89] *Only movements from below,* challenging these stereotypes, will create an atmosphere that makes scientific study possible. To overcome the role of such prejudices in social science, widespread adoption of approximately true theories wiill depend upon class conflict or upon such movements. Note that this argument opposes any relativist notion of a clash of incommensurable "bourgeois" and "proletarian" sciences. Further, nothing in this argument dismisses a grain of truth in Lakatos's view—Marxian political movements have often become conservative and opposed attempts to advance Marxian theory or achieve self-critical insight.

Given Lakatos's recognition of the clash of research programs in determining "crucial experiments" over considerable periods of time, a sophisticated falsificationist could in principle grant the above argument (though Lakatos himself would probably have disapproved of it). But a Popperian, who identifies falsification as the leading feature of a successful scientific research program, could still object that Marxian theories are not sufficiently predictive. As Putnam has argued, however, this Popperian view of the rationality of scientific method is too narrow to characterize even scientific knowledge. For instance, Popper's criterion *rules out* a leading scientific theory, Darwinism, which offers no predictions of the development of particular species. But Darwin's theory explains a great diversity of facts, and links up with later achievements in genetics and molecular biology. It is, as Jacques Monod has stressed, a far wider and "richer" system of explanation than Darwin envisioned: "The theory may be judged precisely by this type of development which more and more falls into its lap even though it was not predictable that so much would come of it."[90] Monod reveals a grain of truth in Lakatos's notion of some "excess corroborated empirical content" (a richness of mutually reinforcing, more powerful explanatory theories); his argument also exposes the impoverishment of the sophisticated Popperian requirement of prediction as a component of even a highly modified notion of falsifiability. Darwinian theory contrasts with implausible theories (creationism) or falsified ones (Lamarckianism). As Putnam argues, this scientific theory can be seen as a very successful, inductive "inference to the best explanation."

A Marxian explanation of racism might qualify as a similar inference. But Marxian explanation of racism might qualify as a similar inference. But Marxian theories are also somewhat more predictive than Darwin's (though less predictive, say, than those of modern astronomy). Marxian strategies, based on multiracial unity, could play and in fact have played (for instance in the 1930s) an important role in reform and revolutionary movements. These strategies project an important political and ethical picture of a movement for a more cooperative society which serves as a basis for action. Though political clashes are complex, cannot be predicted with precision, and always involve an element of daring and risk, such strategies are both a political and moral experiment and a kind of prediction; when successful, they contribute irreplaceably to bringing about the result. Further, Marxian theories plausibly explain many features of the historical situation (i.e., fierce repression, intensification of racism) that led to the ultimate defeat of such movements.[91] No one has yet advanced a telling liberal refutation to the view that a refined Marxian argument, under different circumstances, might have a powerful and desirable political and moral effect. In addition, Reich's study statistically predicts a continuing likelihood of racism in today's United States, with specific effects on income distribution and welfare, in the absence of such multiracial countermovements from below.

Thus, a methodological falsificationist might recognize a Marxian theory of racism (and the Marxian research program) as at least an important competitor for truth along with liberal research programs. On a realist view that reveals the arbitrariness of Popper's dismissal of rich explanatory theories, the claims of sophisticated Marxian arguments are even stronger.

6. CONCLUSION

A comparison of volume 1 of *Capital*, which Marx finished, with the relatively abstract discussion of commodities and money in *Contribution to a Critique of Political Economy* (1859) or the extensive but still general *Grundrisse* demonstrates how dramatically the rebirth of the working-class movement and the political consequences of the theory influenced Marx's actual writing of *Capital*. Echoing occasional complaints in Marx's letters, many scholars have argued that Marx's activity in the IWA hindered the development of his theory (Wolin's claim 1). According to David McLellan, "One of the main reasons why Volume One of *Capital* was so long in appearing and why the subsequent volumes never appeared at all is that Marx's time was taken up by the work forced on him as the leading figure in the International."[92] This view neglects the impetus to finish and publish *Capital* provided by the resurgence of the working class movement. Marx spent the twelve years (1852–1864) which preceded his activity in the IWA studying in the British Museum and writing newspaper articles. In that time, Marx produced the rough drafts for *Capital* and the minor 1859 *Contribution to a Critique*. From 1872 until 1883—another period of lessened political activity—Marx worked at but never finished the later volumes. A relatively calm, scholarly atmosphere did not inspire the completion of *Capital*.

Despite the emergence and reemergence of international working-class movements that Marx had foreseen (the IWA, the German and French socialist parties), the politics of capitalist domination and international ruling class cooperation checked the impact of capitalism's oppressive economic and political trends (including intercapitalist wars) in driving workers and their allies to successful revolution. Concurrently, Marx's theory envisioned revolution as an increasingly complex, though definite, *political* problem. In 1863, just prior to the founding of the IWA, Marx wrote to Engels in praise of the revolutionary youth, enthusiasm, and daring of *Condition of the Working Class in England*: "How freshly and passionately, with what bold anticipations and no learned and scientific doubts, the thing is still dealt with here! And the very illusion that the result will leap into the daylight of history tomorrow or the day after gives the whole thing a warmth . . . compared with which the later "gray [on] gray" makes a damned unpleasant contrast."[93]

This recognition of the increasing political difficulty of revolution reveals the grain of truth in Wolin's characterization of the changes in Marx's theory. But the same Marx celebrated and sought to further the "heavenstorming" of the women and men of the Commune. Wolin's theme treats Marx's later theory as an enervated Weberianism (Weber without the passionate devotion to great power politics, German nationalism and imperialism, and the maintenance of racial status distinctions): an alleged tragic acceptance of the hard facts of industrial life.[94] In Marx's terms, Wolin misinterpreted a powerful dialectical theory of the international movement for a more cooperative society against *apparent* odds as an elegy for unconquerable *alienation*. A productive-forces theory of the omnipotence of capital is simply not Marx's.

Despair was also not his temper. Looking to the abolition of the division of mental and manual work, Marx once wrote that he most admired the indomitable Spartacus, leader of the great Roman slave revolt, and Kepler, whose discoveries contributed to the downfall of the Ptolemaic celestial theory. Marx might have united them in an image of realistic revolutionary and scientific constancy. Toward the end of Marx's life, the English socialist H.M. Hyndman occasionally visited him. Though originally critical of England's colonial policies, Hyndman gradually came to favor a chauvinist socialism for Englishmen that would maintain the Empire, and looked on workers as incapable of political leadership. One day in Marx's study, he expressed his growing conservatism about class conflict: "I remarked [to Marx] that as I grow older, I become more tolerant." On Wolin's thesis, Marx might have amended Hyndman's comment to read "more *despairing*." Marx responded, "Do you? *Do* you?"[95]

NOTES

This paper adapts two sections of my "Social Theory and Revolutionary Activity in Marx," *The American Political Science Review,* **73** (June 1979) with the permission of the publisher. I would like to thank Marianne Gilbert, Syed Rifaat Hussain, and Lucy Rugh for helpful comments.

1. Mary Nolan, *Social Democracy and Society* (Cambridge: Cambridge University Press, 1981), pp. 246–247. V.I. Lenin, *Collected Works* (Moscow: Progress), 26:204, 28:112–113, 187.
2. Angelo Herndon, *Let Me Live* (New York: Harper & Row, 1937).
3. Noam Chomsky and Edward Hermann, *The Political Economy of Human Rights* (Boston: South End, 1979).
4. James R. Prickett, *Communists and the Communist Issue in the American Labor Movement, 1920–1950*. Ph.D. dissertation, UCLA, 1975.
5. Sheldon S. Wolin, "Editorial," *Democracy*, 1 (July 1981), p. 5.
6. George Lichtheim, *Marxism* (New York: Praegar, 1965), pp. 126–129. In a review of Alan Gilbert, *Marx's Politics: Communists and Citizens* (New Brunswick: Rutgers and Oxford: Martin Robertson, 1981), in the *Times Literary Supplement*, Feb. 5, 1982, David McLellan has endorsed Lichtheim's view.
7. Wherever relevant I cite page or section numbers from Wolin's chapter in the text.
8. Wolin, "Political Theory as a Vocation," in Martin Fleisher, ed., *Machiavelli and the Nature of Political Thought* (New York: Atheneum, 1972); "Paradigms and Political Theory," in B.C. Parekh and Preston King, eds., *Politics and Experience* (Cambridge: Cambridge University Press, 1968).
9. Gilbert, *Marx's Politics*, ch. 14.
10. Wolin mentions Marx's internationalism in passing, but does not see its significance.
11. Wolin notes that capitalism exacted an "appalling price" though Marx never claimed that the humanity of workers "was threatened with extinction" (§4, last par.) Wolin reinforces his reductionist argument by asserting that Marx's theory of "an impersonal unity of forces" conflicts with an analysis of the cruel "effects of alienation" (§12).
12. Alan Gilbert, "Historical Theory and the Structure of Moral Argument in Marx," *Political Theory*, 11 (May 1981); "An Ambiguity in Marx's and Engels's Account of Justice and Equality," *The American Political Science Review*, 76 (June 1982); Hilary Putnam, *Reason, Truth and History* (Cambridge: Cambridge University Press, 1981), pp. 171–173.
13. Marx alternately described the need for the dictatorship of the proletariat and the identification of surplus value as his chief discoveries. Marx and Engels, *Selected Correspondance* (Moscow: Progress, 1965), pp. 69, 192 (hereafter *SC*).
14. Wolin's argument reveals the confluence between Kuhnian and Marxian ethical relativism.
15. See Gilbert, *Marx's Politics*, for a detailed treatment.

16. G.W.F. Hegel, *The System of Ethical Life and First Philosophy of Spirit* (Albany: State University of New York, 1979), pp. 248–249.

17. The only post-1848 feature in Wolin's account is the image of the technician "step[ping] to the side" of production.

18. Gilbert, *Marx's Politics*, pp. 40–41, 134.

19. Ibid., ch. 11.

20. Marx, *Capital* (Moscow: Foreign Languages Publishing House, 1957–1962), 1:10.

21. Marx and Engels, *Selected Works* (New York: International, 1974), p. 183.

22. Marx, *Grundrisse* (New York: Vintage, 1973), p. 712.

23. Friedrich Engels, *Condition of the Working Class in England* (Stanford: Stanford University Press, 1968), pp. 243, 224, 246, 297, 259, 255–256 (hereafter *Condition*).

24. Marx and Engels, *SC*, p. 300; *Selected Works* (Moscow: Foreign Languages, 1962), 1:61–64 (hereafter *SW*).

25. Engels, *Condition*, pp. 258–259, 261.

26. Marx, *Poverty of Philosophy* (New York: International, 1963), pp. 172–175.

27. Marx and Engels, *SW*, 1:46, 65.

28. Ibid., 1:373–389. Henry Collins and Chimen Abramsky, *Karl Marx and the British Labor Movement* (London: Macmillan, 1965), pp. 61, 68–70.

29. Marx and Engels, *SW*, 1:47–48, 88–89. Marx, *Poverty of Philosophy* (New York: International, 1963), p. 51. Engels, *Condition*, p. 246.

30. Engels, *Condition*, pp. 246, 252.

31. David Ricardo, *The Principles of Political Economy and Taxation* (London: J.M. Dent, 1948), pp. 61–62.

32. Gilbert, *Marx's Politics*, chs. 1, 10, 11. Marx's analysis of the peasant response to Napoleon shows how a *specific* historical explanation (employing auxiliary statements) can lead to *general* strategic and theoretical conclusions; thus, Marx's explanation of the particular role of "Napoleonic ideas" pointed to the need for strong communist organizing for a worker-peasant alliance *"in all peasant countries."* In such cases, a different kind of interplay or dialectic between historical explanation and general theory exists in Marx than the one between the workers' real movement and the theory in *Capital*.

33. Marx and Engels, *SW*, 1:382, 442–443, 446.

34. Marx, *Capital*, 1:616.

35. Marx and Engels, *SW*, 1:446.

36. Gilbert, *Marx's Politics*, pp. 269–271.

37. Louis Althusser, *Lire le capital* (Paris: Maspero, 1965), 2:116–126.

38. Marx and Engels, *SW*, 1:37. Marx, *Capital*, 1:73–81, 621, 571.

39. For instance, other things being equal, if the rate of exploitation (s/v) increases more rapidly than the organic composition of capital (c/v), the rate of profit (s/c + v) will increase. Marx, *Capital*, 3:229.

40. General Council of the IWA, *Minutes* (London: Lawrence & Wishart, n.d.), 1:348. Marx, *Capital*, 1:644.

41. General Council, *Minutes*, 1:349. Marx, *Capital*, 1:640.

42. Marx, *Capital*, 1:233–234.

43. Ibid., 1:264, 233, 235, 299, 302.

44. Ibid., p. 301. Marx and Engels, *SW*, 1:384. Royden Harrison, *Before the Socialists* (London: Routledge & Kegan Paul, 1965), pp. 66, 64, 76–77.

45. Marx and Engels, *SW*, 1:382. Marx, *Capital*, 1:243–248. Marx and Engels, *SC*, pp. 188, 510.

46. Marx, *Capital*, 1:435–437, 417.

47. Marx and Engels, *Writings on the Paris Commune* (New York: Monthly Review Press, 1971), p. 72.

48. Marx and Engels, *SW*, 1:386.

49. Gilbert, "Marx on Internationalism and War," *Philosophy and Public Affairs*, 7 (Summer 1978).

50. Marx, *Capital*, 1:703.

51. Ibid., 1:616, no. 2. Gilbert, *Marx's Politics*, chs. 1–2.

52. Marx, *Capital*, 1:615.

53. Ibid., 1:654. Marx and Engels, *SW*, 1:379.

54. Marx, *Grundrisse*, p. 705.

55. Ibid., p. 711.

56. Chomsky and Hermann, op. cit. Calling for a cessation of demands for equality in the U.S., Huntington's "Democratic Distemper" asserts ominously: "Democracy will have a longer life if it has a more balanced existence." Samuel P. Huntington, Michel Crozier and Joji Watanuki, eds., *The Crisis of Democracy* (New York: New York University Press, 1975), p. 115.

57. Marx, *Capital*, 1:408–409.

58. Marx, *Grundrisse*, p. 705. Gilbert, "Historical Theory"; "Aristotle's Eudaemonism and Marx's Moral Realism" in Terence Ball and James Farr, eds., *After Marx* (Cambridge: Cambridge University Press, forthcoming).

59. Cohen, op. cit., ch. 11.

60. General Council, *Minutes*, 3:315.

61. H.J. Eysenck, *The IQ Argument* (New York: Library, 1971). Leon J. Kamin, *The Science and Politics of IQ* (New York: John Wiley, 1974).

62. See Aristotle, *Nichomachean Ethics*, bk. 1. In the U.S., Army adver-

tisements counsel unemployed teenagers to "Be *All* That You Can Be."

63. Marx, *Grundrisse*, p. 706.
64. Gilbert, *Marx's Politics*, ch. 2. Marx and Engels, *SC*, pp. 231–232.
65. General Council, *Minutes*, 3:183, 192–194, 458–461. Marx and Engels, *Werke* (Berlin: Dietz, 1959), 32:381, 700; *Ireland and the Irish Question* (New York: International, 1975), pp. 306–308. Jon Elster confuses Marx's emphasis on extending actual examples of working class unity with the hypothesizing of merely imagined tendencies, Elster, "Marxismo," *London Review of Books*, March 18–31, 1982.
66. Marx and Engels, *On the Paris Commune*, pp. 153, 73. Gilbert, "Historical Theory," pp. 185–190.
67. Marx and Engels, *On the Paris Commune*, pp. 154–155. Marx, *Capital*, 1:764.
68. Marx's *Critique of the Gotha Program* stressed the need for radical organizing in unions, a worker-peasant alliance, internationalism and a revolutionary dictatorship of the proletariat. On these points, Lenin's politics—in contrast to those of German Social Democracy—resembled Marx's.
69. Imré Lakatos, "Falsification and the Methodology of Scientific Research Programmes," in Lakatos and Alan Musgrave, eds., *Criticism and the Growth of Knowledge* (Cambridge: Cambridge University Press, 1970), pp. 175–176. For a crude version of this objection, see Elster, op. cit.
70. Gilbert, "Historical Theory."
71. Karl R. Popper, *Conjectures and Refutations* (New York: Harper & Row, 1965), p. 370.
72. Max Weber, *Economy and Society* (New York: Bedminister, 1968), 1:304, 391. Gilbert, "Social Science and the Common Good in Weber and Lenin," *ASPA Proceedings* (Ann Arbor: University Microfilms, 1981), pp. 37–49. Michael Reich, *Racial Inequality: A Political-Economic Analysis* (Princeton: Princeton University Press, 1981), ch. 3.
73. Franz Neumann, *Behemoth* (New York: Harper & Row, 1963), pp. 20–23. R. Palme Dutt, *Fascism and Social Revolution* (San Francisco: Proletarian Publishers, n.d.), chs. v–vii. Allen W. Trelease, *White Terror: The KKK Conspiracy and Southern Reconstruction* (New York: Harper & Row, 1971).
74. Stephan L. Chorover, *From Genesis to Genocide* (Cambridge, Mass.: MIT Press, 1979). Kamin, op. cit. Garland E. Allen, "Genetics, Eugenics and Class Struggle," *Genetics* (1975).
75. George L. Mosse, *The Crisis of German Ideology* (New York: Grosset & Dunlap, 1964), p. 99. Kamin, op. cit., chs. 1–2.

76. Cited in Kamin, op. cit., p. 8.
77. Karl Dietrich Bracher, *The German Dictatorship* (New York: Praeger, 1970).
78. Chorover, op. cit., p. 98. Hans F.K. Günther, *The Racial Elements of European History* (London, 1927), pp. 244–245.
79. Chorover, op. cit., pp. 98–103. Putnam, op. cit., p. 141.
80. Alexander Gerschenkron, *Bread and Democracy in Germany* (Berkeley: University of California, 1943).
81. Otto Friedrich, *Before the Deluge* (New York: Harper & Row, 1972), pp. 201–203.
82. Engels, *Anti-Dühring* (New York: International, 1966), p. 123.
83. See Stephen Gould, *The Mismeasure of Man* (New York, 1981) on craniometry.
84. Reich, op. cit., chs. 4, 7.
85. C. Vann Woodward, *Tom Watson* (New York: Macmillan, 1938), pp. 219–222.
86. Reich, op. cit., p. 311. Kamin, op. cit.
87. Lakatos, op. cit., pp. 153, 167.
88. William Patterson, *We Charge Genocide* (New York: International, 1970).
89. Richard Boyd, "What's Wrong with Prejudice, Methodologically Speaking?" unpublished, Department of Philosophy, Cornell University, 1980.
90. Jacques Monod, "On the Molecular Theory of Evolution" in Romano Harré, ed., *Problems of Scientific Revolutions* (Oxford: Clarendon, 1975), p. 14. Putnam, op. cit., pp. 109, 197–199.
91. Gilbert, *Marx's Politics*, ch. 1.
92. David McLellan, *Karl Marx* (New York: Harper & Row, 1973), p. 360.
93. Marx and Engels, *SC*, pp. 140–141.
94. Marx and Engels, *On the Paris Commune*, pp. 221–222. Gilbert, "Weber and Lenin."
95. McLellan, op. cit., pp. 456–457. Isaiah Berlin, *Karl Marx* (New York: Oxford, 1959), p. 256. Yvonne Kapp, *Eleanor Marx* (New York: International, 1972), 1:209–212.

PART III

MARXISM AND THE LAW

7

IS THERE A MARXIST THEORY OF LAW?

MARK TUSHNET

Ordinarily one would not think that there was much to say on the topic of whether there was a Marxist theory of law. Of course there is. Many people who say that they are Marxists offer us theories of law. But the topic deserves more extended treatment precisely because much of what is offered as Marxist theory of law is patently defective. I want to set two conditions for a Marxist theory of law and explore whether they can be satisfied. To be a Marxist theory of law, a theory must be (a) distinctively Marxist, and (b) a good theory. As I will suggest, much of what is offered as Marxist theory of law satisfies one but not the other condition.

I intend to address the topic by exploring the related question, "What would be the minimum content of a Marxist theory of law?"[1] I divide this into two parts. First, what is the subject of a Marxist theory of law? That is, does it concern the sociological explanation or the normative critique of something like the Sherman Antitrust Act of 1890, or the explanation or critique of "bourgeois law," or something else? Second, what is the minimum substantive content of a Marxist theory of law? That is, must it specify exactly how, for example, the class struggle is reflected in or generates a critique of some item in its subject matter?

Before beginning the exploration, I offer three caveats. First, the theory of which I speak is, in economists' terms, grossly underspecified at present. In my view, the most that one can ask of this kind of theory is that, like scientific theories, it set out a nondegenerating program.[2] Second, although I will do a fair amount of definitional inquiry, I intend to take "law" as an undefined term. I am willing to confine the theory to what Weber called "state law," or, even better, to our vague shared sense of what "law" is.[3] Third, I will avoid exegetical exercises, partly out of personal preference, partly because the texts make exegesis futile,[4] and partly for reasons that I present in the conclusion.

I. THE SUBJECT MATTER

In considering the subject matter of a Marxist theory of law, I address two issues. First, is the theory "sociological/historical" or "normative?" Second, does it deal with the analysis of specific items such as statutes and individual cases, with tort law or contract law, or with bourgeois law or feudal law? I anticipate my conclusion by saying that a Marxist theory of law is a sociology of law at a relatively high level of abstraction.

It is now I think rather generally accepted that one cannot readily distinguish within the Marxist tradition between Marxism as a sociological/historical theory and Marxism as a normative critique of capitalism.[5] We are faced on the one hand with repeated claims that Marxism is a scientific theory rather than utopian, and on the other with the powerfully critical tone of Marx's own writing. Yet surely the weight of tradition falls on the assertedly scientific side, and I believe that it is more fruitful to begin by assuming that a Marxist theory must be sociological, that the normative critique will be immanent in the theory, and that the obvious fact/value problems can be deferred to another forum or author. But serious problems inhere in the idea of a Marxist sociology of law.

A. THE UNIT OF ANALYSIS

I want to approach those problems by analyzing the second issue as to subject matter. Roughly, that issue involves deciding what are the units of analysis—in terms that I ultimately will reject but that serve to locate the issue, the dependent variables—of a Marxist theory of law? The candidates can usefully be ranked by their apparent relative concreteness. For the sake of convenience I will speak of cases and doctrine as the units, though the analysis is, I think, general. Thus, at the most concrete level, we have individual cases like *Hadley v. Baxendale,* and a Marxist theory of law would try to explain why the case was decided as it was.[6] Or a Marxist theory of law could be concerned with the law of expectation damages or of contracts in England in the mid-nineteenth century, or with the law of England at that time, or, ultimately, with feudal, capitalist, and socialist law. I contend that a Marxist theory of law should be concerned with units of the sort described by the next to last of these candidates, English law of the mid-nineteenth century, but I will argue indirectly, by mounting the Legal Realist critique of any units less concrete than individual cases. That critique poses real obstacles to talk about "the law of X" as distinguished from talk about "cases A, B, and C."

We have to begin with what is now called formalism, the legal theory against which Realism reacted. According to formalists, a legal system has two essential elements, a stock of precedents, rules, principles, and so on, and a repertoire of techniques by which items drawn from the stock are combined and manipulated. Formalism claimed that given the stock at a particular time, the techniques restricted the possible outcomes of a new case to one correct decision. The Realist critique demonstrated, conclusively I believe, that because formalism lacked a criterion for correctness,[7] it was mistaken in its claims. But this, in ways that contemporary legal scholars only occasionally acknowledge, seriously undermines any generalizing effort. The Realist critique proceeded in two ways. First, it asked the formalists to produce a case that satisfied their requirements. The critique then demonstrated that a talented lawyer, drawing on the same stock of precedents and repertoire of techniques that the formalists did, could justify an exactly opposite decision. Second, the Realists examined the universe of decided cases and noted the existence of what the formalists had to call minority rules and of contradictory principles. The Realists wondered how this mass of material could be assembled into a single body called "the law of X."[8] What there was, they claimed, was just the accumulation of individual cases. Exemplary Realist works are Corbin's treatise on contracts, which insisted on the relevance of the most minute variations in factual settings even as it tried to discern patterns in the decisions, and Kessler and Sharp's casebook on contracts, which is structured around the contradictory principles of contract law.[9]

Legal Realism, taken as a jurisprudence of rules, argued that one could not determine the proper outcome of a case from the materials traditionally thought of as part of the legal system. It did not rule out the possibility of a sociology of individual cases, but it made it impossible to have a sociology of contract or tort law. Legal Realism denied that traditional legal categories defined coherent entities that could be subjected to unified analysis. There were too many "minority" rules, "exceptions" to the general principles, and so on. Again, however, that the bodies of law have no coherence does no more than require a shift in sociological concern from the content of the categories to the structure of and relations among the categories themselves. The basic point is that even though sophisticated legal scholars can demonstrate that no rule or case can be inserted uniquely into a category like "contract law," in fact lawyers and judges do that classifying daily. The question for the sociology of law and so for a Marxist theory of law is, "Why do those people think that that rule fits into that category and not into another?"

Again I offer some examples. The first is the recent collapse of the categories of contract and tort into what Grant Gilmore calls "a generalized theory of obligation."[10] The second involves the law of industrial accidents. In the mid-nineteenth century it was part of the law of torts. With the rise of workers' compensation schemes, the law of industrial accidents was gradually extruded from the law of torts into the law of social insurance or protective labor legislation, where it was associated not with intentional torts or automobile accidents but with social security, the wage and hour laws, and pension laws. The evolution is of course not complete, for as those who think about the category "torts" come to worry about automobile liability insurance and no-fault compensation, the workers' compensation analogy wiggles its way back into "tort law."

Finally, my third example illustrates the proposition that the relevant question is why certain categories and not others are used. In 1842 the fellow servant rule entered American law when Chief Justice Lemuel Shaw wrote for the Massachusetts Supreme Judicial Court that an employee could not recover from his employer for injuries that had been caused by the negligence of another employee.[11] Shaw defended his result by invoking principles of contract law and tort law. The employee, knowing now that recovery in the case of injury was impossible, could insist on higher pay from employers who hired careless coworkers. In addition, the risk of uncompensated injury would make all employees alert to each others' actions, thus policing the workplace in the name of safety more effectively than the employer could by managerial supervision.

When fellow servant cases arose in the slave South, something interesting happened. The contract and tort rationales become inconsistent, and they were split apart. The North Carolina court relied solely on the contract rationale in adopting the fellow servant rule in a slave case.[12] The suit was solely for the owner's benefit, and the owner could either insure the slave or insist that the rental price include a risk premium. The tort rationale relied on the employee's ability to communicate with the employer about careless coworkers, but, especially where the coworker was white, this was troublesome. In Georgia the court indignantly rejected the contract rationale.[13] Slaves could not leave the employer or alert him to other workers' misconduct; if the fellow servant rule were adopted, "the life of no *hired* slave would be safe."

I have tried to analyze these fellow servant cases elsewhere,[14] and use the example only to show that the way people employ categories, rather than the content they give them, may be an appropriate subject of sociological inquiry. The effect of taking categories as subject matter, however, is to expand the investigation to the law of some geographic area at a particular time. I appreciate that the Legal Realist critique could be levelled against statements about the structure of the categories of legal thought in, say, the slave South. I think the only defense presently available is empirical: though there have been few examinations of such structures, at least few informed by the Legal Realist critique of rules, they seem to have identified relatively stable structures enduring over relatively long periods. And, of course, a full-scale Legal Realist critique would lead to the conclusion, which I think indefensible, that there are no differences between the law of England in 1850 and in 1980.

I have so far identified as potential subject matters of a Marxist theory of law individual cases and structures of legal categories. The second of these might be expanded so that the relevant subject matter was "bourgeois law," defined as the fundamental legal categories that distinguish capitalist from feudal or socialist systems. But that expansion is intuitively implausible and, as I will argue in the next subsection, analytically troublesome. It is implausible because the category would have to identify a thread common to the English law of 1850, American law of 1900, and Japanese law of 1980, and that thread seems unlikely to exist.

B. THE PROBLEM OF LEGAL SOCIOLOGY

The Legal Realist critique of legal rules generates a parallel critique of sociological laws, and, indeed, of generalization regarding social knowledge. I find that line of criticism quite powerful, and so should emphasize at the outset of this subsection that, despite the critique, I believe that we do have social knowledge and that a sociology of law is possible. But I leave to another place the epistemological reconstruction that I think necessary in the face of Legal Realism.

Can we have a sociology of individual cases? Presumably this sociology would take the form of general principles that, when applied to specific circumstances, would explain why a case was decided as it was. In some contexts that form of explanation is called the covering law model of explanation,[15] and it is precisely on the notion of "law" that the Legal Realist critique focuses. I note, however, that the problems that I will discuss arise with whatever version of positivism one chooses. Again, the Realist says that if general principle is to be meaningful, all the circumstances have to be built into the principles at the outset. The two elements, principle and initial conditions, then collapse into one and the law that is said to cover the specific instance becomes indistinguishable from it.[16] I find it helpful to illustrate this point with an example drawn from some historical controversies. Some years ago Robert Fogel examined the contribution that railroads had made to economic development in the nineteenth-century United States.[17] He proceeded in the counterfactual way that the covering law model implies, by supposing that there had been no railroads and by analyzing the costs and benefits of alternative modes of transportation such as canals or postroads. The difficulty with this procedure is suggested by another classic work on nineteenth-century railroads, Leo Marx's *The Machine in the Garden*.[18] Marx examines a painting of a pastoral scene, through which a railroad is peacefully passing, as part of his exploration of the cultural significance of technological change. The point is that we cannot simply imagine a world from which railroads, seen solely as modes of transportation, have been removed. Remove them and you take away an aspect of the way men and women thought about the relation between themselves and the natural environment, with unknowable effects on incentives to work and save and therefore with undeterminable effects on gross national product.

In the historical example, the counterfactual that guides the explanation must therefore be comprehensive: what would things have been like if everything had been different? But that surely is a meaningless question. Before abandoning the quest for a sociology of individual cases, though, I note the possibility that such a sociology might consist not of general principles but of a checklist of things to be sure to think about, perhaps ranked according to some presumptions regarding their likely role, when attempting to explain an individual case.

As I have indicated, the Realist critique of sociology, which collapses general rules into particular instances, applies to all generalization. That is the difficulty with the suggestion that the subject of a Marxist theory of law ought to be "bourgeois, feudal, and socialist" law. At least at first glance, it is hard to see how we could identify "bourgeois" law as something to be explained, without using the very concepts that are at issue. The crude definition of capitalism as private ownership in the means of production, for example, uses the terms "private" and "ownership," both of which are legal concepts, that the sociology of bourgeois law is supposed to explain. This difficulty may perhaps be resolved along the lines that G.A. Cohen has laid out,[19] but it is sufficiently troublesome to make me want to retreat to the intermediate but still fairly abstract level on which we talk about structures of legal categories. As before, my defense against the Realist critique of generalization as applied to that level is empirical and intuitive: scholars who work on that level seem to have social knowledge of a sort that is unavailable at either higher or lower levels.

I end this discussion of the subject matter of a Marxist theory of law, then, with a sociology on a fairly abstract level. The Legal Realist critique, in my judgment, destroys the analytic basis for any other subject matter, and it places even the one that I end with under severe pressure.

II. THE MINIMUM SUBSTANTIVE CONTENT

If I have some uncertainty about the subject matter of a Marxist theory of law, I have even more uncertainty about its substantive content. Here I must say why my uncertainty cannot be resolved by examining what people offer as their versions of Marxist legal theory. Andrei Vyshinsky, Richard Quinney, E.P. Thompson, and Nicos Poulantzas[20] all present such theories, which indicates what the trouble is. If Vyshinsky and Quinney have given us what ought to be regarded as the canonical Marxist theory of law, the theory would deserve attention only by intellectual historians, not by sociologists of law, for their theories are uninteresting and wrong. Thus one of my initial conditions is not satisfied by these works. Conversely, I have cited Thompson and Poulantzas to suggest that their works may fail to satisfy the other condition, that a Marxist theory be distinctively Marxist. It may be, then, that to the degree that a theory is distinctively Marxist, it is not a good theory, and conversely.

This section begins with a brief exercise in exegesis, which demonstrates to my satisfaction that Marx's writings provide the basis for Marxist theories of law that range from strict economic determinism to something just short of the autonomy that liberal theories of law give their subject matter. I follow the exegetical exercise with an analytic one, which attempts to show that the Marxist theories of individual cases are empirically implausible, as are such theories of "bourgeois" law. The section concludes with a modest sketch of what a Marxist theory on the intermediate level would look like.

A. EXEGESIS

Recent controversies in Marxist theory have centered on the validity of a strictly determinist model in which relations of production are the "base" upon which various elements of the "superstructure," including law, are erected. Until G.A. Cohen's *Karl Marx's Theory of History*[21] appeared, the "base/superstructure" model seemed to have been destroyed on analytic grounds. It now seems that the attack must come from where it probably should have come in the first place, from the challenge of the facts. Before discussing the implications of Cohen's analysis, however, I will show that the controversies cannot be resolved by claims of true descent from Marx. Rather, the Marxist texts, from both before and after 1848,[22] support theories of determinism and of great autonomy of the so-called superstructure.[23]

The German Ideology of 1845–1846 contains both determinist and autonomist passages. At one point, for example, Marx and Engels discuss the state as "the form in which the individuals of a ruling class assert their common interests:"

Civil law develops simultaneously with private property out of the disintegration of the natural community. With the Romans the development of private property and civil law had no further industrial and commercial consequences, because their whole mode of production did not alter. With modern people, where the feudal community was disintegrated by industry and trade, there began with the rise of private property and civil law a new phase, which was capable of further development. The very first town which carried on an extensive maritime trade in the Middle Ages, Amalfi, also developed maritime law. As soon as industry and trade developed private property further, first in Italy and later in other countries, the highly developed Roman

civil law was immediately adopted again and raised to authority. . . .

Then, after providing further examples, from France and England, Marx and Engels continue: "Whenever, through the development of industry and commerce, new forms of intercourse have been evolved (e.g., insurance companies, etc.), the
law has always been compelled to admit them among the modes
of acquiring property."[24] Later, however, they discuss the "independent existence" of legal relations: "The hitherto existing
production relations of individuals are bound also to be expressed as political and legal relations. Within the division of
labour these relations are bound to acquire an independent existence over against the individuals."[25]

The post-1848 versions are familiar. The *Preface to a Contribution to the Critique of Political Economy* provides the base/
superstructure model that Cohen defends:

> In the social production of their life, men enter into defi-
> nite relations that are indispensable and independent of
> their will, relations of production which correspond to a
> definite stage of development of their material productive
> forces. The sum total of these relations of production con-
> stitutes the economic structure of society, the real founda-
> tion, on which rises a legal and political superstructure and
> to which correspond definite forms of social consciousness.
> The mode of production of material life conditions the so-
> cial, political and intellectual life process in general. It is
> not the consciousness of men that determines their being,
> but, on the contrary, their social being that determines their
> consciousness.[26]

And finally, Engels' famous letters to Bloch and Schmidt:

> The economic situation is the basis, but the various ele-
> ments of the superstructure . . . also exercise their influ-
> ence upon the course of the historical struggles and in many
> cases determine their *form* in particular. There is an inter-
> action of all these elements in which, amid all the endless
> host of accidents (that is, of things and events whose inner

interconnection is so remote or so impossible of proof that we can regard it as nonexistent and neglect it), the economic movement is finally bound to assert itself. . . .

As soon as the new division of labor which creates professional lawyers becomes necessary, another new and independent sphere is opened up which, for all its general dependence on production and trade, has also a specific capacity for reacting upon these spheres. In a modern state, law must not only correspond to the general economic condition and be its expression, but must also be an *internally coherent* expression which does not, owing to internal conflicts, contradict itself. And in order to achieve this, the faithful reflection of economic conditions suffers increasingly. . . . To a great extent the course of the "development of law" simply consists in first attempting to eliminate contradictions which arise from the direct translation of economic relations into legal principles, and to establish a harmonious system of law, and then in the repeated breaches made in this system by the influence and compulsion of further economic development, which involves it in further contradictions. (I am speaking here for the moment only of civil law.)

The reflection of economic relations in the form of legal principles is likewise bound to be inverted: it goes on without the person who is acting being conscious of it; the jurist imagines he is operating with *a priori* propositions, whereas they are really only economic reflections; everything is therefore upside down. And it seems to me obvious that this inversion, which, so long as it remains unrecognized, forms what we call *ideological outlook,* influences in its turn the economic basis and may, within certain limits, modify it. The basis of the right of inheritance is an economic one, provided the level of development of the family is the same. It would, nevertheless, be difficult to prove, for instance, that the absolute liberty of the testator in England and the severe and very detailed restrictions imposed upon him in France are due to economic causes alone. But in their turn they exert a very considerable effect on the economic sphere, because they influence the distribution of property.[27]

A person interested in defending either the model of relative autonomy or that of base and superstructure would, I think, have little difficulty in reconciling these apparently conflicting statements.[28] The question of pedigree is in general indeterminate. There is, though, one important qualification. In every version of the model of relative autonomy, Marx and Engels insist on the importance of "the division of labor," the "economic movement," and similar phrases—what has come to be called the role of the relations of production "in the last instance." What exactly is "the last instance" has always been, and remains, a mystery to me, but it seems clear that a sociology of law that allowed one to omit reference to the relations of production could not fairly claim to be a Marxist theory of law.

B. ANALYSIS

One immediate consequence of the exegetical exercise is that it probably rules out individual cases as the subject matter of a Marxist theory of law. As Engels suggested, individual cases that can frequently be accounted for without reference to the relations of production. The texts presented above indicate that the outcomes in individual cases might be analyzed as the result of class struggle in a specific context, but that is so implausible that we should put aside individual cases as the units of analysis.

The large abstractions such as "bourgeois law" fare no better. Here I return to G.A. Cohen, who has carefully worked his way around the problem that the economic base appears to be defined in property terms drawn from the superstructure. Cohen's solution is to replace property terms with terms involving the direct exercise of physical force over a material object.[29] This generates a program in which legal terms are systematically replaced. I leave to the philosophers questions about the coherence of Cohen's solution.

My own concerns lie with the possibility of executing Cohen's program. He asserts that "it will generate the appropriate results quite generally."[30] My skepticism takes two forms. First, it seems to me extremely unlikely that the program's execution can be carried on to the level of the large abstractions. If the program works it generates statements that escape tautology because of their functional character. Yet I am unsure of the coherence of functional explanation even after Cohen's defense of it. The second form of my skepticism arises from the examples Cohen uses. He offers six examples of "explanations of property relations and law by production relations."[31] One involves the English Statute of Artificers of 1563, which prevented entry of commoners into the clothing industry. Cohen writes, "It was not conducive to the development of early manufacture, and was widely abused, sometimes with the legal authorities turning a blind eye. Finally, in 1694, the offending clause was repealed, and 'this allowed a proletariat of textile workers to exist *de jure* as well as *de facto.*' "[32] The Legal Realist could not accept so truncated a story, and would insist on all the detail available on the genesis of the 1694 repeal. Although I am unfamiliar with the period in question, my acquaintance with the origins of other statutes makes me confident that when the details accumulate the simple functional account will be implausible. All six of Cohen's examples are on the level of individual cases and rely on a reified concept of what "law" is that the Legal Realist critique has made untenable. If someone as sophisticated as Cohen slips in this manner, we have little reason to be confident that his program can indeed be executed.

It may seem that I have continued to discuss the question of appropriate units of analysis rather than the minimal substantive content of a Marxist theory of law. But the two issues are connected, as the metaphor of "the last instance" shows. It is a commonplace that Marxist theories make the relations of production determinative in the last instance. Yet such a claim is completely implausible on the level of individual cases, and it appears to be tautologous on the level of the large abstractions. Thus, if a Marxist theory of law has a minimum substantive content that refers to relations of production, it will have to be concerned with the intermediate level of structures of legal categories. But what does it mean to say that the relations of production determine those structures in the last instance?[33]

I think it is fair to say that those working within the Marxist

tradition have done little to clarify the concept of "the last instance." One needs only to compare what Althusser has to say
about it with E.P. Thompson's polemical response to see that,[34]
yet there does seem to be something to the idea. In order to
get a handle on the problem, I want to report a personal, possibly idiosyncratic esthetic experience. When I read Althusser
or Poulantzas it takes me about ten pages to be swept into their
system, after which statements on an absurdly high level of abstraction seem to make sense. Yet when I put the book down I
find it exceedingly hard to restate the points that seemed to
make sense a while before, in terms that seem to make sense
now. For whatever reasons, that is, I respond to their presen-
tations as I do to a Morris Louis painting. Similarly, I suggest,
"the last instance" is a metaphor whose function is esthetic rather
than analytic. But if that is its function, all depends on the execution: if *I* let paint flow down on canvas, the product would
not, I am confident, have the impact of a Morris Louis.

This approach, of course, comes close to stripping a Marxist
theory of law of any minimal substantive content. I can come
at the point in a slightly different way. Sometimes "the last instance" is taken to mean this: if you give me a problem to explain in Marxist terms, I can begin by talking about culture,
tradition, partisan politics, what the judge ate for breakfast,
whatever. But after all that is said, if I have not mentioned the
relations of production, my explanation is very likely to be incomplete. Not much is left of a strict sense of "determination"
here, but at least "the relations of production" survive as an
essential element of an explanation. Yet it is now unclear what
is distinctively Marxist about the theory. Liberal sociology would
be entirely comfortable with this checklist approach, especially
if the escape hatch of my "very likely" is left open. I suppose
that we might try to preserve some distinctiveness to a Marxist
theory by asserting that, as a research strategy, it makes sense
to begin our explanations by invoking the relations of production, using other variables to explain what would be treated as
the residuum.[35] For myself, I am comfortable with such an ane-
mic reconstruction of a Marxist theory of law, but it seems so
close to liberal sociology that it now makes sense to ask what
purpose there is in characterizing one's work, as I do my own,
as Marxist.[36]

III. CONCLUSION

If the theory of law that I have described has such an ill-defined subject matter and not much that is distinctively Marxist about it, is there any reason to call it a Marxist theory? I offer three reasons. The first will appeal to others more than it does to me: the effort to produce a sociological theory that is both good and distinctively Marxist may be thought to have failed, but negative results, while rarely reported, are nonetheless important. However, I hope it is clear that I do not think that the result is entirely negative. Second, calling the theory Marxist is a statement of affiliation with an international tradition of struggle for liberation, in which the upheavals in Poland, for example, are seen not only as the herald of the breakdown of Soviet domination, though one hopes they are that too, but also as the struggles of our comrades.

Third, and perhaps more important, calling the theory Marxist emphasizes its political distance from liberalism. For reasons I have discussed elsewhere, I prefer to use a religious metaphor here. Both Marxism and liberalism have known sin. For Marxism the experience was the Gulag and all that it symbolizes. For liberalism the knowledge of sin came in some versions with fascism, against which liberalism could erect no credible defenses, and in other versions with the persistent inequalities of wealth and power in liberal societies, which liberalism had suggested were both improper and destabilizing. Liberals who have known sin have taken two paths, both of which abandon the critical thrust of liberalism. Now, as "neo-conservatives," some celebrate inequality and ground it in the genes. Others merely regard inequality as inevitable and sit as dispassionate observers of the social scene.[37] Like some Christians, Marxists have known sin and still retain their vision that society can be better than it is. That is, I think, worth holding on to. Calling a position Marxist, even though in analytic terms the position is not far from liberalism, is one way of doing so. That, for me, is the contemporary significance of the slogan Gramsci took as his own: "Pessimism of the intelligence, optimism of the will."

NOTES

1. This can be analogized to the question, "what is the family resemblance among those things labelled Marxist theory of law?" The analogy is weakened, however, by my conclusion that most such theories use the wrong units of analysis.
2. See Imre Lakatos, "Falsification and the Methodology of Scientific Research Programmes," in *The Methodology of Scientific Research Programmes* (Cambridge: Cambridge University Press, 1978), pp. 8–101.
3. I suspect, however, (a) that were I to try to define "law" more precisely, I would have to face the general expansionist pressure that appears in section I as I try to define other terms, and (b) that the theory's substantive content would not change much if its subject matter were thus transformed from "law" into something like "culture" under that pressure.
4. See section IIA below.
5. A useful collection is Marshall Cohen, Thomas Nagel, and Thomas Scanlon, eds., *Marx, Justice and History* (Princeton: Princeton University Press, 1980). See also Gary Young, "Justice and Capitalist Production: Marx and Bourgeois Ideology," *Canadian Journal of Philosophy,* VII:3 (Sept. 1978), pp. 421–455.
6. Cf. Richard Danzig, "Hadley v. Baxendale: A Study in the Industralization of the Law," *Journal of Legal Studies,* 4 (June 1975) p. 249.
7. Of course the formalists did have a criterion of correctness. For political reasons they wanted to limit lawmaking discretion, but their theory, which itself rested on a distinction between law and politics, could not incorporate that political ground. See generally Duncan Kennedy, "The Rise and Fall of Classical Legal Thought," unpublished manuscript, 1975.
8. George Priest and others have grappled with this problem but have not solved it. See, e.g., George Priest, "The Common Law Process and the Selection of Efficient Rules," *Journal of Legal Studies,* vol. 6 (Jan. 1977), pp. 65–82; George Priest, "Selective Characteristics of Litigation," *Journal of Legal Studies,* vol. 9 (March 1980) pp. 399–421.
9. Arthur L. Corbin, *Corbin on Contracts: A Comprehensive Treatise on the Rules of Contract Law* (St. Paul: West Publishing Co., 1950); Friedrich Kessler & Malcolm Sharp, *Contracts: Cases and Materials* (New York: Prentice-Hall, 1953).
10. Grant Gilmore, *The Death of Contract* (Columbus, Ohio: Ohio State University Press, 1974), p. 94.
11. *Farwell v. Boston & Worcester R. Co.,* 45 Mass. (4 Metc.) 49 (1842).

12. *Ponton v. Wilmington & Weldon R. Co.*, 51 N.C. (6 Jones) 245 (1848).
13. *Scudder v. Woodbridge*, 1 Ga. 195 (1846).
14. Mark Tushnet, *The American Law of Slavery, 1810–1816* (Princeton: Princeton University Press, 1981), ch. IV.
15. See Carl Hempel, "Explanation in Science and History," in *Frontiers of Science and Philosophy*, R.G. Colodny, ed. (Pittsburgh: University of Pittsburgh Press, 1962).
16. This is what is sensible in the caricature of Legal Realism as explaining decisions on the basis of what the judge ate for breakfast.
17. Robert Fogel, *Railroads and Economic Growth* (Baltimore: John Hopkins University Press, 1964).
18. Leo Marx, *The Machine in the Garden* (New York: Oxford University Press, 1964).
19. G.A. Cohen, *Karl Marx's Theory of History* (Princeton: Princeton University Press, 1979), and section IIB below.
20. Andrei Vyshinsky, "The Fundamental Tasks of the Science of Soviet Socialist Law," in H. Babb, ed., *Soviet Legal Philosophy* (Cambridge: Harvard University Press, 1951); Richard Quinney, *Critique of Legal Order* (Boston: Little, Brown, 1974); E.P. Thompson, *Whigs and Hunters* (New York: Pantheon, 1975); Nicos Poulantzas, *Political Power and Social Classes* (London: New Left Books, 1973).
21. See note 19 above.
22. I make this point because of the emphasis in recent work on Althusser's claim that Marx's thought underwent a major change in 1848. See Louis Althusser, *For Marx* (London: Penguin Press, 1969).
23. A more complete defense of this conclusion emerges from a reading of Maureen Cain and Alan Hunt, *Marx and Engels on Law* (London: Academic Press, 1979), which collects the scattered writings on the subject.
24. Ibid., pp. 53–54.
25. Ibid., p. 61.
26. Ibid., p. 52.
27. Ibid., pp. 56–57.
28. I note, though only as an aside, the implication of the letter to Schmidt that a Marxist theory of law cannot be a sociology of individual cases.
29. Cohen, *Karl Marx's Theory of History*, pp. 217–222.
30. Ibid., p. 223.
31. Ibid., pp. 225–229.
32. Ibid., p. 227.
33. Cohen's functionalism does make this coherent at the higher level of abstraction.
34. Louis Althusser and Etienne Balibar, *Reading Capital* (London: New

Left Books, 1970); E.P. Thompson, *The Poverty of Theory* (London: Merlin Press, 1978).

35. Again this shows the inadequacy of a Marxist theory of individual cases, for there it seems quite likely that "the relations of production" will be the residual variable and that the Marxist research strategy will misdirect energy. For what it is worth, I have come to think that my book on the law of slavery (see note 14 above) does what can be done along the lines I pursue in this paper.

36. An alternative view of Marx's work is that it continues a tradition of total criticism of a society. That tradition, in some ways captured in Hegel's statement that the truth is the whole, insists that we can understand any phenomenon only by understanding the entire society and culture in which the phenomenon occurs. Here the exemplary Marxist text is *The Eighteenth Brumaire of Napoleon Bonaparte*. Of course, on this view there is nothing distinctively Marxist about Marx's own work.

37. It is not impossible, I think, to find this strand of contemporary liberal thought in Lipson's chapter in this volume. This strand no longer takes seriously what used to be at the center of the liberal enterprise, the effort to understand our world.

8

IS THERE A MARXIST THEORY OF LAW? COMMENTS ON TUSHNET

LEON LIPSON

From Mr. Tushnet's paper it is not easy to tell whether he thinks he is moving toward or away from a Marxist theory of law, but it does seem that his reasons for moving are, in his opinion, Marxist reasons. I should like to take up some of the issues that he candidly eludes and then return to consideration of his paper.

I

To me the most fundamental characteristic of a Marxist theory of law is that it purports to look at law from outside law, to disdain the immanent jurisprudence, to relate law to something else that is regarded as being logically or dynamically prior to law. This holds, no matter whether the Marxist is looking at law critically or apologetically; that difference of angle does matter, as I shall try to show soon, for other parts of the subject.

The two main platforms from which the Marxist has looked at law are those of politics and economics. Which of them takes precedence—that is, which comes first "in the last analysis"— has been given various answers in both theory and practice by Marx, Engels, and Marxists, as Mr. Tushnet says. The concept

that for a Marxist reconciles or obviates the conflicting claims
of politics and economics is that of class, for in politics the state
is the executive committee of the ruling class while in economics it is the same class that has been thrown up by the development of relationships of production out of the interaction of
productive forces. The law, by factual coercion and (in non-
Marxist states) ideological mystification, consolidates the predominance of the class that rules the state and even prolongs
that predominance a little, though not forever, past the time
when the changing productive forces have made historically
necessary a change in the relations of production and therewith
a change in class relations.

Mr. Tushnet, like many before him, notes those passages in
the writings of the founders that own the force of *Rückwirkung*,
the influence of the legal ideology upon economic arrangements; thus, by the combination of forehand and backhand,
economic determinism and secondary effects, the strategic universe is closed, there is no danger that counter-example may
invalidate the theory or falsify a crucial hypothesis, every Yin
has its Yang, and all punctures are self-sealed.

In recent Soviet theory, which of course does not lead us to
automatic inferences about Soviet practice, the idea of the state
as executive committee of the ruling class has been joined but
not replaced by a rather less coercive notion of the state as formal expression of the society in its public decision-making, a
notion which though general in terms must be reserved in application to states that have earned the approval of the theoretician. What makes socialism special? The special nature of socialism:

> The interaction of law and politics is dialectical in any class
> society, including socialism. The absence of struggle be-
> tween classes, the existence of people's power, and the su-
> premacy of anti-exploiter relations of production, how-
> ever, inevitably affect this interaction in a radical way and
> exclude objective reasons for conflict between what has been
> established by law and what is done in practical political
> activity. Socialism, by its deepest essence, is able to ensure
> the internal unity of politics and law. The development of
> nation-wide democracy and the growing role of law in its

implementation, and consolidation of the rule of law, are the normal pattern for the political organization of socialist society.[1]

II

Of greater interest, I submit, is the connection made for legal theory between Marxian economics and Marxian politics by E.B. Pashukanis, a Bolshevik jurist of Lithuanian origin, who flourished in the Soviet Union in the 20s, perished in a Soviet prison camp in the 30s and was accorded limited posthumous rehabilitation in the 50s and 60s. His main work, *The General Theory of Law and Marxism,* has recently been reissued in English translation outside the Soviet Union, and several scholars in England and the United States have been mining it.

Pashukanis's theory qualifies for an affirmative answer to Mr. Tushnet's question whether there is a Marxist theory of law, for it is a·theory of law that was devised by a Marxist and rests heavily on Marx as one Marxist understood him. Whether it meets Mr. Tushnet's other criterion, that a defining characteristic of a Marxist theory of law is that it should be a *good* theory, is open to question. Unfortunately almost all of the people who give any thought to the general problem seem to presuppose either that "Marxist" and "good" are redundant or that they are contradictory.

What is most notable in Pashukanis is his attempt to spell out for the theory of law the implications he claims to have found, not invented, in the anthropological and historical constructs used by Marx and Engels. Before and after Pashukanis, official Soviet scholarship had laid down a rough sociological correspondence between a polity and its legal system, focusing at just that distance that leaves Mr. Tushnet unsatisfied in the "Goldilocks" sections of his paper. They combined two basic principles to reach an inference about Soviet law. The first was the universal but qualified principle that law was ultimately derived from relationships of production. The second was a crude version of evolutionist historicism in virtue of which socialism would certainly succeed capitalism and take mankind to a higher stage of social organization and public self-consciousness. From the combination of the two principles they reached the conclusion that socialist law must be or become a higher, more nearly perfect law than bourgeois law, matching the extent to which the socialist socioeconomic system must be or become higher and more nearly perfect than capitalism. For most Soviet jurists of the 20s, to adapt substantive laws from Czarism or central Europe was an expedient that would be either redeemed by new content infused into old concepts or superseded in the fullness of time by proper socialist law.

Pashukanis accepted his colleagues' two premises: law as derivative and evolutionist historicism; but he reached a radically different conclusion. He proposed a different and fundamental distinction between arrangements under capitalism and under socialism, though his distinction was no less triumphalist and even more chiliastic than theirs was. He refused to accept the necessity of a correlation between a society and its law, except within particular limits. He maintained instead that law as a general form—not merely piece by piece, but as a general form—was linked in history to that economic relationship that he said Marx said was at the bottom of all societies that obtained in the interval between the end of primitive family subsistence and the beginning of true socialism: namely, the relationship of commodity exchange. Notice that the course of development of law had terminals: law in history had had a beginning and was about to meet its end. Before goods and services came to be exchanged, whether by barter or through a medium like money, there had been no need for law, and no law; once the allocation of goods and services came to be settled by means other than exchange in equivalent quantity or quality, there would again be no need for law, and no law.

Two things seemed to follow. First, it seemed to follow that talk of new and higher law under socialism was nonsense. Law was *par excellence* the form for regulating exchange of equivalents. Man as rights-bearer had emerged in thought only with the rise of commodity exchange. (Of course the principle of exchange of equivalents is violated in the deeds perpetrated and protected by the rulers and their servants, but the norms are there.) The institutions of exchange—markets, contracts, mints, banks, credit, and the rest—reached not only their empirical but even their theoretical ceiling in bourgeois society.

So, necessarily, did law, which was in the end nothing more than normative justification for the official enforcement of the equivalences decreed by the rulers. Even our morality rested on the is, turned ought, of equivalence: the *lex talionis*, eye for eye and tooth for tooth; as ye sow, so shall ye reap; *suum cuique;* fair exchange is no robbery.

Second, it seemed to follow from Pashukanis's analysis of Marx's analysis that the socialist society superseding bourgeois capitalism would use an allocative device other than law. Here was the promise that law, like the state, would wither away. The horizon was a little blurred. The prospect of abundance in the age of communism could make the problem trivial by reading scarcity out of the givens, but the theoretician claiming the status of scientific thinker could not take refuge yet in the utopian side of Marxian vision. What Pashukanis apparently offered—after a period of transition, in which Bolshevik leaders would frankly make shift with borrowed bourgeois law—was the prospect of allocation of scarce resources through decisions made by technically qualified experts. The victory, at the right time, of the vanguard of the proletariat would have made possible the disappearance of class antagonism and the disappearance (as a social force) of the class enemy. The experts would not so much settle disputes as solve problems. Analogy was made to the difference between resolving a contest over the liability of a railway carrier to a shipper and working out a timetable for trains.

In the post-bourgeois future, to be sure, there would be no room for law as an objective impartial norm; but under bourgeois society that had only been a facade for domination—"the republic of the market masking the despotism of the factory." Once equivalence was transcended, inequality would lose its invidious connotation because justice itself would be seen as an obsolete criterion. A non-Marxist reader might suppose at that point that Pashukanis was proposing to supersede the right with the good, but Pashukanis tried to undermine even that by attacking morality as a fetish of bourgeois society along with commodities, exchange, law, and the state.

Whatever the merits of this approach in theory, it could not please the rulers of the Soviet Union, especially in the 1930s: the authorities practicing their kind of lawlessness under the

label of a search for stability were not about to countenance the
scholarly justification of the transcendence of law. The customary hypocrisy was deployed to justify the necessary murder; but
Pashukanis's ideas survive as one possible answer to Mr. Tushnet's question.

III

To account for the fall of Pashukanis it is not enough, though
it expresses a true tactical judgment, to say that he zigged where
he should have zagged. Nor will it do to add—what may be
true also—that he had shown a capacity for making enemies
when he had been at the top of the heap of Soviet legal politicians. Something more was involved, and that something more
has wider application. I said before that Marxist legal theory
sought to look at law from the outside. While that is so as a
matter of analytical standpoint, it gives trouble when the Marxist theorist is looking at, writing in, and paid by, a Marxist state.
That is when the theorist feels the strain of turning from critique to apology.

For this there are, I suggest, two reasons: a reason of coordination and a reason of contradiction. Coordination: rulers who
call themselves Marxist tend to regard the law and legal scholars alike as tools of state policy and will not tolerate independent observation either of their own legal system or of that of
non-Marxist lands. Legal scholars working in so-called socialist
states are not so much engaged as enlisted. Contradiction: if
independent observation were to be carried out, it would expose the state as false to Marxism, for the political pretensions
of the party have outrun the development of the economic
foundation on which the party's claim to legitimate rule purports to be founded.

If I am right in this, then if we also respect Mr. Tushnet's
constraint that he wants a Marxist theory of law to be a *good*
theory of law, we shall not find a Marxist theory of law in
Marxist countries. As for Marxist legal theory in non-Marxist
countries, it faces, as Mr. Tushnet points out, on one side the
sectarian difficulty of piety and exegesis; on another, the difficulties relished by legal realism. Despite all this, Mr. Tushnet

says he does not wish to relinquish the Marxist perspective, because he finds it wholesome to be reminded of sin and he thinks that liberalism would lull him into the wrong sort of detachment. Mr. Tushnet takes his stand with Gramsci, recalling his slogan of pessimism of the intelligence, optimism of the will. Well, I'm optimistic about Mr. Tushnet's will.

NOTES

1. L.S. Jawitsch, *The General Theory of Law* (Moscow: Progress Publishers, 1980 [transl. 1981]), pp. 49–50.

9

IRON LAW: WHY GOOD LAWYERS MAKE BAD MARXISTS

TOM GERETY

Marxists since Marx have spoken of America as a "special case," for practice and for theory. Are American lawyers, is American law, another such case? As in America at large, so in American law, Marxism has found only a foothold or two, hospitable perhaps but precarious. Nowadays this is not a cause for surprise: if the end of ideology is not at hand there is more than a lull in the successes of the thoroughly centralized "isms." But even in the 30s the Marxist lawyer was a rare bird—and one without a distinctive song. The radical lawyer's clients may have suited his political ideology; but his legal ideology could not have suited them. Marxists among the lawyers are like Christians among the prouder pagans: conversions are rare and often brief. Why so little hold?

There is a Marxist answer.

BOURGEOIS LACKEYS

Law, it used to be said, is the queen of the sciences because it rules all the rest; needless to say, the speaker was a lawyer. To the Marxists this confident innocence sits better on its head: lawyers are the verbal and conceptual servants of capitalism. In *The German Ideology*, Marx and Engels wrote "why the ideolo-

196

gists turn everything upside down."[1] They listed professions back and forth: "Clerics, jurists, politicians. Jurists, politicians (statesmen in general), moralists, clerics." All these are members of the bourgeoisie, the ruling class under capitalism. But they represent "an ideological subdivision," a specialization within that class. Their job is to give the appearance of legitimacy to class privileges based on coercion.

That appearance will prove all the more vivid if those responsible for it come to believe in it. Yes, "[t]he occupation assumes an independent existence owing to the division of labor;"[2] but with that independence goes a point of view, a commitment:

> Everyone believes his craft to be the true one. Illusions regarding the connection between their craft and reality are the more likely to be cherished by [lawyers] because of the very nature of the craft. . . .[3]

Must the lawyer fall prey to this? Or might he play the game without conviction?

Taking a page from Adam Smith, Marx and Engels both suggest that lawyers are "unproductive." They produce no goods; they live off the surplus produced by others. Thus a rising entrepreneurial class might grow impatient with these butlers and valets of coercion. But the more established the bourgeoisie, the more it needs a mask for oppression (and a salve for conscience). The lawyer thus becomes a necessity for the successful ruling class. He in turn requires all the aplomb he can derive from a sure sense of his own place in the order of things.

This account may seem crude, but it is not without subtlety or good sense. American lawyers often talk as if doctrines ruled. Such talk suggests that they themselves rule, or, even better, that through them principles rule. "In *ordinary* consciousness," as Marx put it, "the matter is turned upside down."[4] The lawyers think they hold great power when in fact a great power holds them. Craft consciousness distorts further. The judge thinks of law "as the real, active driving force." An idealization takes place in which he not only thinks he has power because of the law but he thinks he has it because of all the good the law does. "I should rule," the lawyer tells himself, "because I rule in the name of fairness and equity."

Undeniably the lawyer's principles have a relative generality to them. The lawyer understands this generality as a progress of legal history. What he does not understand is the economic necessity for it: "It is precisely because the bourgeoisie rules as a *class* that in law it must give itself a *general* expression."[5]

For markets to exist there must be an ample supply of commodities to exchange. Among those commodities will be labor. People sell, if not themselves, at least their own time and strength. Among the hindrances to such sales were the post-feudal restrictions on alienation of both property and labor. Slavery was only the most obstructive of these. Law reform clears the economic path of these obstructions. Thus women's suffrage, for instance, nearly doubles the labor market for mature capitalism. The market system works itself pure of its hindrances. Where the lawyer sees the 'rights of men', the Marxist sees the 'needs of the market'.

Marx, after Hegel, had a name for this process. He called it "universalization" or "generalization."[6] Where Hegel, much like a lawyer, saw in it the driving force of an idea of the state and citizen, Marx saw in it something at once more concrete and more powerful. Thus his analysis of the French Revolution finds in the rights of man the triumph of the bourgeoisie, of "modern civil society, the society of industry, of universal competition, of private interest freely following its aims. . . ."[7] Human rights are above all an economic or material development. True, it is a development in which lawyers become indispensable. But this is the logic of class, not law. The lawyer who argues for his client's right argues unknowingly for his client's place in bourgeois society. The universalization of rights means that the same argument applies to the factory worker or field hand as to the entrepreneur or professor. The lawyer sees in this a glorious equality of right. What he does not see, what perhaps he cannot see, is the inglorious power of market inequality.

THE MINIMUM MARX

"The greatest of all legal fictions," wrote E.P. Thompson in *Whigs and Hunters,* "is that the law evolves, from case to case, by its own impartial logic, true only to its own integrity, un-swayed by expedient considerations. . . ."[8] May a liberal law-yer retort with a straw man of his own? The greatest of all Marxist fictions is that law evolves by class struggle, by material changes in the means and relations of production, and by noth-ing else. Between these two dictions stand arrayed the mass of those lawyers with enough sense and sensibility to descry in law elements of principle *and* expediency. Marx surely had the sen-sibility; had he the sense?

There are special difficulties in answering this with more than a scarecrow sketch such as the one just given of lawyers. Most obvious are the difficulties of "scarecrowing" itself: the stuffing of a straw man at once easy to push over and made to frighten. Perhaps these difficulties belong exclusively to liberals (like my-self) who find themselves discomfited by the straitjackets of massive, all-explaining theory. There are difficulties, too, for those who call themselves Marxists.

The greatest of these difficulties lies in the relation between Marxist theory and Marxist practice. To Marx theory and prac-tice were inseparable: wrong-headed practice and wrong-headed theory were horse and carriage. When Marx first wrote there were socialists and even communists but no Marxists. The prac-tice and theory of Marx, beyond his own political action, came to little more than words and ideas. Now among socialists and communists we find only Marxists. The practice of Marxism, like the practice of Christianity, has a history. Can a Marxist deny all this and start anew?

As easily as some new sort of Christian, you may say. A new theory of Marxism will have its own practice, untried and un-known. This assumes an innocence that Marx himself would have savaged. A theory has been put into a hundred practices, none very satisfactory. Shall we give it another chance? In pol-itics chances are lives. Liberalism, says the Marxist, when allied to its material conditions in the industrial revolution cost lives. True, but the liberalism that spans parties and practices in the Western democracies can live with its history. Indeed, it must live, as a kind of loyal opposition, within the institutions it takes from history. Not so Marxism, or at least the Marxism we hear of in England or France or America: it is necessarily a new Marxism, cut off from its past practices as if from failed exper-iments.

At the outset, then, we sterilize Marx—as the progenitor of a theory and a practice—in order to make sense of him. Granting this, what is the shape and content of the Marxist *theory* of law? Various shapes and contents, comes the fair response from the new American Marxists, most prominent among them Duncan Kennedy and Mark Tushnet. So, they say, let us devise a best case for Marxism in law, a best theory, or at least a good one.

Variety and identity are not exclusive categories. Marxism may have varieties; it must also have some identity from one variety to the next. Tushnet writes, plausibly if vaguely, of the content as distinguished from the subject matter of a Marxist theory of law.[9] A *minimum* content is the pertinent category for our purposes. The point of saying that such a theory has a minimum content is of course that it has a minimum amount of Marx in it. Can we identify the minimum of Marx that justifies calling a given theory of law Marxist?

It is not easy. Marx may have been, as Kolakowski says,[10] "a German philosopher," but he was no lawyer or philosopher of law. He paid little attention to the workings of the law, to its institutions, doctrines, or methods. Property law was perhaps the one exception, but Marx's attention, which was sustained, was not systematic.

Marx gives us, then, only the materials of a philosophy of law, yet what materials. To begin with, he had a broad conviction about what matters most in society. He was willing, even eager, to test that conviction on all things human. Its rough content is no mystery.

Class conflict is its most essential and characteristic (if not its most general) ingredient. To speak of a Marxist theory of law without speaking of class—and of laws as instruments (if double-edged) of class domination—is something like speaking of Christianity without sin or psychoanalysis without the unconscious. Class is Marx's great insight, his "discovery." Although Marxists, starting with Marx himself, deny it, the conviction about class is at bottom as much a moral insight as a "scientific" one, for "class" remains a naggingly imprecise and controversial concept; much too imprecise for any science.[11] Yet the concept has a *critical* force, as I will call it, that seems all but irrefutable.

That concept requires another, more universal still. As Marx put it in the 1859 *Preface:*[12]

In the social production of their life, men enter into definite relations that are indispensable and independent of their will, relations of production which correspond to a definite stage of development of their material productive forces. The sum total of these relations of production constitutes the economic structure of society, the real foundation, on which rises a legal and political superstructure and to which correspond definite forms of social consciousness. The mode of production of material life conditions the social, political, and intellectual life process in general. It is not the consciousness of men that determines their being, but, on the contrary, their social being that determines their consciousness.

Call it the *primacy of the economic,* or of the productive, or of the material forces. Without it even the concept of class loses its critical and explanatory power. This primacy need not be absolute or mechanical, such that every change in material forces has its precise correlative in intellectual or cultural change. Marx himself spoke of the distinction between "material transformations . . . which can be determined with the precision of natural science" and "ideological forms in which men become conscious of this conflict and fight it out."[13]

To deny or omit some version of this primacy, even as skeptical liberals concede it, seems refined to the point of triviality. Thus Mark Tushnet's agnosticism about the primacy of the economic, in *his* Marxist theory of law, looks like something more than the nice mix of intellectual pessimism and moral optimism he suggests. Indeed, to the untutored eye, it is an intellectual resignation, a surrender, together, somehow, with an unexplained (and inexplicable) access of moral and political enthusiasm for the cause called Marxism.

There is much more to Marx than what I have so far sketched. The theory of ideology, the notion of false consciousness, the concept of alienation—these and other ideas are central to Marx and to Marxism. But the two I have touched on— economic primacy and class struggle—seem to me the essentials. These give us the minimum Marx, without which we may have a theory of law but not a Marxist theory—or even one much aided by the force of Marx's critical insights.

THE NEW MARXISM: THEORY

Theories of law, like juries and the bourgeoisie, seem to come in two basic sizes, grand and (to avoid the French) modest. It is an old saw that where there is thought, there is theory. Surely where there is law there is theory, however rudimentary or confused.

Marxism as we know it in Marx is grand theory. To identify a minimum Marx is not to suggest a minimum of ambition or scope. Quibble endlessly over Marx as philosopher, as historian, as sociologist: that argument conceals the conviction that Marx sought to explain a great deal about the human condition in history. We cannot hold his followers up to that ambition. But we can make sure, first, that they are his followers, at least in the essentials; and, second, that within the compass of their own ambitions, they do good work, good Marxist work.

Is there, in this sense, good Marxist work in American (or English) law? The answer I will give turns on the preposition "in:" good Marxist work on the history of American law, by Marxist historians, *is* available if not abounding; good Marxist work by American lawyers is so far neither very good nor very Marxist (although it begins to abound). But let me begin with the historians, who so far have made our best theorists.

A. LOOKING BACKWARD

Is law autonomous? This is the question that Marxists have pressed in legal history. To put this more plainly, we may substitute for the word autonomous something simpler, say, independent. Still the abstract question becomes vivid and concrete only when we ask, independent of *what?* Marx said again and again that law and morality were not independent cultural forces cut off from the relations of production. What, then, is the relation, over time, between a given legal doctrine and the social system in which the doctrine arose? There are at least three answers in Marx. First there is the weak version of nonautonomy: there must be *some* relation, some influence, of economics on law. Marxists and non-Marxists alike concur in this truism.

Only in the rarest precincts of law have judges and scholars believed in the supremacy of doctrine over fact. Nowadays formalism is an effigy, made, hung, and demolished by its opponents.

The second version of Marx has more content and more currency. Legal relations are *generally* subordinate to economic relations. This is seductive if not always informative. The difficulty is that in history, as in litigation, "general propositions do not decide concrete cases."[14] The real interest in this version comes of its relation to the third and most familiar of Marx's answers to the question of law's independence from economics. In this strong version, so prevalent in Marx's own rhetoric, law always and everywhere submits to economics. No significant legal doctrine has any real autonomy or independence. Free speech means nothing apart from free markets.

Those who take up the middle version of law's subordination to economics permit themselves the flexibility of a kind of situational Marxism. For this they have no need of apologies to Marx, who alternated between heated rhetoric and qualified elaboration.

At times the middle version lapses into an evasion of the ultimate issue: does economics, by hook or by crook, sooner or later, win out over legal (or moral) doctrine? It is no answer to blow alternately hot and cold. We want particular illustrations of the thesis of subordination. If these do not prove the strong version ("always and everywhere") or even the middle ("generally"), they at least show that the Marxists are on to something. And, indeed, as Eugene Genovese will illustrate, they are.

In *Roll, Jordan, Roll,* a study of the culture of slavery in the American South, Genovese gives a clear and subtle statement of the strong version.[15] Under a chapter heading taken from Gramsci, "the hegemonic function of law," Genovese elaborates a view that at first seems to compromise legal autonomy and economic—or, as he prefers, political—primacy. "The decisive means for politics is violence," said Weber.[16] Genovese explains, however, that "this viewpoint does not deny an ethical dimension to state power. . . ." Where does law come in? Law, as Genovese has it, operates as "an ethical sanction" for state coercion. As such, it has a measure of what sounds like autonomy:

In modern societies, at least, the theoretical and moral foundations of the legal order and actual, specific history of its ideas and institutions, influence, step by step, the wider social order and system of class rule, for no class in the modern Western world could rule for long without some ability to present itself as the guardian of the interests and sentiments of those being ruled.[17]

Of course this can be a sham. And what better class to illustrate this than the slaveholders? If ever there was a ruling class with a negligible pretense of deriving its power from the consent of the governed, this was it.

Genovese argues that slave law conformed to the essential mandate of class rule: to maintain and preserve the slave system, social, political, and, above all, economic. This was not easy. A system of outright exploitation of the labor and lives of one caste by another all-but-necessarily maintains itself by raw force. "Such obedience," wrote Judge Ruffin of North Carolina, "is the consequence only of uncontrolled authority over the body."[18] Law, however, knows no "uncontrolled authority." If violence is the only authority, then law is superfluous. How, then, to disguise the violence? If the slave codes "softened" in some respects during the ante-bellum period it only makes the question more pointed. Was the ruling class itself going "soft?" Was it moving toward emancipation?

Here the evidence speaks plainly: the slave codes softened the relative conditions of slavery even as they hardened the one absolute condition, the prohibition on manumission.[19] To protect a slave from his master's rage—by homicide law, for instance—is not to protect him from slavery itself. That peculiar institution itself required protection against abuse. How else to keep the slaves docile? By law, the ruling class disciplined wayward members so as to assure class survival. To the slave jurists this discipline was prudent, right, and just. A bad master was wrong as well as rash. "The heart of the slave law lay with the master's prerogatives."[20] To enforce paternalism was one thing. To carry it toward emancipation was to destroy the world the masters made.

Ultimately the Civil War destroyed that world. Slave society had created a contradiction it could not resolve, by law or by anything short of armed struggle. Genovese describes the contradiction as that between "the bourgeois idea of private property" under conditions of "marketplace equality" and the slaveholder's idea of property in human beings, under conditions of barbaric inequality. Mark Tushnet, cribbing from Beard, calls it the conflict between humanity and "interest," by which he means class interest.[21]

Slave law gave no way out of this conflict. For all its importance, the slave code had no independence within the slave system. The fault lines in the social system ran much deeper than the surface cracks that appeared in the legal code. The human "relations of production" were the real working parts of the slave system. So slave law was, in a sense not far from Marx's own, an epiphenomenon of slave production. Can we generalize, then, from slave law to all law? Does Genovese, in other words, adopt the strongest version of Marxism?

Complex, subtle, and wily as he is, Genovese will not be pinned to our board. He is an historian and a very good one: a man of particulars. Yet he is a Marxist and a theorist as well. He revels in the broad rhetorical strokes of a complex but rigid model. Slavery yields itself up to his superb account of class and caste struggle. It fits the frame. But is it, in some sense, an easy case? To answer this we need a harder case; Thompson's study of the Black Act provides it.

The Black Act prohibited a variety of offenses—epitomized by the 'blacked' faces of poachers—in the forests of eighteenth-century England. Strictly speaking, it had no legislative history. Its motley rigor suggests, however, a frantic concern to impose a lost order on those "green and pleasant" woodlands. The Act touched on everything from breaking dams and felling trees to blackmail; nearly everything it touched it made a capital offense. It was "a complete and extremely severe criminal code. . . ."[22]

Thompson begins his study with the questions of a good historian: "What occasioned the passage of the Act? Who were the 'Waltham Blacks?' " Did any special interests gain from its passage? Finally, "[w]hy was it so easy for the legislators of 1723 to write out this statue in blood?"[23]

The politics of the Black Act in his account reveal a Walpole, and a government and society beneath him, far less serene, far less rational, and no less stern than Whig traditions have taught. Thompson "recovers to view," as he says, an episode otherwise lost even to its contemporaries. It was not so much the passage of a harsh and exotic code of law, a piece of legal barbarism. It was rather a century-long struggle over property rights. Make no bones about it, it was a class struggle. It was a struggle, moreover, for control over a very special, and very primitive, means of production, the forest with its wood and fish and meat. Above all, Thompson studies a piece of legislation; above all, the struggle was over law. Thus Thompson gives a direct comparison to Genovese.

In the last section of his book, Thompson wonders aloud what larger interest his theme holds. Is not "concern with the rights and wrongs of law of a few men in 1723 . . . concern with trivia?"[24] After all, he writes, to some "the rule of law is only another mask for the rule of class."[25] Knowing this, why bother to confirm it:

> I sit here in my study, at the age of fifty, the desk and the floor piled high with five years of notes, xeroxes, rejected drafts, the clock once again moving into the small hours, and see myself, in a lucid instant, as an anachronism. Why have I spent these years trying to find out what could, in its essential structures, have been known without any investigation at all?[26]

His answer comes close to the middle version of Marx that Genovese (like Marx himself) never quite brings himself to reject. Yet it is an answer almost unique in the Marxist tradition for its avowal of law as an institutional and moral good.

"[S]ome parts of this study have confirmed," he writes,[27] "the class-bound and mystifying functions of law." His account to that extent is Marxist, or at least compatible with Marxism. Yet the emphasis contrasts sharply with Genovese. To begin with, Thompson makes no use of what he calls the "typology of superior and inferior (but determining) structures." Nowhere does he rely on the primacy of the economic.

No doubt Genovese would say, "I don't rely on it either." But the "hegemonic function of law" bespeaks precisely this instrumental view of law in an overriding class struggle, call it economic or political.

In Thompson, by contrast, there is a new relativism. Law may be seen as governed by class interest; it may also be seen in other ways. The Black Act itself is a perfect instance of law as a tool of class. The English legal system of 1723 is something else again. As often as not that legal system checks and restrains class oppression. Again, Genovese may adopt this view: law *is* a force in his work and so perhaps an independent force. But Thompson takes this a step farther. For law "[M]ay [also] be seen simply in terms of its own logic, rules and procedures— that is, simply *as law*. And it is not possible to conceive of any complex society without law."[28] Genovese has no necessary quarrel with the anthropology here. But the perspective that Thompson opens up with these assertions moves quickly past culture to ethics.

Recall the insight that becomes Thompson's theme in *Whigs and Hunters*. These oddly assorted Englishmen of the 1720s were fighting over the law itself. "What was often at issue was not property, supported by law, against no-property; it was alternative definitions of property-rights."[29] Nor was the fight purely instrumental, for either class (if there were only two). Even "[w]hen it ceased to be possible to continue the fight at law, men still felt a sense of legal wrong. . . ."[30]

A sense of legitimacy is indispensable even on an orthodox Marxist account. "[P]eople . . . will not be mystified by the first man who puts on a wig."[31] Some pretense of justice is required for the trick to work. You must at least talk about "standards of universality and equity." Talk is cheap, it may be said. But not so cheap as Walpole's men would have liked.

> Most men [and women] have a strong sense of justice, at least with regard to their own interests. If the law is evidently partial and unjust, then it will mask nothing, legitimize nothing, contribute nothing to any class' hegemony. The essential precondition for the effectiveness of law, in its function as ideology, is that it shall display an independence from gross manipulation and shall seem to be just. It cannot seem to be so without upholding its own logic

and criteria of equity; indeed, on occasion, by actually *being* just.[32]

From this point, Thompson's "conclusions and consequences" diverge radically from Genovese's. Law is not simply a stubborn beast, likely to turn on its abuser. It is also, as Thompson argues, "an unqualified human good."[33] Its use—which is inescapable—creates a community of interest between ruler and ruled, even in brutal struggle. At times law transcends even the most deep-seated antagonisms.

Is this still Marxism? Thompson may be forgiven a loyalty to the creed of his youth. But he has given up dogma and system for the particularities of "episode." From Marx he takes more than one critical insight. So may the rest of us. If Genovese shows that there is good Marxist work in the history of law, Thompson shows that the best of that work is only loosely and ambiguously Marxist.

B. LOOKING . . .

In historians such as Genovese and Thompson the "minimum Marx" is a palpable presence. Agree or disagree, they take his questions as their own. When we turn to the writings of the new Marxist lawyers, we find not so much a minimum as a phantom Marx—now appearing, now disappearing, never quite solid or plain. Take Mark Tushnet and Duncan Kennedy as our examples. Between them they have written dozens of articles, a book, and more than one sermon on Marxism. Of this abundance we may well ask: What are their ideas? How good are they? And, finally, how Marxist are they?

If we take the essay in this volume as representative, we find Tushnet entangled in three strands of perplexity. First, he has some trouble identifying a subject matter for his Marxism; second, he has trouble with its content; and third, he has trouble saying how—and why—he is a Marxist. In this, as we shall see, he is not alone.

To most of the neo-Marxist lawyers even the subject matter of a Marxist theory of law remains somehow uncertain. Tushnet speaks in hesitant, almost anguished, terms of various subject matters, more or less well suited to the contemplated theory. Neither "cases" nor "doctrines" will do; "categories" may. Ostensibly this search for a subject becomes necessary because something disastrous has happened in law and jurisprudence. Most of us had not noticed the disaster. So we ask, what happened? His answer comes in thudding anticlimax: legal realism.

Realism, Llewellyn once said, was "not a theory but a method."[34] In philosophical terms it was a method of radical doubt applied to the settled doctrines of law. Until very recently this was the one legacy of realism that no one wanted. Suddenly the Critical Studies Marxists appear in the guise of heirs. To them skepticism is an essential discipline. It is the only way to knowledge.

Now however praiseworthy as an ambition, this search for certainty—for "knowledge"—will almost certainly keep us from getting anywhere. Corrosive skepticism soon eats away at the thin sheetmetal that separates legal concepts from other concepts. When we doubt "the facts" in law we doubt them elsewhere. If a case is an artifice, is not a court, or, for that matter, a country? Marx himself points theory toward no necessary passage by way of naive or radical skepticism. Marxists at large have hardly become notorious for their chronic doubts.

A pervasive doubt about an ostensible subject matter must lead, if not to an abyss, to one of two postures for theory: either a theory with a newly ascertained subject matter—as if by discovery—or else to a theory so laden with qualification, as a hedge against doubt, as to be irrefutable—a kind of theology.

The subject matter of any theory of law must remain obvious. It is law, which is to say all of it, from cases to clients, from the chancellor's foot to the formalist's doctrine. Yes, you may take aim at any one portion of the whole, understanding "portions" in any way you will—in time or space or what have you. You may say, too, that a theory only explains so much, a given period in law or a given body of rules: to modesty its due. But a theory in search of a subject matter is not so much modest as absurd.

This is not a cry to go back to the phenomena. We are always, in social theory, back with the phenomena. What is more, we cannot deny that our experience is laden with inarticulate and unverified theory—a kind of common law of experience.

But to legislate a grand theory without regard to that common law is hopelessly utopian.

To the neo-Marxists such as Tushnet, only "the structures of legal categories" have sufficient resistance to realism to constitute a proper field of application and so of testing. Cases are too crudely particular, and such abstractions as "feudal law" or "Roman law" (favored by both Marx and Engels) are too airily thin upon inspection. So we settle on this new subject matter: the structures of legal categories. The first question is, what do we mean by structure?

Tushnet does not tell us exactly. But his work, along with that of Duncan Kennedy and others, gives at least a clue. To structure something is to build it or plan it. The noun suggests the main lines of construction or composition. "Figuratively," as *Webster's* has it,[35] structure is "the interrelation of parts as dominated by the general character of the whole; as the *structure* of society; the *structure* of a sentence." Kennedy's essay on "the structure of Blackstone's Commentaries"[36] tries to show that the work has one motive—of apology or rationalization—and two contradictory methods or mechanisms—the Lockean argument from natural liberty and the Hobbesian from (literally) social security. To say that these propositions display the "structure" of the *Commentaries* is to say, less elegantly, "this is what they are all about."

Now there is a curious twist in this away from the flat, if complex, cause-and-effect assertions of a Marxist like Genovese. Blackstone did not think his work had either the motive or the methods suggested by Kennedy. No matter, we say with the new criticism, an author's intention does not govern his work. Genovese and company say as much, but for them a particular class and condition do govern. Theirs is the method Kennedy calls contextualization,[37] the method of history. It fills in the details of fact until a pattern of explanation emerges.

Contrast this with structuralism. The idea of structures of thought is owed to two people in a particular tradition of French intellectual eclecticism: Lévi-Strauss in anthropology and Merleau-Ponty in philosophy. The anthropological perspective is obvious. The new Marxists, like the old anthropologists, observe and then catalogue with a pretense of detachment. What they examine are the artifacts of moral and institutional life that we call laws. In them they hope to find a deep structure of hidden but ruling concepts. The philosophical perspective is less obvious but more telling.

Merleau-Ponty was at once a phenomenologist and a Marxist. Unorthodox in both circles, his Marxism was nonetheless all too plain,[38] but it is his phenomenology that gives us a clue to the new Marxist lawyers.

Since Husserl,[39] those who call themselves phenomenologists have sought an objectivity (what becomes authenticity in Heidegger) unavailable to other disciplines. Layer upon layer of preconception and prejudgment hide the phenomena, they say. By methods no outsider can explain, the phenomenologist seeks to recover phenomena—of whatever kind—without the freight of conceptions under which ordinary life (and ordinary theory) labors. The point is to *get behind* the ideas of ordinary life—to ideas truer, surer, better. To study the categories of legal thought is in some sense to go behind our ordinary ideas about law. But what do we take with us as we go on this voyage?

Anthropologists, including Lévi-Strauss, have more baggage than they like to admit; philosophers, like mediums, point the way but rarely take it. The structuralists have at a minimum a commitment to structures: they exist; they matter; they can be studied. The Marxist structuralists, moreover, have a commitment to Marx—or so we assume. But that assumption is precisely the difficulty. How do "structures of thought" relate to "structures of society"—to class, to economics, to exploitation? These are matters, ultimately, of cause and effect. But categories of thought float about elusively in an intellectual ether where content is ineffable. Causation was a curse to Husserl, the founding phenomenologist. At times Kennedy and Tushnet seem to curse with him.

In Kennedy's notoriously ambitious essay on "substance and form in private law adjudication" he confesses that "it is impossible to 'prove' or 'disprove' the validity of [his] two constructs" of individualism and altruism. To identify a judge or legislator, or any given decision, as one or the other is not the point. Rather, it is to display an important typology or polarity in judicial decisions.

Not being a systematic nominalist, I believe that there *is* an altruist and an individualist mode of argument. More, I believe that the rhetorical modes are responsive to real issues in the real world. . . . As with Romanticism, we can believe in the usefulness of the notion of altruism without being able to demonstrate its existence experimentally, or show the inevitability of the association of the elements that compose it.[40]

What this comes to is a method of suggestion: I will show you something that you may not have noticed—in a line of cases or a body of work—and you will see it or not according to the suggestiveness, the persuasiveness, of my account. This is nothing to scoff at, for all interpretation and criticism rely on powers of suggestion in just this sense. Still, suggestiveness is a convenient turn for a theory of law. Whatever else these "structures" are, they are wieldable (and inventable) by clever essayists in the style of, say, Michel Foucault,[41] the historian of culture. This style has already mounted a kind of putsch in certain precincts of literary theory, proceeding first by the "deconstruction" (again by naive skepticism) of received concepts and then by a "reconstruction" of knowledge. Inevitably, and a little ironically, the new Marxist structuralists have much more to say about "mentalities" than about "materialities." But whoever remains uninitiated must reserve some doubt about the realities behind all this. On the new plane of "categories" and structures" of conception the common sense canons of evidence need not apply.

"The way people employ categories, rather than the content they give categories, may be an appropriate subject of sociological inquiry. . . ." writes Tushnet.[42] Yes, we may say, the legal categories of the slave South are worthy of analysis. As instruments of a caste system they will likely prove suggestive about the way the slaveholders, at least, thought about race and class. But this suggestiveness is inverifiable and, if you will forgive me, un- or non-Marxist.

In the new Marxism, then, subject matter and content merge. Take Marx's critical question about class struggle. An endless analysis of categories or structures of thought yields no program for answering that question. The relation between primary or productive forces and the cultural or secondary—such as law—remains at a sharp remove from the subtleties of "category" or "structure" analysis. Thus the conclusions of such efforts have always a kind of take-it-or-leave-it quality, not entirely attributable to Marxism's grandeur.

Why did Blackstone think about law in one way and not in another, Kennedy asks. Might Blackstone—or whoever—have used other categories, intellectually or intrinsically more appealing? Yes, Kennedy answers, but his particular categories—so odd in themselves—find a home in his *particular* society with its own conflicts and contradictions. This is why—and how—they make sense: as a denial of or as an apology for a given social reality. Yet Kennedy has nothing to tell us about that reality itself. He posits its existence and also its "contradictions." These he approaches, moreover, only by way of interpreting the *Commentaries*. That interpretation itself proceeds not on the fairly precise hypotheses of Marxism—of class struggle and economic primacy—but on the much vaguer hypotheses of "fundamental contradictions" in social life.

There is no denying that Marx spoke of such contradictions himself; to that extent the idea is Marxist. But in speaking this way Marx was willing to commit himself: he identified the contradictions with class struggle; he analyzed them in terms of economic primacy; and he even went so far as to predict their resolution. For Kennedy, for Tushnet, and for the others like them, such explicitness is somehow inelegant. Contradictions or polarities abound: humanity and interest, altruism and individualism, community and autonomy. The rhetorical tradition of Marxism heralds some resolution of these contradictions. Yet between the rhetoric and the analysis there is almost no firm ground in evidence. Not only are Marx's concepts too crude but so are those—like causality—on which we all depend for ordinary explanation.

The neo-Marxist turn to a new subject matter and a new content allows, perhaps, a new subtlety and sense. Thus Kennedy's reinterpretation of Blackstone, while sandwiched between truism and dogma, is rich in the kind of detail hitherto left, with mild scorn, to less committed historians. In this return to interpretive detail the new Marxists bear a resemblance to Lukacs: the old Marxist who worked so hard to make sense of the texts of Joyce and Mann and Kafka. Do they also resemble him in their dogmatism?[43] These at least are *attentive* Marxists, who would not put down Blackstone without trying to understand him on his own ground. Attentiveness amounts, nearly always, to an intellectual virtue, or so we liberals hold. But it may depend upon attentiveness to *what.*

I have spoken so far of the content and subject matter of the new Marxists. The word subject in this sense comes to much the same as the word object. We mean by subject matter an object of study. If we mix an Aristotelian vocabulary, in which reality submits to theory, with a Kantian one, in which theory submits to reality, no harm is done. But this slight confusion of terms points up an important question. Marx himself had no doubts about the objectivity of his theory. He was, as he saw it, a student (like Darwin) of things alive and changing but real—and subject (to push the ironies of vocabulary) to testable, provable theory.[44] Yet to search Marx's writings for a discussion of the kind of test suggested for his theory is to end where we began.

Marx's test is reality itself. "[T]heory itself becomes a material force when it has seized the masses,"[45] he wrote. His early criticisms of Hegel's idealism remain in force against idealism in his own work: "Out of too much reverence for the ideas they are not being realized."[46] True, the relation between theory and practice in Marx is never quite that of blueprint and building: "It is not enough that thought should seek to realize itself; reality must also strive toward thought."[47]

Confessedly an ideology, Marxism seeks not so much certainty as adequacy. But the "adequacy" of an "ideology" comes, very literally, to its objectivity: its realization in a world in which "an old dream," as Marx put it, about liberty and community continues to exercise its fascination. Is the dream an illusion? Sadly enough, official Marxism, in its own works and days, in its own history (played out in Warsaw and Kabul even as I write), tells us the dream has died. Unofficial Marxism—Marx's, Kennedy's, Tushnet's—tells us it lives. But if it is to live objectively, as the Marxists have it in Marxism itself, it must live in the grand manner, the grand style that Marx never carried off so well as Hegel. "Once the realm of imagination has been revolutionized reality can no longer hold out."[48]

The new Marxists, in law as elsewhere, have revolutionized

neither reality nor the imagination. They have plundered the structuralists for odd bits and notions. These they have attended to. But at best their work is suggestive and, fainter praise still, interesting. In the end, they make neither very good Marxists nor very good theorists.

THE NEW MARXISM: PRACTICE

What is to be done, asked Lenin in the classic formulation of Marxist urgency and concreteness. The answer is revolution. But over time short answers lose both urgency and concreteness. Preparation has its perplexities; so does waiting. The question then grows more concrete, if less urgent. What *precisely* is to be done by American Marxist lawyers? When? How? And, in a further question Marxists almost never ask (or answer), why?

Why should we do anything revolutionary at all? The moral basis of Marxist action (or praxis, as Marxists call it) has been either scorned or taken for granted since Marx himself.[49] Morality is a bourgeois nicety, concealing the crude inequality and brutality of an oppressive economic system. Even taken in its breadth, morality to the Marxist is but the set of inhibitions favored, for convenience's sake if nothing else, by any given social order at any given time. Judgments of good or bad are never more than realtive to the social order in which they arise and in which they seem to make sense. Marx hated absolutes. It was his favorite technique in argument to say that his opponents reified or absolutized things changeable. Bourgeois morality stood in the way of revolution precisely because of its seeming fixity.

If so, however, there remains an awkward round of very practical questions. If there is no moral point of view outside a given social order, from what point of view do we criticize that order—any order—as oppressive? From what point of view do we commit ourselves to its overthrow? Marx himself indulged in an all but deliberate inconsistency on this question. He was always quick to cry "maudlin" or "sentimental" at moral criticism of societies distant in time or space. Yet he himself waxed positively Dickensian about "wage slavery," child labor, and factory work. Which, then is the true Marxist position?

The answer seems to be, neither. Even without recourse to the young Marx, one can reconcile the detached positivism with the *engagé* rhetoric by the simple device of an accurate prediction of revolution. Marxism can afford to be at once morally detached and politically engaged because, bluntly, Marxism knows the future. There is much mincing among modern Marxists about the inevitability of revolution. Texts are cited for the proposition that it will only come by dint of self-conscious effort, of struggle. Still, whether or not you and I engage in that struggle is, on a strict Marxist account, not so much irrelevant as immaterial. The revolution will happen willy nilly, with us or without us.

Put abstractly this is not a sentiment that many of us can deny: *che será, será.* If it resolves moral doubts with scientific certainties—numbing us, in a sense, to the point of our doubts—it only shifts the ground of difficulty. We can criticize bourgeois economies, say the Marxists, because we know something about what will succeed them. From this privileged vantage point, the logic of capitalism—including class differentiation and the exploitation of labor—looks astonishingly weak. This in turn teaches the possibility of change. Thus the cat leaps out of the bag. The revolution occurs in the realization of its possibility—if not its inevitability—and then in its actual attempt and achievement. Morality is irrelevant to all this. The proletariat will have its reasons, even on a simple Benthamite calculus of individual pleasures and pains. Oppression is painful to many or most. What sustains it is the myth of its inevitability. Take that away and the revolution is at hand.

This simple tale has one curious twist, however. Possibilities come in all shapes and sizes of likelihood. Oppressions, too, vary; some are worse than others. All revolutionary political action has risks. What forces the tale of revolution on toward its conclusion must be either its inevitability—which, after all, begs the question—or else its desirability. If it is inevitable, any given member of the proletariat (or the intelligentsia) can sit idly by until it arrives. The desirability of revolution may make our idle proletarian eager, but why should it make him industrious?

If, on the other hand, the revolution is not inevitable, but only possible, then we will have to argue over the balance between its possibility and its desirability. Once we begin that argument we are bound to come to the question: what is in it for me? A Marxist uncertain of his revolutionary timetable—as all good modern Marxists are—must concede that what is in it for many is a specifically moral commitment to the task of bringing about a better social order. But the very generality of *that* commitment suggests the need for a moral scrutiny of actions. This the Marxist tradition has studiously camouflaged in tactical debates.[50] Marxist lawyers in the United States give poignant example of the need for both moral and tactical scrutiny.

The only continuous source of legal writing on the Left in the United States is the journal of the National Lawyers Guild, originally titled the *Guild Quarterly* but called, since 1965, the *Guild Practitioner*.[51] After lurching from liberal to radical and back again in the late 30s, 40s, and 50s, the *Practitioner*, along with the Guild itself, settled, around the time of the war in Vietnam, into a not always comfortable but usually consistent "left radicalism." Although the *Practitioner*'s editors would have blushed over the lawyerly pieties seen in its pages in the very first numbers,[52] its latter-day radicalism remains eclectic enough to abide a steady dose of mainline professionalism. "First of all be a lawyer," enjoins Ann Fagan Ginger,[53] a radical civil libertarian and one of the staunchest and best of the Guild's longtime leaders. Indeed, most of all be a lawyer, and a good lawyer: this theme, more than any other sounds as the first principle for radical law practice in the *Practitioner*'s pages.

Being a good lawyer, however, does not necessarily make you into a good radical or revolutionary. To the contrary, it may turn you into an unwitting liberal. How will the *Practitioner*'s readers bring off the union of both forms of virtue, professional and revolutionary? The obvious but never quite persuasive answer remains in the 60s (or 80s) what it was in the 30s. Radical lawyers have radical clients; or better, radical lawyers *choose* radical clients. Now with the qualification that radical lawyers have *only* radical clients this simple answer may make sense, particularly Marxist sense.

Professionalism in part suggests detachment. A lawyer may

represent a criminal without espousing the criminal's world-view. So, lawyers will say, they represent all of their various clients with impartiality, with no strings attached. Yet strings have a way of attaching themselves to actions. The repeated representation of the Mafia does not make a lawyer a mafioso. Yet if the fee proves generous it may make the lawyer grateful. Attitudes creep in on even the most casual of arguments. To a Marxist critic of the professions, certainly, a cynicism about protestations of detachment from clients comes with the territory. Most clients are bourgeois, as are most lawyers. Of course the "mystifying" role of lawyers requires the pretense of professional detachment. The lawyer argues best when he argues "neutral" principles of right or justice, attractive even to the class enemies of capitalism. The better the lawyer, the better hidden the client's true interests. To unmask the lawyer is thus to unmask the client.

Putting this account into practice, then, the Marxist lawyer cannot have it both ways, exercising the professional as well as the revolutionary virtues, *unless* he or she has revolutionary clients.

When Guild lawyers represent self-conscious and active revolutionaries they are at their most exuberant. "The radical potential of the law" is nowhere more obvious than when its "reactionary potential" comes into play.[54] Keeping revolutionaries out of jail requires good lawyering, its revolutionary value requires little or no explanation. If only there were enough revolutionaries to go around. Alas, the radical lawyers, too, must survive in a world of scarcity.

On a closer examination, however, the shortage of revolutionaries is hardly the only problem. There is always the nagging question of internal consistency. Does it accord with revolutionary morality to represent revolutionaries in a nonrevolutionary (if winning) fashion? The uncomfortable but sensible answer seems to be, yes. But the nuances bear heavily on the Guild's writer members. Thus Malcolm Burnstein insists on the radical version of lawyerly detachment. Forget your own politics during litigation, he urges, and learn enough about your client's politics to facilitate whatever expression of them the client wants to make.[55] What if the client's use of the court as a political forum will condemn him or her to certain conviction?

Again, the radical lawyer recurs to a version of what, with apologies to Spiro Agnew, we must call radical liberalism. It is the client's business what results he or she wants. If conviction makes revolutionary sense to the client, so be it.

This deference to clients goes at times to very nearly absurd lengths. Thus Charles Garry writes in the *Practitioner* of his defense of Huey Newton: "Frankly, I didn't spend any time with Huey discussing the facts of the case . . . until 3 or 4 days before he took the witness stand. . . ."[56] Garry needed all the pretrial time he could find to learn black history, and thereby the Black Panther ideology of his client. As to Newton's version "of the incident of October 1961, I wasn't particularly interested."[57] The client knows best, he seems to say, not only in politics but in law as well. "I was satisfied that" he was innocent.[58] And that was that; or was it?

Here we meet little of Fagan Ginger's measured good sense. To Garry the client knows best because the court knows worst. "No black person can get a fair trial," he cries. Now Garry does try, and he often succeeds,[59] but he flirts with an attitude that only a conspiratorial theory makes sense of. In theory the courts are tools of class oppression. In theory, then, an aborted process of adjudication teaches the masses that the iron law of capitalist oppression works in the courts as elsewhere. And yet, to take Garry at his word, the lawyer's deliberate ineptitude rigs the process to come out just as he predicts. What began as an effort to "demystify" ends up in a revolutionary mystification. Only now what suffers obfuscation is the possibility of fairness—or even luck—in the courts of law.

If this is the role of the revolutionary lawyer—that of an *agent provocateur* in the courts—then it is a sinister role indeed. The client, consenting or no, is now the victim of his lawyer's politics, specifically his politically inspired litigation tactics. The convicted client now demonstrates the correctness of the lawyer's condemnation of the system. "This court could not give a fair trial anyway," says the radical lawyer—to a black man, a white radical, an illegal alien. Perhaps. So long as a fair trail is possible, however, a lawyer with a client cannot be at once a good lawyer and, in Garry's sense at least, a good revolutionary.

Nonetheless, some American lawyers still try, most often

without the compensations (or exaggerations) afforded by ce-
lebrity. Perhaps the most interesting American lawyers on the
Left are those who work for clients with neither money nor
ideology. If impressions serve at all, the rare species of radical
American lawyer is best sighted at work in the legal services
offices, public or private, with clients at best "objectively" revolutionary.

To these lawyers, the maxim that "radical lawyers have radical clients" requires an extenuation and revision. Most of their
clients have no notion of a revolutionary change in American
society. What they do have—and know they have—are legal
problems. But these problems make up the numbing common-
places of life on the margins of consumer markets and welfare
bureaucracies. Many will doubt that those who suffer from them
want or seek revolution. An end to the hassling may suffice.

The old paradox of antagonism between reform and revolution, better and best, reasserts itself. If their clients are "objectively" revolutionaries then they are enemies of the present
order. If the present order is one of oppression, then it will
seek, in the favorite verb of radicals and vintners, to crush them.
The courts of law provide only an elegant cover for this process. What possible good can be done, then, by defending the
objective revolutionary in the enemy's lair? To answer naively,
the same good as is done by defending a self-conscious revolutionary, namely, keeping him or her on the streets revolutionizing, misses the point. These clients are not out fomenting revolution. What keeps them from doing so is an understandable
failure of imagination, of self-consciousness.

Marxism is a pedagogical faith. The objective revolutionary
must come round to subjective revolutionizing. He must learn
that the system oppresses. Only *then* can he learn to change it.
This requires demystification—consciousness raising. Fair trials,
due process, individual rights—these are connivances of the
present system. Laws, like religion, sanctify. So long as our "objective" revolutionaries remain credulous before bourgeois lib-
erties and bourgeois justice they will be of little or no use to the
struggle. Thus the conundrum: to give them legal help within
the system—assuming a modicum of success—may be to convince them that the system works. To the Marxist faithful this
is as good as making the client into a permanent (if impover-

ished) reactionary. But conversion to the revolution cannot very well be exacted as a fee.

Much to their credit, such lawyers seem to have chosen the path of lawyerly rather than revolutionary righteousness. The costs even on this side of the ledger may remain considerable (if, again, entirely impressionistic). Often one senses in these lawyers a resignation if not a cynicism about the worth of what they do. Poor clients grow neither rich nor revolutionary. Law work in their behalf rarely advances them in any very hopeful direction. Few lawyers can sustain the unrequited ideological commitment for long. Some nurture a more modest apocalypse in the details of just dealing. Those who do must know in their hearts the iron law that good lawyers make bad Marxists.

Is it an iron law that good Marxists make bad lawyers? No law is iron. The incompatibilities of lawyering and Marxism run broad and deep, but neither logic nor history compels them. The good lawyer looks always to detail in argument and fact. By long habit he or she grows skeptical of generalization—and scornful of that commonest generalization, prediction. The good lawyer, whether scholar or counsel, is above all a practitioner. It cannot be blinked that the good Marxist is above all a theoretician, in power or out. To this day the practice of Marxism, in law as in politics, remains an obscure and forbidding suggestion.

NOTES

1. *The German Ideology*, Sec. 12, "Forms of Social Consciousness," in *Marx and Engels on Law*, M. Cain and A. Hunt, eds. (London: Academic Press, 1979), p. 54.
2. Ibid.
3. Ibid.
4. Ibid., p. 54.
5. Ibid., p. 142.
6. *See* S. Avineri, *The Social and Political Thought of Karl Marx* (London: Cambridge University Press, 1968), pp. 162–174.
7. *See The Holy Family*, R. Dixon, trans. (London: Lawrence & Wishart, 1956), pp. 164–165.

8. E.P. Thompson, *Whigs and Hunters: The Origin of the Black Act* (London: Pantheon, 1976), p. 250.

9. Mark Tushnet, "Is There a Marxist Theory of Law," in this volume.

10. Leszek Kolakowski, *Main Currents of Marxism*, Vol. 1, *The Founders* (London: Oxford University Press, 1978), p. 1.

11. As Darwin may or may not have seen in rejecting Marx's proposed dedication to him of one edition of *Capital. See* Colp, "The Contacts Between Karl Marx and Charles Darwin," *Journal of the History of Ideas*, 35 (1974), pp. 329–338.

12. Cain and Hunt, op. cit., p. 52.

13. Ibid.

14. *Lochner v. New York*, 198 U.S. 45, (1905) (Holmes, J., dissenting).

15. Eugene Genovese, *Roll, Jordan, Roll: The World the Slaves Made* (New York: Random House, 1977).

16. Max Weber, "Politics as a Vocation," in H.H. Gerth and C.W. Mills, trans. and eds., *From Max Weber: Essays in Sociology* (New York: Oxford University Press, 1946), p. 121, cited by Genovese at p. 25.

17. Op. cit., p. 25.

18. Cited in Genovese, op. cit., p. 35, from *Papers of Thomas Ruffin*, Hamilton, ed., vol. IV (Raleigh: AMS Press, 1920), pp. 255–257. ——

19. Op. cit., pp. 49–70.

20. Ibid., p. 41.

21. Mark Tushnet, *The American Law of Slavery 1810–1860: Considerations of Humanity and Interest* (Princeton: Princeton University Press, 1981).

22. Leon Radzinowicz, *A History of English Criminal Law and Its Administration from 1750*, vol. I (London, Stevens: 1948), p. 77. Cited in Thompson, op. cit., at p. 22.

23. Thompson, op. cit., p. 24.

24. Op. cit., p. 259.

25. Ibid.

26. Ibid., p. 260.

27. Ibid.

28. Ibid., p. 260.

29. Ibid., p. 261.

30. Ibid.

31. Ibid., p. 262.

32. Ibid.

33. Ibid., p. 266.

34. Quoted in Gilmore, *The Ages of American Law* (New Haven: Yale University Press, 1977), p. 138.

35. *Webster's New International Dictionary,* 2d ed. (Springfield, Mass.: G & C Merriam Co., 1936).

36. Duncan Kennedy, "The Structure of Blackstone's Commentaries," *Buffalo Law Review* 28 (1979), p. 205.

37. *See* Duncan Kennedy, "Form and Substance in Private Law Adjudication," *Harvard Law Review* 89 (1976), p. 1685.

38. *See* Maurice Merleau-Ponty, *Humanism and Terror,* John O'Neill, trans. (Boston: Beacon Press, 1969).

39. *See* Paul Ricoeur, *Husserl: An Analysis of His Phenomenology,* E.G. Ballard and L.E. Embree, trans. (Evanston: Northwestern University Press, 1967).

40. Kennedy, "Form and Substance," p. 1723.

41. *See,* e.g., Michel Foucault, *The History of Sexuality,* Robert Hurley, trans. (New York: Pantheon Books, 1978).

42. *See* Tushnet, this volume,

43. *See* Georg Lukacs, *History and Class Consciousness,* Rodney Livingstone, trans. (Cambridge: MIT Press, 1971), pp. ix–xvii.

44. Thus Marx can write in the *Preface,* of "the general result at which I arrived. . . ."

45. Karl Marx, *Early Writings,* T. Bottomore, trans. (London: Oxford University Press, 1963), p. 52 ("Introduction to a Contribution to the Critique of Hegel's Philosophy of Right").

46. *Rheinische Zeitung,* May 19, 1842. Quoted in Avineri, op. cit., p. 137.

47. *Early Writings,* op. cit., pp. 53–54.

48. Hegel wrote this in a letter to Niethammer that Avineri translates, op. cit., p. 138, n. 2, *Briefe von und an Hegel,* J. Hoffmeister, ed., vol. I (Hamburg: F. Meinert, 1952), p. 253.

49. But *see* A. Buchanan, "Revolutionary Motivation and Rationality," *Philosophy and Public Affairs,* 9 (1979), p. 59.

50. Lenin's attitude in virtually all his writings epitomizes the "hard line" that evades morality with strategy. See Edmund Wilson, *To the Finland Station* (London: Secker & Warburg, 1940).

51. Actually the *Guild Quarterly* turned first into the *Lawyers Guild Review* (in 1940), then (in 1961) into *Law in Transition,* and finally (in 1965) into the *Guild Practitioner.*

52. Only the first of these name changes seems to have masked a definite change in ideology, although the tone and emphasis changed year by year.

53. *See* vol. 28, no. 1 (1969), p. 15.

54. *See* Donald Jelinek, "Evolution of a Radical Lawyer," *Guild Pract.* 28 (1969), p. 20.

55. Malcolm Burnstein, "Trying a Political Case," *Guild Pract.* 28 (1969), p. 40.

56. Charles Garry, "Attacking Racism in Court Before Trial," *Guild Pract.* 28 (1969), p. 86.

57. Ibid.

58. Ibid., p. 87.

59. *See People v. Newton,* 87 Cal. Rptr. 394 (1970).

PART IV

SOME UNRESOLVED ISSUES

10

RECONSIDERING HISTORICAL MATERIALISM

G.A. COHEN

1.

I called my book on Karl Marx's theory of history a *defence*, because in it I defended what I took to be Karl Marx's theory of history.[1] I believed the theory to be true before I began to write the book, and the initial conviction more or less survived the strain of writing it. More recently, however, I have come to wonder whether the theory the book defends is true (though not whether, as I claimed, it is the theory of Karl Marx). I do not now believe that historical materialism is false. It is rather that I am not sure how to tell whether or not it is true. Certain considerations, to be exhibited below, constitute a strong challenge to historical materialism, but though they plainly do represent a serious *challenge* to the theory, it is unclear what kind and degree of revision of it, if any, they justify.

That is unclear because we still have only a very crude conception of how historical materialism is to be confirmed or disconfirmed. My book made the theory more determinate, and consequently contributed to clarifying its confirmation conditions, but it will be apparent from the inconclusive upshot of the challenge I shall describe that substantial further clarification is needed.

I do not, then, reject historical materialism in this essay, but

227

since I am nevertheless in some degree letting the side down, let me emphasize that my belated reservations about historical materialism do not weaken my belief that it is both desirable and possible to extinguish existing capitalist social relations and to reorganize society on a just and humane basis. The political significance of retreat from historical materialism should not be exaggerated. An appreciation of the principal evils of capitalism, which are its injustice, its hostility to the development of the faculties of the individual, and its voracious ravaging of the natural and built environment, does not depend on ambitious theses about the whole of human history. Nor does the claim that it is possible to establish a society without exploitation which is hospitable to human fulfillment require, or perhaps even follow from, those theses. So skepticism about historical materialism should leave the socialist project more or less where it would otherwise be. There are, it is true, Marxist claims about how society works whose falsehood would make supersession of capitalism and installation of socialism less likely. But one can affirm those claims without believing, as I am still sure Marx did, that the fundamental process in history is the material one of the growth of human productive power.

If refinement of historical materialism has political value from a socialist point of view, then it has it mainly for the indirect reason that it increases the prestige of Marxism and the self-confidence of socialists, and not so much, in my opinion, for the more direct reason that it furnishes a guide to action. Historical materialism is a theory about epochs,[2] and to act in the light of possible epochal outcomes of one's action is a formidable business, partly because of difficulties of foreknowledge, and also because there is a limit to the amount of responsibility nongods can take, or even conceive. I believe it is nevertheless possible to make rational political choices, and even when epochal issues are at stake, but that is a topic for a different occasion.

2.

The epigraph of my book reproduces the final sentence of *The Little Boy and His House*,[3] which was my favorite book when I was a child. The sentence is as follows: "For what they all said was, 'It depends . . . It all depends . . . It all depends on where you live and what you have to build with.' "

I thought the sentence was a charming way of communicating a central thesis of my book: that forms of society reflect material possibilities and constraints. But while my book was in press, and perhaps, I confess, a little earlier, I was rereading *The Little Boy and His House,* and I came to see that my use of its final sentence was to some extent exploitative. When the sentence is abstracted from its context what it seems to mean makes it a very suitable epigraph for the book. Seen in context, however, the sentence can be a point of departure for formulating the challenge to historical materialism I want to discuss here.

Let me, then, supply the context. The story concerns an unnamed little boy who, at the outset, has no house to live in. In winter he is too cold, in summer he is too hot, when it rains he gets wet, and when it is windy he is nearly blown away. So he goes to see his uncle, who is sympathetic. They agree that the little boy needs something to live in. His uncle then explains that there exist many different kinds of dwelling, and that it would be wise for the little boy to examine some of them before deciding what he wants for himself. A world tour follows, in which nine types of accommodation are sampled, in nine different countries. But the boy finds each kind of dwelling either inherently unappealing (for example because it is a Romany gypsy's tent too low to stand up in, or because it is an unpleasantly damp Spanish cave) or, however appealing, unattainable in his circumstances (for example because it is a house made of stones which lie around the Irish fields, and none lie around the fields where he lives, or because it is an igloo, and igloos wouldn't last long in the little boy's climate). Returning to wherever they started from—the book does not say but linguistic evidence suggests it is England—the boy sighs and says, "What a lot of different ways of building houses!" whereupon, somewhat surprisingly, he and his uncle set about building a small red-brick bungalow. Having finished building, they invite their nine new friends to see the result, and the friends come with their wives and animals and they are so impressed that they go home determined to build houses just like the little boy's house. But when they get home they change their minds. And now I

shall quote the last couple of pages of the book, which end with
the sentence I used as an epigraph:

>   And they all went home determined to build brick houses
> like the Little Boy had built.
>   But when they all got home again, Don Estaban thought
> that after all it *was* very convenient to have a cave all ready
> made for you, and Johnnie Faa and Big Bear thought how
> convenient it was to have a house you could carry about
> wherever you wanted to go, and Wang Fu thought it was
> even more convenient to have a house that would carry *you*
> about. And E-took-a-shoo saw that where he lived he would
> *have* to build with ice and snow because there was nothing
> else, and M'popo and M'toto saw that they would *have* to
> build with grass and mud because they had nothing else,
> and Mr. Michael O'Flaherty thought that if you had a lot
> of stones lying about the fields it was a shame not to use
> them, and Lars Larsson thought the same about the trees
> in the forest.
>   So
>   what
>   do
>   you
>   think
>   they
>   did?
> THEY ALL WENT ON
> BUILDING JUST AS THEY'D
> ALWAYS DONE.
>   FOR
> WHAT THEY
> ALL SAID
> WAS . . .
> "It depends . . .
>   It all depends . . .
>   It all depends on WHERE YOU LIVE
> and WHAT YOU HAVE TO BUILD WITH."

3.

Let us think about why the Little Boy's friends decide not to build red brick bungalows. In at least most cases, they are said to change their minds for reasons that appear accessible to historical materialism: they reject bungalow-building after reflecting on features of their physical circumstances. But their reasons for carrying on as before could seem favorable to historical materialism without actually being so. The next to last sentence says: they all went on building just as they'd always done. And my present view is that, notwithstanding their sincere and materialist-sounding avowals, they went on building as they'd always done partly just *because* they *had* always built in that way, and they consequently recognized themselves in the ways of life that went with their dwellings. This is a nonmaterialist reason for architectural conservatism, but it can come to appear materialist, because one way that a culture consolidates itself is by misrepresenting the feasible set of material possibilities as being smaller than it is in fact. Culturally disruptive material possibilities are screened out of thought and imagination: in certain contexts people prefer to think that they have no choice but to take a course to which, however, there are, in fact, alternatives.

Big Bear thought it convenient to have a house (i.e., a tepee) he could carry about, whereas Wang Fu thought it more convenient to have one (i.e., a houseboat) that would carry him about, but I do not think they reached these contrasting judgments because they made different technical calculations. I think they were led to them by the potent force of familiarity, which determined where they felt at home: "to be at home," unlike "to be housed," is not a materialist property. It is the dialectic of subject finding itself in object that explains, at least in part, why Big Bear and Wang Fu conceived convenience differently. (I say "at least in part" because I need not deny that houseboats are more likely to appear in territory dense with waterway, and tepees are more likely on riverless plains. But even if the relevant ancestors developed their different housings under pressure of such material determinations, it is entirely implausible to think that Big Bear and Wang Fu stick to custom not at all because it is custom, but just because the plains remain riverless and the rivers haven't dried up.)

If, then, it all depends on where you live and what you have to build with, the importance of where you live is not purely materialist. The way of life where you live counts, as well as what you have to build with there. People live not by mud and bricks alone, but also by the traditions from which they draw their identity, the traditions that tell them who they are.

And now I shall leave the story behind, but I shall presently return to the issue I think it raises.

4.

Marx produced at least these four sets of ideas: a philosophical anthropology, a theory of history, an economics, and a vision of the society of the future.

There are connections among these doctrines, but before we consider some of them, I would like to point out that, despite great differences in their domains of application, the four doctrines have something important in common. In each doctrine the major emphasis, albeit in a suitably different way, is on the *activity of production,* and each of the four is, partly for that reason, *a materialist doctrine.*

The philosophical anthropology says that humans are essentially creative beings, or, in the sexist personification of humanity which Marxists have not always avoided: man is an essentially creative being, most at home with himself when he is developing and exercising his talents and powers.

According to the theory of history, growth in productive power is the force underlying social change.

In the economic theory magnitude of value is explained not, as in rival accounts, at least partly in terms of desire and scarcity, but wholly in terms of labor, and labor is "essentially the expenditure of human brain, nerves, muscles and sense organs,"[4] the using up of a certain amount of human material substance: labor time, the immediate determinant of value, is but a measure of, or a proxy for, the quantity of living matter consumed in the process of production.

Finally, the main indictment of capitalism is that it crushes people's creative potentials, and the chief good of communism is that it permits a prodigious flowering of human talent, in which the free development of the powers inside each person harmonizes with the free development of the powers of all. Communism is the release of individual and collective productive capacity from the confinement of oppressive social structure.

5.

I now believe that the philosophical anthropology is false, because it is one-sided. This has evident consequences for the vision of the desirable future, since it comes from the anthropology (see section 8 below). It should have no consequences for the economic theory, which answers questions about which the anthropology should be silent. Its consequences for the theory of history are, as we shall see (in sections 9 through 11), hard to judge.

6.

The side missing in Marx's anthropology is the one prominent in Hegel. In my book I said that for Marx, by contrast with Hegel, "the ruling interest and difficulty of men was relating to the *world*, not to the *self*."[5] I would still affirm that antithesis, and I now want to add that, to put it crudely, Marx went too far in the materialist direction. In his anti-Hegelian, Feuerbachian affirmation of the radical objectivity of matter,[6] Marx focussed on the relation of the subject to an object that is in no way subject, and, as time went on,[7] he came to neglect the subject's relation to itself, and that aspect of the subject's relation to others which is a mediated (that is, indirect) form of relation to itself. He rightly reacted against Hegel's extravagant representation of all reality as ultimately an expression of self, but he overreacted, and he failed to do justice to the self's irreducible interest in a definition of itself, and to the social manifestations of that interest.

I shall use the phrases "need for a self definition" and "need for self definition" as abbreviated ways of speaking about "the need for (a) definition of self," but the shorter forms could give rise to a misunderstanding that I hope herewith to forestall. The expression "self-definition," particularly when hyphenated, suggests a reference to a process (or the result of a process) in which the self defines itself, in which, that is, the self is not only what gets defined but also what does the defining. I shall not employ the hyphenated form, since when I speak of the need for self definition, I mean the self's need not for the process but for the result, and I do not mean its need to define itself, but its need to be defined, whatever may, or must, do the defining. If self definition, even as I intend the phrase, is necessarily due to the activity of the self, and if the self needs that activity as well as its result, then so be it, but what especially matters here is the self's need to end up defined.

I do not say that Marx denied that there is a need for self definition, but he failed to give the truth due emphasis, and Marxist tradition has followed his lead. The interest in self definition is not catered for by the good Marx and Marxists do emphasize "the development of human powers as an end of itself."[8] For, to begin with, the creative activity characterized by that phrase need not provide self understanding, and it is thought of as good in large part independently of any self understanding it may afford: the perfection and employment of a person's gifts is an attractive idea apart from any insight into himself that results. And even when the person does gain an understanding of himself in and through creative activity, because, as Marxist tradition says, he recognizes himself in what he has made, then his understanding is of what he can do and has done: it is not an understanding of who he is, an acquisition of identity in the sense I am trying to convey.

A person does not only need to develop and enjoy his powers. He needs to know who he is, and how his identity connects him with particular others. He must, as Hegel saw, find something outside himself that he did not create, and to which something inside himself corresponds, because of the social process that created him, or because of a remaking of self wrought by later experience. He must be able to identify himself with some part of objective social reality: spirit, as Hegel said, finds itself at home in its own otherness as such.[9]

I said that what matters here is possession of a definition of self, not struggle to acquire one, and in the last paragraph I tried to suggest how passive a process the acquisition of identity can be: a person does not supervise his own social formation. But creation and enrichment of identity can also result from the agent's own initiatives, from chosen engagements with which he comes to identify. I do not have in mind a deliberate attempt to forge an identity for oneself: apart from special cases, that would be self-defeating, since on the whole one's identity must be experienced as not a matter for choice. Yet even when people engage themselves with people and institutions other than to find out who or what they are, the engagement can persist when whatever was the reason for it is gone, and people are not necessarily irrational when it outlives its original rationale and becomes an identification ungrounded in particular reasons. The reason for abiding in some connections, if this counts as a reason, is that one has invested oneself in them and consequently finds oneself there (which is not to say that the purpose of the investment was to find oneself there), and a person is incomplete without connections of that perhaps nonrational, but certainly not irrational, kind.

I claim, then, that there is a human need to which Marxist observation is commonly blind, one different from and as deep as the need to cultivate one's talents. It is the need to be able to say not what I can do but who I am, satisfaction of which has historically been found in identification with others in a shared culture based on nationality, or race, or religion, or some slice or amalgam thereof. The identifications take benign, harmless, and catastrophically malignant forms. They generate, or at least sustain, ethnic and other bonds whose strength Marxists systematically undervalue, because they neglect the need for self identity underlying them.[10]

7.

Let us turn to the vision of the future, discussed in my book under the heading "Communism as the Liberation of the Content." At the level of the individual, the liberation of the content is the release of his powers: he escapes location within a social role thought of as confining them. But I now suggest that Marx's desire to abolish social roles reflects a failure to appreciate how the very constraints of role can help to link a person with others in satisfying community.

"In a communist society," says Marx, "there are no painters but at most people who engage in painting among other activities."[11] I argued that this means two things: first, and obviously, that no one spends all of his active time painting. But less obviously and more interestingly it also means that there are not even part-time *painters*, where to be a painter is to be identified as, and to identify oneself as, one whose role it is to paint (even if one has other roles too). Under communism people now and then paint, but no one assumes the status painter, even from time to time.

I now wonder why roles should be abolished, and even why, ideally, people should engage in richly various activities. Why should a man or woman *not* find fulfillment in his or her work as a painter, conceived as his contribution to the society to which he belongs, and located within a nexus of expectations connecting him to other people? And what is so bad about a person dedicating himself to one or a small number of lines of activity only? Nothing is wrong with a division of labor in which each type of work has value, even though no one performs more than, say, two types of work, so that many talents in each individual perforce lie underdeveloped. Marx wanted the full gamut of each person's capacity to be realized: " 'free activity,' " he said, "is for the communists the creative manifestation of life arising from the free development of *all* abilities."[12] But that ideal is too materialist. It is neither realizable nor desirable. You will see that it is unrealizable if you imagine someone trying to realize it, in a single lifetime. But it is not even *in general* desirable to realize it as much as possible. There is often a choice between modest development of each of quite a few abilities and virtuoso development of one or very few, and there is no basis for asserting the superiority of either of these choices in the general case. What constitutes the free development of the individual in a given case depends on many things, and his *free* development is never his *full* development, for that is possible only for beings which are sub- or superhuman. A society in which everyone is free to develop in any direction is not the same as a society in which anyone is able to develop in every direction: that kind of society will never be, because there will never be people with that order of ability.

Marx's ideal is properly called materialist because of its demand that the living substance within the individual be allowed to grow and emerge in, as he puts it in the phrase just quoted, a "creative manifestation of life." Elsewhere he indeed himself says that to be free "in the materialistic sense" is to be "free not through the negative power to avoid this or that, but through the positive power to assert [one's] true individuality," and one's individuality, when asserted, is "the vital manifestation of [one's] being."[13] His ideal qualifies as materialist because it is semi-biological, and it is certainly materialist in the sense of the opposition between the material and the social defended in chapter IV of my *Karl Marx's Theory of History.* It is true that for Marx the liberation of the human material is possible only in community with others, since "only within the community has each individual the means of cultivating his gifts in all directions,"[14] but here society is required, as Marx puts it, as a *means,* to an independently specified (and, I argued, absurd) goal. It is not required, less instrumentally, as a field for that self identification the need for which is unnoticed in Marx's vitalistic formulations.

I have criticized Marx's ideal both for being too materialist and for requiring an impossibly total development of the individual. I think these are connected excesses, but I acknowledge that I have not clearly articulated the connection between them. The idea that the human substance within should be nourished and expressed need not, it is true, imply a demand for that plenary development that I claim is impossible. But I do think, even if I cannot show, that the materialism encourages the wish to draw forth everything in the individual, and I note that no corresponding error is naturally associated with an emphasis on the importance of self definition. There is no temptation to think that one has a satisfactory identity only when one identifies with everything that can be identified with.

I argued that Marx's anthropology misses one great side of human need and aspiration, and I have now criticized an extreme version of the ideal of creativity the anthropology exalts, by urging that the *full* development of the individual is an ill-considered notion. To prevent misunderstanding I should therefore add that I do not, of course, reject the ideal of creativity as such, which remains a valuable part of the Marxist inheritance and which has, as we shall see in section 12, important political applications.

8.

The vision of the future inherits the one-sidedness of the anthropology, but the limitations of the anthropology should not influence one's attitude to the labor theory of value, which should never have been defended, as it sometimes has been, on anthropological grounds. The question of the bearing of the anthropology on the theory of history persists, and it is a particularly difficult one.

Now there are phenomena, such as religion and nationalism, whose importance historical materialism *seems* to underrate, and which are intelligible in the light of the self's need for definition. But even if the theory of history really does undervalue what a more Hegelian anthropology would honor, it does not follow that it is because the theory of history depends upon an un-Hegelian anthropology that the undervaluation occurs, for, as I shall argue in section 10, *it is unclear that historical materialism is attached to the materialist anthropology I have criticized.* First, though, a brief discussion of the two phenomena just mentioned.

A certain cliché of anti-Marxist thought is probably true, namely that Marx misjudged the significance of religion and nationalism. He saw and exposed the class uses to which such ideologies are put. But he did not pursue the consequences of what he sometimes acknowledged, that they have origins far removed from class struggle. The power they have when they are used for particular class purposes is applied to those purposes, not derived from them. They might, in consequence, have a social and historical weight beyond their role within the schema of base and superstructure.

Marx's awareness that religion's source is deep in human need is evident in his statement that it is the opium of the people. He did not mean that priests devise it on behalf of exploiters and dispense it to the people to keep them in order. What priests do helps to keep the people still, but religion does not come from priests. It is, instead, "the sigh of the oppressed creature, the soul of a heartless world, just as it is the spirit of a spiritless situation. It is the opium of the people."[15]

Participation in religion is a form of alienation, for it is a search on an illusory plane for what is unavailable in life itself. If religion is the spirit of a spiritless situation, one might expect that it will disappear only when there is spirit in life itself. It would then follow that, since there is no religion under communism, there will be a spirit in the free association of individuals. But where does Marx say anything about it?

Let us turn from religion to nationalism. Two passages in the *Communist Manifesto* warrant mention here. The first is the statement that working men have no country,[16] which expressed an expectation that the various national proletariats would rapidly transcend particularism in favour of international solidarity. It is hard to repel the suggestion that the workers refuted this when they marched to the trenches of World War I. Consider too what the *Manifesto* says about nationality and culture:

In place of the old local and national seclusion and self-sufficiency, we have intercourse in every direction, universal inter-dependence of nations. And as in material, so also in intellectual production. The intellectual creations of individual nations become common property. National one-sidedness and narrow-mindedness become more and more impossible, and from the numerous national and local literatures, there arises a world literature.[17]

Now if Marx means just that locally produced cultural objects become globally available through improved education and communication, then of course he is absolutely right. But I think his remarks go beyond that. I think they reflect a belief and hope that men and women will relate to other men and women as fellow human beings, and on a world scale, not in addition to but instead of finding special fellowship in particular cultures. Against that I would say that literatures are national, or in some other way parochial, because their makers are, as they must be, connected with particular sets of people. Like everybody else they need to, and do, participate in concrete universals. Marxist universalism suffers from the abstractness of the Enlightenment universalism criticized by Hegel. The Enlightenment was wrong because the universal can exist only in a determinate embodiment: there is no way of being human which is not *a* way of being human.

I do not deny that the literature of one nation can be appreciated by the people of another, and they need not think of it as foreign literature to do so. When people from different cultures meet, they get things they do not get at home. But I think Marx is guilty of the different idea that people can, should, and will relate to each other just as people, an idea that ignores the particularization needed for human formation and human relationship. He complained that "in bourgeois society a general or a banker plays a great part, but man pure and simple plays a very mean part."[18] I am not on the side of the generals and bankers, but I do not think they are unattractive because the characterizations they satisfy are too specific, and that man pure and simple is what everyone should try to be.

Marxism is not plausible on the subject of nationalism. In a fine collection of articles, Tom Nairn says valuable things about recent eruptions of nationalism in the British Isles and elsewhere.[19] His phenomenology of national feeling is sensitive, but his description of it as Marxist has no justification.

I have expressed a positive attitude to ties of nationality, so I had better add that I lack the Hegelian belief that the state is a good medium for the embodiment of nationality.[20] It is probably true that whenever national sentiment fixes itself on the state there results a distortion of both thought and feeling, a set of preposterous illusions and mindless passions on which rulers play. But even if that claim is too strong, it is evident that, unlike literature, the state is a terribly dangerous vehicle of self-expression, and it is a good thing that in our own time people are developing identifications of more local kinds, and also international ones, identifications which cut within and across the boundaries of states.[21]

9.

Two questions remain, only the second of which will be pursued in this essay (in sections 10 and 11).

The first is: how much damage to historical materialism is caused by the fact that the phenomenon of attachment to ways of life that give meaning to life is materialistically unexplainable? Is the force of that attachment great enough to block or direct the development of the productive forces, or influence the character of economic structures, in ways and degrees that embarrass the theory of history? This is the question I said at the outset I could not answer, because the confirmation conditions of the theory of history remain unclear. It may seem obvious that the human interest I have emphasized makes historical materialism unbelievable, but it is not obvious in fact. That people have goals that are as important, or even more important, to them than development of the productive forces need not contradict historical materialism, since even if "people have other goals which are always preferred to productive development whenever they conflict with it," the conflict might never determine the direction of events at critical junctures and might therefore never assume epochal significance.[22]

10.

The second question is whether Marxism's one-sided anthropology is the source of historical materialism's lack of focus on the phenomenon referred to in the first question, however damaging or otherwise to historical materialism that lack of focus may be.

It is natural to think that the anthropology and the theory of history are closely related, since each has the activity of production at its center. Yet they seem on further (if not, perhaps, in the final) analysis, to have little to do with one another. Hence although I think the anthropology is false, and also that historical materialism *may* be false because it neglects what the anthropology cannot explain, I also think that *if* historical materialism is false then we might have parallel errors here, rather than one error giving rise to another.

Production in the philosophical anthropology is not identical with production in the theory of history. In the anthropology people are by nature creative beings. They flourish only in the cultivation and exercise of their manifold powers, and they are especially productive—which is to say, *here*, creative—in the condition of freedom conferred by material plenty. But in the theory of history people produce not freely but because they have to, because nature does not otherwise supply their wants; and the development in history of the productive power of *man* (as such, as a species) occurs at the expense of the creative capacity of the *men* who are the agents and victims of that development. They are forced to perform repugnant labor that is a denial, not an expression, of their natures: it is not "the free play of [their] own physical and mental powers."[23] The historically necessitated production is transformation of the world into an habitable place by arduous labor, but the human essence of the anthropology is expressed in production performed as an end in itself, and such production is different, in form and content, from production that has a merely instrumental rationale.[24]

I argued in Chapter I of my book that for Marx there is no development of the productive forces and, therefore, no history, when nature is too generous. When nature is niggardly people must produce, and history consequently unfolds. So in the first instance people produce not because it belongs to their *essence* to do so, but for the almost opposite reason that it is a requirement of survival and comfort in their inclement *situation*. In the argument of Chapter VI for the primacy in history of the development of productive power, the premises are scarcity, intelligence, and rationality: nothing about humanity being by nature productive enters those premises, and that is hard to explain if (as I still believe)[25] they are the right premises and if (as I consequently doubt) the anthropology does bear on the theory of history.

To show how easy it is, and how wrong, to elide the distinction between historical materialism and the Marxist conception of human nature, I quote and criticize Allen Wood:

"Historical progress consists fundamentally in the growth of people's abilities to shape and control the world about them. This is the most basic way in which they develop and express their human essence. It is the definite means by which they may in time gain a measure of freedom, of mastery over their social creations."[26]

Wood's first sentence is ambiguous, because of "people's abilities," which may denote either abilities inherent in individuals or the ability of man; only under the latter interpretation is the sentence true. The second sentence is, consequently, false: people do not develop and express their human essence in activity that thwarts that essence. The third sentence, taken out of context, might still be true, since an essence-frustrating cause could have essence-congenial effects, but if we take it to mean that humanity engages in self-denying labor *in order* "in time" to achieve self-fulfillment, then it is false, since it is false—it could not be true—that the whole of history has a purpose that humanity sets and pursues; in his more sober moments Marx ridiculed just such claims.[27] (In the most ambitious of those readings of historical materialism in which humanity is an agent with a purpose, the historical production whose character is dictated by circumstance is undertaken in order to realize a conquest of nature after which production need no longer be dictated by circumstance: under communism essence-governed creativity is possible for the first time.[28] In a slightly less extravagant reading, there exists no purpose of facilitating creative expression independently of and prior to history, but once production begins under the imperative of survival the latent powers of humanity are roused,[29] and the project of attaining a creative existence is founded.)

I say that the theory of history does not require or derive from the anthropology, but I do not say that the two doctrines contradict one another, and since, as I said, essence-frustrating causes can have essence-congenial effects, it is possible to conjoin them. One could say that humanity is essentially creative, but that its historical creativity, this side of communism, is governed not by its essence but by its circumstances, so that there is a frustration of the human essence that only communism, the ultimate product of essence-frustrating activity, will relieve.

11.

I deal here with objections to the claims of section 10. It might be argued that the anthropology supplies *part* of the explanation of the reworking of the world in history, since even if the thesis that humanity is by nature creative is irrelevant to human *interest* in transforming the environment, it is needed to explain why and how people are *able* to satisfy that interest. The fact that humanity is by nature productive enables it to do what intelligence and rationality would have it do in face of inclement circumstances. That people can transform the world, it might be said, is an implicit premise in the argument of Chapter VI of my book.

But this argument for the relevance of the anthropology to the theory of history is mistaken. For the implicit premise is not that humanity is *essentially* productive, but just that, whether or not this is an essential truth about them, human beings can produce, and perhaps, indeed, in a sense of "produce" different from that in which it is their essence to produce, according to Marx.

One might, however, say that historical materialism requires the anthropology as a basis for its forecast of how human beings will occupy themselves under communism. But I have wanted here to separate the vision of the future from the theory of the past, and I have meant by "historical materialism" the theory of the dialectic of forces and relations of production that comes to an end with the achievement of communism. Historical materialism here is the theory of what Marx called *prehistory*,[30] and the present objection is therefore out of order.

The claim that historical materialism does not contradict the anthropology could also be challenged. For according to historical materialism people produce because of scarcity, because they have to, while the thesis that humanity is by nature creative entails that people would produce even when they do not have to produce, when, indeed, they do not have to do anything. Yet, as I emphasized in my book, Marx represents people as not producing in the Arcadian conditions that stimulate no historical development.[31]

To deal definitively with this objection one would need to be more clear about the concept of essence than I am at the moment. But a rather simple distinction will, I think, get us some-where. Here are two contrasting principles about essence, nei-ther of which is absurd:

E: If an activity is essential to a being, then the being does not *exist* unless it performs it.

F: If an activity is essential to a being, then the being does not *flourish* unless it performs it.

If our understanding of essence includes principle E, then the objection stated above succeeds, unless Marx thought, as perhaps, indeed, he did, that people in Arcadian conditions are, in virtue of their underdevelopment, prehuman. This last sav-ing suggestion might seem to offer only temporary relief, since the objector could then say that post-Arcadians *are* human for Marx, and even though they do produce—so that the objection does not apply in its original form—they do not produce in a way that manifests their essence, as the E conception of essence would require.

But it is not pedantic to rejoin that E may not require that essential activity be performed in a satisfactory fashion. One might, then, silence the objector by saying that people produce because circumstances give them no other choice, but that in producing they exercise their essential powers, yet not, because of situational constraint, in a satisfactory way.[32] Note that in such a view the theory of history and the anthropology remain substantially independent of each other. One might, indeed, at a pinch, imagine two kinds of creature, one whose essence it was to create and the other not, undergoing similarly toilsome histories because of similarly adverse circumstances. In one case, but not the other, the toil would be a self-alienating exercise of essential powers.

Consider now principle F. On its different construal of es-sence, the objection fails, although it would follow that if Ar-cadians are humans, then they are not flourishing ones. Marx strongly implies, of course, that, whatever they are, t'ey are contented, but he did not regard contentment as a sufficient condition of flourishing.[33]

12.

I have been contrasting production that flows from human nature with production that reflects malign human circumstance, and I would like to end by quoting a politically potent commentary by Jon Elster, which relates to that distinction. In a liberating inversion of conventional wisdom about "the problem of incentives," he claims that they are needed not in order to get people to produce, but to get them to produce in circumstances of scarcity that prevent their natural creativity from expressing itself. Having quoted Marx's statement that in the future society "the free, unobstructed, progressive and universal development of the forces of production is itself the presupposition of society and hence of its reproduction,"[34] he goes on:

> Behind this statement, and many others in the same vein, lies the image of man worked out in the *Economic and Philosophic Manuscripts of 1844*. According to this view, innovative and creative activity is natural for man, and springs from the inner sources of his being. Contrary to the usual approach in political economy, the problem is not one of creating the incentives to innovate, but of removing the obstacles to the natural innovative drive of the individual "in whom his own realization exists as an inner necessity."[35] Special incentives are required only in conditions of scarcity and poverty, in which the needs of the individual are twisted and thwarted. In the early stages of capitalism there was indeed a great deal of scarcity and poverty

so that incentives to innovation, such as the patent system, and extravagant rewards to entrepreneurship, were required. But

> "given the technology developed by capitalism itself, it is materially feasible to install a regime in which the level of want satisfaction is so high that innovation as a spontaneous activity comes into its own—at a rate far in excess of anything that has existed before."[36]

13.

The main contentions of this essay are as follows:

1. Marxist philosophical anthropology is one-sided. Its conception of human nature and human good overlooks the need for self definition than which nothing is more essentially human (see sections 6 and 7).

2. Marx and his followers have underestimated the importance of phenomena, such as religion and nationalism, that satisfy the human need for self definition (section 8).

3. It is unclear whether or not phenomena of that kind impinge in a damaging way on historical materialism (section 9).

4. Historical materialism and Marxist philosophical anthropology are independent of, though also consistent with, each other (sections 10 and 11).

5. If historical materialism is, as (3) allows it may be, false, then, in virtue of (4), it is not false because it relies on a false anthropology, but it and the anthropology are false for parallel reasons.[37]

NOTES

1. G.A. Cohen, *Karl Marx's Theory of History: A Defence* (Oxford and Princeton, 1978), henceforth referred to as *KMTH*.

2. A truth people are inclined to forget. The late Harry Braverman's *Labor and Monopoly Capital* (New York: Monthly Review Press, 1974) is often invoked against the *KMTH* thesis that productive forces are explanatorily more fundamental than production relations, since Braverman claimed that the way the forces develop under capitalism is determined by the class antagonism between potentially insurgent workers and capitalists who forestall insurgency by introducing technologies that deskill and so demean the workers. But Braverman would not himself have objected to the primacy thesis in this fashion, since he realized that historical materialism was about epochs: "The treatment of the interplay between the forces and relations of production occupied Marx in almost all his historical writing, and while there is no question that he gave primacy to the forces of production in the long sweep of history, the idea that this primacy could be used in a formulistic way on a day-to-day basis would never have entered his mind" (Op. cit., p. 19).

It would follow that the pattern of development of productive power in relatively restricted time periods is not probative with respect to historical materialist theses.

3. Stephen Bone and Mary Adshead, *The Little Boy and His House* (London: Dent, 1936).

4. *Capital*, volume I, (Harmondsworth: Penguin, 1976), p. 164; see also p. 274.

5. *KMTH*, p. 22.

6. One of Feuerbach's achievements, according to Marx, was "his opposing to the negation of the negation, which claims to be the absolute positive, the self-supporting positive, positively based on itself." *Economic and Philosophic Manuscripts of 1844*, in Karl Marx-Frederick Engels, *Collected Works*, volume 3 (London: Lawrence and Wishart, 1975), p. 328.

7. For he is less guilty as charged in the *1844 Manuscripts* than he comes to be later.

8. *Capital*, volume III (Harmondsworth: Penguin, 1981), p. 959.

9. I quote from memory, and I am afraid I have lost my record of where Hegel says this (or nearly this).

10. I agree with Frank Parkin that what I would call divisions of identity are as deep as those of class, and that they cannot be explained in the usual Marxist way. But I think he is wrong to suppose that this weakness in Marxism casts doubt on its treatment of domination and exploitation as centering in class conflict. Parkin commits a category mistake when he maintains that domination or exploitation is predominantly racial in one society, religious in another, and of a class nature in a third, for racial exploitation and class exploitation are not two species of one genus. Racial exploitation is (largely) relegation to an exploited class because of race. And if, as Parkin thinks, Protestants exploit Catholics in Northern Ireland, then the exploitation is economic, and not in a comparable sense religious. Catholics are denied access to material values, not religious ones.

So while I think Marxism lacks an explanation of the potency of identities as bases of allocation to classes, I do not think it is also mistaken in refusing to put religious and racial exploitation on a par with economic exploitation. It is false that "closure on racial grounds plays a directly equivalent role to closure on the basis of property." Unlike racism, property is not, in the first instance, a means of protecting privilege. It *is* privilege, although, like any privilege, it offers those who have it ways of protecting what they have. See Frank Parkin, *Marxism and Class Theory* (London: Tavistock, 1979), especially pp. 94, 114.

11. *The German Ideology*, in Karl Marx-Frederick Engels, *Collected Works*,

volume 5 (London: Lawrence and Wishart, 1976), p. 394, translation amended. This passage is discussed at pp. 132–133 of *KMTH*.

12. Ibid., p. 225.

13. *The Holy Family*, in Karl Marx-Frederick Engels, *Collected Works*, volume 4 (London: Lawrence and Wishart, 1975), p. 131. I would argue that the ideal figured forth in the following much-quoted passage also deserves to be called materialist:

> . . . when the limited bourgeois form is stripped away, what is wealth other than the universality of individual needs, capacities, pleasures, productive forces, etc., created through universal exchange? The full development of human mastery over the forces of nature, those of so-called nature as well as of humanity's own nature? The absolute working out of his creative potentialities . . . which makes this totality of development, i.e. the development of all human powers as such the end in itself, not as measured on a *pre-determined* yardstick?

Grundrisse, Martin Nicolaus, trans. (Harmondsworth: Penguin, 1973), p. 488.

14. *The German Ideology*, op. cit., p. 78.

15. *Contribution to the Critique of Hegel's Philosophy of Law: Introduction*, in Karl Marx-Frederick Engels, *Collected Works*, volume 3, op. cit., p. 175, translation amended.

16. *The Communist Manifesto*, in Karl Marx-Frederick Engels, *Collected Works*, volume 6 (London: Lawrence and Wishart, 1976), p. 502. Note how false the predictions made at this point in the *Manifesto* are.

17. Ibid., p. 488.

18. *Capital*, volume I, op. cit., p. 135, translation amended.

19. Tom Nairn, *The Break-Up of Britain* (London: New Left Books, 1981).

20. No one was keener on nationality than Johann Gottfried Herder, and yet he hated states. See Isaiah Berlin's "Herder and the Enlightenment," in that author's *Vico and Herder* (London: Hogarth Press, 1976), pp. 158–165, 181.

21. Marx was not alone in his tendency to underestimate the strength of national bonds. For a brilliant evocation of general intellectual failure on that score, see Isaiah Berlin's essay on "Nationalism" in his *Against the Current* (London: Hogarth Press, 1979). A good summary statement appears on p. 337.

22. The quotation is from Allen Wood, to whom I am here indebted, but I have modified his point, since he says the conflict might be

too infrequent to threaten historical materialism, and the crucial question is not how many times it occurs, but whether, as I have said, it assumes epochal significance. See Allen Wood, *Karl Marx* (London: Routledge and Kegan Paul, 1981), p. 30.

23. *Capital*, volume I, op. cit., p. 284.

24. It does not follow that these categories of production cannot overlap, and it may be that their potential intersection is greater than Marx allowed himself to hope. See *KMTH*, pp. 324–325.

25. This does not mean that I am sure the argument whose premises they are is successful. For a challenging critique of it, see the review of *KMTH* by Joshua Cohen, *The Journal of Philosophy*, May, 1982.

26. Wood, *Karl Marx*, op. cit., p. 75.

27. Such claims are usually called "teleological", and I have myself argued that teleological or (as I prefer to consider them) consequence explanations are fundamental to historical materialism, but there follows no commitment to the grandiose idea rejected here. For defence of the place of consequence explanation in historical materialism, see *KMTH*, chapter X; "Functional Explanation: Reply to Elster," *Political Studies*, 28 (March, 1980) pp. 129–135; "Functional Explanation, Consequence Explanation, and Marxism," *Inquiry*, 25 (January, 1982), pp. 27–56; and "Reply to Elster on 'Marxism, Functionalism and Game Theory,' " *Theory and Society*, 11 (July, 1982), pp. 483–495.

28. Or possible, that is, for people in general, since it is false that essence-based creativity is never exhibited in history: one person who exhibited it was John Milton, who "produced *Paradise Lost* for the same reason that a silk worm produces silk. It was an activity of *his* nature." Karl Marx, *Theories of Surplus Value*, volume I, (London: Lawrence and Wishart, 1969), p. 401. On creativity before and after the advent of communism, see *KMTH*, p. 205. By the way: would a communist Milton lack the historical Milton's singleness of vocation? Would he function not as a *writer* but as one who engages in writing "among other activities?" The idea is neither attractive nor plausible.

29. It is adversity that "spurs man on to the multiplication of his needs, his capacities, and the instruments and modes of his labour." *Capital*, volume I, op. cit., p. 649.

30. See the reference to prehistory at the end of the famous extract from the Preface to *A Contribution to the Critique of Political Economy*, quoted at p. viii of *KMTH*.

31. *KMTH*,. P. 23–24.

32. The view just sketched bears comparison with the following difficult *Manuscripts* passage:

> We see how the history of *industry* and the established *objective* existence of industry are the *open* book of *man's essential powers,* the perceptibly existing human *psychology.* Hitherto this was not conceived in its connection with man's essential being, but only is in external relation of utility . . . We have before us the *objectified essential powers* of man in the form of *sensuous, alien, useful* objects, in the form of estrangement, displayed in *ordinary material industry* . . . all human activity hitherto has been labour—that is, industry—activity estranged from itself. . . .

> *Economic and Philsophical Manuscripts of 1844,* op. cit., pp. 302–303.

33. See the personal views he expressed in a "Confession" available in David McLellan, *Karl Marx* (London: Macmillan, 1973), pp. 456–457.

34. *Grundrisse,* op. cit., p. 540.

35. *Economic and Philosophical Manuscripts of 1844,* op. cit., p. 304.

36. Jon Elster, "The Contradiction Between Forces and Relations of Production," typescript, pp. 11–12.

37. For their comments on a draft of this essay I am indebted to Dick Arneson, Annette Barnes, Isaiah Berlin, Jon Elster, Keith Graham, Helge Høibraaten, Margaret Levi, Keith McLelland, John McMurtry, Philip Pettit, Jack Pitt, Hillel Steiner, Chuck Taylor, Ian Vine, David West, Erik Wright, the editors of *Nomos,* and, above all, Arnold Zuboff, who provided many hours of acute criticism and constructive suggestion.

11

MARX'S ENTERPRISE
OF CRITIQUE

PETER G. STILLMAN

Marx's predominant form of theoretical discourse is the critique (*Kritik*). His central and most famous work is labelled a critique: *Capital: A Critique of Political Economy* (1867).[1] He announced other works similarly: for instance, *The Holy Family, or Critique of Critical Criticism* (1844) and *A Contribution to the Critique of Political Economy* (1859). His major unpublished works also bear that title. His first important political work is *The Critique of Hegel's Philosophy of Right* (1843). His preferred title for the 1844 *Economic and Philosophical Manuscripts* was *A Critique of Politics and Political Economy*.[2] The full title of his next long, unprinted effort, *The German Ideology* (1845), included "critique."[3] While the frequent appearance of *Kritik* has often been noted, only rarely has anything more than a brief and superficial analysis been given.[4]

There is one sense of "critique" for which Marx is justly notorious: vitriolic destruction or devastation of the theoretical formulations of fellow socialists, would-be allies, and bourgeois opponents. No one can read Marx's works without being struck by his often vicious critical polemics and his continuing criticisms of others. Burdened with carbuncles, burning with indignation, and convinced of his own scientific accuracy, Marx took the theories of others, examined them, and then disagreed with, censured, and sometimes excoriated them, using as his basis

252

the conclusions that he had arrived at in the course of his own studies.[5]

As can be discerned in *Capital* and his other works titled *Kritik*, Marx also engages in "critique" in a different and technical sense of the term, with a complex, far-reaching, and unique meaning. For Marx, critique involves insightful assessment that can produce knowledge even in a society permeated by illusion and constrained by power, knowledge that can become part of the consciousness—and hence the bases for thought and action—of a part of that society, the proletariat. The presentation of Marx's sense of critique also indicates his indebtedness to his predecessors in philosophy and economics, like Hegel and Ricardo; shows how critique is integral to Marx's idea of science; reveals that critique forms the locus for his claim to unify theory and practice, science and revolution, knowledge of the world and action to change it; and suggests that attention to critique may help clarify some recurrent issues in the interpretation of Marx and Marxism.

1. THE MEANING OF CRITIQUE

As a technical term for Marx, critique encompasses three distinguishable steps of analysis and evaluation: immanent criticism, critical reconstruction, and critical supersession.[6] Each step occurs on two levels, consciousness and reality, as Marx indicates in the ambiguity of *Capital*'s full title: it is a "critique of political economy," where "political economy" refers both to those thinkers who analyze the economic order and to the actual workings of that economic order, i.e., to both economists and economics, both theory and the reality it describes.

As the first step (and using political economy as the example), critique involves an immanent criticism of contemporary economists and economy, pointing up errors, inconsistencies, and irrationalities. But such internal criticism is not merely negative and does not stop with the discovery of the errors of a Nassau Senior (CI, 224–29) or of the misleading appearances and practices of capitalism (CI, 583). Rather—and as the second step—critique includes the discovery and reconstruction of the way the economic world works, i.e., an interpretation of capital and its laws of motion (CI, 10). Since this theoretical reconstruction illuminates the historical and developmental aspect of capitalism, it includes some hints toward the reconstruction of reality, some suggestions of the new world of associated producers that will grow out of the old world of capital. In other words, critique reconstructs both theory and reality, as the reinterpretation of the laws of capital and completes the immanent criticism of the political economists, and the hints of the new society show the results of the immanent criticism of economic activity. Finally, critique takes on its concluding meaning: it is the criticism of political economy as such, as an autonomous enterprise of thought and action. Bound up with the bourgeois world, political economy is to be replaced by theories that account for the full range of human potentials and activities, and by practical human life and actions motivated by and aiming for more than money and capital.

The meaning of critique, with its three steps and two levels, needs to be described in more detail and with examples from the range of Marx's work.[7] At first, critique entails an analysis of theory, thought, or consciousness.[8] This immanent criticism does not look outside the theory but examines the theory's categories, statements, and conclusions with the intention of discovering internal limitations and defects: logical inconsistencies, insuperable internal contradictions or aporias, unasked questions or unexamined assumptions, gaps in reasoning, and failure to realize the goals posited for the theory. Thus, for instance, Marx criticizes Hegel's assertion that the bureaucracy is the universal class by showing how, in Hegel's own construction, the bureaucracy and bureacrats pursue their own particular interests (CHPR, 45–48, 50–51). Marx begins his essay "Alienated Labour" by accepting the "presuppositions" of British political economists; he notes, for instance, that "political economy begins with the fact of private property; it does not explain it"; and then he goes on to "explain" it, starting from their facts and ideas (EW, 120). His later analyses of Smith, Ricardo, and the others lead Marx to conclude that "it is the weak point of the classical school of Political Economy that it nowhere, expressly and with full consciousness, distinguishes between labour, as it appears in the value of a product and the same labour, as it appears in the use-value of that product" (CI,

80 n. 1). They fail even though both uses occur in their writings.

Critique also includes an analysis that builds on this immanent criticism of theories: having exposed the theory's problems, Marx does not rest content with an academic or polemic victory, but rather he asks *why* these inadequate theoretical categories and conclusions exist. To answer that question, Marx moves from the realm of pure theory to an examination of the society that can give rise to such internally insufficient or incoherent theoretical constructs. In other words, Marx does not allow his criticism to stay at the level of theory (GI, 148–49); he insists that consciousness is always consciousness *of* something (CI, 154–55; CIII, 313); and, even "if in all ideology men and their circumstances appear upside-down as in a *camera obscura,* this phenomenon arises just as much from their historical life-process as the inversion of objects on the retina does from their physical life-process" (GI, 154; CIII, 209). So Marx engages in an immanent criticism of the "historical life-process" of men.

For instance, Hegel's misunderstanding of the bureaucracy derives in part from the "uncritical idealism" that simply reproduces the institutions and conundrums of his world (CHPR, 3–10). Thus, "the criticism of the German philosophy of right and of the state . . . is at once the critical analysis of the modern state and of the reality connected with it, and the definitive negation of all the past forms of consciousness in German jurisprudence and politics" (ICHPR, 59). The inability of Adam Smith and James Mill to "explain" private property leads Marx to the concept of alienated labor (EW, 120, 129). To discover why Smith and Ricardo fail to understand the value form and hence the commodity, Marx examines the form of value in its different historical manifestations (CI, 80 n. 2) and is able to draw out the "two-fold nature" of labor and value in commodities (CI, 41). So the criticism of a theory gives insight into the "historical life-processes" of men and makes possible the criticism of these processes: the state's sovereignty is only "imagined" (EW, 14); labor in capitalism is alienated; and Ricardo's problems with value reflect the historical nature and complexity of the commodity itself.

Critique includes immediately a second step. Since a fully completed immanent criticism gives insights into the deficiences of theories of reality and of the reality they describe, it results in the clarification of reality: consequently, critique is reconstruction, as reality is redescribed by an alternate theory or interpretation. Since the immanent criticism of Hegel's political philosophy leads Marx to see that Hegel's "uncritical positivism and [equally] uncritical idealism" (EW, 201) simply reproduce the dilemmas of the bourgeois world he describes, Marx can then redescribe and reformulate that world, accounting for its (and Hegel's) contradictions, as a world in which civil society dominates the state. Throughout the 1844 *Economic and Philosophical Manuscripts,* Marx uses his immanent criticism to arrive at reformulations like alienated labor.

Similarly, in one important theme of *Capital,* Marx describes the liberal ideology of "liberty, equality, property, and Bentham" as the ideology and reality of the sphere of simple circulation (CI, 176) and then shows how that sphere (with that ideology) does not yield the answer to the question, posed by Smith and Ricardo via Marx, about where and how surplus value is created (CI, 166). Marx's analysis drives him to see that the sphere of circulation is the "phenomenon of a process taking place behind it" (G, 255), the sphere of production, in which, as Marx concludes four hundred pages after posing the question, the apparently equal and "ever repeated purchase and sale of labour-power is now the mere form; what really takes place is this—the capitalist again and again appropriates, without equivalent, a portion of the previously materialised labour of others, and exchanges it for a greater quantity of living labour" (CI, 583). Through the criticism of ideology and the world that produces it, Marx arrives at a theoretical recontruction of the process of the appropriation of labor.

Marx intends practical reconstruction also; he suggests the critical reconstruction of bourgeois society according to the possibilities implicit in his immanent criticism and theoretical reconstruction. Because reconstruction grows out of immanent criticism, Marx finds the image of the future in the present: as he wrote in a letter of 1843, "we do not attempt dogmatically to prefigure the future, but want to find the new world only through criticism of the old" (to Ruge, Sept. 1843); and in 1875, "what we have to deal with here is a communist society, not as it has *developed* on its own foundations, but, on the contrary, just as it *emerges* from capitalist society . . . still stamped with the birth marks of the old society from whose womb it emerges" (Gotha, I).

For example, from his study of Hegel's political philosophy, Marx discovers the inadequacy of purely political emancipation (EW, 11–13) and the need for the proletariat as the revolutionary class (ICHPR, 64). The analysis in "Alienated Labor" leads Marx to see the inadequacy of "radical" measures like equality of wages (EW, 132) and the need to abolish the conditions of labor that result in alienation (EW, 132–33). *Capital* contains many allusions to a reconstructed society. Where capitalism imposes a limited form, Marx sees the possibility for breadth: "When the limited bourgeois form is stripped away, what is wealth other than the universality of individual needs, capacities, pleasures, productive forces, etc., created through universal exchange? The full development of human mastery over the forces of nature . . .? The absolute working-out of his creative potentialities . . ." (G, 488; CI, 645)? Where capitalism has introduced new possibilities but maintains them in destructive forms, Marx sees the potential: "Modern Industry . . . compels society, under penalty of death, to replace the detail-worker of to-day, crippled by life-long repetition of one and the same trivial operation, and thus reduced to the mere fragment of a man, by the fully developed individual, fit for a variety of labours, ready to face any change of production, and to whom the different social functions he performs, are but so many modes of giving free scope to his own natural and acquired powers" (CI, 488). Furthermore, Marx is clear about the means to be used to attain these goals: since the theoretical reconstruction of capitalism demonstrates the centrality of time (as in labor time), the "basic prerequisite" for the "true realm of freedom" is "the shortening of the working-day" (CIII, 820).

Finally, the last step of critique is critical supersession, in which the narrow area being criticized—whether it be philosophy, politics, or economics—is seen to be deficient as a theoretical and practical enterprise and therefore to be superseded or *aufgehoben*.[9] Thus, Marx wishes to "realize and abolish philosophy" (ICHPR, 59). He wishes, in 1844, to reverse the situation in which "everything which the economist takes from you in the way of life and humanity, he restores to you in the form of money and wealth" (EW, 171). In his later critiques, Marx continues his early theme. Following Hegel, Marx sees that political economy has arisen "out of the conditions of the modern world" (PR, 189R[10]; CI, 80 n. 2). For Marx, the theory of political economy is too narrow: it treats the worker as a worker, not as a man (EW, 76; CI, 407–409); it sees work only in a limited sense (G, 610–11; CI, 177–78); and it generally looks only to the economic (G, 650–52). Similarly, economic activity is too narrow: the capitalist lives by only one commandment—"Accumulate, accumulate! That is Moses and the prophets!" (CI, 595)—and the worker has only one existence—"it is self-evident that the labourer is nothing else, his whole life through, than labour-power to be devoted to the self-expansion of capital" (CI, 264). So Marx looks to a future society in which the narrow issues of political economy will be replaced by the central issues of human freedom and self-development (CM, II; Gotha, I), and political economy, like politics and philosophy, will no longer exist as a separate theoretical undertaking or distinct sphere of activity. While his contemporaries are writing the "principles of political economy," Marx writes about a specific historical form, capital, and engages in a critique of its theoretical and practical companion, political economy, in order to supersede them.

Marx's critique, then, involves three steps, each on the two levels of theory and reality. Writing more than half a century before Marx's "early writings," Kant presaged that "our age is the age of critique, to which everything must be subjected."[11] Kant's critiques, which discover the conditions for the proper employment of the faculties of knowledge, differ from Marx's critique, which examines what others know—their consciousness of the world and the world of which they are conscious. Marx's critique, nevertheless, aims at subjecting everything to the process of critique, so as to resolve the difficulties and realize the potentials of human knowing and acting.

2. THE NECESSITY FOR IMMANENT CRITICISM

Marx insists on and requires immanent criticism as the first step in critique because he sees that there can be no immediate access to reality, no direct route to truth, "no royal road to science" (CI, 21). Both reality and the logic of access to it are in question. Marx faces exactly the same dilemma that Hegel sees confronting philosophy: "Philosophy misses an advantage enjoyed by the other sciences. It cannot like them rest the existence of its objects on the natural admissions of consciousness, nor can it assume that its method of cognition, either for starting or continuing, is one already accepted" (Enc. 1). German idealism since Kant recognized that human subjects participate in the constitution of the world, building up the world and knowledge of it at the same time that they create constraints and distortions—as each stage in Hegel's *Phenomenology* testifies. Marx follows Hegel in seeing that the world as it appears is the result of a prior social construction of reality (Enc. 41A). Appearances have been constituted or constructed by "everyday concepts" (CIII, 820) that "have already acquired the stability of natural, self-understood forms of social life" (CI, 75). As Marx is aware, in this world of appearances all facts gain their place and meaning for human discourse by the labels and categories that are attached to them: "brute" social facts, i.e., facts that exist independently of human categories, do not exist. The categories with which human beings order their observations and experiences are a "social product as much as language" (CI, 74). But, for Marx, this preconstituted world of appearances, categories, and mediated facts ultimately masks the essential relations of capital.

Moreover, the logic of analysis is not self-evident. German idealism since Kant had subjected previous modes of thought to critiques of reason, and Hegel did the same to Kant (Enc. 41–60). So all pre-Hegelian methods of cognition are problematical by Marx's youth, and Marx's critique of Hegel's *Philosophy of Right* and *Phenomenology* made clear to him that he could not just appropriate Hegel's logic outright (CHPR, 3–10; EW, 201; CI, 19–20).

As a result of the process of critique, Marx concludes that "the final pattern of economic relations as seen on the surface, in their real existence and consequently in the conceptions by which the bearers and agents of these relations seek to understand them, is very much different from, and indeed quite the reverse of, their inner but concealed essential pattern and the conception corresponding to it" (CIII, 209). Marx tries to discover and present logically the inner, concealed, and frequently inverted (CI, 537) "essential pattern" hidden behind "real existence" and "conceptions" of it.[12] He uses immanent criticism for the discovery.

But the voyage of discovery is difficult because, for Marx, capitalism produces "an enchanted, perverted, topsy-turvy world" (CIII, 830) in which appearances mask essence in a double way: the conceptions and ideas that actors hold about "capitalist relations" (CIII, 818) (or, synonymously, "real existence" [CIII, 209]) may be more or less accurate and unastigmatic representations of those relations; and those capitalist relations themselves frequently invert, hide, or otherwise mystify the "essential pattern" (or, synonymously, "essential relations" or "essence") of human interaction.

For Marx, "false appearance and illusion" (CIII, 830) characterize the conceptions "in the ordinary consciousness of the agents of production themselves" (CIII, 25) and in the texts of the vulgar political economists, whose theories are "no more than a didactic, more or less dogmatic, translation of everyday concepts of the actual agents of production" (CIII, 830; CI, 537). These illusions nonetheless are not simply "false"[13] but derive from observation and reasoning. Marx explains at some length how a superficial observer of a surface of capitalist relations could perceive these false appearances (CIII, 826–29); for instance, because capital increases productive forces, "all of labour's social productive forces appear . . . to issue from the womb of capital itself" (CIII, 827). If the superficial observer writes in justification of capitalism, as do the vulgar political economists, then illusions multiply: one example that releases Marx's indignation, learning, and sarcasm is Nassau Senior's replacement of "capital" with "abstinence" and J.S. Mill's further claim, that profits are "remuneration of abstinence" (CI, 596 n. 3 and 596–98).

The illusory conceptions of everyday life invade the consciousness of even the best economists, the school of "classical Political Economy . . . which, since the time of W. Petty, has investigated the real relations of production in bourgeois society" (CI, 80 n. 2). As Marx notes in connection with an important argument about wages and the value of labor power, classical economists "borrowed from every-day life the category of 'price of labour' without further criticism" (CI, 537) and "accepted uncritically the categories 'value of labour,' 'natural price of labour,' &c., as final and as adequate expressions for the value-relations under consideration, and [were] thus led . . . into inextricable confusion and contradiction" (CI, 538).

Even when conceptions conform to the "real existence" of "capitalist relations," the "real existence" may mask and mystify the essential pattern. In capitalist relations, exchange value exists, circulation of commodities exists, but "exchange-value . . . is only the mode of expression, the phenomenal form, of something contained in" the commodity (CI, 37); and circulation is the "phenomenon of a process taking place behind it" and is "pure semblance," not self-grounding, dependent on production (G, 255).

Commodities and other central aspects of capitalism are "enigmatic" (CI, 71) in other ways. For instance, "a commodity is . . . a mysterious thing . . . because the relation of the producers to the sum total of their own labour is presented to them as a social relation, existing not between themselves, but between the products of their labour" (CI, 72); human relations are reified relations. Similarly, the social becomes the natural: "The special difficulty in grasping money in its fully developed character as money . . . is that a social relation, a definite relation between individuals, here appears as a metal, a stone, a purely physical, external thing which can be found, as such, in nature, and which is indistinguishable in form from its natural existence" (G, 239). Human creations have power over humans in capitalism, "in which the process of production has the mastery over man, instead of being controlled by him" (CI, 81, 92–93). Finally, both reality and thought in capitalism are ahistorical. While money, commodities, and the like have evolved historically, "the intermediate steps of the process vanish in the result and leave no trace behind" (CI, 92; Phen. 68). So crucial economic forms have a social fixity because nothing remains of their "genesis" (CI, 47). Moreover, for Marx, even the best bourgeois political economist "seeks to decipher, not their historical character, for to him they are immutable, but their meaning" (CI, 75); the economist remains within the "bounds of the bourgeois horizon" (CI, 14), looks upon the "capitalist regime . . . as the absolutely final form of social production, instead of as a passing historical phase of its evolution" (CI, 15), and thus evinces no interest in history and change except to treat them in the essentially ahistorical way that as "the Fathers of the Church treated pre-Christian religions" (CI, 81).

To accept appearances uncritically—to accede to common conceptions and to look only for "real existence"—is the mark of an inadequate science (CIII, 817; CI, 542), a vulgar political economy, or a radicalism manqué. Proudhon, for instance, failed as a radical thinker, according to Marx, because he accepted the categories of thought that appeared to him in bourgeois society and so he always spoke and thought in the concepts of a capitalist (G, 248; PofP, 161), with whom he shares the illusions of the epoch (GI, 165).

On the other hand, appearances must be taken seriously: they are not mere illusion or mere "real existence" unconnected or irrelevant to essence; rather, they are manifestations that both reveal and conceal essence. In Hegel's words, appearance is the "illusory being of essence itself" (Logic, 398): i.e., both illusory and being. As Marx wrote of some categories of British political economists, "these imaginary expressions arise from the relations of production themselves. They are categories for the phenomenal forms of essential relations" (CI, 537; CI, 586).

The discovery of essential relations behind appearances requires criticism of the categories or forms of thought in which appearance is cast. Marx agrees with Hegel that "forms of thought must be made an object for investigation" (Enc. 41; CI, 80 n. 2). So Marx analyzes the category of free laborer and discovers estranged labor (EW, 123), and he analyzes labor and value in order successfully to break labor conceptually into its relations with use value and exchange value (CI, 80 n. 1). Immanent criticism of theories—that discovers the inconsistencies and other inadequacies in their concepts—discloses deficient categories and exposes them as categories of appearance, in need of rejection or modification.

Marx needs previous philosophical and economic theories as a mine for his critical excursions. They also assist Marx because previous theories do contain partial insights or show where interpretive problems exist (CI, 542; CIII, 313). He also needs good prior philosophical and economic analyses that have asked important questions and have refined or resolved many major difficulties (CIII, 830). Both the number of reference footnotes in *Capital* and Marx's modesty about the number of his own theoretical insights [14] indicate his reliance on past theories; Marx is here like Hegel, for whom "the half-truth" should not be rejected as wrong but maintained as a "mere element . . . included in the truth" (Enc. 32A). Consequently, Marx is also like Hegel in wishing not to eliminate previous theories as though replacing falsehood with truth; rather, both Hegel and Marx see themselves as fulfilling the previous theoretical development and rendering the previous theories *aufgehoben*, both cancelled and preserved (HF, 38; Phen. 68). Marx is therefore a part of the traditions of German idealism and British political economy at the same time that he is trying to burst them open to discover their liberatory potentials.

Marx insists that criticism be immanent because, in the analysis of categories, he agrees with Hegel that criticism or "refutation must not come from the outside, that is, it must not proceed from assumptions lying outside the system in question and inconsistent with it. . . . The genuine refutation must penetrate the opponent's stronghold and meet him on his own ground; no advantage is gained by attacking him somewhere else and defeating him where he is not" (Logic, 580–81). The critic must, in a sense, know the theory better than its author, to discern its internal inadequacies and inconsistencies.

Thus, for Marx (as for Hegel), there is little value in criticizing one theory by holding it against another theory asserted dogmatically, as Marx knew from his youth (letter to Ruge, Sept. 1843; Enc. 32A). Equally, there is little point in criticizing a theory with moral imperatives or dogmas brought in from outside. Since the very need for critique stems from the problematic status of "reality" and the ubiquity of illusion, there is little point in opposing "reality" to the theory to be criticized. Nor is there need to discover new facts or ascertain if hypotheses can be falsified empirically with new data. Rather, immanent criticism analyzes and reconceives existing concepts and categories of theories and the real existence they reflect.[15]

In his concern with categories of analysis or forms of thought, Marx indicates how bourgeois ideology—with its categories that reflect the phenomenal appearances of capitalist society—permeates the very basis of the thinking of individuals in that society and thus how the illusions of the epoch are maintained and solidified; as Marx sees, cultures create and maintain illusion.[16] At the same time, concern with categories leads Marx to concern with logic. He demonstrates the intimate relation between form (or categories or concepts) and content: a content (like labor [CI, 177–85] or value [CI, 80 n. 2]) takes many different forms, each of which is characteristic of a specific historical period and involves different defining aspects. In his concern with forms, Marx rejects the Kantian approach that concepts are a priori categories of reasoning, fixed and immutable; he also rejects the alternative, empiricist formulation, that they are "mere" concepts, abstract generalizations arbitrarily abstracted from arbitrarily assembled empirical data or merely stipulated, as a convenient means to order data; and he rejects the approach of a formal logic that, seeing no inherent essence or necessary connections in the external world, develops in the human mind a set of principles that are then to be applied, from the outside, to the world. As I.I. Rubin has written:

> One cannot forget that on the question of the relation between content and form, Marx took the standpoint of Hegel, and not of Kant. Kant treated form as something external in relation to the content, and as something which adheres to the content from the outside. From the standpoint of Hegel's philosophy, the content is not in itself something to which forms adheres from the outside. Rather, through its development, the content itself gives birth to the form which is already latent in the content. Form necessarily grows out of the content itself.[17]

Whereas Hegel's *Logic* develops by a process of thought analyzing thought (Enc. 83), for Marx both content and form derive from human practical life. For instance, labor's content is universal: "it is the everlasting Nature-imposed condition of human existence, and thus is independent of every social phase of that existence, or rather, is common to every such phase" (CI, 184). As men relate to each other in different social phases, the form of labor differs: e.g., slavery, wage labor. So the form grows from the common content, differently in different social arrangements. Through his study of Hegel, Marx decided that Hegel's logic (like his politics) was inverted: for Hegel, the categories of thought determined social and political life. Marx's logic therefore turns Hegel's right-side-up; the categories, the forms of life, must be discovered as they essentially exist in economic and social life (CI, 19–20; G, 93, 101).[18]

3. THE VALIDATION OF CRITICAL RECONSTRUCTION

Immanent criticism needs to be followed by critical reconstruction. Marx is well aware of the limited value of "that kind of criticism which knows how to judge and condemn the present, but not how to comprehend it" (CI, 505 n.) Ever since Hegel's portrayal of master and slave (Phen. 228–40) showed how human beings create the relations that oppress them and demonstrated that the form of liberation is conditioned by the form of domination (G, 98), outrage at oppression must be matched by analysis of its exact form and legitimation. So, for instance, awareness that the capitalist "robs" the worker must be matched by the comprehension of how he "earns surplus value with full right."[19]

For Marx as for Hegel, however, immanent or philosophical criticism is not only negative but contributes to knowledge. As Hegel said, "For the negative, which emerges as the result of dialectic, is, because a result, at the same time the positive: it contains what it results from, absorbed into itself, and made part of its own nature" (Enc. 81A, 82; G, 90). Marx's youthful criticism of the political economist's "free laborer" led him to see "alienated labor." *Capital* as a whole stands as the central example of the positive contribution.

Capital is the critical reconstruction of the essential relations of capitalist interaction. Deriving from his immanent critique, it is justified in two ways. First, Marx claims that *Capital* is science—and by "science" Marx means systematic knowledge, the goal of German idealists and British political economists.[20] In other words, Marx's is an interpretive science.[21] Moreover, Marx asserts his science is superior to his predecessors'. By this, he makes multiple claims. His science is internally more consistent than theirs, for his immanent criticism has discovered the inconsistencies in classical political economy that his critical reconstruction can overcome. His science explains as wide or wider a scope than theirs, as is indicated by his continual references to their work, to show that he has mastered *their* scope. His science, finally, is a better reflection of reality, as Marx strikingly and unfortunately phrased it, using a metaphor that later positivists, "Marxist" or not, have misread: in an "adequate" description, "the life of the subject-matter is ideally reflected as in a mirror" (CI, 19). In discussing commodities, Marx gives an example of such a reflection: "When I state that coats or boots stand in a relation to linen, because it is the universal incarnation of abstract human labour, the absurdity of the statement is self-evident. Nevertheless, when the producers of coats and boots compare those articles with linen, or, what is the same thing, with gold or silver, as the universal equivalent, they express the relation between their own private labour and the collective labour of society in the same absurd form" (CI, 76; CIII, 25). Marx's mirror does not simply reflect nature, but restates the categories and the categorical relations in their essential pattern.

In his interpretive science, Marx does not reify laws or facts, i.e., he does not place them beyond human thought or activity. Even Marx's central laws are subject to recurring modifications and exceptions: of a law so important it is italicized, *"the absolute general law of capitalist accumulation"* (CI, 644), Marx writes: "Like all other laws it is modified in its workings by many circumstances, the analysis of which does not concern us here" (loc. cit.) Moreover, these "natural laws of capitalist production" can take forms that are "more brutal or more humane" and can be overthrown more rapidly by the effective formation of the proletariat into a class (CI, 8–10). Similarly, for Marx facts cannot be used immediately for evidence or falsification, because he distinguishes essence from appearance and because for him "brute" facts do not exist independent of the categories that subsume them and give them meaning.

But Marx does not scorn laws, for he does try to develop the essential pattern of capitalism. Nor does he dismiss facts; rather, he uses them to buttress and amplify the results of his interpretive science. As he wrote to a follower, Sigfried Meyer, about

Capital: "Besides the general scientific exposition, I describe in great detail, from hitherto unused *official* sources, the condition of the English agricultural and industrial proletariat *during the last 20 years,* ditto *Irish* conditions. You will, of course, understand that all this serves me only as an *argumentum ad hominem*' " (letter of 30 April 1867). So, for instance, Marx derives and presents "the absolute general law of capitalist accumulation," i.e., that "accumulation of wealth at one pole is . . . at the same time accumulation of misery, agony of toil, slavery, ignorance, brutality, mental degradation at the opposite pole" of laborers, paupers, and unemployed (CI, 644–45). Then he illustrates the law by presenting multiple types of evidence (CI, 648–712), such as statistics of all sorts, conclusions of economists, visible conditions like the terrible housing for the poor, quotations from government documents, reports in Tory newspapers, and the like.

While Marx's interpretive science does make distinctions between essence and appearance (CIII, 817) and does distinguish between capitalism's narrow view of human essence, wealth, and labor and communism's broad and exalted view (G, 611, 488), Marx would not consider these discriminations as "value judgments" or "normative statements" in the contemporary positivisitic, social science senses of the phrases. Rather, the "values" and "norms" are part and parcel of the interpretation itself: distinctions about relative importance are integral to any interpretive comprehension of any broad scope of human life; equally integral are reflections about human activities, human potentials, and the possible forms of social life. In other words, any interpretive science—Marx's, Ricardo's, Hegel's, anyone's— must include, explicitly or implicitly, a view of man. As sciences, they must be judged, not by the absence or prevalence of "value judgments" nor by the "realism" or "idealism" of those judgments, but by which interpretation can marshall the force of the better argument.

Marx does not, however, hinge the validity of his critique of political economy solely on its superiority as an interpretive science. He understands and explains the limited efficacy of persuasion and the limited validity of intersubjective agreement in a society marked by constrained communication and by individual self-understandings so firmly rooted in objective life situations as to be virtually unchangeable. Marx looks to the consciousness of the working class for his ultimate justification. Just as vulgar political economy represents the point of view of the businessman, so, Marx thinks, *Capital* represents the working class: "So far as . . . criticism [of 'the bourgeois economy'] represents a class, it can only represent the class whose vocation in history is the overthrow of the capitalist mode of production and the final abolition of all classes—the proletariat" (CI, 16; see PofP, 109). Marx here is restating his youthful stand: "Just as philosophy finds its *material* weapons in the proletariat, so the proletariat finds its *intellectual* weapons in philosophy" (ICHPR, 65).

In presenting the standpoint of the proletariat, Marx wishes to amplify and clarify the workers' feelings of unease, unfairness, or oppression and to recast them into systematic, scientific form. "Theory is only realized in a people so far as it fulfils the needs of the people" (ICHPR, 61). So *Capital* is the demonstration that the felt problems of the workers derive from the essential relations of capitalism, that oppression takes the form of the class exploitation inherent and necessary to capitalism (EW, 69–76; CI, 583), and that capitalism is a transitory economic system. Marx's systematic presentation, then, develops and expands the workers' thoughts, explains to them, "as in a mirror" (CI, 19), their situation, and gives them categories for thinking and acting that can illuminate the enigmatic face of capitalism. In other words, it is their critical self-consciousness.

But, for Marx, *Capital* requires self-clarification by the workers. The conclusions of *Capital* cannot simply be accepted and memorized by rote, or adopted immediately on authority "as if shot out of a pistol" (Phen. 89)—or, at least, they make little sense if they are (CI, 76).[22] While the laws of Newton's physics or Euclid's geometry can be memorized and applied, critique is a process in which existing categories and logic must be criticized and overthrown, new ones developed, and a system constructed. Consequently, Marx's science includes both the conclusions and the process by which they were reached, and the individual learning the science has to "go through the stages" (Phen. 89), i.e., has to engage in a formative education (*Bildung*) in which his whole perspective on the world may be changed.

Just as the character Socrates tries, in Plato's *Republic,* to speak directly to the particular characteristics and concerns of his interlocutors, Marx tries to speak directly to the interests of the workers, in order to persuade. This persuasion to new knowledge involves, for Socrates, a transformation of the souls of individuals to a new and just ordering and, for Marx, a *Bildung* that reorders the attitudes and activities of each of the workers who reads and comprehends *Capital.* Quietism, reconciliation, reformism—none of these is possible, Marx thinks after *Capital* has been taken to heart (CI, 644, 583, 235); only possible is opposition to capital,[23] through action focusing on the shortening of the working day (CIII, 820).

Socrates sees the trip out of the cave as arduous and hazardous. Marx lacks the overpowering image but shares the concern: the power of bourgeois culture blocks comprehension and insight into cultural illusions. "The ideas of the ruling class are in every epoch the ruling ideas" (GI, 172). Whereas Socrates addresses himself to single individuals to convince them to undertake the struggle out of the cave, Marx makes clear to workers that opposition to capital can be effective only when they cooperate: "the isolated labourer, the labourer as 'free' vendor of his labour-power . . . succumbs without any power of resistance" (CI, 299). So the persuasion of workers aims at the formation of the proletariat into a class (CM, II), i.e., the creation of its consciousness of itself as a class.

As the action-orienting consciousness of the proletariat as a class, *Capital* is revolutionary; it entails the critical reconstruction of society in practice. As a systematic statement of interpretation, it is science, and involves the critical reconstruction of society in theoretical terms. Marx's critique of political economy is, as he wrote his friend Weydemeyer, "a scientific victory for our party" (letter of 1 Feb. 1859). While some might see a conflict between advocacy of revolution and science, Marx does not. He sees that all science has a bias or interest. Even at its most scientific and "unprejudiced," classical political economy supported the bourgeoisie against the "feudal aristocracy" (CI, 14). After about 1825, when the bourgeois-proletariat "class struggle, practically as well as theoretically, took on more and more outspoken and threatening forms" (CI, 15), major economists end up supporting either capital or labor in the struggle.

For Marx in 1867, this struggle has been "a civil war of half a century" (CI, 295) in which the capitalist has tried to expand and intensify the working day, the worker to reduce it. "There is here, therefore, an antinomy, right against right, both equally bearing the seal of the law of exchanges. Between equal rights [,] force decides" (CI, 235). Within the rules of capitalism, both capital and labor have equal right; like the characters in Aeschylus' *Oresteia* or the cultures in Hegel's world history, both sides have justifiable claims; without Athena or the world-spirit to constitute a tribunal or cast the deciding vote, parties claiming irreconcilable rights must resort to force. The political economist represents capital; Marx, the worker. Marx's science is inherently revolutionary.

4. THE PROMISE OF CRITICAL SUPERSESSION

For Marx, the proof of the effective unity of science and revolution is the transformation of society. "Man must prove the truth, that is, the reality and power, the this-sidedness of his thinking in practice" (Theses on Feuerbach, II). Marx expects that the victory of the proletariat will vindicate his interpretive science with its view of human life and activity. Then, his immanent criticism will be seen as accurate; his assessments will be shown to be not "value judgments" but valid comprehension; the horizons of bourgeois life will appear as constricting; and the separate spheres and divisions of bourgeois life, with their separate ideologies, will dissolve in a new society in which philosophy (and the critique of philosophy) and political economy (and its critique) will be superfluous because "the practical relation of every-day life offer to man none but perfectly intelligible and reasonable relations with regard to his fellowmen and to Nature" (CI, 79).

5. MARX'S CRITIQUE TODAY

Almost immediately after Marx's death, one important segment of his "disciples," the theoreticians of the Second International, dissolved Marxism into a dogmatic economics that eliminated most dimensions of "critique" found in his thought, retaining only critique in the sense of polemics based on pre-established dogma. Leading the workers, these theoreticians—and their theoretical successors in the Soviet Union and elsewhere—drowned themselves like lemmings in a sea of positivistic social theory. The comment of a Dutch Marxist around the time of World War I has recurring accuracy: "Because the proletariat masses were still wholly ruled by a bourgeois mode of thought, after the collapse [of November 1918] they rebuilt with their own hands bourgeois domination."[24]

Among some Marxists ostracized by the "orthodox," a commitment to "critical theory" remained. But for the Frankfurt School, for instance, part of the justification of Marx's critique gradually became problematical, as the revolutionary character of the working class was questioned. Undermined on one side by uncritical ideologues and on the other by the apparent integration of the proletariat, what remains of Marx's critique today?

Since critique involves not only the bare conclusions but also the process by which they were discovered, the vital strands of Marx's critique today almost always include an emphasis on reflecting upon and thinking through again Marx's full theory. So theorists stressing critique usually do not ossify Marx's theoretical conclusions, much less his tactical remarks or the later accretions to his theory. Occasionally, theorists stressing critique may accept more or less uncritically Marx's own use of critique as the definition of "critical theory" or they may attempt to deduce from Marx's critique some method or methodology that is to be applied universally—in both instances, however, losing some essential aspects of Marx's process of critique.

But critique is alive today. Clearly, critique as immanent criticism of ideology and the reality that generates it does remain. This dimension of critique has been the self-appointed task of, among others, the Frankfurt School: for an American audience, Herbert Marcuse's *One-Dimensional Man* is probably the best-known exemplar.[25] The anguish of the book's last chapter, however, as well as Marcuse's later writings, suggest that critique as reconstruction and as supersession could not be or has not been maintained.

The critique of political economy also remains, whether as renewed critique of classical political economy, as critique of current economic thought, or as critique of current economic activity. At present, this last seems to be the most theoretically interesting and practically promising, in its Marxist and non-Marxist forms of workers' self-management. Concern with workers' participation and control grew in part from analysis of the relation of the worker to the process of production, the focus of Marx's critique in "Alienated Labour." André Gorz, for instance, has drawn on Marx's insights to make an immanent criticism of that relation and its ideological accompaniments and legitimations, and has attempted to construct some new modes of interaction on the basis of his criticisms.[26]

Marx's sense of critique is alive today in another way. Some contemporary theorists—of whom Jürgen Habermas is the most famous, but not the only nor necessarily the paradigmatic example—have tried to readdress the issue of critique by looking back to Marx and examining how he undertook the process of critique. So, for instance, Habermas has worked his way through the major philosophers since Kant, as well as other thinkers important to contemporary dilemmas, and subjected their theories to an immanent criticism that allows at least the reconstruction of a critical social theory with a practical intent. As Albrecht Wellmer has written, "Habermas's work is critical theory attempting, in a debate with analytical scientific theory and social science [and, since Wellmer wrote, with theories of linguistics and communication], to determine its critical position anew."[27] While Haberman's own work is marred by a number of problems from a Marxist—or Hegelian—point of view (including especially some Kantian turns), nonetheless he is following Marx's own development of critical theory.

In his attempt to respond theoretically to "a changed historical situation,"[28] Habermas is also following Marx's stance. For Hegel, "philosophy is its own time comprehended in thought" (PR, Preface); for Marx likewise, critique comprehends, analyzes, and evaluates its own time, to criticize, reconstruct, and —unlike Hegel—suspersede it. Both Hegel and Marx evince a radical concern with the present. Although interested in confronting questions that concerned their predecessors, they refuse to be bound by those questions. Hegel and Marx do not ask, as their central explicit questions, Kant's question of the limits to reason or the Cartesian question about certain human knowledge. Rather, Hegel and Marx rephrase issues into their contemporary dilemmas and concerns. To follow through on Marx's critique in the late twentieth century poses the same challenge that Hegel put, in the Preface to the *Philosophy of Right:* "Hic Rhodus, hic salta!"

NOTES

1. Citations to Marx's works are usually in the text, in parentheses, and to page number (except as noted below). The most frequently cited texts are *Capital*, vol. I (abbreviated CI) and *Capital*, vol. III (abbreviated CIII) (New York: International Publishers, 1967). Other cited works, in the order Marx wrote them, are: J. O'Malley, ed., *Critique of Hegel's 'Philosophy of Right'* (Cambridge: Cambridge University Press, 1970), abbreviated as CHPR; "Introduction to the Critique of Hegel's 'Philosophy of Right'," abbreviated as ICHPR and cited according to Robert C. Tucker, ed., *The Marx-Engels Reader* (New York: Norton, 1978; second edition); "On the Jewish Question" and the 1844 *Economic and Philosophical Manuscripts*, in T.B. Bottomore, ed., *Karl Marx: Early Writings* (New York: McGraw-Hill, 1964), abbreviated as EW; *The Holy Family, or Critique of Critical Criticism* (Moscow: Progress, 1975), abbreviated as HF; *The German Ideology*, cited according to *The Marx-Engels Reader* and abbreviated as GI; *The Poverty of Philosophy* (Moscow: Progress, 1955), abbreviated as PofP; *The Communist Manifesto,* cited according to *The Marx-Engels Reader*, by section number, and abbreviated as CM; *Grundrisse,* Martin Nicolaus, trans. (New York: Vintage, 1973), abbreviated as G; and the *Critique of the Gotha Program,* cited according to *The Marx-Engels Reader*, by section number, and abbreviated as Gotha. Marx's letters can be found in Marx and Engels, *Selected Correspondence* (Moscow: Progress, 1975; third edition); they are cited by recipient and date. In cases of more than one citation in parentheses, the first is the origin of the quotation cited; other citations can be seen for elucidation.
2. Gary Teeple, "The Development of Marx's Critique of Politics, 1842–1847," doctoral dissertation, 1981, University of Sussex, p. 276, n. 12.
3. *The German Ideology: A Critique of the New German Philosophy as represented by Feuerbach, B. Bauer, and Stirner, and of German Socialism and its various Prophets.* Other texts that are "critiques" in the tech-

nical sense are the *Poverty of Philosophy* (see HF, 38) and the "Theses on Feuerbach" (see the fourth thesis).

4. For the best treatments of critique, see Jürgen Habermas, "Between Philosophy and Science: Marxism as Critique" in his *Theory and Practice* (Boston: Beacon, 1973); Karl Korsch, *Three Essays on Marxism* (London: Pluto Press, 1971); Geoffrey Pilling, *Marx's Capital: Philosophy and Political Economy* (London: Routledge & Kegan Paul, 1980); and Teeple, "Marx's Critique of Politics." On related topics, see Lucio Coletti, "Marxism: Science or Revolution?" and Norman Geras, "Marx and the Critique of Political Economy," both in Robin Blackburn, ed., *Ideology in Social Science* (New York: Vintage, 1973).

5. For one famous example, see the *Critique of the Gotha Program* (not Marx's title); also, CI, 224–29.

6. The German word *Kritik* can be translated as either "critique" or "criticism." In titles, it is usually translated as "critique," a practice I follow. I take advantage of the existence of two English words to use "critique" as the technical term and "criticism" (and its other grammatical forms) as a short synonym for "analysis, assessment, and evaluation."

7. While most of this chapter stresses the critique of political economy, because Marx saw that as central, in this section I use evidence from his *Critique of Hegel's 'Philosophy of Right'* and his 1844 *Economic and Philosophical Manuscripts* as well to indicate the basic stability of his use of critique. For a more detailed examination, see Teeple, "Marx's Critique of Politics."

8. While "consciousness" is the umbrella term, I use these terms— and "ideology"—not synonymously but with overlapping ranges of meaning. I think that greater precision is not necessary for the arguments of this chapter, except for "science," for which see section 3 below.

9. Korsch, *Three Essays*, p. 41.

10. Citations to G.W.F. Hegel's works are also in the text, in parentheses. Hegel, [*Encyclopedia*] *Logic*, William Wallace, trans. (Oxford: Oxford University Press, 1892; second edition), abbreviated as Enc. and cited to section (not page) number; where an "R" follows the number, the citation is not to the main paragraph but to Hegel's written elucidatory "remarks"; where an "A," to students' notes of Hegel's lectures collated by them in posthumous editions; Hegel, *The Science of Logic*, A.V. Miller, trans. (London: George Allen & Unwin, 1969), abbreviated as Logic and cited to page number; Hegel, *The Phenomenology of Mind*, J.B. Baillie, trans. (London: Macmillan, 1931), abbreviated as Phen. and cited to page

number; and Hegel, *The Philosophy of Right*, T.M. Knox, trans. (Oxford: Oxford University Press, 1942), abbreviated as PR and cited as is the [*Encyclopedia*] *Logic*.

11. I. Kant, *Critique of Pure Reason*, Preface to the First Edition. See also Marx's letter to Ruge, Sept. 1843.

12. As is the case with many other issues, Hegel makes a similar distinction between "reality" and "actuality" (PR, Preface). Hegel is frequently cited and referred to because one subsidiary theme of this chapter is the close relation between Hegel's thought and *Capital*. Indeed, Hegel's idea of critique in much of the *Phenomenology* directly parallels Marx's technical sense of the term.

13. For Marx, I think, the opposite of "true" consciousness is not "false" consciousness (as though consciousness were wayward only by erring) but "mystified" consciousness (led astray by both illusion and error). Illusion can derive from a misperception of the world or from an accurate perception of mystified real existence.

14. See Marx's letters to Weydemeyer on 5 March 1852 and to Engels on 8 January 1868.

15. As is frequently apparent in the section on the fetishism of commodities (e.g., CI, 73, 75), existing concepts may well accurately reflect real existence, but that real existence itself is an inversion and mystification of essential human relations (G, 640), needing criticism.

16. Marx himself may have fallen victim to the objectivism of bourgeois society (CI, 57–85, 71–76), according to some critics like Albrecht Wellmer; see his "The Latent Positivism in Marx's Philosophy of History" in his *Critical Theory of Society* (New York: Seabury, 1974).

17. I.I. Rubin, *Essays on Marx's Theory of Value* (Detroit: Black and Red, 1972), p. 117; see Pilling, *Marx's Capital*, p. 74. For Hegel and Marx, the intimate connection between form and content means that logic can only be discovered in the process of undertaking science. To attempt a prior epistemology or critique of pure reason commits "the error of refusing to enter the water until you have learnt to swim" (Enc. 41R). To develop specific rules of sociological method before studying the subject matter results in the same problem.

18. A full statement of Marx's logic—especially in its relations to Kant's and Hegel's—would require writing the book that Marx promised but never started. Briefly, the distinction in this paragraph is between Hegel's logic of ideas and Marx's logic of practical (or material) life, i.e., between Hegel's idealism and Marx's materialism. One implication, central for *Capital*, is that, whereas Hegelian me-

diations between opposites produce a higher synthesis on the path to thought thinking thought, Marx's mediations can simply retain the conflict and opposition of what is (CHPR, 91–92; e.g., CI, 644).

19. Karl Marx, *Notes on Adolph Wagner*, pp. 185–186, in Terrell Carver, *Karl Marx: Texts on Method* (New York: Barnes & Noble, 1975).

20. Phen., 70–71; James Steuart, *Principles of Political Economy* (1767), Preface.

21. "Interpretive" in a sense like that of, for instance, Charles Taylor, "Interpretation and the Sciences of Man," *Review of Metaphysics*, XXV, no. 1 (Sept. 1971).

22. For Marx's concern about reaching the working class, see CI, 13 and 21.

23. As a part of persuading workers to see *Capital* as the scientific statement of their interests and consciousness, Marx uses rhetorical devices throughout: classical allusions, metaphors, tropes, irony, the whole range of expressive forms. As with Socrates in Plato's presentation of him, Marx's rhetoric should be seen as part of an appeal to the entire individual, not just to his rational or theoretical faculties—because both Socrates and Marx realize that individuals are not persuaded exclusively by logic, because both aim at the transformation of the whole individual (and not just his reason), and because both assert that their rhetoric is in the service of rationality. In other words, Marx's rhetoric is not primarily evaluative, subjective, or superfluous, but an essential element of a persuasive text.

24. Anton Pannekoek, "World Revoluti on and Communist Tactics" (1920), quoted in Russell Jacoby, "Toward a Critique of Automatic Marxism," *Telos*, no. 10 (Winter 1971), p. 125. See also Korsch's 1923 comment: "the neglect of the problem of philosophy [or critique] by the Marxists of the Second International [is] . . . related to the fact that problems of revolution hardly concerned them," in his *Marxism and Philosophy* (New York: Monthly Review Press, 1970), pp. 52–53.

25. Herbert Marcuse, *One-Dimensional Man* (Boston: Beacon, 1964).

26. André Gorz, *Strategy for Labor* (Boston: Beacon, 1967).

27. Wellmer, *Critical Theory of Society*, p. 53.

28. Ibid.

12

EXPLOITATION, FREEDOM, AND JUSTICE

JON ELSTER

Exploitation is the generation of economic injustice through free market transactions. This is the thesis I want to discuss, and to a large degree to defend, in the present paper.* The thesis will provoke disagreement along two different lines. First, Marxists might want to say that the worker is forced to sell his labor power; hence the wage agreement is not a free transaction. Conversely, libertarians might want to argue that if the transactions are free, the outcome cannot be unjust. Each of the objections has some merit; hence my defence of the thesis is not unconditional. I shall proceed by discussing in turn each of the three notions appearing in the title, exploitation, freedom, and justice. Since I am also concerned to elucidate what I take to be a major strand in Marx's thought, I shall often refer to his writings, but the exegetical issue is secondary to the substantive ones.

1. THE STRUCTURE OF CAPITALIST EXPLOITATION

I shall define Marxian exploitation as the intersection of two more general categories. On the one hand it is a special case of the more general Marxian notion of extraction of surplus labor, on the other hand it is a special case of a more general notion of exploitation that also encompasses non-Marxist varieties.

Surplus labor, according to Marx, may be extracted by "direct coercion"[1] or "extraeconomic compulsion"[2] on the one hand, by "the force of circumstances"[3] or "the dull compulsion of economic relations"[4] on the other. The former is the mode of surplus labor extraction characteristic of slavery and feudalism, or at least of the nonmarket sectors of these systems. The latter is found in capitalism, and more generally in market economies. I shall reserve the term "exploitation" for the latter, referring to the former as "forcible extraction of surplus labor." This terminology, while contrary to that of Marx,[5] is supported by the more general usage as well as by certain substantive considerations.

From consultation of the *OED*, Littré, Duden, and Harrap's *German-English Dictionary*, it would appear that "exploit," "exploiter" and *"ausbeuten"* have three central meanings that are relevant for our purposes. First, there is the morally neutral sense of "making use of," as in the exploitation of natural resources. In German this is rather rendered by *"ausnützen,"* hence Marx's suggestion in *The German Ideology* of a link between utilitarianism and exploitation.[6] Secondly, there is a morally negative sense of "turning to account for selfish purposes" (*OED*) or *"/skrupellos/ für sich ausnützen"* (Duden). When applied to persons considered as "mere workable material" (*OED*), exploitation means treating another not as an end in itself, only as a means to one's own satisfaction or profit. Exploitation in this sense can be mutual, as in the act of exchange. In *The German Ideology* Marx does in fact speak of "mutual exploitation," when referring to the general tendency in capitalism to evaluate other people according to their utility.[7] Marx certainly believed this to be a morally deplorable phenomenon, but it is more akin to alienation than to what in the later economic writings he was to call exploitation.[8] Thirdly, there is the asymmetrical notion of "taking unfair advantage of someone" (Harrap) or *"tirer un peu profit illicite ou peu honorable de quelque chose"* (Littré). This, I believe, best caputres the notion of capitalist exploitation found in *Capital*.

As I understand it, the phrase "taking unfair advantage of someone" not only does not imply, but actually excludes the idea of physically forcing someone to work for one's own profit. As I shall argue in section 2 below, this does not exclude that the person being taken advantage of is in some sense "forced" or "coerced," but this sense cannot be the one that implies an infringement of his physical liberty. Such infringement, on the other hand, was at the heart of surplus labor extraction from slave or serf. In an important special case, that of perfectly competitive markets, exploitation also differs from other forms of surplus labor extraction in that it is to the benefit of both parties.[9] There cannot be mutual exploitation, but there can be mutually beneficial exploitation. These differences between capitalist exploitation and precapitalist modes of surplus labor extraction provide the substantive reason behind the terminology I am using.

The starting point for my discussion of Marxian exploitation will be one of the models developed by John Roemer, in his recent, pathbreaking analysis of exploitation and class.[10] Roemer's work offers a series of models of exploitation. The most general approach (briefly explained in note 15 below) enables him to characterize exploitation in socialist no less than in capitalist economies. Here, however, I shall only draw on the models in Part II of his book. These try to explain how exploitation and class division can arise endogenously through market exchange, thus breaking with the usual Marxist practice of taking these phenomena as given. More specifically, imagine a set of individuals all equipped with the same amount of labor power (or the same skill), but differentially endowed with other factors of production. In addition to the individuals, we must assume the presence of a state that guarantees their property rights and enforces contracts. There are well-defined techniques for producing all goods except labor power, which is the only scarce resource. Given the existence of a labor market, "an agent can engage in three types of economic activity: he can sell his labor power, he can hire the labor power of others, or he can work for himself. His constraint is that he must be able to lay out the operating costs, in advance, for the activities he chooses to operate, either with his own labor or hired labor, funded by the value of his endowments."[11]

Here the endowments and the labor power are evaluated at the prices and wage rate that obtain at the competitive equilibrium.[12] In addition to the capital constraint, Roemer assumes that there is a constraint on the length of the working day. Within these constraints, agents are supposed to maximize their net revenue. We can then ask three questions with respect to the economic agents:

1. What is their revenue?

2. Do they work for themselves, sell their labor power, or hire labor?

3. Do they work longer hours than are embodied in the commodities they can buy with their net revenue?

The first question concerns the *wealth* of the economic agents, the second their *class* membership and the third their *exploitation* status. In a series of important theorems, Roemer proves that these are highly correlated.[13] Exploiters are rich people that hire others to work for them. This may not come as a surprise, yet earlier Marxists have tended to assume this to be true by definition, not seeing that a proof is required.

Roemer's model is admirably clear and instructive. Although highly abstract, it brings out very well many of the central features of the Marxian theory of exploitation and class. On the other hand, because of the high level of abstraction, it tends to obscure other important aspects of exploitation. To be specific, I shall argue that the model brings out very well the *modal* and *structural* nature of exploitation, while unduly restricting it by the *static* and *competitive* setting.

Class membership is a *modal* notion in the following sense. A worker is not defined as any agent who actually sells his labor power, but as an agent who *must* sell his labor power in order to optimize. Some agents have the option of optimizing by selling their labor power, but they may do equally well by working for themselves; hence they are petty bourgeois rather than workers. The workers are "forced to sell their labor power." Similarly, a capitalist is an agent who must hire labor to optimize, as distinct from the petty bourgeois who may have this as one optimal solution among others. We cannot look at actual behavior to define class membership; rather we must look at constraints, necessities, and possibilities. The class-exploitation correspondence principle holds only for classes thus modally defined: a person who must sell his labor power in order to optimize is always an exploited agent, while a petty bourgeois who chooses to do so may or may not be exploited.[14] I should add that there is another reason as well why behavior is an inadequate indicator of class: some agents may choose not to optimize. A well-endowed person does not become a worker if he chooses to sell his labor power if this is not among his optimizing solutions. He remains a capitalist as long as his endowments would make him a compulsory hirer of labor were he to optimize. To leave the capitalist class he would have to give away his endowments, rather than using them inefficiently. This, I believe, makes good sociological sense. The analogous possibility for the worker is less interesting, since the worker is not only forced to sell his labor power in order to optimize, but also forced to optimize. I discuss this issue further in section 2 below.

The idea of *structural* exploitation can be taken in a variety of ways. In a wide sense, for instance, one might say that the unemployed are structurally exploited, even though they expend no labour, since they would be better off were they given their share of society's capital goods.[15] This is not the sense I have in mind here. Rather I use it to bring out the fact that exploitation is not a face-to-face phenomenon, but a general-equilibrium one—the net effect of all the various transactions an agent undertakes in different markets. In Roemer's models it is not possible, in fact, to define the relation "A exploits B," only the predicates "A is an exploiter" and "B is an exploited." Although it may be possible to identify a specific transaction between two individuals by virtue of which one is an exploiting and the other an exploited agent, this need not always be so. Marx, for instance, observes that a landlord who leases his land to a capitalist tenant is an exploiter, although he does not directly exploit labor.[16] On this structural understanding of exploitation, it is the capitalist class as a whole that takes unfair advantage of the working class as a whole, but it may prove impossible to define similarly clear-cut confrontations between individuals. I believe that for normative purposes, this structural sense of exploitation is indeed the proper one, but for explanatory purposes it may be less relevant. Managers rather than shareholders may be the target of collective action by the working class.[17]

The *static* character of Roemer's model is a serious drawback, for two reasons. First, part of the surplus accruing to the exploiter may be used for investment in future production, and part of that future production may benefit the workers. Marx writes in *Capital I* that "the greater part of the yearly accruing surplus-product [is] embezzled because abstracted without return of an equivalent."[18] If this is what constitutes the moral wrongness of exploitation, the return later of part of the surplus would make it less wrong.[19] Hence the injustice of exploitation would depend on the size and distribution of unearned capitalist consumption, not on the size of the surplus.[20] Secondly, workers no less than capitalists may save and invest, if wages are above subsistence. If workers save differentially, an equal initial distribution of resources might over time change into an unequal one that could in turn be the basis for exploitation of workers by ex-workers. It is not obvious that this is subject to the same moral condemnation as exploitation due to endowments that are not in this sense "deserved." Summing up, the static or one-period approach to exploitation is misleading because both the future use of profits and the past origin of capital are morally relevant. I return to these issues in section 3 below.

The *competitive* nature of the model makes it inapplicable to capitalist economies with collective bargaining or other modes of interaction involving coalitions, such as "divide and conquer" tactics by the capitalists.[21] To determine the rate of exploitation in a one-period model of collective bargaining, one will have to invoke some theory of bilateral monopoly, e.g. the Zeuthen-Nash-Harsanyi theory that makes the outcome dependent in a precise way on the relative bargaining strength of the parties.[22] It may then be true in a literal sense that the capitalist class is taking unfair advantage of the working class, as distinct from the more indirect sense in which that phrase was used above. In the more interesting case of multi-period bargaining, both the working class and the capitalist class will have to take account of the impact of the present wage settlement on the future stream of income. There are elements of such reasoning in Marx, when he suggests that it is in the interest of the capitalist class to restrain its greed because otherwise the physical reproduction of the workers will be threatened,[23] and in the interest of the working class to restrain its wage demands in order not to jeopardize economic growth and future wage increases.[24] More recently, Kelvin Lancaster has proposed an analogous model in which the capitalists are restrained by the fear that the workers might retaliate against high levels of capitalist consumption with high wage demands and welfare payments.[25] Unlike Marx's hints at a temporally defined model, the Lancaster model is a genuinely strategic one, in which the decisions of both classes are interdependent in the sense of being "best replies" against each other.

In conclusion, I should say that the above discussion has not yet provided any grounds for normative statements about the injustice of exploitation. I have been concerned to bring out what exploitation *means,* in the technical Marxian sense of working more than the amount of labor embodied in the goods one can purchase for one's income, and to sketch some of the ways in which it can *come about,* by competition or collective bargaining based on differential ownership of the means of production. I have stated that for Marx this was no doubt also a case of exploitation in the wider sense of taking unfair advantage, but I have yet to state and discuss the criteria of fairness that are involved.

2. FREEDOM, COERCION, AND FORCE UNDER CAPITALISM

Is the worker coerced or forced to sell his labor power? If so, how can this be made compatible with the fact that capitalism, unlike earlier modes of production, offers a good deal of freedom to the worker? I shall begin with the last question, and explore the sense in which and the limits within which the worker has a freedom of choice in capitalism. I then ask whether the worker can be said to be *coerced* to sell his labor power, assuming that this expression implies the existence of an agent coercing him. Finally, focusing on the cases in which this question is answered negatively, I shall consider whether the worker might not yet be *forced* to sell his labor power, assuming this phrase to be neutral with respect to the existence of an agent forcing him.

Following Marx, the worker has freedom of choice with respect to (at least) three different economic decisions. First, he is free to leave the working class altogether; secondly, he is free to choose his employer; and thirdly, he is free to spend his wage as the pleases. I shall discuss these in turn, but first let me make a distinction between two senses of freedom. One we may refer to as "formal freedom:" it simply consists in the absence of coercion, in the broad sense indicated below. The other I call "real ability," and is defined by the fact that the real ability to do x and the desire to do x implies doing x.[26] Formal freedom to do x and the desire to do x, on the other hand, do not imply doing x, unless the required material or personal resources are present. Real ability is unconditional, formal freedom is conditional in the sense that it requires resources to be effective.

Marx argues that in "bourgeois society every workman, if he is an exceedingly clever and shrewd fellow, and gifted with bourgeois instincts and favoured by an exceptional fortune, can possibly be converted himself into an *exploiteur du travail d'autrui.*"[27] As is evident from the conditional clause, this is a mere formal freedom, whose transformation into real ability depends inter alia on personal talents. The freedom to choose one's employer on the other hand, is a real ability, under the competitive conditions usually assumed by Marx.[28] Hence we see that the worker is free in the more important sense (i.e., real ability) with respect to the less important freedom (the freedom to choose one's employer), while free in the weaker sense with respect to the more important freedom. Marx argued that the latter freedom tends to generate the illusion that the worker is free not only with respect to the individual capitalist, but with respect to capital as such.[29] This illusion is reinforced by the formal freedom with respect to capital as such, i.e., the conditional freedom to leave the working class altogether. Marx sometimes suggests that it is further reinforced by the (unconditional) freedom of the worker as a consumer,[30] but he equally suggests that this freedom tends to develop the self-control and autonomy of the worker, making him fit for his future revolutionary role.[31]

G.A. Cohen has argued that the workers are unconditionally free to leave the working class, yet in another sense are unfree to do so.[32] Starting from the empirical observation that in contemporary Britain a great many poor immigrants are able to enter the petty bourgeoisie, through their willingness to work long hours, he argues that this option is in fact open to any worker. There are, he argues, more exits available from the working class than there are actual exiters, although far fewer than there are workers, i.e., potential exiters. *Any* worker may leave the class, but not *all* of them can do so.[33] The reason why any worker *has* the unconditional freedom to leave the working class is that almost all workers choose not to *use* it. Cohen suggests, moreover, that a possible explanation for their not using it may be solidarity: no worker wants to use an option that is not collectively available. In his phrase, the workers are collectively forced to sell their labor power, although individually free not to do so. The tendency to confuse individual and collective freedom is an additional reinforcement of the illusion of independence mentioned above.

I now turn to the question whether the worker is coerced into selling his labor power. To discuss this, I must first explain what I mean by coercion. The paradigm case of coercion is making someone do something he would otherwise not have done by threatening him with physical punishment, but I shall use the term in a much wider sense. It then covers all cases of threats, whether in the form of inflicting punishment or withholding benefits. It covers, moreover, threats that invoke economic as well as physical sanctions or benefits. It covers, finally, a more general class of manipulations of the environment: intentionally depriving the coerced agent of some options that he would otherwise have had. This may or may not go together with adding an extra option—i.e., an offer—to the original feasible set.[34] The common feature of these cases is that an agent A performs an action X that has the intended and actual consequence of making another person B perform an action Y that differs from the action Z that B would have performed had A instead pursued his "normal" course of action W. We must also stipulate that B prefers the counterfactual situation in which A does W and he does Z to the actual one in which A does X and he does Y. We need not add, however, that A prefers the actual situation to the counterfactual one, although standardly this will indeed be the case. (A may be coercing B just to flex his muscles.) Clearly, much depends on how we determine the "normal" course of action for A. It may be defined in some cases as what A usually does, in other cases as what he would have done had B not been present. I shall not here try to resolve this question of the proper baseline for imputations of coercive behavior, except to note that it should not be defined as the course that A *ought* to have taken.[35] This would make it impossible, for instance, to say that the police justly coerce people to abstain from crimes.

If this account of coercion is accepted, at least in broad outline, one implication immediately follows: when an individual capitalist makes a wage offer to an individual worker in a competitive labor market, the latter is not coerced into accepting it. This was the case that Marx, mainly for methodological reasons, took as the paradigmatic one. He tended, in fact, to disregard the intermediate cases between physical compulsion and uncoerced labor contracts. Such intermediate cases arise in "thin markets," i.e., when there is some degree of monopoly or monopsony.[36] If a capitalist has a local monopsony as a purchaser of labor power, he can coerce the worker into accepting lower wages than he would have to offer to attract workers from elsewhere. Yet even in this case the worker is not necessarily coerced into selling his labor power, only into selling it at a particularly low price. An example of the worker being coerced into selling his labor power could be that the capitalist first takes steps to render the alternative of self-employment an unfeasible or unattractive one, and then makes his wage offer.

Consider now the case of collective bargaining. Against the contention that the workers are coerced into such bargaining, a standard objection is that nothing prevents the unions from setting up their own firm. They have the capital, and indeed the manpower to do so. If they choose not to do so, it must be because they expect that they would do less well for themselves than they will as wage laborers, for instance because they lack organizational skill or, more farfetchedly, because they do not trust themselves to retain some of the current revenue for investment.[37] Yet there is another possible explanation, paralleling the suggestion made above with respect to individual workers. The capitalist class might actively seek to undermine the profitability of worker-owned firms, e.g., by making external financing more difficult or by underselling them (over and above what takes place in competition between capitalist firms). In that case it would be true to say that workers are coerced into selling their labor power.[38]

A more complex case is the following. The workers in a given firm or industry are unorganized. If they were to organize themselves, they might set up their own firm; hence the employers take steps to prevent them from organizing themselves. I do not have in mind here such political measures as anticombination acts, which fall outside the present discussion. Rather, the employers might use their economic power to influence the variables that determine the probability of successful collective action by the workers. As an example, one may cite the use of "divide and conquer" tactics, e.g., by hiring workers from different ethnic or national backgrounds. If this is done purposively to prevent the workers from liberating themselves from the "invisible threads" of the wage contract, they are indeed coerced into selling their labor power. I believe, however, that this is mainly a theoretical possibility. Far more importantly, employers might use such tactics because organized workers could command a higher wage, not because they could break away from the wage relationship altogether. In that case, the workers are coerced into accepting a low wage, not into selling their labor power.

Is the worker forced to sell his labor power? This notion can be taken in one of three distinct senses. First, given the various constraints facing him, the worker has only two options: selling his labor power or starving to death. Secondly, while the worker can survive without selling his labor power, he can do so only under conditions that are so bad that the only acceptable option is to sell his labor power. Thirdly, the worker must sell his labor power to optimize, but there may be acceptable ways of surviving that do not involve wage labor. The third sense may be set aside as distinctly spurious. Being forced to sell one's labor power in order to optimize does not count as being forced to sell one's labor power unless one is also forced to optimize,[39] in either of the first two senses.

As to the first sense, observe that this idea is not equivalent to that of wages being at subsistence. Wages might be above subsistence, and yet the only alternative to wage labor could be below subsistence, if the worker has no access to capital. Conversely, wages might be at subsistence because of the existence of a mass of peasants similarly living at subsistence, forcing wages down to their level but also providing an alternative occupation to wage labor. Hence evidence concerning trends in the wage level is not direct evidence on the issue whether workers are forced to sell their labor power or starve. One might invoke the process of primitive accumulation, but this largely implied that the workers were coerced into wage labor, rather than forced by "the dull compulsion of economic relations." In any case, the idea of starvation is irrelevant for modern capitalist economies.

The most reasonable way of understanding the contention that the worker is forced to sell his labor power is by taking it in the second of the senses indicated above. The existence of alternative occupations that might allow him to survive is irrelevant if they are so unattractive that no one could be expected to choose them. Of course, this depends on how we define what is acceptable and what is not.[40] I do not have any ideas about how to do this, except for some general remarks. The notion of what is acceptable will have to be defined both in relative and in absolute terms. If wages are high, a person may be said to be forced to sell his labor power if the alternative just allows him to survive, but if wages are at subsistence, the existence of such an alternative implies that he is not forced to sell his labor power. On the other hand, some alternatives are so good that even should the wage offer be raised to astronomical levels, the worker is not forced to take it. The worker is forced to sell his labor power if (1) the alternative is below some critical level and (2) the offered wage is well above the alternative. Presumably we do not want this critical level to be determined by moral considerations,[41] but I find myself unable to spell out the non-moral criteria that underlie our intuitions in this respect.

What is the moral relevance of being forced to sell one's labor power? There is a well-known bourgeois answer to this question: you've made your bed, so you can lie in it. The answer can be rephrased in terms of a distinction between static and dynamic considerations. A worker may at any time of his life be forced to sell his labor power, but at any time he could take steps that at a later time would make him free not to do so. If moving out of the working class is only a matter of time preferences, i.e., a preference for saving over consumption, this answer has some force. It is further discussed in section 3 below. If, however, it is a matter of being exceptionally gifted, the answer is blatantly ideological, since it turns on the confusion between conditional and unconditional freedom. If, finally, the reason why the worker remains a worker is solidarity with his fellow workers, the answer turns on a confusion between individual and collective freedom.

3. CAPITALIST INJUSTICE AND SOCIALIST JUSTICE

In this section I shall try to set out Marx's theory of justice, partly with a view to explaining why it condemns exploitation as unjust, partly to examine its validity. I shall first discuss the widespread idea that Marx had no theory of justice, because he thought the notions of right and justice would be transcended in the fully developed communist society. I then go on to consider the idea that property is theft, with an application to two central cases of exploitation. I end by discussing the principles from *Critique of the Gotha Program:* "to each according to his contribution" in the lower phase of communism, "to each according to his need" in the higher phase.

Marx's critique of justice should be distinguished from his general critique of *ideals.* Writing in *The Civil War in France* that the workers "have no ideals to realize,"[42] he appears to suggest that the class struggle is in no way moved by normative considerations. Yet any reader of *Economic and Philosophical Manuscripts* or *Grundrisse* knows that Marx himself held very strongly the ideal of autonomy or self-realization. The most plausible reading of the cited phrase is that Marx believed ideals to be politically inefficacious, not that he believed them to be nonexistent or strictly relative in nature. It has been suggested, however, that moral and nonmoral goods, e.g., justice and autonomy, differ in this respect.[43] The value of self-realization is unconditionally good, that of justice only "good because necessary" within a given society. There are certainly plenty of texts in which Marx appears to deny the existence of transhistorical ideals of justice, e.g., by asserting the justice of capitalist exploitation[44] or by suggesting that fully developed communism is a society in which rights are transcended rather than transformed.[45] Yet closer inspection of his views concerning both capitalism and communism shows that he was simply wrong about what he was doing. Marx may have thought that he had no theory of justice, but his actual analyses only make sense if we impute such a theory to him.

Why I think Marx's analyses of capitalism require an underlying criterion of justice will appear below. As to the analysis of communism, the passage in *Critique of the Gotha Program* in which Marx asserts the withering away of justice and rights in fully developed communism comes close to being self-contradictory. Here he first explains why the contribution principle is inadequate, because, for instance, it does not take account of differences between the workers: "one is married, another not; one has more children than another, and so on and so forth." He then goes on to conclude:

> But these defects are inevitable in the first phase of communist society as it is when it has just emerged after prolonged birth pangs from capitalist society. Right can never be higher than the economic structure of society and its cultural development conditioned thereby.

> In a higher phase of communist society, after the enslaving subordination of the individual to the division of labor, and therewith also the antithesis between mental and physical labour, has vanished; after labour has become not only a means of life, but life's prime want; after the productive forces have also increased with the all-round development of the individual, and all the springs of social wealth flow more abundantly—only then can the narrow horizon of bourgeois right be crossed in its entirety, and society inscribe on its banners: from each according to his ability, to each according to his needs.[46]

When Marx here refers to the "defects" of the contribution principle, he is implicitly invoking a higher principle of justice. Moreover, he then goes on to spell out the principle: to each according to his needs. No doubt Marx thought that in this passage he set out an argument against any abstract theory of justice, and did not notice that he could do so only by invoking himself a theory of the kind he wanted to dispense with.

Is property theft? Marx often refers to the transaction between capitalist and worker as "robbery," "embezzlement," "theft," etc. One passage is especially striking. It occurs in a discussion of expanded reporduction, where Marx supposes the existence of an "original capital" of £10,000, which then creates a surplus of £2,000. Even if the former were acquired honestly, the latter, according to Marx, is not:

> The original capital was formed by the advance of £10,000. How did the owner become possessed of it? "By his own labour and that of his forefathers", answer unanimously the spokesmen of Political Economy. And, in fact, their supposition appears the only one consonant with the laws of the production of commodities.

> But it is quite otherwise with regard to the additional capital of £2,000. How they originated we know perfectly well. There is not a single atom of its value that does not owe its existence to unpaid labour. The means of production, with which the additional labour-power is incorporated, as well as the necessaries with which the labourer is sustained, are nothing but component parts of the surplus-product, of the tribute exacted annually from the working-class by the capitalist class. Though the latter with a portion of that tribute purchases the additional labour-power even at its full price, so that equivalent is exchanged for equivalent, yet the transaction is for all that only the old dodge of every conqueror who buys commodities from the conquered with the money he has robbed them of.[47]

The argument is somewhat disingenuous or question-begging. To see this, consider G.A. Cohen's gloss on the last sentence: "capitalists pay wages with money they get by selling what workers produce."[48] But of course workers produce with the help of capital goods, that by the assumption of the argument is the legitimate possession of the capitalist. I return to this issue shortly. First I want to consider the passage as evidence that Marx thought the capitalist appropriation of surplus value an unjust one. Cohen, in his further comment on the passage, argues that "Now since . . . Marx did not think that by capitalist criteria the capitalist steals, and since he did think he steals, he must have meant that he steals in some appropriately non-relativist sense. And since to steal is, in general, wrongly to take what rightly belongs to another, to steal is to commit an injustice, and a system which is "based on theft" is based on injustice."[49]

I shall argue that this view, while not quite false, is misleading. Marx himself explains why it is inappropriate to say that the capitalist robs the worker:

> In my presentation, the earnings on capital are not in fact "only a deduction or 'robbery' of the worker". On the contrary, I present the capitalist as a necessary functionary of capitalist production, and show at length that he does not only "deduct" or "rob" but forces the production of surplus value, and thus helps create what is deducted; further I show in detail that even if in commodity exchange *only equivalents* are exchanged, the capitalist—as soon as he pays the worker the actual value of his labour-power—earns *surplus-value* with full right, i.e. the right corresponding to this mode of production.[50]

The notion of theft as usually employed presupposes that the stolen object exists prior to the act of stealing it. It is because the object exists that someone might want to steal it. In capitalist exploitation it is the other way around: it is because the surplus can be appropriated or robbed that the capitalist has an incentive to create it. Had there been no capitalist, the workers would not be robbed, but nor would they have anything he could rob them of. Hence I submit that it is misleading to speak of theft in this case. This terminology plays on the moral connotations of standard cases of theft, in order to condemn non-standard cases. The latter may or may not be relevantly different from a moral point of view, but the question should at least be confronted, not obscured, as it is by this language. In my view the issue should be formulated as one of distributive justice: exploitation is wrong because it violates the principle "to each according to his contribution." The capitalist gets something for nothing, or much for little, at the expense of others. I shall first apply the contribution principle to two polar cases of exploitation, and then discuss two correlated objections.

First, consider the pure capitalist coupon-clipper, who hires a manager at a poor wage to exploit the workers for him. Disregarding for the time being the question of how the capitalist came to acquire his capital, this violates the contribution principle, since the capitalist makes no contribution (in terms of work), yet receives an income. (To say that he contributes capital would be relevant only if his capital was accumulated "by his own labor and that of his forefathers," which is the issue I prefer to postpone for a moment.) The capitalist is not entitled to profit on his capital. This does *not* mean that the working class is somehow collectively entitled to the whole product, because directly or indirectly its labor accounts for all that is produced. The "indirect" contribution of past labor to present capital is quite irrelevant if the past workers are no longer alive. There is no collective historical subject called "the working class" whose current incarnation is entitled to the current product by virtue of the contributions of past incarnations. The issue should be posed squarely as one of the distribution of the current product among those currently living. Of the latter, only the workers make a contribution; hence no one else is entitled to any part of the product.[51]

At the other pole, consider the pure capitalist entrepreneur, who has no capital, but exploits the worker by virtue of his organizational skill. By bringing together workers whose abilities complement one another, he is able to make them much more productive collectively than they could be in isolation. He "helps create what is to be deducted." Yet this does not entitle him to an income vastly greater than that of his workers. One is not morally entitled to everything one is causally responsible for creating. The thief has no claim to the proceeds from the sale of theft-alarm devices, nor the slavedriver to the produce of his slaves, nor finally the broker or mediator to the gains that he makes possible by bringing together people of complementary skills. Similarly, the capitalist entrepreneur should at most be rewarded for the actual effort of bringing the workers together, not for the work done by those whom he assembles. (I say "at most" because he would not be entitled to anything if he is also instrumental in preventing the workers from setting up their own firm.)

To these polar cases there correspond two powerful and widespread objections to the view that exploitation is unjust. With respect to the first, we must face the problem whether there could not be a "clean path" to capitalist accumulation,[52] morally unobjectionable unlike the "primitive accumulation" in early capitalism. If some workers, who for the sake of argument we may assume differ from others only in their time preferences, choose to save and invest rather than consume immediately, could anyone object if they offer others to work for them at a wage above what the latter could earn elsewhere? (To simplify matters, let us assume that our self-made capitalist arises within an initially egalitarian communist economy, not within a capitalist economy in which the alternative wage would be part determined by past and current injustice.) This is a variant of Nozick's "Wilt Chamberlain" argument:[53] can anyone forbid capitalist acts between consenting adults? There are at least two grounds on which one could justify intervention to prevent this. First, the individual worker might be imperfectly informed, by no fault of his own, about the consequences of accepting the offer.[54] Secondly, even if it were in the fully informed interest of the worker to accept the offer, it might not be in the collective interest of the class of workers to accept it.[55] Hence, if the workers are unorganized by no fault of their own, and a fortiori if the capital owner was instrumental in bringing about their lack of organization, the Wilt Chamberlain argument breaks down. I must add, however, that if workers are both well-informed and well-organized, the argument appears irrefutable. One might try to temper it by arguing for curtailment of inheritance rights,[56] but it is not easy to do so in a way that avoids violation of the Pareto principle. My conclusion on this issue, therefore, must be twofold. First, in present-day capitalism the objection is largely irrelevant, since the situation is unjust through and through. Secondly, in an egalitarian economy there is a possibility, hardly quantifiable, that well-informed and well-organized workers would not start upon the slippery slope to income inequalities.

The second case points to the *incentive problem* that is at the heart of current discussions about the viability of socialism. How could it be unjust to reward someone for a task that he would not have undertaken in the absence of the promise of a reward? The problem of organizational skill is only one special case of this general issue. Again the objection can be stated in terms of Pareto efficiency: No one is made worse off by people reaping a reward for the use of skills that would otherwise have lain dormant. If one accepts this general type of argument, the best one can do is along the lines of Rawls's "difference principle," i.e., accepting inequalities up to the point where further inequality would make the worst-off group even worse off.[57]

Marx would probably have dismissed these problems as belonging only to the initial stage of communism, in which material incentives are still needed to elicit work or the deployment of skills. In the higher phase this will be forthcoming out of solidarity with the community[58] or because work has become "life's prime want." This, however, is an unproven and unprovable statement. At present, higher communism does not appear to be historically feasible, if we are to judge from the experience of the countries that call themselves socialist. On the basis of the principle that "Ought implies can," one might then be tempted to reject the idea that there is anything unjust about exploitation. To say that exploitation is unjust is to say that it ought to be abolished, which only makes sense if it can be abolished, which is false. It is not obvious, however, that historical feasibility is the relevant sense of "can" in this context. The nonexploitative state is feasible in a different and more relevant sense, that is, physical feasibility. Since workers under capitalism work hard and entrepreneurs use their skills, we know that the proposed alternative is physically feasible.[59] It is not utopian in the sense in which it is utopian to assert, as did Marx, that under communism everybody could be a Raphael or a Leonardo.[60] Hence I suggest that "Ought implies can" holds only if "can" is taken in the narrow sense of physical feasibility. If it is taken in the broader sense of historical feasibility, the principle works equally well the other way around: that something is perceived as morally obligatory may contribute to making it historically feasible, given the physical possibility. Historical feasibility is a relative and highly volatile notion. It should not be absolutized to serve as an argument for the perpetuation of inequalities that may be unavoidable today, but need not remain so indifinitely.

Let me consider finally the two principles of distribution asserted in *Critique of the Gotha Program,* the contribution principle and the needs principle. The former is a Janus-like notion. Looked at from one side, it serves as a criterion of justice that condemns capitalist exploitation as unjust. Looked at from the vantage point of fully developed communism, it is itself inadequate by the higher standard expressed in the needs principle. An able-bodied capitalist who receives an income without working represents an unjustified violation of the contribution principle—a violation, that is, not justified by the needs principle. By contrast, an invalid who receives welfare aid without contributing anything in return represents a violation of the contribution principle that is justified by the needs principle.[61] I believe that the best way of making sense *both* of Marx's critique of capitalism and of the remarks on communism in *Critique of the Gotha Program* is by imputing to him a hierarchical theory of justice, in which the contribution principle provides a second-best criterion when the needs principle is not yet historically ripe for application.[62]

I now turn to the needs principle itself. From what Marx says in *Critique of the Gotha Program,* it is most plausibly understood as a principle of equal welfare. He says, for instance, that it is a defect of the contribution principle that a worker with many children will receive the same income as a worker with few, presumably because each member of the former's family will have a lower level of welfare. The needs principle, if it is to correct this defect, must ensure equality of welfare. Alternatively, the needs principle could be read as saying that each person receives the maximal amount of welfare he is capable of enjoying, assuming such maxima, which might differ across individuals, to exist. This idea is perhaps more plausible exegetically, but too utopian to merit further discussion. I shall focus on the more realistic idea of equal welfare, and consider some objections to it that cumulatively make it rather unattractive as a principle of justice.

Observe first that the needs principle also embodies a contribution principle, although a different one from the principle regulating the initial phase of communism. If a person decides to work less in order to have more leisure, he must expect to receive correspondingly less income. This is so for two reasons. First, as a result of his decision less is produced, and hence even with an equal distribution of goods and services there will be less for everybody. Next, such a person should also receive fewer goods and services than a person whose income-leisure trade-off makes him work longer hours. They achieve the same welfare levels (including the maximal level of equal welfare for all) at different income-leisure combinations.

The issue is complicated by the notion of work becoming "life's prime want." I believe this is to some extent true of everybody and to some extent false of everybody. For every person there comes a point when he would rather stop working than continuing, if only because he needs to sleep and eat. Similarly, although more controversially, every person would rather do some work than do no work at all. When forced to work very hard, one may think that a life of complete leisure is the best, but in the first place many people who have that option do not use it, and, in the second place, people who are forced to use it, i.e., the unemployed, typically do so because they are forced to, not because they welcome the opportunity to earn an income without working.[63] Hence the question of work becoming life's prime want is a question of *when* the marginal utility of work crosses the line from positive to negative, not *whether* it does so. A person, then, might prefer to work long hours because he enjoys the work, not because it allows him to earn more. Strict adherence to the principle of equal welfare should then allow him less income than someone who, for the sake of more income, works long hours in an occupation he finds irksome. This, clearly, creates difficulties for the application of the principle, since it might be hard for the person concerned, not to speak of others, to tell whether he works long hours because he likes the job or because he wants the income it provides him. The anticipation of the income might make him enjoy the work more, and he might falsely believe that his enjoyment is due to the nature of the work itself.[64]

A more fundamental difficulty is posed by the fact that some people have expensive needs. These fall in three classes. First, there are the needs stemming from mental and physical handicaps either present from birth or acquired involuntarily in later life. Next, there are the consumption needs that to a large extent are within the control of the individual. Fat people need more food, but they need not be fat. Some people have a craving for luxury goods, but they could undertake a planned change of preferences. People with large families need large incomes, but they could have chosen to have fewer children. The last example is a borderline case. It could also belong to the third class, the need to realize oneself through the sometimes expensive exercise of one's capacities. To write poems requires little by way of material resources, to make films a great deal more.

I am not saying that all of these cases present a problem for the needs principle. It was, after all, designed precisely to take care of such instances. At least this holds for the first class of expensive needs, and perhaps to some extent for the second. Yet not all sorts of extravagant consumption tastes merit support from society. If free rein was given to the development of tastes, with a guarantee that they would be fulfilled to an extent compatible with the same level of welfare for all, expensive tastes might emerge in an amount that would make it possible to satisfy them only very partially. Hence, to prevent this kind of anarchy of preferences, people could be told at the early stages of preference formation that society will not underwrite all sorts of expensive tastes. Since consumption tastes belong in general to the periphery of the individual rather than to the core, this would not seem too objectionable. Nevertheless, it would involve a very different understanding of the needs principle from the usual one. The principle would here be invoked to shape preferences so that it can be satisfied: "To each according to needs that allow equal satisfaction of needs." It is not obvious that this is in any way superior to giving everyone the same amount of resources, and then leaving them free to decide on how they want to use them.[65]

The anarchy problem could also arise with respect to the third set of expensive needs. In capitalism many people are frustrated in their self-realization because they lack the means to do what they would most like to do. If they knew that society would underwrite their preferred activity, so many might choose expensive ways of realizing themselves that few would be able to do so to a large extent. This, however, cannot be dealt with analogously to the previous problem. *Self*-actualization is so close to the core of the individual that one cannot expect that people will cease wanting to do the things that society tells them are too expensive; they will only cease trying to do them. Hence it is hard to see how one could avoid the source of frustration and inequality of welfare that stems from not everyone being able to do what they would most like to do. In addition, there is the problem that even were they able to do what they most want to do, they might be frustrated when they discover that they are not very good at doing it. It would be facile and Panglossian to suggest that the frustration due to lack of resources has the useful consequence of preventing people from experiencing the more profound frustration due to lack of talent, but it does seem true that these kinds of frustration vary inversely with one another, and that if the first kind of frustration were eliminated for all the second kind would create unavoidable welfare inequalities. Once again, equality of resources might be a better aim for society to set itself.

4. EPILOGUE

I have little to say by way of conclusion. The above discussion is clearly very tentative. It represents an attempt to rethink some basic Marxian notions in the light of the challenges of Rawls, Nozick, Dworkin, and others over the last decade or so. These authors have not succeeded fully in disturbing the dogmatic slumber of Marxism, but there are signs that it is becoming increasingly difficult to reassert the traditional views without more vigorous arguments than the traditional ones. In addition, of course, the increasingly repulsive character of many socialist regimes makes it obligatory for Marxists to reexamine the feasibility of their traditional ideals, and the desirability of the feasible arrangements. Broadly speaking, Marxist political theory is on the defensive for theoretical as well as practical reasons. It would be too much to say that I have mounted a counteroffensive, but perhaps I can claim to have tried to stabilize the lines of defense. If one were to accept the possibility of a clean path to capitalist accumulation, it would still be true that accumulation in actually existing capitalism has a long and unclean history that, by the principle of rectification invoked by the foremost champion of political libertarianism, would justify massive redistribution from capitalists to workers.[66] If one were to accept that a society not based on material incentives is historically unfeasible at present, one could still claim that the notion of justice need not be constrained by such feasibility.

NOTES

*Many, perhaps most, of the ideas in this paper are unoriginal. They derive from the work of G.A. Cohen and John Roemer, and from numerous discussions I have had with them over the last few years. I have full responsibility, of course, for the use made of their ideas. I would also like to thank Ottar Dahl, Philippe van Parijs and Robert van der Veen for helpful criticism and comments.

1. Karl Marx, *Capital III* (New York: International Publishers, 1967), p. 795.
2. Ibid., p. 791.
3. Ibid., p. 795.
4. Karl Marx, *Capital I* (New York: International Publishers, 1967), p. 737.
5. Marx finds exploitation both in slavery (*Capital III*, p. 809) and in feudalism (*Capital I*, p. 715). These are, however, isolated instances.
6. *The German Ideology*, in Marx and Engels, *Collected Works* (London: Lawrence and Wishart, 1975 ff.), vol. 5, p. 409.
7. Ibid., pp. 409, 410, 416.
8. See Stanley Moore, *Marx on the Choice between Socialism and Communism* (Cambridge, Mass.: Harvard University Press, 1980), pp. 14 ff. and passim.
9. Karl Marx, *Theories of Surplus-Value* (London: Lawrence and Wishart, 1972), vol. 3, p. 106; see also John Roemer, *A General Theory of Exploitation and Class* (Cambridge, Mass: Harvard University Press, 1982), p. 206.
10. Roemer, *A General Theory*. In Parts I and II of this work Roemer develops a series of models of exploitation, that differ in the *motivation* imputed to the agents (subsistence vs. accumulation) and in the *markets* in which the transactions between agents take place (nonlabor commodity market, labor market, credit market).
11. Roemer, *A General Theory*, p. 113.

12. See Roemer, *A General Theory*, pp. 44–45 for a discussion of multiple price equilibria and their relation to exploitation.

13. Roemer, *A General Theory*, Theorems 4.3, 4.6, and 4.7.

14. See Roemer, *A General Theory*, pp. 131–132 for an explanation of this indeterminacy.

15. According to the *general* theory of exploitation proposed in Part III of Roemer's book, a group is capitalistically exploited if it would be better off, and its complement worse off, were it to withdraw from society with its per capita share of the means of production. This, for instance, would mean that the unemployed form an exploited group, contrary, I think, to intuition. Roemer's recent article "Property Relations vs. Surplus Value in Marxian Exploitation," (*Philosophy and Public Affairs*, 1983) adds the condition that the complementary group should also be worse off were it to withdraw with its *own* endowments (not its per capita share). According to this definition the unemployed are not exploited, but rather, as Roemer now says, "Marxian-unfairly treated." In my "Roemer vs. Roemer" (*Politics and Society*, 1982) I give an example of a group that satisfies all three conditions of Roemer's revised definition of exploitation, and yet could not be said to be exploited in any intuitive sense. In that article I also give my reasons for believing that no definition of exploitation in terms of counterfactual statements can capture the essentially *causal* nature of that concept.

16. *Capital III*, p. 829.

17. Max Weber, *Economy and Society* (New York: Bedminster Press, 1968), p. 305.

18. *Capital I*, p. 611.

19. See also C.C. von Weizsäcker, "Modern Capital Theory and the Concept of Exploitation," *Kyklos*, 1975.

20. This must be modified in one important respect. The size of the surplus could be a good indicator of the injustice stemming from unequal access to investment decisions. Some writers (e.g., Leszek Kolakowski, *Main Currents of Marxism* [Oxford: Oxford University Press, 1978], vol. I, p. 305) take this "exclusive power of decision" to *be* exploitation, but I think the more usual definition in terms of excess labor worked is to be preferred. One could well argue, however, that in contemporary capitalism inequalities of *power* matter more than inequalities of *consumption*, but I cannot here go into this issue.

21. On divide and conquer, see Lloyd Shapley and Martin Shubik, "Ownership and the Production Function," *Quarterly Journal of Economics*, 1967, and John Roemer, "The Simple Analytics of Di-

vide and Conquer," working paper number 203 from the Department of Economics, University of California at Davis.

22. For a brief exposition with application to exploitation, see my "Marxism, Functionalism and Game Theory," *Theory and Society*, 1982.

23. *Capital I*, p. 239.

24. Karl Marx, "Wages," in *Collected Works*, vol. 6, pp. 420, 428, 435.

25. Kelvin Lancaster, "The Dynamic Inefficiency of Capitalism," *Journal of Political Economy*, 1973.

26. More precisely, my being really able to do *x*, and preferring *x* over all other actions, implies my doing *x*. Given this definition of real ability, one can go on to say that my being really able to do *x*, and preferring *x* over all other things that I am really able to do, implies my doing *x*.

27. *Results of the Immediate Process of Production*, appendix to *Capital I* (New York: Vintage Books, 1977), p. 1079.

28. Ibid., pp. 1032–1033.

29. *Capital I*, pp. 574, 614.

30. Karl Marx, "Reflections," in *Collected Works*, vol. 10, p. 591.

31. Karl Marx, *Results of the Immediate Process of Production*, p. 1033.

32. See his articles "Capitalism, Freedom and the Proletariat," in Alan Ryan, ed., *The Idea of Freedom: Essays in Honour of Isaiah Berlin* (Oxford: Oxford University Press, 1979); "Illusions about Private Property and Freedom," *Issues in Marxist Philosophy* 4 (Sussex: Harvester Press, 1981); "The Structure of Proletarian Unfreedom," *Philosophy and Public Affairs*, 1983.

33. For the logical structure involved, see my *Logic and Society* (Chichester: Wiley, 1978), pp. 97 ff.

34. See David Zimmerman, "Coercive Wage Offers," *Philosophy and Public Affairs*, 1981, p. 133.

35. Ibid., pp. 127 ff.

36. I own this point (and the phrase "thin markets") to Pranab Bardhan.

37. See Finn Kydland and Edward Prescott, "Rules Rather than Discretion," *Journal of Political Economy*, 1977, p. 486.

38. Against this Robert Nozick (*Anarchy, State and Utopia* [Oxford: Blackwell, 1974], pp. 252–253) writes: "And don't say that it is against the class interest of investors to support the growth of some enterprise that if successful would end the enterprise system. Investors are not so altruistic. They act in their personal and not their class interest." This may indeed be so, but the history of capitalism shows that investors nevertheless are able to organize themselves *politically* on behalf of their class interests.

39. Roemer, *A General Theory*, p. 81.
40. Cohen, "The Structure of Proletarian Unfreedom."
41. See Cohen, "Capitalism, Freedom and the Proletariat."
42. *Marx-Engels Werke* (Berlin: Dietz, 1964 ff.), vol. 17, p. 343.
43. This is the argument of George Brenkert, "Freedom and Private Property in Marx," *Philosophy and Public Affairs*, 1979, pp. 135–136 and of Allen Wood, *Karl Marx* (London: Routledge, 1981), pp. 126 ff.
44. E.g., *Capital I*, p. 194; *Capital III*, pp. 339–340. Ziyad Husami, "Marx on Distributive Justice," *Philosophy and Public Affairs*, 1978, p. 36, note 11, argues that these passages are not to be taken literally. I agree, however, with Allen Wood ("Marx on Right and Justice: A Reply to Husami," *Philosophy and Public Affairs*, 1979) that the relativistic reading is the only unstrained one. On the other hand I agree with Husami against Wood on the substantive issue: Marx had a theory of justice, even if he denied that he had one.
45. See the passage referenced in the following note.
46. *Marx-Engels Werke*, vol. 19, p. 21.
47. *Capital I*, p. 582.
48. G.A. Cohen, Review of Allen Wood, *Karl Marx*, in *Mind*, 1982.
49. Ibid.
50. "Marginal Notes on Wagner," in *Marx-Engels Werke*, vol. 19, p. 359.
51. I am indebted to Ottar Dahl for making me see the inadequacy of what one could call "normative collectivism."
52. For this idea, see Richard Arneson, "What's Wrong with Exploitation?" *Ethics*, 1981, p. 204; G.A. Cohen, "Freedom, Justice and Capitalism," *New Left Review* 126 (1981), p. 13; and John Roemer, "Are Socialist Ethics Consistent with Efficiency?" *The Philosophical Forum*, 1983.
53. Nozick, *Anarchy, State and Utopia*, pp. 161–162.
54. See my *Ulysses and the Sirens* (Cambridge: Cambridge University Press, 1979), p. 83.
55. G.A. Cohen, "Robert Nozick and Wilt Chamberlain: How Patterns Preserve Liberty," in John Arthur and William Shaw, eds., *Justice and Economic Distribution* (Englewood Cliffs, N.J.: Prentice Hall, 1978).
56. See Roemer, "Are Socialist Ethics Consistent with Efficiency?"
57. Strictly speaking, application of the difference principle leads to Pareto improvement only if one has what Rawls calls a "chain connection" between the welfare of individuals; see Rawls, *A Theory of Justice* (Cambridge, Mass.: Harvard University Press, 1971), pp. 80 ff.

58. For an argument along these lines, see Amartya Sen, *On Economic Inequality* (Oxford: Oxford University Press, 1973), pp. 96 ff.

59. See Roemer, *A General Theory*, pp. 241 ff.

60. See the exposition and discussion of his views in Chapter 1 of my *Making Sense of Marx*, forthcoming from Cambridge University Press, 1984.

61. What about the case (suggested by G.A. Cohen) of the invalid capitalist whose unearned income is exactly that to which he is entitled by the needs principle? By the definition of exploitation, he exploits his workers, but one might argue that the ensuing income distribution is nevertheless just. On closer inspection, however, this is seen to be false. Although *his* income corresponds to the canons of justice, the workers he employs receive less than they should, since his income is deducted from *their* wages, not from a social welfare fund to which all workers contribute. In any case the source of injustice mentioned in note 20 above would remain.

62. See Roemer, *A General Theory*, pp. 265 ff. and Serge-Christophe Kolm, *Justice et Equité* (Paris: Editions du CNRS, 1972), pp. 114 ff.

63. I realize that both of these arguments are incomplete, and that the (alleged) facts are open to other explanations.

64. This could be so, for instance, because of the tendency to reduce cognitive dissonance.

65. See Ronald Dworkin, "What Is Equality? Part 2: Equality of Resources," *Philosophy and Public Affairs*, 1981.

66. Nozick, *Anarchy, State and Utopia*, pp. 152–153.

BIBLIOGRAPHY

JOHN W. CHAPMAN

Given the amount of work on Marx, Marxisms, and communism, this bibliography is of necessity selective. It deals mainly with recent books; only a few articles of exceptional interest are listed. Theoretical studies having to do with Marxism are emphasized at the expense of, but not entirely to the exclusion of, analyses of communist politics. The reader will wish to refer to the bibliographies published in *Political Theory* during the 70s.

SOME CLASSIC STUDIES

Acton, H.B. *The Illusion of the Epoch: Marxism-Leninism as a Philosophical Creed.* Routledge & Kegan Paul, 1955.

Avineri, Shlomo. *Social and Political Thought of Karl Marx.* Cambridge University Press, 1968.

Berlin, Isaiah. *Karl Marx: His Life and Environment.* 4th ed. Oxford University Press, 1978.

Kolakowski, Leszek. *Main Currents of Marxism: Origins, Growth, and Dissolution.* Translated by P.S. Falla. 3 vols. Oxford University Press, 1978.

Lindsay, A.D. *Karl Marx's* Capital: *An Introductory Essay.* Oxford University Press, 1925.

Meyer, Alfred G. *Marxism: The Unity of Theory and Practice.* Harvard University Press, 1954.

Plamenatz, John. *German Marxism and Russian Communism.* Longmans, Green, 1954.

———. *Karl Marx's Philosophy of Man.* Clarendon Press, 1975.

Tucker, Robert C. *Philosophy and Myth in Karl Marx.* Cambridge University Press, 1961.

PHILOSOPHICAL STUDIES

Althusser, Louis. *For Marx.* Translated by Ben Brewster. Schocken Books, 1978.

Anderson, Perry. *Considerations on Western Marxism.* Schocken Books, 1979.

Aron, Raymond. *Marxism and the Existentialists.* Simon and Schuster, 1970.

Bologh, Roslyn Wallach. *Dialectical Phenomenology: Marx's Method.* Routledge & Kegan Paul, 1979.

Chiodi, P. *Sartre and Marxism.* Translated by K. Soper. Harvester, 1976.

Cornforth, Maurice. *Communism and Philosophy: Contemporary Dogmas and Revisions of Marxism.* Lawrence and Wishart, 1980.

D'Amico, Robert. *Marx and Philosophy of Culture.* University of Florida Press, 1981.

Della Volpe, Galvano. *Rousseau and Marx.* Translated by John Fraser. Lawrence and Wishart, 1978.

Desan, Wilfrid. *The Marxism of Jean-Paul Sartre.* Doubleday, 1966.

Germino, Dante. *Machiavelli to Marx: Modern Western Political Thought.* University of Chicago Press, 1972.

Gouldner, Alvin W. *The Dark Side of the Dialectic.* 3 vols. Oxford University Press, 1982.

Hook, Sidney. *Marxism and Beyond.* Rowman and Littlefield, 1983.

Hudson, C. Wayne. *The Marxist Philosophy of Ernst Bloch.* Macmillan, 1980.

Jacoby, Russell. *Dialectic of Defeat: Contours of Western Marxism.* Cambridge University Press, 1982.

Kissin, S.F. *Farewell to Revolution: Marxist Philosophy and the Modern World.* St. Martin's Press, 1978.

Labica, Georges. *Marxism and the Status of Philosophy.* Humanities Press, 1976.

Lecourt, D. *Marxism and Epistemology: Bachelard, Foucault, Canguilhem.* Translated by B. Brewster. New Left Books, 1975.

Lobkowicz, Nikolaus. *Theory and Practice: History of a Concept from Aristotle to Marx.* Notre Dame University Press, 1967.

——, ed. *Marx and the Western World.* Notre Dame University Press, 1967.

Loewenstein, Julius I. *Marx against Marxism.* Translated by Harry Drost. Routledge & Kegan Paul, 1980.

Löwith, Karl. *Max Weber and Karl Marx.* Translated by Hans Fantel. Allen & Unwin, 1982.

Mandelbaum, Maurice. *History, Man & Reason: A Study in Nineteenth-Century Thought.* Johns Hopkins University Press, 1971.

McBride, William Leon. *The Philosophy of Marx.* St. Martin's Press, 1977.

McMurty, John. *The Structure of Marx's World-View.* Princeton University Press, 1977.

Mepham, John and D.H. Ruben, eds. *Issues in Marxist Philosophy.* 3 vols. Humanities Press, 1979.

Novack, George, ed. *Existentialism versus Marxism: Conflicting Views on Humanism.* Dell, 1966.

Odajnyk, Walter. *Marxism and Existentialism.* Doubleday, 1965.

Parkinson, G.H.R., ed. *Marx and Marxisms: Royal Institute of Philosophy Lectures 1979–1980.* Cambridge University Press, 1982.

Petrovic, Gajo. *Marx in the Mid-Twentieth Century: A Yugoslav Philosopher Reconsiders Karl Marx's Writings.* Doubleday, 1967.

Poster, Mark. *Existential Marxism in Postwar France: From Sartre to Althusser.* Princeton University Press, 1976.

———. *Sartre's Marxism.* Cambridge University Press, 1982.

Quinney, Richard. *Social Existence: Metaphysics, Marxism, and the Social Sciences.* Sage, 1982.

Ruben, David-Hillel. *Marxism and Materialism: A Study in Marxist Theory of Knowledge.* Humanities Press, 1977.

Rubinstein, David M. *Marx and Wittgenstein: Social Praxis and Social Explanation.* Routledge & Kegan Paul, 1981.

Sartre, Jean-Paul. *Critique of Dialectical Reason.* Schocken Books, 1978.

Sayer, Derek. *Marx's Method: Ideology, Science and Critique in* Capital. Harvester Press, 1979.

Schmidt, Alfred. *The Concept of Nature in Marx.* Schocken Books, 1978.

Somerville, John and Howard L. Parsons, eds. *Dialogues on the Philosophy of Marxism.* Greenwood Press, 1974.

Vree, Dale. *On Synthesizing Marxism and Christianity.* Wiley, 1976.

Zeleny, Jindrich. *The Logic of Marx.* Translated by Terrell Carver. Rowman and Littlefield, 1980.

PSYCHOLOGY AND MORALITY

Axelos, Kostas. *Alienation, Praxis, and Techne in the Thought of Karl Marx.* Translated by Ronald Bruzina. University of Texas Press, 1976.

Barbu, Zevedei. *Society, Culture and Personality: An Introduction to Social Science.* Basil Blackwell, 1971.

Bauer, Raymond A. *The New Man in Soviet Psychology.* Harvard University Press, 1952.

Bier, William C., ed. *Alienation: Plight of Modern Man?* Fordham University Press, 1972.

Buchanan, Allen E. *Marx and Justice: The Radical Critique of Liberalism.* Methuen, 1982.

Carver, Tyrell. *Marx's Social Theory.* Oxford University Press, 1982.

Cohen, G.A. "Capitalism, Freedom and the Proletariat." In *The Idea of Freedom: Essays in Honour of Isaiah Berlin,* edited by Alan Ryan. Oxford University Press, 1979.

Cohen, Marshall, et al., eds. *Marx, Justice, and History.* Princeton University Press, 1979.

De George, Richard T. *Soviet Ethics and Morality.* University of Michigan Press, 1969.

Duncan, Graeme. *Marx and Mill: Two Views of Social Conflict and Social Harmony.* Cambridge University Press, 1974.

Fetscher, Iring. "Karl Marx on Human Nature." 40 Social Research (1973).

Fisk, Milton. *Ethics and Society: A Marxist Interpretation of Value.* New York University Press, 1979.

Fromm, Erich. *Marx's Concept of Man.* Frederick Ungar, 1977.

Gallie, W.B. "Liberal Morality and Socialist Morality." In *Philosophy, Politics and Society,* edited by Peter Laslett. Macmillan, 1956.

Geyer, R. Felix and David Schweitzer, eds. *Alienation: Problems of Meaning, Theory and Method.* Routledge & Kegan Paul, 1981.

Godelier, Maurice. *Perspectives in Marxist Anthropology.* Translated by Robert Brain. Cambridge University Press, 1977.

Gould, Carol C. *Marx's Social Ontology: Individuality and Community in Marx's Theory of Social Reality.* MIT Press, 1980.

Gray, John N. "Philosophy, Science and Myth in Marxism." In *Marx and Marxisms,* edited by G.H.R. Parkinson. Cambridge University Press, 1982.

Heller, Agnes. *The Theory of Need in Marx.* St. Martin's Press, 1976.

Hook, Sidney. *Revolution, Reform and Social Justice: Studies in the Theory and Practice of Marxism.* Basil Blackwell, 1976.

Israel, Joachim. *Alienation: From Marx to Modern Sociology.* Humanities Press, 1979.

Kamenka, Eugene. *Marxism and Ethics.* St. Martin's Press, 1969.

———. *The Ethical Foundations of Marxism.* Revised ed. Routledge & Kegan Paul, 1972.

Lane, Robert E. "Capitalist Man, Socialist Man." In *Philosophy, Politics and Society: Fifth Series,* edited by Peter Laslett and James Fishkin. Yale University Press, 1979.

Lebedev, Alexander, et al. *The Rights of the Individual in Socialist Society.* Progress Publishers, 1982.

LeBon, Gustav. *The Psychology of Socialism.* Transaction Books, 1980.

Lefebvre, Henri. *The Sociology of Marx.* Columbia University Press, 1982.

Lichtmann, Richard. *The Production of Desire: The Integration of Psychoanalysis into Marxist Theory.* Free Press, 1982.

Lukes, Steven. "Marxism, Morality and Justice." In *Marx and Marxisms,* edited by G.H.R. Parkinson. Cambridge University Press, 1982.

Markovic, Mihailo. *From Affluence to Praxis.* University of Michigan Press, 1974.

Meszaros, Istvan. *Marx's Theory of Alienation.* Harper and Row, 1970.

Meynell, Hugo. *Freud, Marx and Morals.* Macmillan, 1981.

Monnerot, Jules. *Sociology and Psychology of Communism.* Greenwood Press, 1977.

Nielsen, Kai and Steven C. Patten. "Bibliography on Marx and Morality." Supplementary Volume VII, *Canadian Journal of Philosophy* (1981).

O'Rourke, J.J., ed. *Problem of Freedom in Marxist Thought: Analysis of the Treatment of Human Freedom by Marx, Engels, Lenin and Contemporary Soviet Philosophy.* Reidel, 1974.

Ollman, Bertil. *Alienation: Marx's Conception of Man in Capitalist Society.* 2nd ed. Cambridge University Press, 1976.

Passmore, John. *The Perfectibility of Man.* Duckworth, 1970.

Quinton, Anthony. "Has Man an Essence?" In *Nature and Conduct,* edited by R.S. Peters. 8 Royal Institute of Philosophy Lectures, 1973–1974, 14–35. Macmillan, 1975.

Schaff, Adam. *A Philosophy of Man.* Dell, 1963.

———. *Marxism and the Human Individual.* McGraw-Hill, 1965.

Seliger, Martin. *The Marxist Conception of Ideology: A Critical Essay.* Cambridge University Press, 1977.

Seve, Lucien. *Man in Marxist Theory and the Psychology of Personality.* Translated by John McGreal. Humanities Press, 1978.

Smirnov, Georgi. *Soviet Man: The Making of a Socialist Type of Personality.* Translated by Robert Daglish. Progress Publishers, 1973.

Stojanovic, Svetozar. *Between Ideals and Reality: A Critique of Socialism and Its Future.* Oxford University Press, 1973.

Tucker, David F.B. *Marxism and Individualism.* Basil Blackwell, 1980.

Tucker, Robert C. "Marx and Distributive Justice." In *Justice: NOMOS VI,* edited by Carl J. Friedrich and John W. Chapman. Atherton Press, 1963.

Vygotsky, L.S. *Mind in Society: The Development of Higher Psychological Processes.* Edited by Michael Cole, et al. Harvard University Press, 1978.

Walicki, Andrzej. "The Marxian Conception of Freedom." Unpublished paper presented to History of Ideas Unit, The Australian National University, 30 June 1982.

HISTORY AND POLITICS

Allen, Victor L. *Social Analysis: A Marxist Critique and Alternative.* Longman, 1975.

Althusser, Louis. *Politics and History: Montesquieu, Rousseau, Hegel and Marx.* Translated by Ben Brewster. New Left Books, 1972.

Aronowitz, Stanley. *The Crisis in Historical Materialism: Class, Politics, and Culture in Marxist Theory.* Praeger, 1980.

Baechler, Jean. *Revolution.* Translated by Joan Vickers. Harper & Row, 1978.

Berlin, Isaiah. *Historical Inevitability.* Oxford University Press, 1954.

Cleaver, Harry. *Reading* Capital *Politically.* University of Texas Press, 1979.

Cohen, G.A. *Karl Marx's Theory of History: A Defence.* Oxford University Press, 1978.

Cohen, Marshall, et al., eds. *Marx, Justice, and History.* Princeton University Press, 1979.

Draper, Hal. *Karl Marx's Theory of Revolution.* 2 vols. Monthly Review Press, 1978, 1981.

Gandy, D. Ross. *Marx and History: From Primitive Society to the Communist Future.* University of Texas Press, 1979.

Giddens, Anthony. *Capitalism and Modern Social Theory: An Analysis of the Writings of Marx, Durkheim and Weber.* Cambridge University Press, 1971.

———. *Between Capitalism and Socialism: A Contemporary Critique of Historical Materialism.* Macmillan, 1981.

Gilbert, Alan. *Marx's Politics: Communists and Citizens.* Rutgers University Press, 1981.

Gombin, Richard. *The Radical Tradition: A Study in Modern Revolutionary Thought.* Translated by Rupert Swyer. St. Martin's Press, 1979.

Goran, Therborn. *What Does the Ruling Class Do When it Rules? State Apparatuses and State Power under Feudalism, Capitalism and Socialism.* New Left Books, 1978.

Harnecker, Marta. *The Basic Concepts of Historical Materialism.* Harvester, 1978.

Heller, Agnes. *A Theory of History.* Routledge & Kegan Paul, 1982.

Holloway, John and Sol Picciotto, eds. *State and Capital: A Marxist Debate.* University of Texas Press, 1979.

Hook, Sidney. *Revolution, Reform and Social Justice: Studies in the Theory and Practice of Marxism.* New York University Press, 1975.

Hunt, A., ed. *Marxism and Democracy.* Lawrence & Wishart, 1980.

Jakubowski, Franz. *Ideology and Superstructure in Historical Materialism.* St. Martin's Press, 1976.

Jessop, Bob. *The Capitalist State: Marxist Theories and Methods.* New York University Press, 1982.

Kautsky, John H. *The Politics of Aristocratic Empires.* University of North Carolina Press, 1982.

Laclau, Ernesto. *Politics and Ideology in Marxist Theory: Capitalism, Fascism, Populism.* Schocken Books, 1978.

Maguire, John M. *Marx's Theory of Politics.* Cambridge University Press, 1978.

McCarthy, Timothy. *Marx and the Proletariat: A Study in Social Theory.* Greenwood Press, 1979.

Milliband, Ralph. *The State in Capitalist Society.* Basic Books, 1969.

————. *Marxism and Politics.* Oxford University Press, 1977.

Miller, James. *History and Human Existence—From Marx to Merleau-Ponty.* University of California Press, 1979.

Moore, Stanley. *Marx on the Choice Between Socialism and Communism.* Harvard University Press, 1980.

Parkin, Frank. *Marxism and Class Theory: A Bourgeois Critique.* Tavistock, 1979.

Perez-Diaz, Victor M. *State, Bureaucracy and Civil Society: A Critical Discussion of the Political Thought of Karl Marx.* Macmillan, 1978.

Poggi, Giovanni. *Images of Society: Essays on the Sociological Theories of Tocqueville, Marx and Durkheim.* Stanford University Press, 1972.

Poulantzas, Nicos. *Classes in Contemporary Capitalism.* New Left Books, 1975.

Rader, Melvin. *Marx's Interpretation of History.* Oxford University Press, 1979.

Schmidt, Alfred. *History and Structure: An Essay on Hegelian-Marxist and Structuralist Theories of History.* MIT Press, 1981.

Shaw, William H. *Marx's Theory of History.* Stanford University Press, 1979.

Torrance, John. *Estrangement, Alienation, and Exploitation: A Sociological Approach to Historical Materialism.* Columbia University Press, 1977.

Tucker, Robert C. *The Marxian Revolutionary Idea.* Norton, 1969.

Ulam, Adam B. *The Unfinished Revolution: Marxism and Communism in the Modern World.* Revised ed. Westview Press, 1979.

Wells, David. *Marx and the Modern State: An Analysis of Fetishism in Capitalist Society.* Harvester, 1981.

Weiner, Richard R. *Cultural Marxism and Political Sociology.* Sage, 1981.

LAW AND LEGAL STUDIES

Arthur, C., ed. *Law and Marxism*. Ink Links, 1978.

Balbus, Isaac D. *The Dialectics of Legal Repression*. Russell Sage, 1973.

Beirne, Piers and Robert Sharlet, eds. *Pashukanis: Selected Writings on Marxism and Law*. Translated by Peter B. Maggs. Academic Press, 1980.

———— and Richard Quinney, eds. *Marxism and Law*. Wiley, 1982.

Black, Donald. *The Behavior of Law*. Academic Press, 1976.

Butler, W., ed. *Russian Law: Historical and Political Perspectives*. Sijthoff, 1977.

Cain, Maureen and Alan Hunt. *Marx and Engels on Law*. Academic Press, 1980.

Chambliss, William J. and Robert Seidman. *Law, Order, and Power*. Addison-Wesley, 1971.

Chkhikvadze, V.M., ed. *The Soviet State and Law*. Translated by Yuri Sdobnikov. Progress Publishers, 1969.

Critique of Law Editorial Collective. *Critique of Law: A Marxist Analysis*. U.N.S.W. Critique of Law Society, 1978.

Edelman, Bernard. *Ownership of the Image: Elements for a Marxist Theory of Law*. Translated by Elizabeth Kingdom. Routledge & Kegan Paul, 1980.

Fine, Bob, et al., eds. *Capitalism and the Rule of Law*. Hutchinson, 1979.

Griffith, J.A.G. *The Politics of the Judiciary*. Fontana, 1977.

Hazard, John N. *Communists and Their Law: A Search for the Common Core of the Legal Systems of the Marxian Socialist States*. University of Chicago Press, 1969.

————, et al. *The Soviet Legal System: Fundamental Principles and Historical Commentary*. 3rd ed. Oceana, 1977.

Hirst, Paul. *On Law and Ideology*. Humanities Press, 1979.

Hunt, Alan, ed. *Law, State and Economy*. Croom Helm, 1981.

Kahn-Freud, O., ed. *Karl Renner: The Institutions of Private Law and Their Social Functions*. Routledge & Kegan Paul, 1949.

Kamenka, Eugene. "Demythologizing the Law." *Times Literary Supplement* (1 May 1981), 475–476.

Lipson, Leon. "The New Face of 'Socialist Legality.' " *Problems of Communism* 7 (July–August 1958), 22–30.

Lukes, Steven. "Marxism, Morality and Justice." In *Marx and Marxisms*, edited by G.H.R. Parkinson. Cambridge University Press, 1982.

Makepeace, R.W. *Marxist Ideology and Soviet Criminal Law*. Croom Helm, 1980.

Minogue, Kenneth. "The Biases of the Bench." *Times Literary Supplement* (6 January 1978), 11–12.

Pashukanis, Evgeny. *Law and Marxism: A General Theory.* Translated by Barbara Einhorn. Ink Links, 1980.

Phillips, Paul. *Marx and Engels on Law and Laws.* Martin Robertson, 1980.

Schlesinger, R. *Soviet Legal Theory.* Routledge & Kegan Paul, 1945.

Solomon, P.H. *Soviet Criminologists and Criminal Policy: Specialists in Policy-Making.* Macmillan, 1978.

Struchkov, Nikolai. *Correction of the Convicted: Law, Theory, Practice.* Translated by Oleg Stieffelman. Progress Publishers, 1982.

Sumner, Colin. *Reading Ideologies: An Investigation into the Marxist Theory of Ideology and Law.* Academic Press, 1979.

Thompson, E.P. *Whigs and Hunters: The Origins of the Black Act.* Pantheon Books, 1975.

ECONOMIC THEORY AND POLITICAL ECONOMY

Amin, S. *The Law of Value and Historical Materialism.* Monthly Review Press, 1978.

Baechler, Jean. *The Origins of Capitalism.* Translated by Barry Cooper. Basil Blackwell, 1975.

Bailey, Anne M. and Josep R. Llobera, eds. *The Asiatic Mode of Production: Science and Politics.* Routledge & Kegan Paul, 1981.

Balinky, Alexander. *Marx's Economics: Origin and Development.* D.C. Heath, 1970.

Becker, James. *Marxian Political Economy: An Outline.* Cambridge University Press, 1977.

Blaug, Mark. *A Methodological Appraisal of Marxian Economics.* North-Holland, 1980.

Bose, Arun. *Marx on Exploitation and Inequality: An Essay in Marxian Analytical Economics.* Oxford University Press, 1980.

Brewer, Anthony. *Marxist Theories of Imperialism: A Critical Survey.* Routledge & Kegan Paul, 1980.

Croce, Benedetto. *Historical Materialism and the Economics of Karl Marx.* Transaction Books, 1981.

Cutler, Anthony, et al. *Marx's* Capital *and Capitalism Today.* 2 vols. Routledge & Kegan Paul, 1977, 78.

Desai, Meghnad. *Marxian Economics.* Basil Blackwell, 1980.

Dumont, Louis. *From Mandeville to Marx: The Genesis and Triumph of Economic Ideology.* University of Chicago Press, 1978.

Fine, B. *Marx's* Capital. Macmillan, 1975.

Fine, Ben and Laurence Harris. *Rereading* Capital. Columbia University Press, 1979.

Harris, Donald J. *Capital Accumulation and Income Distribution.* Stanford University Press, 1978.

Harvey, David. *The Limits to Capital.* University of Chicago Press, 1982.

Hindess, Barry and Paul Q. Hirst. *Pre-Capitalist Modes of Production.* Routledge & Kegan Paul, 1975.

———. *Mode of Production and Social Formation: An Auto-Critique of Pre-Capitalist Modes of Production.* Macmillan, 1977.

Hodgson, Geoffrey. *Capitalism, Value and Exploitation.* Martin Robertson, 1981.

Horvat, Branko. *The Political Economy of Socialism: A Marxist Social Theory.* M.E. Sharpe, 1982.

Howard, Michael C. and John E. King. *The Political Economy of Marx.* Longman, 1975.

Hutchinson, T.W. *The Politics and Philosophy of Economics: Marxians, Keynesians and Austrians.* Basil Blackwell, 1982.

Kuhne, Karl. *Economics and Marxism.* Translated by Robert Shaw. 2 vols. St. Martin's Press, 1980.

Levine, David. *Economic Theory: Vol. 2: The System of Economic Relations as a Whole.* Routledge & Kegan Paul, 1981.

Mandel, Ernest. *Long Waves of Capitalist Development: The Marxist Interpretation.* Cambridge University Press, 1980.

Meek, Ronald L. *Smith, Marx and After: Ten Essays in the Development of Economic Thought.* Chapman & Hall, 1977.

Morishima, Michio. *Marx's Economics: A Dual Theory of Value and Growth.* Cambridge University Press, 1973.

Pilling, Geoffrey. *Marx's* Capital: *Philosophy and Political Economy.* Routledge & Kegan Paul, 1980.

Ransom, B. "Rival Economic Epistemologies: The Logics of Marx, Marshall, and Keynes." 14 *Journal of Economic Issues* (March 1980), 77–98.

Roberts, Paul Craig and Matthew A. Stephenson. *Marx's Theory of Exchange, Alienation and Crisis.* Hoover Institution Press, 1973.

Roemer, John E. *Analytical Foundations of Marxist Economic Theory.* Cambridge University Press, 1981.

Rosdolsky, Roman. *The Making of Marx's* Capital. Translated by P. Burgess. Pluto Press, 1980.

Steedman, Ian. *Marx After Sraffa.* Schocken Books, 1979.

Sweezy, Paul M. *Four Lectures on Marxism.* Monthly Review Press, 1981.

Urry, John. *The Anatomy of Capitalist Societies: The Economy, Civil Society and the State.* Macmillan, 1981.

Weeks, John. *Capital and Exploitation.* Princeton University Press, 1981.

Wiles, P.J.D. *The Political Economy of Communism.* Harvard University Press, 1962.

———. *Communist International Economics.* Praeger, 1969.

————. *Economic Institutions Compared.* Basil Blackwell, 1977.

Winner, Langdon. *Autonomous Technology: Technics-out-of-control as a Theme in Political Thought.* MIT Press, 1977.

Wolfson, Murray. *A Reappraisal of Marxian Economics.* Columbia University Press, 1966.

MARX AND MARXISMS: GENERAL INTERPRETATIVE AND CRITICAL STUDIES

Aron, Raymond. "Karl Marx." In *Main Currents in Sociological Thought: I.* Translated by Richard Howard and Helen Weaver. Weidenfeld and Nicolson, 1965.

Avineri, Shlomo, ed. *Marx's Socialism.* Lieber-Atherton, 1973.

————. *Varieties of Marxism.* Martinus Nijhoff, 1977.

Bottomore, Tom, ed. *Karl Marx.* Basil Blackwell, 1979.

————. *Modern Interpretations of Marx.* Basil Blackwell, 1981.

Burke, John P., et al., eds. *Marxism and the Good Society.* Cambridge University Press, 1981.

De George, Richard T. *The New Marxism: Soviet and East European Marxism Since 1956.* Pegasus, 1968.

Elster, Jon. "Marxismo." 4 *London Review of Books* (18 to 31 March 1982), 6–8.

————. *Explaining Technical Change: A Case Study in the Philosophy of Science.* Cambridge University Press, 1982.

Georgopoulos, N., ed. *Continuity and Change in Marxism.* Harvester, 1981.

Gouldner, Alvin W. *The Two Marxisms: Contradictions and Anomalies in the Development of Theory.* Seabury Press, 1979.

Heilbroner, Robert L. "Inescapable Marx." *The New York Review of Books* (29 June 1978), 33–37.

————. *Marxism: For and Against.* Norton, 1980.

Hobsbawm, Eric J., ed. *The History of Marxism.* 4 vols. Harvester, 1981–.

Hook, Sidney. "Spectral Marxism." 49 *The American Scholar* (Spring 1980), 250–271.

Hunt, Richard N. *The Political Ideas of Marx and Engels: Vol. 1: Marxism and Totalitarian Democracy, 1818–1850.* University of Pittsburgh Press, 1974.

Hyppolite, Jean. *Studies on Marx and Hegel.* Translated by John O'Neil. Basic Books, 1969.

Jacobs, Dan N., ed. *From Marx to Mao and Marchais: Documents on the Development of Communist Variations.* Longman, 1979.

Lichtheim, George. *Marxism: An Historical and Critical Study.* Columbia University Press, 1982.

Lindsay, Jack. *The Crisis in Marxism.* Barnes & Noble, 1981.

Lowy, Michael. *The Marxism of Che Guevara.* Translated by Brian Pearce. Monthly Review Press, 1974.

MacIntyre, Alasdair. *Marxism and Christianity.* Schocken Books, 1968.

Mandel, Ernest. *Introduction to Marxism.* 2nd ed. Ink Links, 1979.

Marcuse, Herbert. *Soviet Marxism: A Critical Analysis.* Routledge & Kegan Paul, 1958.

Martin, Joseph. *A Guide to Marxism.* St. Martin's Press, 1980.

McLellan, David. *The Thought of Karl Marx.* 2nd ed. Macmillan, 1980.

———. *Karl Marx.* Penguin Books, 1980.

———. *Marxism after Marx: An Introduction.* Macmillan, 1980.

———. *Marx before Marxism.* Revised ed. Macmillan, 1980.

Mehring, Franz. *Karl Marx: The Story of His Life.* Translated by Edward Fitzgerald. Harvester, 1981.

O'Malley, Joseph and Keith Algozin, eds. *Rubel on Karl Marx: Five Essays.* Cambridge University Press, 1981.

Padover, Saul K. *Karl Marx: An Intimate Biography.* McGraw-Hill, 1978.

Plamenatz, John. *Man and Society: A Critical Examination of Some Important Social and Political Theories from Machiavelli to Marx.* 2 vols. Longman, 1963.

Prawer, S.S. *Karl Marx and World Literature.* Oxford University Press, 1976.

Raddatz, Fritz J. *Karl Marx: A Political Biography.* Translated by Richard Barry. Little, Brown, 1978.

Rauch, Leo. *The Political Animal: Studies in Political Philosophy from Machiavelli to Marx.* University of Massachusetts Press, 1981.

Rubel, Maximilien and Margaret Manale. *Marx Without Myth: A Chronological Study of His Life and Work.* Basil Blackwell, 1979.

Rubel, Maximilien. *Marx: Life and Works.* Macmillan, 1980.

Seigel, Jerrold. *Marx's Fate: The Shape of a Life.* Princeton University Press, 1977.

Singer, Peter. *Marx.* Oxford University Press, 1980.

Steenson, Gary P. *Karl Kautsky, 1854–1938: Marxism in the Classical Years.* University of Pittsburgh Press, 1979.

Tönnies, Ferdinand. *Karl Marx: His Life and Teachings.* Michigan State University Press, 1974.

Walker, Angus. *Marx: His Theory and Its Context.* Longman, 1978.

Wolfson, Murray. *Karl Marx.* Columbia University Press, 1971.

———. *Marx: Economist, Philosopher, Jew—Development of a Doctrine.* Macmillan, 1981.

Wood, Allen. *Karl Marx.* Routledge & Kegan Paul, 1981.

Worsley, Peter. *Marx and Marxism.* Tavistock/Horwood, 1982.

Wylczynski, Josef. *An Encyclopedic Dictionary of Marxism, Socialism and Communism.* Macmillan, 1980.

MARX AND MARXISMS: COGNATE AND SPECIAL STUDIES

Abercrombie, Nicholas. *Class, Structure, and Knowledge.* New York University Press, 1980.

Anderson, Perry. *Arguments within English Marxism.* New Left Books, 1980.

Balbus, Isaac D. *Marxism and Domination.* Princeton University Press, 1982.

Benson, Leslie. *Proletarians and Parties.* Tavistock, 1978.

Bottomore, Tom and Patrick Goode, eds. *Austro-Marxism.* Oxford University Press, 1978.

Callinicos, Alex. *Is There a Future for Marxism?* Macmillan, 1982.

Cohen, Carl. *Four Systems.* Random House, 1981.

Corrigan, P., et al. *Socialist Construction and Marxist Theory.* Monthly Review Press, 1978.

Dobb, Maurice, et al. *The Transition from Feudalism to Capitalism.* Schocken Books, 1978.

Dunn, John. *Western Political Theory in the Face of the Future.* Cambridge University Press, 1979.

Goff, Tom W. *Marx and Mead: Contributions to a Sociology of Knowledge.* Routledge & Kegan Paul, 1980.

Gombin, Richard. *The Origins of Modern Leftism.* Translated by Michael K. Perl. Penguin Books, 1975.

Guarasci, Richard. *The Theory and Practice of American Marxism, 1957–1970.* University Press of America, 1980.

Herod, C.C. *The Nation in the History of Marxian Thought: Concept of Nations with History and Nations without History.* Nijhoff, 1976.

Howard, Dick. *The Marxian Legacy.* Macmillan, 1977.

Hussein, Athar and Keith Tribe. *Marxism and the Agrarian Question.* 2 vols. Macmillan, 1980.

Kiernan, V.G. *Marxism and Imperialism.* St. Martin's Press, 1975.

Kolakowski, Leszek and Stuart Hampshire, eds. *The Socialist Idea.* Weidenfeld and Nicolson, 1974.

Kubalkovka, V. and A.A. Cruickshank. *Marxism-Leninism and Theory of International Relations.* Routledge & Kegan Paul, 1980.

Larrain, Jorge. *The Concept of Ideology.* University of Georgia Press, 1980.

Lewy, Guenter. *False Consciousness: An Essay on Mystification.* Transaction Books, 1982.

Ling, Trevor. *Karl Marx and Religion: In Europe and India.* Macmillan, 1980.

Macintyre, Stuart. *A Proletarian Science: Marxism in Britain, 1917–33.* Cambridge University Press, 1980.

McLellan, David, ed. *Karl Marx: Interviews and Recollections.* Macmillan, 1981.

Parekh, F. *Marx's Critique of Ideology.* Croom Helm, 1982.

Plamenatz, John. *Ideology.* Praeger, 1970.

Portis, Larry. *Georges Sorel.* Pluto Press, 1980.

Roth, Jack J. *The Cult of Violence: Sorel and the Sorelians.* University of California Press, 1980.

Salvadori, Massimo. *Karl Kautsky and the Socialist Revolution.* Schocken Books, 1979.

Sarup, Madan. *Marxism and Education: A Study of Phenomenological and Marxist Approaches to Education.* Routledge & Kegan Paul, 1978.

Selucky, Radoslav. *Marxism, Socialism, Freedom: Towards a General Theory of Labor-Managed Systems.* St. Martin's Press, 1979.

Semmel, Bernard, ed. *Marxism and the Science of War.* Oxford University Press, 1981.

Sharp, Rachel. *Knowledge, Ideology and the Politics of Schooling: Towards a Marxist Analysis of Education.* Routledge & Kegan Paul, 1980.

Sik, Ota. *The Third Way: Marxist-Leninist Theory and Modern Industrial Society.* M.E. Sharpe, 1976.

Smart, Barry. *Phenomenology and Marxian Analysis: A Critical Discussion of the Theory and Practice of a Science of Society.* Routledge & Kegan Paul, 1976.

Stanley, John. *The Sociology of Virtue: The Political and Social Theories of Georges Sorel.* University of California Press, 1982.

Thomas, Paul. *Karl Marx and the Anarchists.* Routledge & Kegan Paul, 1980.

Turner, Bryan S. *Marx and the End of Orientalism.* Allen & Unwin, 1979.

Ulam, Adam B. *Ideologies and Illusions: Revolutionary Thought from Herzen to Solzhenitsyn.* Harvard University Press, 1976.

Utechin, S.V. *Russian Political Thought: A Concise History.* Praeger, 1963.

Voeglin, Eric. *From Enlightenment to Revolution.* Edited by John H. Hallowell. Duke University Press, 1975.

Walicki, Andrzej. *A History of Russian Thought: From the Enlightenment to Marxism.* Translated by Hilda Andrews-Rusiecka. Stanford University Press, 1979.

Weil, Simone. *Oppression and Liberty.* Translated by Arthur Wills and John Petrie. University of Massachusetts Press, 1973.

Wessell, Leonard P. *Karl Marx, Romantic Irony, and the Proletariat: Studies in the Mythopoetic Origins of Marxism.* University of Louisiana Press, 1980.

Williams, Raymond. *Marxism and Literature.* Oxford University Press, 1977.

Wittfogel, Karl A. *Oriental Despotism: A Comparative Study of Total Power.* Yale University Press, 1957.

ENGELS

Carver, Terrell. *Engels.* Oxford University Press, 1981.

McLellan, David. *Friedrich Engels.* Penguin Books, 1980.

Woolfson, Charles. *The Labour Theory of Culture: A Re-examination of Engels' Theory of Human Origins.* Routledge & Kegan Paul, 1982.

LENIN, BOLSHEVISM, AND THE RUSSIAN REVOLUTION

Acton, Edward. *Herzen and the Role of the Intellectual Revolutionary.* Cambridge University Press, 1979.

Althusser, Louis. *Lenin and Philosophy and Other Essays.* Translated by Ben Brewster. New Left Books, 1971.

Ascher, Abraham. *Pavel Axelrod and the Development of Menshevism.* Harvard University Press, 1972.

Berlin, Isaiah. *Russian Thinkers.* Edited by Henry Hardy and Aileen Kelly. Penguin Books, 1980.

Besancon, Alain. *The Rise of the Gulag: Intellectual Origins of Leninism.* Continuum, 1980.

Bradley, John. *Civil War in Russia, 1917–1920.* St. Martin's Press, 1975.

Carr, Edward Hallett. *The Russian Revolution from Lenin to Stalin (1917–1929).* Macmillan, 1979.

Cohen, Stephen F. *Bukharin and the Bolshevik Revolution: A Political Biography.* Oxford University Press, 1980.

Corrigan, Philip, et al. *Socialist Construction and Marxist Theory: Bolshevism and Its Critique.* Macmillan, 1978.

Crankshaw, Edward. *The Shadow of the Winter Palace: The Drift to Revolution, 1825–1917.* Penguin Books, 1980.

Dukes, Paul. *October and the World: Perspectives on the Russian Revolution.* Macmillan, 1979.

d'Encausse, Hélene Carrère. *Lenin: Revolution and Power.* Translated by Valence Ionescu. Longmans, 1981.

Ferro, Marc. *October 1917: A Social History of the Russian Revolution.* Translated by Norman Stone. Routledge & Kegan Paul, 1980.

Fitzpatrick, Sheila. *Education and Social Mobility in the Soviet Union, 1921–1934.* Cambridge University Press, 1979.

————. *The Russian Revolution.* Oxford University Press, 1982.

Frolich, Klaus, ed. *The Emergence of Russian Constitutionalism, 1900–1904.* Nijhoff, 1982.

Gill, Graeme J. *Peasants and Government in the Russian Revolution.* Macmillan, 1979.

Gleason, Abbott. *Young Russia: The Genesis of Russian Radicalism in the 1860s.* Penguin Books, 1980.

Haimson, Leopold H. *The Russian Marxists and the Origins of Bolshevism.* Beacon Press, 1966.

————, ed. *The Mensheviks: From the Revolution of 1917 to the Second World War.* University of Chicago Press, 1974.

Harding, Neil. *Lenin's Political Thought.* 2 vols. Macmillan, 1977, 80.

Hasegawa, Tsuyoshi. *The February Revolution: Petrograd, 1917.* State University of Washington Press, 1981.

Hill, Christopher. *Lenin and the Russian Revolution.* Penguin Books, 1980.

Katkov, George. *Russia 1917: The Kornilov Affair.* Longman, 1980.

Kelly, Aileen. "Good for the Populists." *New York Review of Books* (23 June 1977), 10–15.

Koenker, Diane. *Moscow Workers and the 1917 Revolution.* Princeton University Press, 1981.

Lane, David. *Leninism: A Sociological Interpretation.* Cambridge University Press, 1981.

Leggett, George. *The Cheka: Lenin's Political Police.* Oxford University Press, 1981.

Lukács, Georg. *Lenin: A Study on the Unity of His Thought.* Translated by Nicholas Jacobs. MIT Press, 1971.

Manning, Roberta T. *The Crisis of the Old Order in Russia: Gentry and Government.* Princeton University Press, 1982.

McNeal, Robert H. *The Bolshevik Tradition.* Prentice-Hall, 1975.

Medvedev, Roy A. *The October Revolution.* Translated by George Saunders. Constable, 1979.

Meyer, Alfred G. *Leninism.* Harvard University Press, 1957.

Nahirny, Vladimir C. *The Russian Intelligentsia: From Torment to Silence.* Transaction Books, 1982.

Owen, Thomas C. *Capitalism and Politics in Russia: A Social History of the Moscow Merchants, 1885–1905.* Cambridge University Press, 1981.

Pearson, Raymond. *The Russian Moderates and the Crisis of Tsarism, 1914–1917.* Macmillan, 1977.

Pintner, Walter McKenzie and Don Karl Rowney, eds. *Russian Officialdom: The Bureaucratization of Russian Society from the Seventeenth to the Twentieth Century.* University of North Carolina Press, 1980.

Pipes, Richard, ed. *Revolutionary Russia.* Harvard University Press, 1968.

————. *Struve.* 2 vols. Harvard University Press, 1970, 80.

Read, Christopher. *Religion, Revolution and the Russian Intelligentsia, 1902–1913.* Macmillan, 1980.

Rigby, T.H. *Lenin's Government: Sovnarkom 1917–22.* Cambridge University Press, 1979.

Rosenberg, Arthur. *A History of Bolshevism: From Marx to the First Five Years' Plan.* Translated by Ian F.D. Morrow. Doubleday, 1967.

Schapiro, Leonard and Peter Reddaway, eds. *Lenin: The Man, the Theorist, the Leader: A Reappraisal.* Hoover Institution Press, 1967.

Schapiro, Leonard. *The Origin of the Communist Autocracy: Political Opposition in the Soviet State, First Phase 1917–1922.* 2nd ed. Macmillan, 1977.

Schwartz, Solomon M. *The Russian Revolution of 1905: The Workers' Movement and the Formation of Bolshevism and Menshevism.* University of Chicago Press, 1967.

Service, Robert. *The Bolshevik Party in Revolution: A Study in Organizational Change.* Macmillan, 1979.

Skocpol, Theda. *States and Social Revolutions: A Comparative Analysis of France, Russia, and China.* Cambridge University Press, 1979.

Solzhenitsyn, Alexander. *Lenin in Zurich.* Translated by H.T. Willetts. Farrar, Straus and Giroux, 1976.

Talmon, J.L. *The Myth of the Nation and the Vision of Revolution: The Origins of Ideological Polarization in the Twentieth Century.* Secker & Warburg, 1981.

Taylor, A.J.P. *Revolutions and Revolutionaries: From Jacobinism to Bolshevism.* Hamish Hamilton, 1980.

Theen, Rolf H.W. *Lenin: Genesis and Development of a Revolutionary.* Princeton University Press, 1979.

Ulam, Adam B. *The Bolsheviks: The Intellectual and Political History of the Triumph of Communism in Russia.* Collier Books, 1968.

———. *In the Name of the People: Prophets and Conspirators in Prerevolutionary Russia.* Viking Books, 1977.

———. *Russia's Failed Revolutions: From the Decembrists to the Dissidents.* Basic Books, 1981.

Venturi, Franco. *Studies in Free Russia.* University of Chicago Press, 1982.

Vucinich, Alexander. *Social Thought in Tsarist Russia: The Quest for a General Science of Society 1861–1917.* University of Chicago Press, 1976.

Weber, Gerda and Herman. *Lenin: Life and Works.* Macmillan, 1980.

Weeks, Albert L. *The First Bolshevik: A Political Biography of Peter Tkachev.* New York University Press, 1968.

Wesson, Robert G. *Lenin's Legacy: The Story of the CPSU.* Hoover Institution Press, 1978.

Wildman, Allan K. *The Making of a Workers' Revolution: Russian Social Democracy, 1891–1903.* University of Chicago Press, 1967.

Wolfenstein, E. Victor. *The Revolutionary Personality: Lenin, Trotsky, Gandhi.* Princeton University Press, 1967.

LEON TROTSKY

Alexander, Robert J. *Trotskyism in Latin America.* Hoover Institution Press, 1973.

Carmichael, Joel. *Trotsky: An Appreciation of His Life.* Hodder and Stoughton, 1975.

Deutscher, Isaac. *The Prophet Armed: Trotsky, 1879–1921.* Oxford University Press, 1954.

———. *The Prophet Unarmed: Trotsky, 1921–1929.* Oxford University Press, 1959.

———. *The Prophet Outcast: Trotsky, 1929–1940.* Oxford University Press, 1963.

Heijenoort, Jean Van. *With Trotsky in Exile: From Prinkipo to Coyoacan.* Harvard University Press, 1978.

Howe, Irving. *Leon Trotsky.* Penguin Books, 1979.

Mandel, Ernest. *Trotsky: A Study in the Dynamic of His Thought.* New Left Books, 1979.

Mavrakis, Kostas. *On Trotskyism.* Routledge & Kegan Paul, 1976.

Paz, Baruch Knei-. *Social and Political Thought of Leon Trotsky.* Clarendon Press, 1979.

Segal, Ronald. *The Tragedy of Leon Trotsky.* Hutchinson, 1979.

Stokes, Curtis. *The Evolution of Trotsky's Theory of Revolution.* University Press of America, 1982.

Wistrich, Robert. *Trotsky: Fate of a Revolutionary.* Robson Books, 1979.

STALIN AND STALINISM

Bailes, Kendall E. *Technology and Society Under Lenin and Stalin: Origins of the Soviet Technical Intelligentsia, 1917–1941.* Princeton University Press, 1977.

Dunham, Vera. *In Stalin's Time: Middleclass Values in Soviet Fiction.* Cambridge University Press, 1976.

Dunmore, T. *The Stalinist Command Economy: The Soviet State Apparatus and Economic Policy 1945–1953.* Macmillan, 1981.

d'Encausse, Hélene Carrère. *Stalin: Order through Terror.* Translated by Valence Ionescu. Longmans, 1981.

Fischer, Ruth. *Stalin and German Communism: A Study in the Origins of the State Party.* Transaction Books, 1980.

Grey, Ian. *Stalin: Man of History.* Weidenfeld and Nicolson, 1979.

Lewin, Moshe. *Political Undercurrents in Soviet Economic Debates.* Pluto Press, 1975.

Medvedev, Roy A. *On Stalin and Stalinism.* Translated by Ellen de Kadt. Oxford University Press, 1979.

————. *Bukharin: The Last Years.* Norton, 1980.

Nove, Alec. *Stalinism and After.* Allen & Unwin, 1975.

Pethybridge, Roger. *The Social Prelude to Stalinism.* St. Martin's Press, 1974.

Rosenfeldt, Niels Erik. *Knowledge and Power: The Role of Stalin's Secret Chancellery in the Soviet System of Government.* Rosenkilde and Bagger, 1978.

Souvarine, Boris. *Staline: Apercu historique de bolchevisme.* Champ Libre, 1977.

Taubman, William. *Stalin's American Policy: From Entente to Detente to Cold War.* Norton, 1982.

Tucker, Robert C. *The Soviet Political Mind: Studies in Stalinism and Post-Stalin Change.* Praeger, 1963.

————. *Stalin as Revolutionary, 1979–1929: A Study in History and Personality.* Chatto & Windus, 1974.

————., ed. *Stalinism: Essays in Historical Interpretation.* Norton, 1978.

Ulam, Adam B. *Stalin: The Man and His Era.* Viking Press, 1973.

Urban, G.R., ed. *Stalinism.* Maurice Temple Smith, 1982.

Zaleski, Eugene. *Stalinist Planning for Economic Growth, 1933–1952.* Macmillan, 1980.

MAO TSE-TUNG AND MAOISM

Boorman, Scott A. *The Protracted Game: A Wei-ch'i Interpretation of Maoist Revolutionary Strategy.* Oxford University Press, 1969.

Brugger, Bill. *China: Liberation and Transformation 1942–1962.* Barnes & Noble, 1981.

————. *China: Radicalism to Revisionism 1962–1979.* Barnes & Noble, 1981.

Corrigan, Philip and Derek Sayer. *For Mao.* Macmillan, 1979.

Dirlik, Arif. *Revolution and History: Origins of Marxist Historiography in China, 1919–1937.* University of California Press, 1978.

Eckstein, Alexander. *China's Economic Revolution.* Cambridge University Press, 1979.

FitzGerald, C.P. *Mao Tsetung and China.* Holmes & Meier, 1976.

Gurley, John G. *Challengers to Capitalism: Marx, Lenin, and Mao.* New 2nd Edition. Norton, 1979.

Hiniker, Paul J. *Revolutionary Ideology and Chinese Reality: Dissonance under Mao.* Sage, 1977.

Ho, Ping-ti and Tsang Tsou, eds. *China in Crisis.* 2 vols. University of Chicago Press, 1968.

Howard, Roger. *Mao Tse-tung and the Chinese People.* Allen and Unwin, 1978.

Kraus, Richard Curt. *Class Conflict in Chinese Socialism.* Columbia University Press, 1981.

Lee, Hong Yung. *The Politics of the Chinese Cultural Revolution: A Case Study.* University of California Press, 1978.

Leys, Simon. *The Chairman's New Clothes: Mao and the Cultural Revolution.* St. Martin's Press, 1978.

Lieberthal, Kenneth G. *Revolution and Tradition in Tiensin, 1949–1952.* Stanford University Press, 1980.

Lifton, Robert Jay. *Thought Reform and the Psychology of Totalism: A Study of "Brainwashing" in China.* Norton, 1963.

———. *Revolutionary Immortality: Mao Tse-tung and the Chinese Cultural Revolution.* Norton, 1976.

MacFarquhar, Roderick. *The Origins of the Cultural Revolution: Contradictions Among the People.* Columbia University Press, 1974.

McDonald, Angus W., Jr. *The Urban Origins of Rural Revolution: Elites and Masses in Hunan Province, China, 1911–1927.* University of California Press, 1978.

Meisner, Maurice. *Mao's China: A History of the People's Republic.* The Free Press, 1979.

Metzger, Thomas A. *Escape from Predicament: Neo-Confucianism and China's Evolving Political Culture.* Columbia University Press, 1977.

Murphey, Rhoads. *The Fading of the Maoist Vision: City and Country in China's Development.* Methuen, 1980.

Nathan, Andrew. *Peking Politics, 1918–1923: Factionalism and the Failure of Constitutionalism.* University of California Press, 1976.

Oksenberg, Michel and Richard Bush. "China's Political Evolution: 1972–82." XXXI *Problems of Communism* (September–October 1982), 1–19.

Pepper, Suzanne. *Civil War in China: The Political Struggle, 1945–1949.* University of California Press, 1979.

Perry, Elizabeth J. *Rebels and Revolutionaries in North China, 1845–1945.* Stanford University Press, 1980.

Pye, Lucian W. *Mao Tse-tung: The Man in the Leader.* Harper and Row, 1978.

———. *The Dynamics of Factions and Consensus in Chinese Politics: A Model and Some Propositions.* Rand Corporation, 1980.

Rice, Edward E. *History of the Ruling Communist Party of China.* Hoover Institution, 1982.

Robinson, Thomas W., ed. *The Cultural Revolution in China.* University of California Press, 1971.

Rue, John W. *Mao Tse-tung in Opposition, 1927–1935.* Stanford University Press, 1966.

Schram, Stuart R. *Mao Tse-tung.* Penguin Books, 1967.

————. *The Political Thought of Mao Tse-tung.* Revised and enlarged ed. Praeger, 1969.

Schwartz, Benjamin I. *Chinese Communism and the Rise of Mao.* Harvard University Press, 1979.

Shue, Vivienne. *Peasant China in Transition: The Dynamics of Development toward Socialism, 1949–1956.* University of California Press, 1980.

Solomon, Richard H. *Mao's Revolution and the Chinese Political Culture.* University of California Press, 1971.

Soo, Francis Y.K. *Mao Tse-Tung's Theory of Dialectic.* Reidel, 1982.

Starr, John Bryan. *Continuing the Revolution: The Political Thought of Mao.* Princeton University Press, 1979.

Suyin, Han. *Wind in the Tower: Mao Tse-tung and the Chinese Revolution, 1949–1975.* Cape, 1976.

Terrill, Ross, ed. *The China Difference.* Harper & Row, 1980.

————. *Mao: A Biography.* Harper & Row, 1980.

Thornton, Richard C. *China: A Political History, 1917–1980.* Westview Press, 1981.

Vogel, Ezra F. *Canton under Communism: Programs and Politics in a Provincial Capital, 1949–1968.* Harvard University Press, 1980.

Wilson, Dick, ed. *Mao Tse-tung in the Scales of History.* Cambridge University Press, 1978.

Womack, Brantly. *The Foundations of Mao Zedong's Political Thought, 1917–1935.* University of Hawaii Press, 1981.

Wu, Tien-wei. *Lin Bao and the Gang of Four: Contra-Confucianism in Historical and Intellectual Perspective.* Southern Illinois University Press, 1983.

Wylie, Raymond F. *The Emergence of Maoism: Mao-Tse-tung, Ch'en Po-ta, and the Search for Chinese Theory, 1935–1945.* Stanford University Press, 1980.

THE FRANKFURT SCHOOL AND CRITICAL THEORY

Abercrombie, Nicholas, et al. *The Dominant Ideology Thesis.* Allen & Unwin, 1981.

Bottomore, Tom. *Marxist Sociology.* Holmes & Meier, 1975.

Buck-Morss, Susan. *The Origin of Negative Dialectics: Theodor W. Adorno, Walter Benjamin, and the Frankfurt Institute.* The Free Press, 1977.

Connerton, Paul. *The Tragedy of Enlightenment: An Essay on the Frankfurt School.* Cambridge University Press, 1980.

Ealy, Steven D. *Communications, Speech and Politics: Habermas and Political Analysis.* University Press of America, 1981.

Feenberg, Andrew. *Lukács, Marx and the Sources of Critical Theory.* Rowman and Littlefield, 1981.

Friedman, George. *The Political Philosophy of the Frankfurt School.* Cornell University Press, 1981.

Fry, J. *Marcuse.* Harvester, 1979.

Geuss, Raymond. *The Idea of a Critical Theory: Habermas and the Frankfurt School.* Cambridge University Press, 1982.

Goulding, James W., et al., "Jürgen Habermas: An International Bibliography." 8 *Political Theory* (May 1980), 259–85.

Held, David. *Introduction to Critical Theory: Horkheimer to Habermas.* University of California Press, 1980.

Huff, Toby E., ed. *Benjamin Nelson, On the Roads to Modernity: Conscience, Science and Civilizations.* Rowman and Littlefield, 1981.

Keat, Russell. *The Politics of Social Theory: Habermas, Freud, and the Critique of Positivism.* University of Chicago Press, 1981.

Kettler, David. "Herbert Marcuse: Alienation and Negativity." In *Contemporary Political Philosophers,* edited by Anthony de Crespigny and Kenneth Minogue. Dodd, Mead, 1975.

Kilminster, Richard. *Praxis and Method: A Sociological Dialogue with Lukács, Gramsci and the Early Frankfurt School.* Routledge & Kegan Paul, 1979.

Kortian, Garbis. *Metacritique: The Philosophical Argument of Jürgen Habermas.* Translated by John Raffan. Cambridge University Press, 1980.

McCarthy, Thomas. *The Critical Theory of Jürgen Habermas.* MIT Press, 1978.

Schoolman, Morton. *The Imaginary Witness: The Critical Theory of Herbert Marcuse.* The Free Press, 1981.

Schroyer, Trent. *The Critique of Domination.* Beacon Press, 1975.

Sensat, Julius, Jr. *Habermas and Marxism: An Appraisal.* Sage, 1979.

Skinner, Quentin. "Habermas's Reformation." XXIX *The New York Review of Books* (7 October 1982), 35–38.

Slater, Phil. *Origin and Significance of the Frankfurt School: A Marxist Perspective.* Routledge & Kegan Paul, 1980.

Steuernagel, Gertrude A. *Political Philosophy as Therapy: Marcuse Reconsidered.* Greenwood Press, 1979.

Thompson, John B. and David Held, eds. *Habermas: Critical Debates.* MIT Press, 1982.

GEORG LUKÁCS

Arato, Andrew and Paul Breines. *The Young Lukács and the Origins of Western Marxism.* Seabury Press, 1979.

Arvon, Henri. *Georges Lukács ou le Front populaire en litterature.* Éditions Seghers, 1968.

Goldmann, Lucien. *Lukács and Heidegger: Towards a New Philosophy.* Translated by William Q. Boelhower. Rutledge & Kegan Paul, 1977.

Heller, Agnes., ed. *Lukács Revalued.* Basil Blackwell, 1983.

Parkinson, G.H.R. *George Lukács.* Routledge & Kegan Paul, 1977.

ANTONIO GRAMSCI

Adamson, Walter L. *Hegemony and Revolution: Antonio Gramsci's Political and Cultural Theory.* University of California Press, 1981.

Apple, Michael W. *Ideology and Curriculum.* Routledge & Kegan Paul, 1979.

Buci-Glucksmann, Christine. *Gramsci and the State.* Translated by David Fernbach. Lawrence & Wishart, 1979.

Cammett, J. *Antonio Gramsci and the Origins of Italian Communism.* Stanford University Press, 1967.

Clark, Martin. *Antonio Gramsci and the Revolution That Failed.* Yale University Press, 1977.

Davidson, Alastair. *Antonio Gramsci: Towards an Intellectual Biography.* Merlin Press, 1977.

Davis, John A., ed. *Gramsci and Italy's Passive Revolution.* Barnes & Noble, 1979.

Entwistle, Harold. *Antonio Gramsci: Conservative Schooling for Radical Politics.* Routledge & Kegan Paul, 1979.

Femia, Joseph V. *Gramsci's Political Thought: Hegemony, Consciousness, and the Revolutionary Process.* Oxford University Press, 1981.

Joll, James. *Antonio Gramsci.* Penguin Books, 1980.

Mouffe, Chantal, ed. *Gramsci and Marxist Theory.* Routledge & Kegan Paul, 1979.

Pellicani, Luciano. *Gramsci: An Alternative Communism?* Hoover Institution, 1981.

———. *Gramsci and the Communist Question.* Hoover Institution, 1982.

Salamini, Leonardo. *The Sociology of Political Praxis: An Introduction to Gramsci's Theory.* Routledge & Kegan Paul, 1981.

Sassoon, Anne Showstack. *Gramsci's Politics.* St. Martin's Press, 1980.

CRAWFORD BROUGH MACPHERSON

Chapman, John W. "Natural Rights and Justice in Liberalism." In *Political Theory and the Rights of Man,* edited by D.D. Raphael. Macmillan, 1967.

————. "Justice, Freedom, and Property." In *Property: NOMOS XXII*, edited by J. Roland Pennock and John W. Chapman. New York University Press, 1980.

Kontos, Alkis, ed. *Powers, Possessions and Freedom: Essays in Honour of C.B. Macpherson.* University of Toronto Press, 1979.

MARXISM, SOCIALISM, AND COMMUNISM

Brown, Archie and Jack Gray, eds. *Political Culture and Political Change in Communist States.* Macmillan, 1979.

Brus, Wlodzimierz. *Socialist Ownership and Political Systems Under Socialism.* Routledge & Kegan Paul, 1975.

Cummins, Ian. *Marx, Engels and National Movements.* St. Martin's Press, 1980.

Curtis, Michael. *Totalitarianism.* Transaction Books, 1979.

Hegedus, Andras. *Socialism and Bureaucracy.* St. Martin's Press, 1977.

Hirszowicz, Maria. *The Bureaucratic Leviathan: A Study in the Sociology of Communism.* New York University Press, 1981.

Hodges, Donald C. *The Bureaucratization of Socialism.* University of Massachusetts Press, 1981.

Holmes, Leslie, ed. *The Withering Away of the State? Party and State under Communism.* Sage, 1981.

Jancar, Barbara Wolfe. *Women Under Communism.* Johns Hopkins University Press, 1978.

Luard, Evan. *Socialism Without the State.* Macmillan, 1979.

Kaplan, Morton A., ed. *The Many Faces of Communism.* The Free Press, 1978.

Lane, David. *The Socialist Industrial State: Toward a Political Sociology of State Socialism.* Westview Press, 1976.

————. *The End of Social Inequality? Class, Status and Power under State Socialism.* Allen & Unwin, 1982.

Lindblom, Charles E. *Politics and Markets: The World's Political-Economic Systems.* Basic Books, 1978.

Löwenthal, Richard. *World Communism: The Disintegration of a Secular Faith.* Oxford University Press, 1964.

Narkiewicz, Olga A. *Marxism and the Reality of Power 1919–1980.* Croom Helm, 1981.

Nelson, Daniel N., ed. *Communism and the Politics of Inequalities.* Lexington Books, 1982.

Parekh, Bhikhu, ed. *The Concept of Socialism.* Holmes & Meier, 1975.

Poulantzas, Nicos. *State, Power, Socialism.* New Left Books, 1978.

Rosefielde, S., ed. *World Communism at the Crossroads.* Nijhoff, 1980.

Rosenberg, William G. and Marilyn B. Young. *Transforming Russia and*

China: Revolutionary Struggle in the Twentieth Century. Oxford University Press, 1982.

Seton-Watson, Hugh. *The Imperialist Revolutionaries: Trends in World Communism in the 1960s and 1970s.* Hoover Institution Press, 1978.

Schapiro, Leonard. *Totalitarianism.* Macmillan, 1972.

Selucky, Radoslav. *Marxism, Socialism, Freedom: Towards a General Democratic Theory of Labour-Managed Systems.* Macmillan, 1979.

Stojanovic, Svetozar. *In Search of Democracy in Socialism.* Prometheus Books, 1982.

Szajkowski, Bogdan, ed. *Marxist Governments: A World Survey.* 3 vols. St. Martin's Press, 1980.

Szporluk, Roman. *The Political Thought of Thomas G. Masaryk.* Columbia University Press, 1981.

Urban, G.R., ed. *Communist Reformation: Nationalism, Internationalism and Change in the World Communist Movement.* Temple Smith, 1979.

Waller, Michael. *Democratic Centralism: An Historical Commentary.* University of Manchester Press, 1981.

Wesson, Robert. *The Aging of Communism.* Praeger, 1980.

Westoby, Adam. *Communism Since World War II.* Harvester, 1981.

Whetten, Lawrence L., ed. *The Present State of Communist Internationalism.* Lexington Books, 1982.

MARXISM AND COMMUNISM IN WESTERN EUROPE

Albright, David E., ed. *Communism and Political Systems in Western Europe.* Westview Press, 1979.

Amyot, G. *The Italian Communist Party.* Croom Helm, 1981.

Blackmer, D.L.M. and S. Tarrow, eds. *Communism in Italy and France.* Princeton University Press, 1975.

Childs, David, ed. *The Changing Face of Western Communism.* Croom Helm, 1980.

Elliott, Charles F. and Carl A. Linden, eds. *Marxism in the Contemporary West.* Westview Press, 1980.

Johnson, Richard. *The French Communist Party versus the Students: Revolutionary Politics in May–June 1968.* Yale University Press, 1972.

Kelly, Michael. *Modern French Marxism.* Johns Hopkins University Press, 1982.

Kriegel, Annie. *The French Communists: Profile of a People.* University of Chicago Press, 1972.

Middlemas, Keith. *Power and the Party: Changing Faces of Communism in Western Europe.* Andre Deutsch, 1980.

Serfaty, Simon and Lawrence Gray, eds. *The Italian Communist Party: Yesterday, Today, and Tomorrow.* Greenwood Press, 1980.

Tannahill, R. Neal. *The Communist Parties of Western Europe: A Comparative Study*. Greenwood Press, 1978.
Tiersky, Ronald. *French Communism, 1920–1972*. Columbia University Press, 1974.

EUROCOMMUNISM

Aspaturian, Vernon V., et al., eds. *Eurocommunism Between East and West*. Indiana University Press, 1980.
Boggs, Carl and David Plotke, eds. *The Politics of Eurocommunism: Socialism in Transition*. Macmillan, 1980.
Boggs, Carl. *The Impasse of European Communism*. Westview Press, 1981.
Claudin, Fernando. *Eurocommunism and Socialism*. Schocken Books, 1978.
Godson, Roy and Stephen Haseler. *Eurocommunism: Implications for East and West*. Macmillan, 1979.
Griffith, William E., ed. *The European Left: Italy, France, and Spain*. Lexington Books, 1979.
Kindersley, R., ed. *In Search of Eurocommunism*. Macmillan, 1982.
Kriegel, Annie. *Eurocommunism: A New Kind of Communism?* Hoover Institution Press, 1978.
Mandel, Ernest. *From Stalinism to Eurocommunism*. Translated by Jon Rothschild. New Left Books, 1978.
Ranney, Austin and Giovanni Sartori, eds. *Eurocommunism: The Italian Case*. American Enterprise Institute, 1978.
Schwab, George, ed. *Eurocommunism: The Ideological and Political-Theoretical Foundations*. Greenwood Press, 1981.
Tőkes, Rudolf L., ed. *Eurocommunism and Detente*. New York University Press, 1981.

MARXISM AND COMMUNISM IN YUGOSLAVIA

Bombelles, Joseph T. *Economic Development of Communist Yugoslavia, 1947–1964*. Hoover Institution Press, 1968.
Borowiec, Andrew. *Yugoslavia After Tito*. Praeger, 1977.
Carter, April. *Democratic Reform in Yugoslavia: The Changing Role of the Party*. Princeton University Press, 1982.
Comisso, Ellen Turkish. *Workers' Control under Plan and Market: Politicoeconomic Implications of Yugoslav Self-Management*. Yale University Press, 1979.
Crocker, David A. *Praxis and Democratic Socialism: The Critical Social Theories of Markovic and Stojanovic*. Harvester, 1982.

Denitch, Bogdan Denis. *The Legitimation of a Revolution: The Yugoslav Case.* Yale University Press, 1976.

Djilas, Milovan. *Tito: A Critical Portrait.* Weidenfeld & Nicolson, 1981.

Gruenwald, Oskar. *The Yugoslav Search for Man: Marxist Humanism in Contemporary Yugoslavia.* J.F. Bergin, 1981.

Horvat, Branko. *The Yugoslav Economic System: The First Labor-Managed Economy in the Making.* M.E. Sharpe, 1980.

Moore, John H. *Growth With Self-Management: Yugoslav Industrialization 1952–1975.* Hoover Institution Press, 1979.

Rusinow, Dennison. *The Yugoslav Experiment: 1948–1974.* University of California Press, 1977.

Seibel, Hans Dieter and Ukandi G. Damachi. *Self-Management in Yugoslavia and the Developing World.* Macmillan, 1980.

Sher, Gordon S. *Praxis: Marxist Criticism and Dissent in Socialist Yugoslavia.* Indiana University Press, 1977.

Singleton, Fred. *Twentieth-Century Yugoslavia.* Columbia University Press, 1976.

Sirc, Ljubo. *The Yugoslav Economy under Self-Management.* Macmillan, 1979.

Stankovic, Slobodan. *The End of the Tito Era: Yugoslavia's Dilemmas.* Hoover Institution Press, 1981.

Tyson, Laura D'Andrea. *The Yugoslav Economic System and Its Performance in the 1970s.* University of California, Institute of International Studies, 1981.

Vanek, Jaroslav. *The General Theory of Labor-Managed Market Economies.* Cornell University Press, 1970.

Wilson, Duncan. *Tito's Yugoslavia.* Cambridge University Press, 1979.

USSR: POLITICAL

Bellis, Paul. *Marxism and the USSR: The Theory of Proletarian Dictatorship and the Marxist Analysis of Soviet Society.* Macmillan, 1979.

Bialer, Seweryn. *Stalin's Successors: Leadership, Stability and Change in the Soviet Union.* Cambridge University Press, 1980.

———— and Thane Gustafson, eds. *Russia at the Crossroads: The 26th Congress of the CPSU.* Allen & Unwin, 1982.

Besancon, Alain. *The Soviet Syndrome.* Translated by Patricia Ranum. Harcourt Brace Jovanovich, 1978.

Breslauer, George W. *Khruschev and Brezhnev as Leaders: Building Authority in Soviet Politics.* Allen & Unwin, 1982.

Brown, A. and M. Kaser, eds. *The Soviet Union Since the Fall of Khrushchev.* The Free Press, 1976.

Brown, Archie, et al., eds. *The Cambridge Encyclopedia of Russia and the Soviet Union.* Cambridge University Press, 1982.

Brzezinski, Zbigniew. *Ideology and Power in Soviet Politics.* Greenwood Press, 1977.

Cohen, Stephen F., et al., eds. *The Soviet Union since Stalin.* Macmillan, 1980.

Hahn, Werner G. *Postwar Soviet Politics: The Fall of Zhdanov and the Defeat of Moderation, 1946–53.* Cornell University Press, 1982.

Hill, R.J. and P. Frank. *The Soviet Communist Party.* Allen & Unwin, 1982.

Hoffmann, Erik P. and Robin F. Laird. *The Politics of Modernization in the Soviet Union.* Cornell University Press, 1982.

Hough, J.F. and M. Fainsod. *How the Soviet Union is Governed.* Harvard University Press, 1979.

Kelley, Donald R. *Soviet Politics in the Brezhnev Era.* Praeger, 1980.

Lane, David. *Politics and Society in the U.S.S.R.* 2nd ed. New York University Press, 1981.

McAuley, Mary. *Politics and the Soviet Union.* Penguin Books, 1980.

Rigby, T.H., et al., eds. *Authority, Power and Policy in the USSR: Essays Dedicated to Leonard Schapiro.* St. Martin's Press, 1980.

Schapiro, Leonard. *The Government and Politics of the Soviet Union.* 6th ed. Hutchinson, 1977.

Shatz, Marshall S. *Soviet Dissent in Historical Perspective.* Cambridge University Press, 1981.

Skilling, H. Gordon and Franklin Griffiths, eds. *Interest Groups in Soviet Politics.* Princeton University Press, 1970.

Wesson, Robert, ed. *The Soviet Union: Looking to the 1980s.* Hoover Institution Press, 1981.

White, Stephen. *Political Culture and Soviet Politics.* St. Martin's Press, 1979.

USSR: ECONOMIC AND SOCIAL

Bergson, Abram and Herbert J. Levine, eds. *The Soviet Economy: Toward the Year 2000.* Allen & Unwin, 1982.

Bornstein, Morris, ed. *The Soviet Economy: Continuity and Change.* Westview Press, 1981.

Grossman, Gregory. "The 'Second Economy' of the USSR." 26 *Problems of Communism* (September–October 1977), 25–39.

Hunter, Holland, ed. *The Future of the Soviet Economy: 1978–1985.* Westview Press, 1978.

Lane, David and Felicity O'Dell. *The Soviet Industrial Worker: Social Class, Education and Control.* St. Martin's Press, 1978.

Matthews, Mervyn. *Privilege in the Soviet Union: A Study of Elite Life-Styles under Communism.* Allen & Unwin, 1978.

————. *Education in the Soviet Union: Policies and Institutions Since Stalin.* Allen & Unwin, 1982.

McAuley, A. *Economic Welfare in the Soviet Union: Poverty, Living Standards, and Inequality.* Allen & Unwin, 1979.

Nove, Alec. *Political Economy and Soviet Socialism.* Allen & Unwin, 1979.

Rosefielde, Steven, ed. *Economic Welfare and the Economics of Soviet Socialism: Essays in Honor of Abram Bergson.* Cambridge University Press, 1981.

COMMUNISM IN EASTERN EUROPE

Bahro, Rudolf. *The Alternative in Eastern Europe.* Schocken Books, 1981.

Brown, A. and M. Kaser, eds. *The Soviet Union Since the Fall of Khrushchev.* The Free Press, 1976.

Connor, Walter D. *Socialism, Politics, and Equality: Hierarchy and Change in Eastern Europe and the USSR.* Columbia University Press, 1980.

Drachkovitch, Milorad, ed. *East Central Europe: Yesterday, Today, Tomorrow.* Hoover Institution Press, 1982.

Faber, Bernard Lewis, ed. *The Social Structure of Eastern Europe: Transition and Process in Czechoslovakia, Hungary, Poland, Romania and Yugoslavia.* Praeger, 1976.

Fehér, Ferenc, et al. *Dictatorship over Needs.* Basil Blackwell, 1982.

Fischer-Galati, Stephen, ed. *The Communist Parties of Eastern Europe.* Columbia University Press, 1981.

————, ed. *Eastern Europe in the 1980s.* Westview Press, 1981.

Granick, David. *Enterprise Guidance in Eastern Europe: A Comparison of Four Socialist Economies.* Princeton University Press, 1975.

Janos, Andrew C., ed. *Authoritarian Politics in Communist Europe: Uniformity and Diversity in One-Party States.* University of California, Institute of International Studies, 1981.

Rakovski, Marc. *Towards an East European Marxism.* St. Martin's Press, 1978.

Rakowska-Harmstone, Teresa, ed. *Perspectives for Change in Communist Societies.* Westview Press, 1979.

Staar, Richard F. *Communist Regimes in Eastern Europe.* 4th ed. Hoover Institution Press, 1982.

Tőkes, Rudolf L., ed. *Opposition in Eastern Europe.* Macmillan, 1979.

Triska, Jan F. and Charles Gati, eds. *Blue-Collar Workers in Eastern Europe.* Allen & Unwin, 1981.

Tudjman, Franjo. *Nationalism in Contemporary Europe.* Columbia University Press, 1981.

POLAND

Ascherson, Neal. *The Polish August: The Self-Limiting Revolution.* Viking Press, 1982.

Davies, Norman. *God's Playground: A History of Poland.* 2 vols. Clarendon Press, 1981.

Dziewanowski, M.K. *Poland in the Twentieth Century.* Columbia University Press, 1980.

Experience and the Future Discussion Group. *Poland Today: The State of the Republic.* M.E. Sharpe, 1981.

Fiszman, J. *Revolution and Tradition in People's Poland: Education and Socialization.* Princeton University Press, 1972.

Goldfarb, Jeffrey C. *On Cultural Freedom: An Exploration of Public Life in Poland and America.* University of Chicago Press, 1982.

Karpinski, Jakub. *Countdown: The Polish Upheavals of 1956, 1968, 1970, 1976, 1980.* Karz-Cohl, 1982.

Kolakowski, Leszek. "Light in August." *The New Republic* (14 April 1982), 24–28.

Leslie, R.F., et al. *The History of Poland since 1863.* Cambridge University Press, 1980.

MacShane, Denis. *Solidarity: Poland's Independent Trade Union.* Spokesman Books, 1981.

Malia, Martin. "Poland: The Winter War." *The New York Review of Books* (18 March 1982), 20–26.

Montias, J. Michael. "Poland: Roots of the Economic Crisis." XXIV *The Aces Bulletin* (Fall 1982), 1–19.

———— and Susan Rose-Ackerman. "Corruption in a Soviet-Type Economy: Theoretical Considerations." In *Economic Welfare and the Economics of Soviet Socialism,* edited by Steven Rosefielde. Cambridge University Press, 1981.

Middlemas, Keith. "Poland's Special Way." 4 *London Review of Books* (4–18 February 1982), 14–15.

Polonsky, Anthony and Boleslaw Drukier, eds. *The Beginnings of Communist Rule in Poland: December 1943–June 1945.* Routledge & Kegan Paul, 1980.

Pomian-Srzednicki, Maciej. *Religious Change in Contemporary Poland: Secularization and Politics.* Routledge & Kegan Paul, 1982.

Simon, Maurice D. and Roger E. Kanet, eds. *Background to Crisis: Policy and Politics in Gierek's Poland.* Westview Press, 1981.

Singer, Daniel. *The Road to Gdansk: Poland and the USSR.* Monthly Review Press, 1981.

Walicki, Andrzej. *Philosophy and Romantic Nationalism: The Case of Poland.* Clarendon Press, 1982.

Weschler, Lawrence. *Solidarity: Poland in the Season of Its Passion.* Simon & Schuster, 1982.

de Weydenthal, Jan B. *The Communists of Poland: An Historical Outline.* Hoover Institution Press, 1978.

Woodall, Jean. *The Socialist Corporation and Technocratic Power: The Polish United Workers' Party, Industrial Organization and Workforce Control 1958–1980,* Cambridge University Press, 1982.

CZECHOSLOVAKIA

Bloomfield, Jon. *Passive Revolution: Politics and the Czechoslovak Working Class, 1945–8.* St. Martin's Press, 1979.

Bradley, J.F.N. *Politics in Czechoslovakia, 1945–1971.* University Press of America, 1981.

Eidlin, F.H. *The Logic of "Normalization:" The Soviet Intervention in Czechoslovakia of 21 August 1968 and the Czechoslovak Response.* Columbia University Press, 1980.

Fisera, Vladimir, ed. *Workers' Councils in Czechoslovakia: Documents and Essays, 1968–69.* St. Martin's Press, 1979.

Krystufek, Zdenek. *The Soviet Regime in Czechoslovakia.* Columbia University Press, 1981.

Mlynar, Zdenek. *Night Frost in Prague: The End of Humane Socialism.* C. Hurst, 1980.

Myant, M.R. *Socialism and Democracy in Czechoslovakia: 1945–1948.* Cambridge University Press, 1981.

Oxley, Andrew, et al., eds. *Czechoslovakia: The Party and the People.* St. Martin's Press, 1973.

Paul, David W. *Czechoslovakia: Profile of a Socialist Republic at the Crossroads of Europe.* Westview Press, 1980.

Pelikan, Jiri. *Socialist Opposition in Eastern Europe: The Czechoslovak Example.* St. Martin's Press, 1976.

Sik, Ota. *Czechoslovakia: The Bureaucratic Economy.* M.E. Sharpe, 1972.

Skilling, H. Gordon. *Czechoslovakia's Interrupted Revolution.* Princeton University Press, 1976.

———. *Charter 77 and Human Rights in Czechoslovakia.* Allen & Unwin, 1981.

Suda, Zdenek. *Zealots and Rebels: A History of the Ruling Communist Party of Czechoslovakia.* Hoover Institution Press, 1981.

Valenta, Jiri. *Soviet Intervention in Czechoslovakia 1968: Anatomy of a Decision.* Johns Hopkins University Press, 1980.

Wallace, William V. *Czechoslovakia.* Westview Press, 1977.

HUNGARY

Irving, D. *Uprising: One Nation's Nightmare: Hungary 1956.* Hodder, 1981.

Janos, Andrew C. *The Politics of Backwardness in Hungary, 1825–1945.* Princeton University Press, 1981.

———— and William B. Slottman. *The Revolution in Perspective: Essays on the Hungarian Soviet Republic.* University of California Press, 1972.

Kovrig, Bennett. *Communism in Hungary from Kun to Kadar.* Hoover Institution Press, 1979.

Lomax, Bill. *Hungary, 1956.* St. Martin's Press, 1977.

Molnar, Miklos. *A Short History of the Hungarian Communist Party.* Westview Press, 1978.

GERMAN DEMOCRATIC REPUBLIC

Baring, Arnulf M. *Uprising in East Germany: June 17, 1953.* Cornell University Press, 1972.

Schneider, Eberhard. *The GDR: The History, Politics, Economy and Society of East Germany.* St. Martin's Press, 1978.

Sontheimer, Kurt and Wilhelm Bleek. *The Government and Politics of East Germany.* St. Martin's Press, 1976.

Wettig, Gerhard. *Community and Conflict in the Socialist Camp: The Soviet Union, East Germany and the German Problem.* St. Martin's Press, 1975.

ROMANIA

Jowitt, Kenneth. *Revolutionary Breakthroughs and National Development: The Case of Romania, 1944–1965.* University of California Press, 1971.

King, Robert R. *History of the Romanian Communist Party.* Hoover Institution Press, 1981.

Nelson, Daniel N. *Democratic Centralism in Romania: A Study of Local Communist Politics.* Columbia University Press, 1980.

————., ed. *Romania in the 1980s.* Westview Press, 1981.

INDEX